Mediating the Message in the 21st Century

Hailed as one of the "most significant books of the 20th century" by *Journalism & Mass Communication Quarterly*, this new edition of the classic media sociology textbook now offers students a comprehensive, theoretical approach to media content in the 21st century. *Mediating the Message in the 21st Century* provides a broad perspective on the ways in which mass media content is subject to external influences, ranging from the content producer's personal values to national ideologies, and argues that in order to understand the effects of media, it is first necessary to understand how media content is created. This updated edition expands upon Pamela J. Shoemaker and Stephen D. Reese's earlier editions, with an added focus on entertainment media and the Internet. The updated edition of *Mediating the Message in the 21st Century* is an essential text for media effects scholars and students of media sociology.

Pamela J. Shoemaker is John Ben Snow Professor at the S.I. Newhouse School of Public Communications at Syracuse University. Her books include *News Around the World*, *How to Build Social Science Theories*, and *Gatekeeping Theory*. She is co-editor of the journal *Communication Research*. She is former president of the Association for Education in Journalism and Mass Communication.

Stephen D. Reese is Jesse H. Jones Professor and Associate Dean for Academic Affairs in the College of Communication at the University of Texas at Austin, where he has been on the faculty since 1982 and was previously director of the School of Journalism. He is co-editor of *Framing Public Life: Perspectives on Media and Our Understanding of the Social World*.

Mediating the Message in the 21st Century

A Media Sociology Perspective

Pamela J. Shoemaker and
Stephen D. Reese

Routledge
Taylor & Francis Group

NEW YORK AND LONDON

Third edition published 2014
by Routledge
711 Third Avenue, New York, NY 10017

and by Routledge
2 Park Square, Milton Park, Abingdon, OX14 4RN

First edition published 1991 by Longman Publishers USA

Second edition published 1996 by Longman Publishers USA

Routledge is an imprint of the Taylor & Francis Group, an informa business

Library of Congress Cataloging-in-Publication Data

Shoemaker, Pamela J.
Mediating the message in the 21st century: a media sociology perspective /
  Pamela J. Shoemaker, Stephen D. Reese. – Third edition.
    pages cm
  Includes bibliographical references and index.
 1. Mass media.   2. Content analysis (Communication)   I. Title.
II. Title: Mediating the message in the twenty-first century.
  P91.S46   2013
  302.23—dc23   2013008502

ISBN: 978-0-415-98913-8 (hbk)
ISBN: 978-0-415-98914-5 (pbk)
ISBN: 978-0-203-93043-4 (ebk)

Typeset in Stone Serif
by Apex CoVantage, LLC

Printed and bound in the United States of America by Sheridan Books, Inc. (a Sheridan Group Company).

CONTENTS

FOREWORD

Living in what they viewed as a new modern world experiencing rapid social change, the classical 19th century social science theorists worried about the relationship between the individual and society. They phrased this issue in a myriad of ways: What does the individual owe society? What kind of responsibility does a society have for the individuals who live in it? Does social change result from individual or group action and if from both factors, how are they related to one another? How do ideas circulate around a society and among individuals? What is the relationship between an individual's ideas and the institutions of which she is a part?

As Pamela Shoemaker and Stephen Reese remind us in *Mediating the Message in the 21st Century*, we are once again living in a period of critical change and these compelling questions still resonate throughout the social sciences, especially when it comes to understanding the transformation of the media. Today as yesterday, the media filter our experiences and shape our understandings of the world. At the turn of the 19th century, European social critics charged that, with its emphasis on romantic love, the then newly popular novel was undermining parents' ability to arrange the marriages of their children and so was undermining the stability of society. Today, a new generation of critics bemoans how violent digital games encourage aggression and disrespect; they also claim that the new social media are not only hampering the academic achievements of young people, but even their ability to make friends in face-to-face interactions. Whether voiced in the 19th or the 21st century, these sorts of accusations can be understood as attempts to untangle how individuals, the media, and societies influence one another. As Shoemaker and Reese also explain, it is difficult to discuss where the media have been, how they have been changing, and where they are going without addressing the complex relationships among global forces, nations, institutions, organizations, and individuals.

Those relationships are rendered more complex by the evidence that each of these kinds of social organization have both direct and indirect effects upon each other. The days when social scientists drew a simple diagram to explain the interactions among these levels of social organization has gone the way of the large-circulation, independent, afternoon "ink" newspaper. Each is difficult to find, but finding and understanding a seemingly basic diagram or a successful old-fashioned newspaper makes it easier to analyze more contemporary and complex media arrangements, such as how bloggers act as both media users and media producers, how networks transcend nation states, and how new forms of digital literacy are emerging.

Reese and Shoemaker's solution to explaining the complexity of today's media is to discuss what they call "the hierarchy of influences"—a necessarily simplified map showing how levels of social organization influence media and also affect one another as they link patterns of symbols to each other and to the societies in which they are embedded. As Reese and Shoemaker explain their model, they move from large sociocultural units, such as international corporations and nation states, to smaller ones, such as the individual. Consistent with American ideology, the individual stands at the center of their diagram and is affected by routines that have been developed within (usually capitalist and bureaucratic) organizations, which in turn are affected by social institutions contained within social systems. But, they instruct us, reality—the world in which we live—is much more complex. Some of the great 19th century social scientists stressed how the actions of individuals affect larger social structures, while others emphasized the impact of the larger structures on a person's life. So, too, Reese and Shoemaker note that some research moves from the inner level of their hierarchy to the outer and larger one. One scholar might explore how individuals may organize social movements that use the media to affect social change and how the media resist their efforts, while another analyzes the impact of global organizations—how the great transnational oligarchies influence everything from national ideologies to even how people express their appreciation (:-D) or likes and dislikes (👍👎). I read their hierarchy as a guide to asking questions about the impact of the media on society and on the people who have given the media a significant place in their lives—even if they have not meant to do so. Like capitalism, the media are omnipresent.

Today as more and more activities are performed through the media, both mass and interactive, other institutions and organizations have shaped themselves to conform to media logic, a process called *mediatization*. Like the media themselves, this process is everywhere. Students take online courses, whose readings, lessons, and assignments are designed to conform to the logic of the Internet. In secular Western societies, people are increasingly attending religious services on their televisions, tablets, and smart phones; participation in organized religion is waning, and religious belief is becoming an individual matter; some denominations are trying to present themselves in ways that will attract an audience (as opposed to "real-life" congregants) and so encourage religious belief. Politics are geared to the media. Even as campaign finances revolve around the high cost of media ads, politicians use social media to attract supporters and raise money. To seem vote-worthy, they try to have their activities covered on news shows, and, to display what they believe to be their appeal, they appear as "guests" on news, talk, and comedy shows. Media have even become implicated in self-presentation, as people boast about how many "friends" and "followers" they have on Facebook and Twitter. Students standing or walking alone on campus seem to have their cell phones pasted to their ears as though announcing to observers that they do indeed have friends.

How religions present themselves, how individuals find love and found families, how politicians woo supporters—all these matters have varied historically and cross-culturally. Centuries ago in the West, such social institutions as political regimes and economic markets conformed to the demands of the church, but, with the advent of contemporary forms of globalization, politics and religion began to conform to the market. As, at the turn of the 21st century, the media became increasingly independent of national and international regulation, they also become ever more powerful—so dominant that they can demand that economic markets transform their operations to meet media logic, so important to individual success that when corporate managers are hiring new personnel, they consult the social media to learn about job applicants or hire firms that specialize in discovering what individuals have recently deleted from their social-media pages.

Throughout their text, Shoemaker and Reese refer to the research on the social construction of news published in the 1970s and early 1980s, a significant period of "media sociology" in which I myself was involved. In this period, cable television was beginning to flourish, and personal computers were entering the homes of the educated upper middle classes, who lived on the prosperous side of the digital divide. Recognition of the power of media permeates the pages of these studies. However, looking back, I don't think that the authors of those newsmaking studies—Mark Fishman, Herbert Gans, Todd Gitlin, Harvey Molotch, Michael Schudson, and I—realized that we were documenting what Dan Hallin has since called the "high modernism" of American journalism, a period when newsworkers pledged obeisance to codes of professionalism and claimed their news coverage was independent of the financial interests of the large corporations, then beginning to consolidate their grasp on the media landscape and eventually to hold it in thrall.

We were all sociologists. With the exception of Gans, all of us were at the start of our careers. (Fishman, Gitlin, Schudson, and I started our work on news as research for our dissertations. Molotch had been recently tenured.) We knew one another. I recall a conversation with Professor Gans, while I was still working on my dissertation. I read a draft of Schudson's book, and I think he read a draft of mine. Gitlin and I had lunch in New York, and I lent him the pages about "framing" written for the first draft of *Making News*. While still a graduate student working with Harvey Molotch, Fishman read drafts of my work, and I read chapters of the excellent dissertation that was to become his *Manufacturing the News*. Molotch and I had extensive conversations about news during the year that he was a visiting professor of sociology at State University of New York, Stony Brook. Together with his student Marilyn Lester, we taught an informal graduate seminar on phenomenological sociology and ethnomethodology; it probably influenced their classic article "News as Purposive Behavior," published in the *American Sociological Review* in 1974.

All of us had started our work on news in a period when political debate was lively and passions ran high. Mostly, we identified with the political left. I cannot speak for others' political experiences, though Gitlin makes no bones about his involvement with Students for a Democratic Society. In my case, as a moderately radical graduate student in sociology at Brandeis University, I was surrounded by people who cared deeply both about the civil rights movement and the antiwar movement. To me and others, understanding the forces that shaped news coverage seemed essential to analyzing why news organizations provided seemingly favorable coverage of "responsible" political actors, were highly critical of radical social movements, and cultivated a belief in the free press as the bulwark of democracy.

At the time, I had wanted to use phenomenological sociology to analyze how the routinization of work influences news as a form of knowledge. That concern permeates the early pages of *Making News* that I had shared with my colleagues. They were based on "Telling Stories," an article about framing that I had published in the *Journal of Communication* in 1975, the year after Goffman had discussed theater and novels in his path-breaking *Frame Analysis: An Essay on the Organization of Experience*. So far as I know, "Telling Stories" was the first work to apply Goffman's concepts about the organization of experience to newswork. I felt fairly confident about the thrust of my treatment of framing, because Erving Goffman had also read a draft of *Making News*, mentioned it briefly to me, and discussed it more extensively with my editor, the now legendary Gladys Topkis, who then worked at Free Press. (Some ten years after the publication of *Making News*, a prominent researcher told me I had misinterpreted Goffman's use of "frames" and "strips," but I have always felt that Goffman had given me his imprimatur.)

I don't know whether other researchers read political concern into the media sociology that emerged in the 1970s and early 1980s, although such British researchers as Stuart Hall used our works. Certainly, the theories that I used—the phenomenological sociology of Alfred Schutz, the constructivist approach of his students Peter Berger and Thomas Luckmann, the ethnomethodological ideas of Aaron Cicourel and Harold Garfinkle, and Goffman's frame analysis—were not at all politically radical. However, that set of ideas explicitly rejected the functionalism that had dominated both American sociology and communication research on gatekeeping. These new theories and the temper of the times enabled all of us to ask new questions, and those new questions inevitably led to new answers. After all, question and answer are inextricably linked. In different ways, while investigating newsmaking, each of us explored aspects of the power of media, especially the formation of ideology.

In *Mediating the Message in the 21st Century*, Pamela Shoemaker and Stephen Reese present the hierarchy of influence to help us to think about the power of the media today. They also present new ways to think about older questions that still seem vital as mass media and social media permeate our lives: who we are and how we fit into the families, organizations, institutions, and nations in which we are embedded.

Gaye Tuchman
University of Connecticut
November 2012

PREFACE

Mediating the Message in the 21st Century has been in the works a long time. It began with the 1991 and 1996 incarnations of our original book *Mediating the Message*, which we wrote during an early phase of our academic lives. The framework of this book remains much the same as the previous two editions, but much has happened in the media world and along our scholarly paths. Returning to this topic brings an opportunity to be retrospective and consider "the making of" *Mediating the Message*. Through this completely revised book, we've been able to take stock of a project that has figured prominently in both of our careers.

In 1999, the second edition was designated by *Journalism & Mass Communication Quarterly* as one of the most significant journalism and communication books of the 20th century. It was an unexpected honor, and we were grateful to have been recognized in a list of such distinguished company, especially since it was published in the final decade of the century. It was gratifying to see our work's value ratified by our scholarly peers, a judgment we assume stemmed from the book helping to legitimate and bring helpful conceptual tools to what had been a marginal, far flung, and rather eclectic part of the communication field. It was difficult to create a fully satisfactory title to reflect this new area, and we had considered simply calling it *Media Sociology*. That's a familiar term, coming closest to what we are interested in (and an adequate descriptor we continue to use), but labeling it "sociology" would have limited the disciplinary scope of the subject (an issue we discuss further in Chapter 1). So, we've stuck with the original title, which emphasizes mediation: particularly the construction, production, and control of specific patterns of meaning contained in media *content*. Although our goal is the same, this book is a new work that reflects the changing media world and the rich scholarly world we now review. We finally recognized that we were writing a book that included almost completely new material when compared to the 1996 edition. Our new publisher Routledge agreed and so *Mediating the Message in the 21st Century* was born. Note that *media sociology* made its way into the secondary title, emphasizing our preferred name for this area of scholarship.

Of course, we still embrace our original editions of *Mediating the Message*, particularly given how widely they have been cited over the years, therefore keeping the "brand" intact. But doing so has presented a challenge. Little of the subject matter in the 1996 edition has escaped the transformations at work in the media and larger society: Forces of technology and globalization have made our objects of study themselves newly problematic, including the news profession, the boundaries of the media organization, and the institutional media–society relationships. The intensification of social relations transcends national boundaries, making it important to acknowledge that the US- and UK-based version of media sociology must be extended and understood more globally. We both have travelled widely in this interim and have collaborated with international colleagues in research projects, and so we are more sensitive to the global context. Nevertheless, we are admittedly much more aware of trends and examples from the USA. We do try to be cautious, however, in universalizing them.

Reflecting upon the earlier books, we found ourselves striking a polemical tone, advocating for greater attention to this area even as we critiqued it and drew together the various strands of existing work into a more unified theoretical framework. Now the tone has changed, because what we advocated has to a great extent come to pass. A burgeoning amount of work now does take the production and control of media seriously, and this part of the field has grown steadily. Our books' organizing device has become more formally known as the Hierarchy of Influences Model and has been widely adopted. A major section of the *International Encyclopedia of Communication*, the most comprehensive map to date of the research field, was set aside for the related area "Media Production and Content." But this proliferation of scholarship has made more difficult our job of synthesizing it in a useful way.

We approach *media* broadly, recognizing that there is much to be done in applying the Hierarchical Model to the entertainment industry; however, our backgrounds and research interests still means that this new book has a focus on the public sphere, in which journalism plays such an important role. And journalism, in spite of the crisis in the US news industry, has enjoyed major international growth as a focus of training and an academic research subject in the last two decades. The International Communication Association, for example, launched a journalism interest group which quickly grew to division status; the Association for Education in Journalism and Mass Communication has continued to grow in size; and new journals with international editorial boards with a focus on journalism have been launched in recent years: *Journalism: Theory, Practice, Criticism* and *Journalism Studies*, to be followed soon by *Digital Journalism*. So this surge in journalism scholarship—driven in large part by scholars outside of the USA—naturally brings renewed interest in media sociology. With this global impulse spurring research collaboration across national lines, the Hierarchy of Influences Model seems to adapt well to cross-national comparative media studies. By beginning work early on in this field we've been the beneficiaries of these subsequent trends.

We both come out of the Wisconsin-Madison tradition of doctoral training, which then and now emphasizes variable analysis and theory building, with media content (and exposure of content) as a cause that leads to effects. But *Mediating the Message* was and is still more about the forces that shape media content, with content variables as effects. One could say that our book has been a reaction to the "audience and effects" tradition we absorbed in graduate school. We recognize that this new book intersects with other intellectual traditions that don't fit as easily into that variable-analytic language, including the more humanistic Zelizer approach to journalism as an *interpretive community*, the critical study of ideology with its dynamics of *hegemony*, and the *network society* model of Castells (2007) that describes "articulations" rather than effects. Indeed, the online world naturally lends itself to new spatial models, with *public spheres, fields, networks,* and global news *arenas*. Destabilized and reconstituted relations among citizens, media, and society make it harder to easily partition and completely contain the influences we examine within specific levels of analysis. Nevertheless, we still take from our Wisconsin years the value of explicating concepts, developing models, and proposing analytical frameworks—in short, theoretical thinking. We continue to see the value of thinking systematically about even these slippery phenomena, so that we can bring some order to an eclectic area and thus make it easier for scholars to better collaborate, share, and accumulate insights.

We have been thinking about this revision since the 1996 edition, as we have each pursued our respective independent yet complementary research programs. We've included examples of that research where relevant. Both of us have embraced an international perspective, with Shoemaker, for example, conducting large-scale empirical cross-national work in *News around the World* (2006) and Reese considering globalization more generally as it relates to journalism (2010). We have both continued to teach courses organized around the book's chapters and have extended our thinking about many of these concepts since those early efforts. In *Mediating the Message in the 21st Century*, we have reversed the presentation of the levels of analysis, now moving from macro to micro (an argument can be made to logically proceed in either direction). We have also switched some chapter responsibilities to reflect our new understanding of media sociology. Reese took primary charge of the introduction, the introduction of the Hierarchical Model, the chapter on influences on content from individuals, and the social institutional (what we earlier referred to as extra-media) level. Shoemaker drafted the mediated reality (patterns of media content) chapter, the social system level (formerly ideology), the routines level, and the organizational level. We both contributed to the final chapter on research conducted using the Hierarchical Model. Much of our earlier material can be identified in this new book, but it is surrounded by new research and thinking.

Much has changed in the communication world, and we've worked hard to overhaul each chapter to also reflect the evolution of our own thinking. Although some chapter titles have changed, the format remains the same:

- Chapter 1, now titled "Media Content and Theory" instead of "Studying Influences on Media Content," describes the focus of the book, the major conceptual issues, and establishes the value of a levels of analysis approach to understanding the influences on content.

- Chapter 2, still titled "Beyond Processes and Effects," takes a historical perspective to explain why 20th century media scholarship so strongly emphasized media effects. Our old chapter "Linking Influences on Content to the Effects of Content" has been folded into discussion of the model.

- Chapter 3, "Mediating Reality," is more theoretical than previously. Instead of just describing *Patterns of Media Content*, we now consider the symbolic environment created by the media and how this interacts with the social reality of people. We even consider whether reality as we know it actually exists.

- Our new macro-to-micro organization results in Chapter 4, "Social Systems," beginning with a consideration of how macro variables within this level can affect content, including those from structural functionalism, Marxism, critical and cultural studies, hegemony, political economy, democratic pluralism, and world systems. This extends the previous "Ideology" chapter.

- What we now call the "Social Institutions" level (Chapter 5) was awkwardly titled in earlier editions as "Influences on Content from Outside Media Organizations." This was often shortened as the *extra-media* level and seemed to consist of "everything else." We now take a more theoretical perspective, accounting for the growing work in fields, institutions, and the shifting boundaries among them—an area that features some of the most interesting research now underway, as the media reshape themselves along with their relationships with other powerful institutions.

- Chapter 6 still covers influences from "Organizations," but it has expanded to include theories of how people interact in organizations, plus the transformation of media on the Internet. We now talk about the many new types of media organizations in the world, including social media such as Facebook and Twitter.

- Chapter 7, "Routines," now addresses how the practices of traditional media have meshed with those of similar media on the Internet and with the social media.

- Chapter 8, "Individuals," recognizes new international work, the more politicized environment for understanding media workers, and the critical debates over journalism education itself.

- Chapter 9, "Studying the Hierarchical Model," takes stock of the theoretical progress of media sociology studies. Our old chapter "Building a Theory of News Content" has been replaced with an analysis of research that has used our model over more than 20 years.

As we looked back over the research cited in previous editions, we realized that several decades have gone by since some of the studies were conducted. Some of these, such as the 1950s studies of gatekeeping and social control and the pioneering ethnographies of sociologists like Herbert Gans, have become classics, and we have retained them for their timeless insights and as models for what was to follow, while also being sensitive to a significantly different world. Other work seemed dated and has been refreshed with more current insights. And, of course, we've tried to provide more current examples and to update trends where necessary (without becoming too topical and easily dated). In providing such a range of material, from the classic studies to current research, this book takes on more of an historical aspect than previous editions.

Sometime back in the early 1990s we planned to write a related, more historical book, with Reese taking the lead, and featuring *key works* in media sociology. Our goal was to identify works that exemplified each level—with insights solicited from the authors into their historical and intellectual context. Regrettably, that book never came to fruition, but we gained some insights and material that we've folded into this volume—a portion of which was published in Reese and Ballinger (2001) and Reese (2009b). We thank Herbert Gans, David Weaver, Todd Gitlin, and the late David Manning White and Warren Breed for sharing their reflections on their scholarly works. Gaye Tuchman was also in that group, one of a confluence of sociologists in the 1970s discovering the news media as a worthy subject, and we are delighted that she agreed to write the Foreword for this edition.

We have been working on this book for many years and would thank our colleagues who have used these ideas in their own research and teaching and who encouraged us to keep at it and finish the job. To see that our ideas have been useful for research in other parts of the world has been particularly gratifying, and we greatly appreciate the invitations and hospitality from our many colleagues abroad. We thank our supporters at the University of Texas and Syracuse University, particularly the many graduate students who over the years have contributed to our intellectual life and growth. As always we are grateful to our families for their love and support, and with this book we commemorate a collaborative friendship that now has reached the 30-year mark.

Stephen D. Reese
Austin, Texas

Pamela J. Shoemaker
Syracuse, New York
February 2013

ACKNOWLEDGMENTS

We thank the many people in both our professional and personal lives—with many occupying special places in both—who helped us make this book possible. Because the work has spread over virtually the course of our careers, acknowledging everyone who had a hand in it would be an encyclopedic and daunting task. Going back, however, to those who helped launch our efforts, we single out our doctoral advisers at Wisconsin, Steve Chaffee (Shoemaker) and Dan Drew (Reese), followed by the chairman at Texas who hired us both in 1982, Dwight Teeter, and our colleague and collaborator at Texas, Wayne Danielson. Every scholar should have such excellent mentors in the early years.

We certainly thank the many students at our home institutions, Syracuse and Texas, who have read and responded to our work for many years, and we appreciate our many colleagues, both locally and around the world, using *Mediating the Message* in their own classes and research. We are grateful to those who generously invited us for lectures and visits, creating many warm memories and friendships. Through it all, they have helped encourage us to pursue this new volume. Special thanks go to the Syracuse assistants who helped with the final push, Jaime Riccio and Christi MacClurg.

Closer to home, Pam thanks her husband and son, John and Jack Parrish, for loving her and keeping her sane. Steve thanks his family for their love and support: Carol, Aaron and Kate, and Daniel.

CHAPTER 1

Media Content and Theory

In this book we examine the forces that shape media content, the *messages* that constitute the symbolic environment. This is an ambitious task, given the multitude of factors that exert influence on the media. Not only that, but questions of media operation, bias, and control have moved to the center of the public arena, with an increasing number of media-literate citizens developing and promoting their own views. Media questions are often highly normative and highly politicized. Thus, the scholarly research questions we consider are very much in the public sphere, closely related to press criticism that circulates among activists, policy elites, and media professionals themselves. Reconciling these conflicting and often partisan-based charges can be difficult. What is more, a cynical public appears increasingly skeptical of the possibility of settling questions with evidence, substituting instead a combination of ironic detachment and impressionistic theories of personal media experience. But systematic media research on even the most controversial subjects is possible. That is why we must bring conceptual and theoretical organization to this area of research, to build understandings and research into a more comprehensive pattern. The same research tools used so extensively to examine media effects can be turned on those media and their links with culture, other organizations, and institutions. In developing *Mediating the Message in the 21st Century*, we hope to strengthen the case that these questions can be generated and examined with rigor given a clear and accepted conceptual framework. We expect the field of communication to devote the same sustained research to the creation, control, and shape of the mediated environment as it has to the effects on audiences of that environment.

Our approach to studying media messages comes from a social science perspective: We try to be clear about our definitions, assumptions, and perspectives, developing a model to locate our questions and suggesting how that model can be used to organize research and to suggest other hypotheses and fruitful areas for additional study. We call the model we have developed the *Hierarchy of Influences*, or more formally the Hierarchical Influences Model, and use it to organize the major chapters and studies discussed in this book. This model takes into account the multiple forces that simultaneously impinge on media and suggests how influence at one level may interact with that at another. The personal bias of an individual journalist, for example, may be relevant to reporting, but journalists of a particular leaning often self-select into organizations because of their preexisting policies, history, and organizational culture. The media organizations and their employees, in turn, must function within the ideological boundaries set by the larger society.

We do not assume that the Hierarchical Model captures all of the complex interrelationships involved in the media. Models, by definition, are meant to simplify, highlight, suggest, and organize. But in doing so, they can exert a powerful guiding effect in determining how questions are posed and defining the relationships singled out for investigation. In retrospect, the model used in our work has had a greater impact on the field than we imagined when we brought out the 1991 edition of *Mediating the Message*. Certainly a survey of the current field shows that research has grown, classes have been organized, and professional academic organizations have been launched. In addition, this area of study has been legitimated, and we suggest some reasons why this has been so. In part this can be attributed to the model providing a compelling way to think about the subject matter and more firmly integrating it into the existing communication field. As we prepare this work for the third edition, we take the opportunity to reflect further on how our ideas have changed, why we chose to emphasize certain ideas before, and why we have made different choices today. So, in setting out the book's plan we may at several points draw comparisons with our previous editions and set them in historical context. We hope that this may be of interest in revealing our own thinking as we re-confront and make sense of this growing field.

We use the term *media sociology* to refer to the scholarship in this book, because it comes closest to describing what we are interested in. The term, however, does come with ambiguities and disadvantages. Certainly, many of the newsroom and other media ethnographies are typically referred to as media sociology, particularly given their use of traditional sociological fieldwork methods. But within the "influences on content" perspective we also include the more psychological studies of individual media workers and how their personal traits affect their decisions. Outside of the US fieldwork tradition, media sociology has been used in international contexts—particularly Europe and Latin America—to refer to the entire context of media production and performance, the entire social structural context. We use media sociology to refer to this larger body of interests concerning how patterns of symbols are linked to social structure—how the mediated symbolic environment gets constructed—by individuals within a social, occupational, institutional, and cultural context. Before laying out a broader model, we review below some of the key issues that must be understood.

MEDIA CONTENT

Analyzing the shaping of this symbolic environment means a central role for the concept of media *content*. As we develop a theory of media content, the shape of the symbolic environment is obviously a crucial component to be established. By media content, we mean the complete range of visual and verbal information carried in what were once called the mass media and increasingly by smaller more interactive and targeted channels. The features of this content have been measured in a number of ways, and we attempt to include a variety of perspectives—quantitative and qualitative. In some ways, *content* is a sterile-sounding term, but we will elaborate it with discussion of its specific shapes and patterns. As it takes on certain culturally significant features, it becomes more importantly the *symbolic environment*. Understanding content, even as a general term, is a crucial bridge between key areas of research: what shapes it and what impact it has (Reese & Lee, 2012).

Media Mirror?

When discussing content, particularly news content, there is a tendency to ask how "objectively" it reflects reality. For the sake of completeness, in our previous editions we included a reference in this discussion to the mirror hypothesis—the expectation that media reflect social reality with little distortion. This lack of distortion is sometimes vigorously defended in self-serving attempts by professionals to argue the accuracy of their work by holding it up as a "mirror to society." In a subtle version of this idea, media are rendered neutral or objective by reflecting the self-regulating and balancing compromises between those who sell information to the media and those who buy it. This notion—the repudiation of which has launched countless media critiques—now seems rather quaint and self-evidently untrue (although that has not been sufficient to squelch it altogether). Certainly, the problematic issue of content—a disconnect between *reality* and its mediated counterpart—is a basic scholarly premise, not to mention an article of faith of the many media watchdog groups that monitor press performance. They find fault with those media for not adequately representing the reality they have in mind.

The notion of *bias* used by many press watchdog groups itself suggests that media deviate in some measurable way from a desirable standard that can be independently known. Of course, it is problematic to think of a reality out there with which we can compare mediated content. The postmodernists have been ridiculed by lay critics for rejecting the more traditional concept of a single, unified external reality, which suggests that there can be no independent standard for distinguishing among rival interpretations. But we all apprehend reality within the framework provided by our senses; even the concept of "empirical" reality refers to those things that can be measured using our senses. The simple fact is that we ultimately cannot lift ourselves out of our human context and apprehend reality apart from it. We address this more in Chapter 3.

We need not get too hung up on such philosophical problems. On a practical level we will often find it useful to compare *media reality* with *social reality*, people's view of the world that is socially derived, what society knows about itself. Our assessment of social reality relies on numerous sources of information, including opinion polls, census surveys, historical records and other documents, all of which have their socially constructed qualities. But to the extent that media reality differs in systematic ways from these other forms of social self-knowledge, we can draw important conclusions about the structures underpinning these differences. Even if we were to accept the possibility of objectively portraying a "world out there," the numerous studies over the years of media distortion have compared media content with other *social* indicators of reality. We assume that the media portray people, events, and ideas in ways that differ systematically from their occurrence in both various social realities.

Viewed another way, media content is fundamentally a social construction, and as such can never find its analog in some external benchmark, a "mirror" of reality. Distortion in this sense becomes irrelevant; social reality is meaningful in and of itself. Media-constructed reality has taken its place alongside other social constructions, such as mental illness, criminality, sexuality, gender, race, and other identities that are no longer considered self-evidently "natural." If content is a construction, then to understand its special quality it is essential to understand the "constructing." This realization in turn assigns greater importance to the research in media sociology, which is about exactly that. Therefore, it is a basic premise of this approach, rather than some tentative theoretical perspective, that the media exert their own unique shaping power on the symbolic environment, a shaping that is open to explanation using various theoretical perspectives—which we combine into the Hierarchy of Influences Model.

BUILDING THEORY

We attempt to place the subject of this book within the larger context of the field by locating it in relation to content. Accepting the problematic nature of content calls for a larger organizing theoretical framework. Therefore, when we first conceptualized this area, we took the idea of media content as a jumping off place, and we took pains to critique the "content research" that we were able to identify. It may seem self evident that content is the basis for media effects and needs to be closely examined, but many of the field's most important lines of research have often not done so. Studies in the communication field that describe the features of media content proliferated, but they were largely unconnected and lacked any consistent theoretical framework. We noted in earlier versions of *Mediating the Message* how early, largely descriptive content research made little attempt to connect across studies, which often limited themselves to measuring the "number of" and "image of" (fill in the blank). We previously identified Warren Breed (1955) and David Manning White (1950) as among the first scholars showing the influences *on* content in a more research-based mode, with their examinations of social control in the newsroom and the news gatekeeper, but others did not follow their lead in communication until more recently (Reese & Ballinger, 2001), something we'll explore more fully in the next chapter.

Our first effort to organize media sociology was strongly oriented toward theory building, and we began with a discussion of hypothesis testing. If the traditional communication field emphasized the transmission of effects from media to audiences, we argued for a just as important need to explain how those media and their messages were acted upon by a variety of influences. Thus, we promoted the idea of regarding media content within a variable analytic framework: that is, treating content as a dependent variable with which a number of independent variables were related and could be said to shape it. But if the traditional field was marked by surveys and controlled experiments, isolating an effect of interest, the media sociology domain has been much more diverse and messy, ranging across many levels of analysis and research traditions. Looking back we recognize that not all useful perspectives bearing on media sociology can be reduced to such straightforward linear relationships. Many of them are qualitative, interpretive, and naturally resistant to being described in more quantitative variable analytic terminology. Nevertheless, it seems more evident to us now that placing this messy area into a more clearly defined container—the stricter language of variables and influence—imposes a drive toward clarification, definitions, assumptions, empirical indicators, and relationships that are the hallmark of useful investigation.

This is what we have tried to do, even if calling that container "theory" may sound grandiose. Looking back, our goal was simply to begin to think seriously about assumptions, relationships, and ways of measuring. This makes it possible to draw connections, find similarities, and in short to build theory. Audience and effects theories have a longer tradition and are more finely drawn and focused, such as the social-psychological approaches to attitude change and, more recently, information processing. Perhaps, we should have been more cautious in making such a daunting claim to theory in assembling previously disparate strands of research. Nevertheless, we did just that and are glad others have found it useful. Hooking up the audience and effects side of the field with the shaping and control of content—within a consistent style of explanation—makes it easier to conceptualize the extension of the field into this less studied domain (as illustrated in Figure 1.1). For example, the intuitively appealing idea of media *agenda-setting* popularized by McCombs and Shaw (1972) suggests the powerful ability of the media to tell people what they should attend to. Given the extensive body of research into the idea of how the media set the agenda for the public, it is an easy rhetorical step to ask an equally important question: What sets the media's agenda? Just by locating such a question within the framework of communication research gives it a certain legitimacy (Reese, 1991).

Integrating Effects on Content with Effects of Content

The broad field of mass or mediated communication research can be laid out as a combination of these two kinds of effects, with the content agenda itself as the bridge and a crucial element in our formulation (Figure 1.1). In our previous editions, we stressed the importance of incorporating measures of content into research, and much of the research in this book addresses the forces operating to shape specific

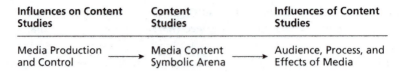

Influences on Content Studies	Content Studies	Influences of Content Studies
Media Production and Control	Media Content Symbolic Arena	Audience, Process, and Effects of Media

FIGURE 1.1 *Communication research foci: Influences on content compared with influences of content*

media messages. Others have taken media content into account, but have linked it either primarily to audience evaluations (such as, how certain content features affect television ratings, print circulation, or website traffic) or directly to effects on those audiences (for example, agenda-setting research requires some measure of the media content agenda, and experimental studies of media effects evaluate some aspect of the message). In other studies, media content is not assessed directly. These research areas include examinations of the active audience (the uses and gratifications tradition of media use), traditional effects studies measuring media behavior of audiences (exposure and attention), without explicitly measuring the nature of the content they consume.

In the next chapter we discuss why the field chose its particular emphases, but suffice it to say here that the more we know about how content is shaped and what form it takes, the more guidance we have in developing theories of effects—historically the main question of interest. Because many of the field's theories come to us second-hand, particularly from social psychology and political science, we argue that the development of mass communication theory, by being largely derivative from other disciplines, was stuck on a plateau and would not grow until it began to deal with media content as a crucial feature, itself open to explanation. Much of the early theorizing in the field seized on media opportunistically as just another setting in which to examine individual response and behavior. Elaborate models of voting behavior, for example, may include one box, among many others, labeled "media." Media use measures, included in countless surveys, show that news consumption is positively related to other desirable outcomes—such as informedness, political interest, and likelihood to vote. It seems like a simple idea to state that exposure to a medium is not the same as exposure to specific content, but many studies work around the task of specifically measuring it. The content of that media consumption remained implied rather than examined directly, and we have cited Gerbner's many studies of television violence as an example of this idea (Gerbner, Gross, Jackson-Beeck, Jeffries-Fox, & Signorielli, 1978). His research typically asked respondents how many hours of television they watched, and from this it was inferred the number of acts of violence they would have likely seen. (Of course, in his case, numerous of his previous content studies of the "television world" confirmed key patterns of representation.) The "communication mediation model" of communication effects developed by the Wisconsin group falls in this category, targeting in the political realm, for example, the effects of exposure to campaign advertising and news consumption on political behavior, a relationship mediated by personal reflection and political discussion (Cho et al., 2009).

Audience research has tested how people feel about various media, including more recently mobile phones, the Internet, and video games—and current studies of news behavior are repeating this tendency. A recent study of young news consumers, for example, asked about their behavior and attitudes toward newspapers, local television, cable television, and "the Internet" (Brown, 2005). Of course, the Internet incorporates information from all of these sources; a news portal on the web is simply another vehicle for delivering content, "aggregated" and with a different format. Keeping track of specifically what content people consume, already a difficult task, is made more difficult with the proliferation of media and should at least hasten the need to abandon simplistic survey measures, such as "where do you get your news?" Eventually, however, we must move beyond issues of "use" and grapple with the specific features in the symbolic mediated environment, linking these to larger social pressures and audience outcomes.

Visualizing these research questions within the larger context of the field, we hope to show that some questions are open for investigation particularly because of their connection to media content. As we have said before, it is easy to take media content as a given, not questioning its origins, especially if we assume it to be a starting point for dealing only with the level of audience evaluation and response. Connecting media to the influences that impinge on them opens up a host of normatively charged questions—but questions that can and should be examined empirically. That is why the notion of media framing has become so popular as a research concept. It takes content seriously, tying those frames to larger structures, and develops new ways of capturing the power of media to define issues visually and verbally, thereby shaping audience perceptions (Reese, 2001a, 2009a).

THE HIERARCHICAL MODEL

Factors affecting media content can be usefully classified at several levels of analysis, leading us to organize them into a larger model. Various theoretical perspectives have been laid out previously on the shaping of media content, including as follows the suggested categories of Gans (1979) and Gitlin (1980).

- *Content is influenced by media workers' socialization and attitudes.* This is a communicator-centered approach, emphasizing the psychological factors impinging on an individual's work: professional, personal, and political.

- *Content is influenced by media organizations and routines.* This approach argues that content emerges directly from the nature of how media work is organized. The organizational routines within which an individual operates form a structure, constraining action while also enabling it.

- *Content is influenced by other social institutions and forces.* This approach finds the major impact on content lying external to organizations and the communicator: economic, political, and cultural forces. Audience pressures can be found in the "market" explanation of "giving the public what it wants."

- *Content is a function of ideological positions and maintains the status quo.* The so-called hegemony approach locates the major influence on media content as the pressures to support the status quo, to support the interests of those in power in society.

A Theoretical Umbrella for Research

From these ideas, it is a logical next step to more formally propose an organized theoretical framework, which we have termed the Hierarchical Model. It comprises five levels of influence, hierarchically arrayed from the macro to micro: social systems, social institutions, organizations, routines, and individuals, levels that we will use to organize the chapters that follow. As seen in Figure 1.2, at the center is the micro *individual* level, which includes the characteristics of the individual communicator. The *routines* level includes the most immediate constraining and enabling structures, larger patterns, or routines within which the individual operates. The *organization* level is distinguished from routines in describing the influences of the larger organized entity within which the individual operates, the larger context of the routinized activities, which includes occupational roles, organizational policy, and how the enterprise itself is structured. The *social institution* level describes the influences arising from the larger trans-organizational media field, how media organizations combine into larger institutions that become part of larger structured relationships as they depend on and compete with other powerful social institutions. The macro *social system* level is the outer-most ring of the model, including influences on content from the system as a whole. This includes ideological forces in the sense that they concern ideas and meaning in the service of interests and power—encompassing how all the other levels add up to a larger result. This perspective also lends itself to cross-national comparisons of how the national and cultural context affect media performance. As we move through the levels, we take different expressions of power into account: from the momentary and situational to the more patterned and repetitive and from the structural and institutional to the systemic and societal.

As we discuss below—and return to in our concluding chapter—the sequence of these levels can be approached in different directions, and we don't mean to single out any one level as more powerful than another. In this case, however, the darker outer ring in Figure 1.2 implies primacy for the social systems level, which suits the order in which we will take them up. Progressing from darker to lighter shadings suggests that different emphases are possible depending on one's research focus. As a further refinement, the stronger border in the figure between the media organizations and social institutions levels simply reflects an intuitive media sociology distinction—between those things that reside within media organizations and the forces that lie beyond their boundaries.

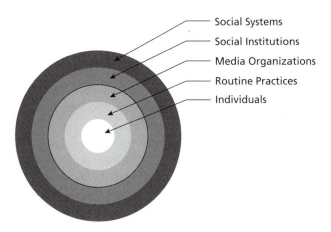

Social Systems
Social Institutions
Media Organizations
Routine Practices
Individuals

FIGURE 1.2 *The Hierarchy of Influences Model uses five levels of analysis*

In our previous books we paid relatively little attention in the first chapter on what we now understand as the appealing contribution of the Hierarchical Model. We organized our own thinking and chapter structure around these levels, but now we can see the ways that simply setting out such a model has affected research, by proposing important distinctions between levels of analysis and locating individuals within a web of organizational and ideological constraints.

Particularly for journalism, such a model untangles many criticisms of press performance, identifies their implicit normative and theoretical assumptions, and suggests appropriate kinds of evidence. For example, conservative media critics have located the source of bias with the individual journalist, calling for more balance in hiring practices and regularly scolding specific news anchors. Left-leaning critics, on the other hand, find fault more with the structure and ownership of the commercial media system, arguing for more public control and protections from the corruption of big advertisers. The irony is that journalists are more apt to give respectability to attacks from their right flank, which, even if targeting them as individuals, at least grants them the professional latitude to be blamed for bias in the first place. The left critique is less professionally satisfying, given that it relegates journalists to mere tools of a larger corporate system. Both critiques can be more easily understood when we know the level about which they are mainly conceived.

Studying Professionalism on Five Levels

The utility of such a model also helps us explicate key concepts on which research is based and unpack those that have multiple levels of meaning. Reese (2001b), for example, uses this model as a way of explicating the different levels of meaning associated with the concept of *professionalism* (whether journalistic or more broadly media), a basic interest within media sociology but one with widely varying connotations. Professionalism can be considered on one level as an individual value that is espoused, a trait of individuals that indicates the extent to which they belong to a professional group, which calls them to certain shared norms and outlooks. Alternatively, at the next level, to the extent that it embodies a set of procedures on how to report an event, professionalism is a routines level phenomenon. What Tuchman (1972) calls a "strategic ritual" suggests that news workers are considered professional to the extent that they adhere to the procedures, the accepted practices of deadlines, and simply getting the work done. Following the procedures provides a useful professional defense when challenged by audience members or other critics. At the organizational level, professionalism is a negotiated set of values worked out to satisfy the organization's needs. Concerns of individual bias and commercial ownership, for example, are rendered more manageable and defused by invoking the buffering power of professionalism said to distance the product from these threats. Here we would ask how professionalism is negotiated within an organization to facilitate both owner and journalistic needs? Indeed, media organizations selectively promote certain aspects of professionalism, not all of which place a strong emphasis on individual freedom.

At the larger *trans-organizational*, social institutional level, media find themselves within institutional relationships, and professionalism takes a different form depending on the nature of those relationships. Blumler and Gurevitch (1995), for example, contrast a "sacerdotal" role of British journalists with a more pragmatic attitude. In the first, it is accepted that official institutions like Parliament have the right to be broadcast because of their "priestly" function in society, as opposed to their actual newsworthiness. Thus, professionalism within media institutions is understood in relation to other key institutions in society. Finally, at the broader ideological level, professionalism takes on a still broader implication, that professional values must be consistent with the prevailing power structure. These values are often invoked to support the status quo and are tied to certain interests. For the press to question a US president's "war on terror" frame was considered unpatriotic in the aftermath of 9/11, and to refer to it as the "so-called" war on terror might be unprofessional (Lewis & Reese, 2009). The levels of the Hierarchical Model alert us to shifting meanings and implications in such important concepts and help generate research questions appropriate to each level.

ISSUES RAISED BY THE HIERARCHICAL MODEL

It is tempting to regard the larger structures within the model as relatively impersonal. Given our interest in *human* behavior, even the levels beyond the individual are still ways of conceptualizing the organized actions of people. No matter the level, we are still trying to explain human behavior and their organized creative products and relationships. Structures are abstractions that only become visible when we name them and begin to look for regularities and norms in human behavior. So, at the heart of this outlook is the interplay between structure and agency, between actions people take and the conditions under which they act that are not of their own making. To paraphrase Marx, they make history but not their circumstances, which they inherit from the past. They participate in a conversation that began before they arrived. Individuals work within social structures, and as these become more complicated they lead us to give less emphasis to specific situational choices, which become lost in the emphasis on larger macro structures. Thus, the distinction among these levels is not between people and non-people, individuals or non-individuals—or even individuals and social structures. It is between the immediate actions of specific individuals, and the more organized and historically situated actions of larger collections of people. Ideology, after all, is the meanings that people have become accustomed to attaching to certain interests of collectivities in control of significant social resources, including power.

In laying out these levels, it could be possible to prioritize their importance and sequence in different ways. We can certainly make a case for stepping through them in both directions: from micro to macro, or vice versa. Does everything begin with the individual, who is progressively hemmed in by more and more layers of constraint? Or is the macro, social system (historical) context logically prior to any actions of its member individuals? These are matters of analytical emphasis and preference and concern the interplay between agency and structure—that is, what we control and what is controlled for us. Previously we began with the individual as the basic building block and proceeded from there to introduce ever more complex and macro-level layers of influence. Intuitively for many, the actions of individuals are closest at hand, most easily visualized and observed. Institutional and ideological forces, although their effects are readily seen, are intuitively more distant and more difficult to grasp analytically.

There is also the tendency in this model to view individuals as relatively more powerless as we view them as increasingly "constrained" by successive layers of influence. Job routines do limit individuals in what they can do. The teacher, for example, must conform to student expectations, usually involving a clear syllabus, stated exam dates, and requirements for class assignments. Every job, however, must have structure, and every creative activity is processed through certain structured rules. Mozart may have been constrained by the symphonic form, but it was also the enabling structure through which he expressed creativity. Giddens (1984) refers to this idea as *structuration*, that structures can be both constraining and enabling. So, within the Hierarchical Model, although higher-level factors do not eliminate influences from a lower level, we must take both levels into account and consider how the lower level sets certain boundaries within which other influences range. Studies cannot take all these levels into account simultaneously, but we expect scholars to pick and choose locations for measurement while interpreting findings within the context of other levels.

Multiple Levels of Explanation

Once researchers begin to understand and express their questions and studies within a levels of analysis framework, it becomes easier to compare them to others' research, to see connections among different levels, and to generally begin a much more systematic approach to a diverse area of the field. The Hierarchical Model helps to organize an array of eclectic research by directing us to the level or perspective at which explanation is primarily sought. Although scholars implicitly recognize that media phenomena have a variety of causes and that explanation within a web of interconnected forces is indeed a matter of emphasis, they naturally still gravitate toward the explanation that fits their disciplinary and political leanings. We must ask, beyond these matters of personal preference, which explanation is theoretically most parsimonious and best makes sense. Empirically, our model suggests that one must determine the conditions under which certain factors are most determinative and how they interact with each other. And it reminds us to make sure the evidence presented is most appropriate to the level of analysis. The policies of a media organization, for example, may not directly translate into knowing the political views of its employees, who may not as individuals share or even resist the higher-level policy.

Recognizing the distinctiveness of the five levels makes possible more powerful studies with the benefit of methodological advances. In a study of news gatekeeping (Shoemaker, Eichholz, Kim, & Wrigley, 2001), newsworthiness (a routines level factor) was assessed by surveying a sample of editors (organizational level) about a list of Congressional Bills, and journalists who wrote stories about the Bills were surveyed about their personal characteristics. Editor data were aggregated and analyzed in an individual level data file to assess whether organizational or individual variables most accounted for the prominence of Bill coverage. The aggregation of editor judgment, however, concealed the variability *among* media organizations, preventing the assessment of *relative* influence of the organization, routines, and individuals. Multi-level modeling statistical procedures (Scherbaum & Ferreter, 2008), which hierarchically assess the effects of variables from two or more levels of analysis, allow us to take advantage of the detail contained in each level. Hierarchical linear modeling has changed how we study influences from more than one level of analysis by helping to assess the relative effects on news content, for example, from organizations, routine practices, and journalists. In our 1991 and 1996 books, we suggested some between-level hypotheses, recognizing that adequate data analysis procedures were not available at the time. Now scholars can test more complex hypotheses about the relationships among levels, giving us a much clearer picture of their overall impact.

Comparative Research

As media sociology grows as a field and across international settings, a consistent theoretical framework allows more comparative research to accumulate. Traditionally, the media sociology associated with newsroom ethnographies has been limited to the North American and British contexts, with a focus on single cases and contexts. But the global media have attracted a similarly global group of media scholars.

As these and other kinds of studies become popular in other national settings, it is important that they be integrated with other research. Shared theoretical perspectives allow these scholars to produce work fitting into a larger more integrated field, even if their respective national contexts vary widely. The work by Hanitzsch (2007) and his international team studying the *Worlds of Journalism* is a good example, as is the comparative project of Shoemaker and Cohen (2006), *News Around the World*. The Hierarchy of Influences Model lends itself to encouraging this kind of comparative framework. It helps move from the most common approach, simply comparing things, to comparing structures formed by things, processes within structures, and finally functions of seemingly different things, structures, and processes.

For example, the Japanese kisha press club system seems in isolation like a quaint set of customs and norms that oblige reporters to become an integral part of a government minister's life, following them around, even going out drinking at night to be assured of getting a story. Each official agency has a press club, and only its members can attend the press conferences it holds. But when we consider the function it serves, to get news, it is much the same as the pack journalism routine followed by US journalists. It is in the interest of the government official to restrict information and develop relationships with journalists who can demonstrate their trustworthiness over time. Although different in type, the press routines in Japan and the USA serve the same purpose.

The Issue of Importance

When looking at our target-like figure that represents the Hierarchical Model, do you assume that individuals are the most important? Or that social systems are most important? The answer to this question reveals assumptions about the nature of the world. For example, think of Figure 1.2 instead as a three-dimensional model of a multi-layer cake, perhaps complete with figurines of people being married at the top. There are two ways of thinking about this theoretical cake:

1. *Individuals are key.* The newlyweds are full of hope and ideas about their future together. If young, they may rejoice at leaving the controlling family power structure of their parents' homes. They may move far away, begin new jobs, and become their own new family. They may not call their parents very often. When they think of their ancestors and the country they live in—if they do—they assign little relevance to them. They are individuals and they make their own success in life. The rest of the theoretical cake is just cake.

2. *Social systems are key.* The base of the cake, being the largest of all layers, is the most important. The cake could not exist without the bottom layer, and if the base crumbles, the other layers fall. If the base is strong, the cake is strong. Representing the social system level in our model, the base defines everything above it. The system creates certain structures and institutions in order

to maintain itself and among these are the mass media, the communications structure. Media organizations, other social institutions, and society itself define the ways in which media work is carried out, the routine practices of information gathering and processing. Media work, not being fully automated, requires people to accomplish it, and so the figurine workers balance precipitously on the top of the cake, knowing that they could be knocked off, or lose their jobs, at any moment.

These examples represent two ways of thinking about the Hierarchical Model. In our 1991 and 1996 books, we chose to represent the model as a flat target that did not emphasize either micro or macro. That these first editions began with the individual level of analysis, however, may have reflected our socialization as American individualists. We had no discussion about the relative importance of the levels—we just put the individual level first. A long five chapters later, we concluded with the ideological chapter, which we now enlarge to be the social system. Figure 1.2 is just a flat set of concentric circles, but is the most important part of a target the center?

Would you put the most important chapter first or last? Since 1996 we have had many discussions about this issue, debating this very question. Moreover, we have both traveled extensively outside of the American hegemonic sphere, and after so many years not only recognize our early assumption, but also question it. The truth generally lies in the middle way between the extremes. Of course we also recognize that the world is a web of structures, relationships, and people, all of which interact. However, it is difficult to study—even theorize about—the billions of concepts attributed to multiple levels of all parts of a world system at the same time. As social scientists, we deconstruct the effects of variables within relatively controlled circumstances, hence the simplicity of the Hierarchical Model. It is a theoretical structure on which scholars can locate and compare their studies, whether comparing 2 or 2,000 variables.

Still, we had to decide whether to begin this new book at the micro or macro level and so switched the order of the core five chapters. This could represent a search for something new or it could reflect our growing recognition that we can never step off of the bottom, hegemonic layer of the cake. We hope that by doing something new scholars will think thoughts they have never thought before. And that's the way to build theory.

SUMMARY

The structure of this new book remains close to previous versions, in that we organize our key chapters around the Levels of Influence Model, taking up each in turn and considering the kinds of research associated with each. In Chapter 2 we locate our research themes in relation to the dominant process and effects approach that has characterized media communication research. Our discussion of mediated reality in Chapter 3 leads to a discussion of the nature of social reality and of reality itself. We organize the levels of influence to proceed from the macro social system level to the micro individual level. We treat each successive level as subsumed within the other.

We conclude this volume with a review of selected studies that have examined hypotheses developed from the Hierarchy of Influences Model. As we will examine in the next chapter, analytical models—even simple ones—can have a powerful effect on directing our thinking and helping to organize a field of research. The media world has grown more complex since our first venture into this area, but that means the need for clarifying tools has grown as well. Although we try to review as much research as possible in the following chapters, our main goal is to bring an organizing framework to a diverse area, helping us understand its historical roots and laying out the key issues. These are issues that have made their way from academic research into the public square, with debates over media performance fueled by citizen activists and powerful interest groups. But communication research is charged with bringing light rather than heat, to explain with evidence how it all works. We hope the Hierarchy of Influences perspective continues to be a valuable approach, as we seek greater understanding of the many forces shaping the symbolic arena so central to modern life.

CHAPTER 2

Beyond Processes and Effects

In this chapter we advocate a particular focus in communication theory and research—the production and control of the media symbolic arena. Before developing our own perspective, however, it is helpful to consider the broader context, locating our questions within the larger trends in social science and the field of communication itself. Mapping the field both theoretically and historically shows where research has been and where it's developing, particularly within the Hierarchy of Influences taken up in the rest of this volume. An historical view shows how the dominant directions in the social sciences left behind the serious study of the mass media themselves. In large measure, the questions posed by media sociology were not compatible with the prevailing methods and theories of the relatively young field of communication research. Some of the blind spots that characterized the early years have been corrected, and the focus has broadened since this book's first edition. We argue, however, that the general thrust has remained true to our earlier picture. For example, in a 20-year analysis of research trends in major mass communication journals, most studies were related to uses and effects of media. Between 1980 and 1999 only 39 percent mentioned a theory by name and, of those, two were related to media sociology: "media construction of social reality" (10 percent of mentions) and "hegemony theory or media as maintainer of status quo" (8 percent). Research was dominated by quantitative methods—arguably a method less tied to studying media production and control—in a pattern that remained consistent over the period (Kamhawi & Weaver, 2003).

INTRODUCING THE FRAMEWORK

Imposing a coherent framework on the media content body of research presents a challenge, given the diversity of methods and perspectives. Using the agenda metaphor, what sets the public's agenda is a better defined area of inquiry than what sets the media's agenda. The latter opens us to a whole range of philosophical issues and methodological approaches. To guide our discussion, we can outline a simple framework that maps the field according to two dimensions, based on unit and level of analysis. Starting in this framework with the unit of analysis, we identify the thing that is being studied. One of the earliest and most often quoted ways of describing the communication process was suggested by Harold Lasswell (1948), who proposed this framework model formed around questions:

- Who?

- Says what?

- Through which channel?

- To whom?

- With what effect?

These units can be arranged as steps in a process of mediated communication. But in conceptualizing that process, communication research has examined the audiences for the media messages and how effects are produced on them. The message itself (or exposure to it) has been the *independent variable*, or cause, and the effects of the message the *dependent* variables—dependent on exposure to content. In this book, we define the message itself as a *dependent variable*, the result of a number of causes. We want to consider how the message, or media content, is influenced by a wide variety of factors both inside and outside of media organizations. This kind of "variable" influence model, using social science language of cause and effect, has been a compelling and useful approach in understanding the entire communication process.

If we take just two examples from political communication we can see how content provides a useful linkage in bridging these perspectives. We already mentioned that the *agenda setting* tradition of media research provides compelling terminology for us to consider not only how the media set the public agenda, but also how the media agenda itself is set by broader factors. The tradition of *media framing* research also cuts across these major domains, considering how issues are constructed, or framed, for the public. We can study not only the resulting interpretations of frames, but also the factors that those media frame in the first place. Scheufele (1999) uses this process model to divide studies of media frames as independent or dependent variables depending on whether they are the cause (of the way audiences think about issues) or effect (the result of a number of factors shaping those frames). He considers those factors to be *inputs*, affecting the process of *frame building* and in turn the *outcomes*, that is, *media frames*. They in turn produce *frame setting* for the audience, yielding various results on attitudes and behaviors. Figure 2.1 shows this process using agendas and frames as specific examples of media content. Thinking this way about the process of communication, from production and content to content and effects, allows us to consider where the relative emphasis has been within the communication field historically.

Mass communication studies have examined all of these elements, or units of analysis—the communicator (who); media content (says what); the medium (through which channel); the audience (to whom); and the effects (with what effect)—but most have concentrated on the final two elements, audience and effects.

FIGURE 2.1   *Agenda-setting and framing: Media content as both independent and dependent variable*

They may have focused on more than one component within the same project's study design, but even those tend to concentrate on part of the communication process more than the others. To understand this emphasis, we offer the early classic voting study conducted in Erie County, Ohio, in 1940 by Paul Lazarsfeld and his colleagues (Lazarsfeld, Berelson, & Gaudet, 1948). Three thousand residents were interviewed about their voting intentions, personal characteristics, and the attention they paid to newspaper and radio messages about a particular political campaign. The researchers concluded that media messages *reinforced* (but did not determine) people's political predispositions. Personal characteristics of the audience members were found to determine campaign interest, and audience members were found to have used media selectively to filter out political messages that ran contrary to their preexisting political stances. In this study, as in many others, a number of components were involved ("says what"—campaign messages; "through which channel"—radio and newspapers; "to whom"—voters; "with what effect"—reinforcement); however, the primary focus, the thing measured directly, was the audience.

For the other dimension of the map we take the levels of analysis in communications research, which can be thought of as forming a continuum ranging from micro to macro—from the smallest units of a system to the largest. A *micro-level* study examines communication as an activity engaged in and affecting individuals; a *macro-level* study examines social structures beyond the control of any one individual—social networks, organizations, and cultures. These levels function hierarchically: what happens at the smaller levels is affected by, even to a large extent determined by, what happens at larger levels.

Locating the Milestones

If we add Lasswell's framework to the level of analysis dimension, we can construct a larger matrix within which to locate the landmark communications studies (see Fig. 2.2). The studies we illustrate are those identified by Shearon Lowery and Melvin DeFleur in their book, *Milestones in Mass Communication Research* (1995). Note that although many of these studies have macro-societal theoretical implications or deal with society-wide problems, the milestone studies were conducted at the individual level of analysis. Thus we use the measurement variables actually employed in the studies to locate them, not their level of theorizing. Only four of these studies directly examined media content, and none was devoted solely to communicators themselves. Most studies (and arguably the most influential) fall into the upper right quadrant of the matrix—the "to whom" and "with what effect" columns, and on the micro or individual level row. We next look briefly at each of these studies.

Who (communicator)	Says What through Which Channel (media content)	To Whom (audience)	With What Effect (effects)
Micro/Individual	*Seduction of the Innocent,* 1954	*The Payne Fund Studies: Motion Pictures and Youth,* 1933	
	Violence and the Media, content analysis, 1969	*The Invasion from Mars,* 1940	*Hovland's Experiments in Mass Communication,* 1949
	Television and Social Behaviour, 1971	*Radio Research,* 1942–43	*Communication and Persuasion,* 1953
	Media Content and Control, 1971	*The Diffusion of Hybrid Seed Corn,* 1943	*Television and Social Behaviour,* 1971
	Television and Behavior, 1982	*The People's Choice,* 1948	*Television and Social Learning*
	Television in the Lives of Our Children, 1961	*Personal Influence,* 1955	*Television and Adolescent Aggressiveness*
		Television and Behavior, 1982	
		Violence and the Media, audience survey, 1969	
		Television and Social Behaviour, 1971	
		TV in Day-to-Day Life	
Macro/Social System		*The Flow of Information,* 1948	*The Agenda-setting Function of the Mass Media,* 1972

FIGURE 2.2 *Matrix approach to describing communication research, adapted from Lowery and Defleur's* Milestones in Mass Communication Research *(1995) and Lasswell's (1948)* Process Model of Communication

Content

Lowery and DeFleur identified only three landmark studies of media content in their 1995 edition, with previous editions containing another: Frederic Wertham's *The Seduction of the Innocent* (Wertham, 1954). His sensational book caused considerable public commotion by linking an analysis of sexual and violent content in comic books with an assumption that such content would negatively affect readers, even to the extent of causing an increase in juvenile delinquency. A more recent and evidence-based study of content was George Gerbner's analysis of violence in the report of the Commission on the Causes and Prevention of Violence, *Violence and the Media* (Baker & Ball, 1969). (This study also includes research on media professionals—the "who"—but this comprised only two of eleven reports in the volume.) Another content analysis by Gerbner was included in the later Surgeon General's report, *Television and Social Behavior* (Gerbner, 1971). The 1982 follow-up to the 1971 studies on television reviewed literature published since the previous report, including studies defining the concept *violence* and determining how much violence is present in television programming. The report also discussed the proportion of women and minorities in television shows as compared to the real world.

Audience

Most of the "milestone" studies fall into the "to whom" category. The first of these, the Payne Fund Studies of 1933, is comprised of 12 separate volumes that are less easily pigeonholed in our matrix. The goals of these studies included measuring film content and audience composition, with the primary object of determining how movies influenced children; the resulting research bridges the "audience" and "effects" categories. *The Invasion from Mars* study (Cantril, 1940) is easier to locate squarely in the "audience" category of our matrix. Cantril explored audience factors associated with panic behaviors through personal interviews with audience members who heard Orson Welles's famous 1938 radio broadcast, the *War of the Worlds*.

The People's Choice, the Erie County voter study referred to earlier (Lazarsfeld et al., 1948), examined the formation of voting decisions over time, with a primary focus on audience social categories and predispositions. Researchers began with the assumption that voters who changed their voting intentions between May and November did so because of campaign communication, but the study did not bear this out. *Personal Influence* (Katz & Lazarsfeld, 1955) was equally influential in its focus, a survey to determine on whom women relied for various kinds of information. This study has a macro-level aspect by exploring networks of relationships but measured using individual respondents.

Using the *Personal Influence* study and other data collected by the Office of Radio Research at Columbia University in the 1940s, Herta Herzog (1944) examined in *Radio Research* the *ways* in which the audience used the mass media (a precursor to the media uses and gratifications approach, what the audience "does" with media). In 1943 another prolific area of research got its start—the diffusion of innovations and of information. Bryce Ryan and Neal Gross examined *The Diffusion of Hybrid Seed Corn in Two Iowa Communities*. Schramm, Lyle, and Parker's study of the child audience, *Television in the Lives of Our Children* (1961), was the first large-scale investigation of television and children, which it regarded as an active audience. The *Violence and the Media* report (1969) mentioned above contained a more general study of the audience for media violence, concentrating on audience media habits, with effects inferred from those behaviors.

Television and Social Behavior: Television in Day-to-Day Life: Patterns of Use (Comstock & Rubinstein, 1971a), the fourth in a four-volume series on television and behavior issued by the United States Surgeon General's office, shed more light on audience uses of television. Only the last study in this "to whom" category approaches the macro level of analysis. *The Flow of Information* (DeFleur & Larsen, 1948) examined how information flows through a social system by studying how slogans included in leaflets dropped in a community were retained and distorted by the audience.

Effects

Justly famous effects studies included those conducted with American soldiers by psychologist Carl Hovland and his colleagues during World War II (Hovland, Lumsdaine, & Sheffield, 1949), which systematically varied content to determine the most persuasive message. Other components in the communication process (such as communicator credibility and the structure of the arguments) were of interest only in terms of the effects they produced. Later studies by Hovland solidified the central role of persuasion effects in communications research (Hovland, Janis, & Kelley, 1953). Two other effects milestones were part of the Surgeon General's multivolume report (Comstock & Rubinstein, 1971b, 1971c) Volumes II *(Television and Social Learning)* and III *(Television and Adolescent Aggressiveness)* summarized research and made the strongest case up to that time linking television viewing and aggression. The 1982 *Television and Behavior* report showed 10 years of additional evidence to support this relationship. The final study in our matrix (McCombs & Shaw, 1972) examined media agenda setting, finding that residents of Chapel Hill, North Carolina, perceived issues to be important to the extent that the media emphasized those issues; in other words, the media effect was guiding not people's attitudes but the topics they perceived as most important to their community: what to think *about*. Although the public agenda was based on the priorities of specific individuals, their responses were presented in the community-level aggregate, leading us to place this study toward the macro side of our matrix.

Distortion in the Field

Mapping these studies, which have been identified as landmarks, shows the thrust of early communications research toward the individual, or micro, level of analysis and toward a focus on the audience and the effects on that audience. To the extent that content was examined, it was to make inferences about its potential effects rather than about the people, organizations, and society that produced it. What led to this skew, favoring some questions over others? To answer this we need to look more closely at the society in which the questions were asked. In the remainder of this chapter, we discuss the factors that have affected what social scientists study and how they study it and identify several key influences on mass communications research. We first trace the main intellectual currents in communication and social science, showing the historical, institutional, professional academic preferences (for theory) within the field, and other pressures that led to the largely individual level study of the audience and communication effects within the existing media framework.

SOCIAL SCIENCE PARADIGMS

To understand the history of any field is to recognize that nothing in it is preordained by "science." Specific choices are made by individuals to study some things and not others, creating the structure of any area of study in the form of these accumulated choices. Of course, these choices are not completely free to the extent that they are made within frameworks not under the control of individual scholars—intellectual currents, institutional support and disciplinary boundaries, fortuitous social networks ("invisible colleges"), funding patterns, chance meetings of like-minded scholars, and political pressures.

Social science, like journalism, is a knowledge system of information gathering that makes truth claims, yet by its nature results in an imperfect approximation of truth. Indeed, no system of information gathering is ever completely adequate. Instead, we rely on what Kuhn (1962) called *paradigms*—ways of representing reality based on widely shared assumptions about how to gather and interpret information. These paradigms do not yield truth as such but generate useful information in ways found acceptable. Because paradigms are based on shared beliefs and expectations, we tend to take them for granted and lose sight of the fact that those beliefs and expectations change not only over time but also from one cultural environment to another. Paradigms, therefore, cannot be understood apart from the cultures that produce and support them.

The journalistic process has perhaps become more obviously problematic to the public, but the social sciences have not escaped public skepticism. In fact, since the 1960s the paradigms for both journalism and social science have undergone serious challenges both from without and within. The ability of news to convey "truth" has become increasingly questioned by a wary public, media "watchdog" monitors, and journalists themselves, who became more active and cynical following the Vietnam and Watergate eras. Postmodern currents in the social sciences have led to "critical" studies that question core philosophical assumptions about the study of human phenomena. The public has become wary of the scientific project in general, distrusting evidence for the process of evolution and climate change, among others. The irony is that critical scholars, in emphasizing the socially constructed nature of science and other knowledge systems as a human enterprise, have helped to undermine the legitimacy of these systems. Thus, there is increasing appreciation for the fact that in the social sciences, just as in journalism, the answers we find depend on the questions we ask.

To what, for example, can we attribute communicator questions being posed primarily at the individual level? US social science has been shaped in part by the larger individual-centered culture. The cultural ideal emphasizes self-contained individualism and tends to look unfavorably on those who rely too heavily on others. Conformity has negative overtones in this context of individualism. The ideal individual is self-sufficient, self-actualized, and autonomous; the dependent person is considered weak and psychologically underdeveloped. In theory, if not in practice, we value the independent thinker over the organizational conformist. Individualism is also the religious and social norm in the USA. The dominant Protestant and particularly evangelical denominations emphasize a personal relationship with God and individual salvation, and the average American aspires to a single-family house with a yard and a fence around it. Alternative living arrangements that involve interdependency—collectives, communes, and the like—arouse skepticism and suspicion. Politically, of course, communism is considered patently un-American, and even mild forms of socialism such as government-sponsored medical care are highly suspect. Critics regularly exploited this ethos in attacking President Obama with the "socialist" label.

Social behavior generally has many causes, but American theorists arguably have preferred the individual explanation. After World War II, communication research incorporated many important areas from its allied field of social psychology—including group dynamics, norms, interpersonal relations, and attitudes—and used them to explain how mass communication was mediated by the audience (Delia, 1987). Thus, communication could be said to track the same tendencies in social psychology, which in spite of an ostensibly group orientation, continued to explain the social with reference to the psychological rather than the other way around. For example, during that period the commonly accepted concept of *androgyny* referred to the presence of both male and female traits in an individual personality and was assumed to define a "standard of psychological health" (Bem, 1974, p. 1962). Critics such as Edward Sampson (1977) suggested, however, that a more cooperative, interdependent cultural ideal would not be as likely to favor the self-contained androgynous personality but would regard it as excessively isolated from others. Such an alternative to the individualist cultural ideal would have placed greater value on a person who "recognizes his or her interdependency on others in order to achieve satisfaction and completion as a human being" in a mutually interdependent relationship. Traits like androgyny are not intrinsically healthy, as Sampson pointed out, but are simply better suited to individually centered cultures like our own. Pepitone (1976) argued that other prominent theories of cognitive dissonance and aggression ignored culturally based explanations for behavior. These may seem to be minor semantic differences in how behavior is interpreted, but they can make a major difference in how we see and interpret the social world.

Roots of the Field

To better understand the paradigmatic tendencies of communication research we need to look at the more general historical context. All research, of course, is affected in some way by the larger currents within the discipline, the direction of which often becomes taken for granted and not made explicit. For this reason, a continual effort to acknowledge and lay out these histories helps to remind us of their blind spots, strengths, and weaknesses. During a period of historic introspection, several efforts were made from within the maturing field to chart the development of the communication discipline by Everett Rogers (1986), Daniel Czitrom (1982), David Sloan (1990), and Jesse Delia (1987). Part of this task involved identifying the key scholarly figures who helped shape the field.

Whether in psychology, sociology, or political science, scholars can usually agree on the "classics" of their field, the studies that were the most influential in shaping other research. In sociology, for example, the foundation was laid by Max Weber, Karl Marx, and Émile Durkheim. What followed has been built on the works of men like these, whether acknowledged or not. In the field of communication, which emerged from a number of related disciplines, Everett Rogers (1986) has identified the "founding fathers" as political scientist Harold Lasswell, social psychologist Kurt Lewin, psychologist Carl Hovland, and sociologist Paul Lazarsfeld. The questions asked about mass communication in society have been profoundly shaped, some would say distorted, by the early work of these men. Most importantly, from our perspective, is the thrust of the field toward the study of audience and effects of mediated communication and away from questions of institutional control and other forces shaping the media. These latter concerns have never been quite at home in the field laid out by founding fathers. Those more radical traditions, such as Marxism, which are directly concerned with issues of control of media content, were not among those absorbed into the beginnings of the communication field in the years following World War II.

From Chicago to Columbia

A central axis on which the early postwar field turned was exemplified by the shift in influence from the University of Chicago to the kind of sociology carried out at Columbia University. Katz and colleagues actually identify five "schools" contributing to communication research: adding to Chicago and Columbia, the Frankfurt School associated with the critical studies of Adorno and others; Toronto and the technological determinism of Innis and McLuhan; and the cultural studies tradition of Stuart Hall and Birmingham, in the UK (Katz, Peters, Liebes, & Orloff, 2003). Of these, the tensions between Chicago and Columbia are most relevant to our interest in media sociology. The broad vision of communication and mass media held by the Chicago School would become more narrow with the professionalization of the social sciences, as the eclectic blend of traditions, concepts, and techniques of observation gave way to what critics have called an over-absorption in method and quantification of social structure. The interplay of influence between these two campuses exemplifies many of the critical issues that have shaped the direction of the communication field: the question of administrative or critical research focus, the nature of theory and what kind of theory is privileged, the appropriate level of analysis, and the professionalization of statistical methods. All of these issues were resolved in such a way as to restrict the field to the individual level audience and effects side of our map.

Chicago Sociology

Four University of Chicago scholars are identified by Rogers (1986) as the "four American roots" of communication science: John Dewey, Charles Horton Cooley, Robert Park, and George Herbert Mead. The Progressive spirit that marked these four led them to see social science as a tool for tackling social problems, and each included an important role for mass media in their conception of a better society. Dewey, Cooley, Park, and Mead had a Progressive's faith in the mass media as a tool for building social consensus, and the newspaper as a tool for social betterment. The "Chicago School" approach to sociology took a broad view of communication as a rich web in which human communities are constituted and maintained, producing a wealth of research into communities, especially urban centers, with their slums and newly arrived immigrants. Communication was viewed as an essential element and unifying force in these increasingly varied and complex communities, leading to some of the earliest studies of mass communication.

As the first scholar to pay serious attention to the press using systematic first-hand observation, Robert Park examined issues of audience, content, and ownership structure (Rogers, 1986). A former journalist, Park had been a student of Dewey, and together they even started a small newspaper. Thus, not only was Park an original figure in communication, but he should also be regarded as the founder of media sociology (Frazier & Gaziano, 1979). Park saw the media as extending the networks of community beyond interpersonal communication, increasing personal interaction and allowing society to adapt and achieve stability. Although Park took a broader, more central view of media than those who followed, he by no means mounted a radical critique of the press. Of course, the media that Park confronted were a far cry from the system in place today, but his acceptance of the prevailing institutional framework is similar in kind to the dominant American liberal pluralist perspective that characterized later scholars, including Wilbur Schramm, the great codifier and institution builder of the communication discipline. According to Park, "the ordinary function of news is to keep individuals and societies oriented and in touch with their world and with reality by minor adjustments" (quoted in Frazier & Gaziano, 1979, p. 24). Thus, Park's view of the media yielded a functionally benign approach to the press, seeing it as an institution that evolved in order to serve important societal needs. That functional view would continue to be an important theme in the field in its shift eastward, carrying the assumption that if social institutions exist they must serve some useful function.

Columbia: Dominant Paradigm and Its Critics

To understand the emerging character of social sciences, it is helpful to look particularly closely at Columbia as the main center of sociology after World War II—a setting that was emblematic of the prevailing currents within the disciplines. Unlike Chicago's engagement with the community, Columbia adopted the individual as the primary unit of study, inspired by such influential attitude change studies as the *American Soldier* volumes produced by Harvard's Samuel Stouffer and his group during the war (Coleman, 1990).

At Columbia, Paul Lazarsfeld and Robert Merton were the most influential figures on the subsequent development of communication research. Lazarsfeld was a problem solver and surrounded himself with other faculty and students who could be set to work on his problems (Coleman, 1990). One of the major books growing out of his projects was *Personal Influence: The Part Played by People in the Flow of Mass Communication*, by Elihu Katz and Paul Lazarsfeld (1955). In their study of women in Decatur, Illinois, Katz and Lazarsfeld developed their two-step flow hypothesis— that ideas often flow from the media to opinion leaders who in turn spread them to other less active members of the population. This focus on social relationships as a filter between media and audience added to the limited effects view. According to Todd Gitlin (1978, p. 75) in his critique of the reigning approach to media research:

> The dominant paradigm in the field since World War II has been, clearly, the cluster of ideas, methods, and findings associated with Paul F. Lazarsfeld and his school: the search for specific, measurable, short-term, individual, attitudinal and behavioral "effects" of media content, and the conclusion that media are not very important in the formation of public opinion.

The "dominant paradigm" had particular implications for larger societal critique in its conception of power.

The Administrative Impulse

The emphasis on audience and effects was part of the early field's narrow focus within prevailing media systems. Indeed, one of the most common criticisms of the Columbia-influenced research approach was its unquestioning acceptance of the media systems around which it developed an "administrative" style of research more focused on day-to-day operations of the media and on more practical concerns of the industries themselves. Lazarsfeld spearheaded the Bureau of Applied Social Research at Columbia University, originally founded in 1937 as the Office of Radio Research, and the word *applied* was not chosen lightly. The Bureau actively sought corporate funding for early studies of consumer and voter uses of the media; in return, those studies provided practical, applied knowledge to their sponsors (Delia, 1987). Because academic concerns have mirrored those of the large media institutions, the early history of the field is inseparable from the history of the mass media. In their review of research on children and the media, for example, Wartella and Reeves (1985) found that each new medium—whether books, newspapers, movies, radio, comics, or television—has prompted a new wave of research devoted to its effects. And this medium-specific focus is not limited to the media and children area. To the extent that research concentrates on one media form at a time, the field is less apt to consider the commonalities across media, which together represent a potent interconnected web of symbolic cultural content. This makes it more difficult to mount a critique of the commercial and political system that gives rise to a system of media.

This was a weakness pointed out early on for the social sciences in general by Robert Lynd (1939), also on the Columbia faculty, as being in the nature of the beast. Economists, for example, spend most of their time measuring the operations of the current economic system and evaluating ways to fine-tune it, rather than contemplating alternative systems. As Lynd pointed out, political science has been preoccupied with minor adjustments to the political system, rather than with the larger impact of the system or possible alternatives. Lynd was particularly critical of large-scale, data-gathering bureaucracies, such as the former National Bureau of Economic Research, which purported to be objective analyzers of data. Such research "asks no questions that fundamentally call into question or go substantially beyond the core of the folkways" (Lynd, 1939, p. 144), and was lured into provisional acceptance of "the system's" definition of problems. In the *Sociological Imagination*, C. Wright Mills (1959), another Columbia sociologist, famously joined Lynd in attacking the new model of research he observed emerging from this academic–corporate alliance. Both felt that large-scale, data-gathering projects made academic researchers too dependent on similarly large-scale funding. This institutional patronage exerted a profound influence on communication by promoting the *administrative* style of research. This new academic model of scholarship, exemplified by Paul Lazarsfeld, was characterized by data-gathering bureaucracies, funded from business-oriented foundations, and resulted in projects of relevance to corporate interests.

More recent historical scholarship has somewhat rehabilitated the reputation of Lazarsfeld, pointing out that he himself coined the distinction between the administrative and more "critical" research styles—and as an émigré was well aware of the larger European tradition of social analysis (Simonson & Weimann, 2003). His work clearly raised the larger systemic questions, even if declining to pursue them in great detail. In his essay, for example, with Robert Merton, on *Mass Communication, Popular Taste, and Organized Social Action* (1971, p. 567), they asked:

What role can be assigned to the mass media by virtue of the fact that they exist? . . . Since the mass media are supported by great business concerns geared into the current social and economic system, the media contribute to the maintenance of that system . . . For these media not only continue to affirm the status quo but, in the same measure, they fail to raise essential questions about the structure of society.

Nevertheless, the administrative style of pursuing questions of interest to media and government interests shifted attention away from a more macro-level, critical examination of media institutions themselves.

The problems addressed by this administrative style of research—in other words, the main concerns of the big media organizations—focused on what the audience was doing *with* media products. Radio in particular had no way of estimating audience size without survey research, a concern television would later share. In the mid 1930s Lazarsfeld worked closely on radio research with Frank Stanton, then research director at CBS. *Life* magazine helped fund the Erie County voting study, which intrigued McFadden Publications (*True Story, True Confessions*) founder Bernarr McFadden, who funded Lazarsfeld's follow-up study, *Personal Influence*, on opinion-leading in fashion, buying, movies, and politics (Gitlin, 1978). In the "uses and gratifications" approach to follow, media were simply sources of material that audience members did something with—"using" it in a functional sense to satisfy their needs, yielding "gratifications." It's not difficult to see how in this benign context, media were seen, as Carey notes (1996), in concert with rather than opposed to the fundamentally democratic and egalitarian forces in the culture.

Government also wanted information about media effects. Carl Hovland's earliest experimental tests of persuasion via a mass medium (Hovland et al., 1949) were funded by a US government that needed to convince soldiers of the value of fighting Germans and Japanese during World War II. DeFleur and Larsen's *Flow of Information* was also government funded (US Air Force), since dropping leaflets was a common "propaganda" technique, and the military was vitally interested in measuring the method's effectiveness. This cooperation among government, business, and scholars came at a time of shared national purpose, when defeating the Axis powers clearly required a concerted effort. Later, widespread prosperity during the Eisenhower years encouraged complacency and general acceptance of the political, economic, and media systems; taking these systems for granted led logically to a research focus on their effects rather than on the systems themselves.

This sort of industry–academic relationship continues to be influential. Media organizations continue to fund various research projects, and media professionals continue to serve on boards of colleges and universities. Many professors in communication-related departments (variously called journalism, mass communication, telecommunication, radio–TV–film, and so on) have themselves worked in the media and often bring values of their former organizations to their teaching and research. Funds for basic research have become harder to come by, producing even greater pressure to seek external funding for studies, with the resulting influence on how those studies are designed. Academic researchers still find themselves under attack from professionals in media organizations for not doing more useful studies of practical problems. Other social science academic departments—sociology or psychology, for example—also rely on external grants for research funding, but they have neither the professional link that communications scholars often have nor quite as concentrated a grant-giving constituency. Such ties between research and industry do not prevent critical questions from being asked, but they do create an unavoidable climate of pressure, toward some questions more than others and asking them from an industry perspective. Studies that don't appeal to grant givers won't be proposed, much less funded.

Spirit of Positivism

Many scholars find nothing wrong with this arrangement, arguing that working on applied problems can produce interesting results of general theoretical value. This is no doubt true, but this attitude rests partly on the positivist view held by many behavioral scientists, who assume the epistemological possibility of eventually gaining a complete understanding of the social world. In Jerald Hage's (1972) view, theories approximate knowledge, a limit toward which they get closer and closer. In this discussion we've focused on the social "science" side of the field, which in its very name indicates its aspiration to the rigor of the natural sciences. With enough time, some social researchers argue, a theory of behavior may be developed that is similar in power to those in the physical sciences. Hage argues that in this respect, it's just a matter of time: "The awarding of a Nobel Prize in economics is indicative of how far that discipline has developed. Physics and chemistry have better approximations to their limits than do psychology and economics. Each discipline is at a different stage of development" (1972, p. 186).

The continuing search for predictive theories in both the social and the physical sciences assumes that, given enough observations, the many discrete research results may ultimately be ordered up into a complete understanding of physical and social life. The development of new knowledge, therefore, becomes self-justifying, with the hope that in the long run it will all make sense.

Columbia's Robert Merton was said to excite students with his positivist vision of sociology (even with an ironic anti-administrative twist), which although its goal was a long way off, could strive to understand society.

> It's not the sociologist's fault that society is in bad need of his help today, when his science is still immature . . . If sociology in its present state were to address itself only to practical problems, it would never become the science . . . whose benefits will be as wonderful as they are unpredictable.
>
> (Hunt, 1961, p. 63)

One can see how this ultimate "knowability" of the social world would make the Bureau's projects more palatable—they provided much grist for the big mill and were all part of the larger project of sociological understanding. But Mills and Lynd attacked this notion. They saw it as a justification for not addressing the larger questions of power, values, and social structures. It is, however, a notion that is fully compatible with American free-market, laissez-faire capitalism: If all knowledge is good, and if it eventually must be known, then why should the scientist not begin with those questions that also interest big—and wealthy—institutions outside academia, questions that primarily concern media impact on audience buying, voting, reading, viewing (and "clicking")?

Methodological Individualism

One of the key shifts in the Columbia–Chicago transition was the greater emphasis on variable analysis and survey research that characterized the work of Lazarsfeld and others. This methodological individualism helps explain the tendency of communication research to focus in our map on the micro level. Indeed, the rise of statistical methods at Columbia was part of an increasing professionalization of the social sciences after World War II, leading to the desire to codify research procedures to make them more standardized and "scientific." The statistical techniques used to analyze survey data had adopted the same sampling techniques developed for use in manufacturing. The beer bottler discovered early in the 20th century that randomly checking a small number of bottles for quality would give reasonable assurance that the entire batch was good, within certain bounds of probability (see Tankard's description [1984] of W.S. Gosset's work for Guinness Brewery). Before long, someone discovered that this same procedure could accurately describe groups of people, forming the basis for a huge polling and audience-measurement industry. The beer bottler, however, has no interest in the relationship between and among the bottles—a macro-level concern.

Sociology, called the "tool maker" for the social sciences, was especially concerned with refining the measurement of individual response through these methods. Although this approach does give greater precision in measuring some human behavior, it has greater difficulty capturing other group and community qualities. Blumer, for example, argued that

> the crucial limit to the successful application of variables analysis to human group life is set by the process of interpretation or definition that goes on in human groups. This process, which I believe to be the core of human action, gives a character to human group life that seems to be at variance with the logical premises of variable analysis.
>
> (Quoted in Hammersley, 1989, p. 116)

Beyond their relative strengths and weaknesses, these methods served to strengthen an individual level research bias and work against the study of larger social structures. C. Wright Mills (1959) was deeply involved early on in helping to run Lazarsfeld's research projects and, after a time, deeply critical of them, deriding them as "the statistical ritual." Like Blumer, Mills argued that we cannot understand larger social structures simply by adding up data about individuals, a style he termed "molecular," characterized by small-scale problems and statistical models of verification. This style, he argued, was usefully fitted to and strengthened by studies of "problems connected with media of mass communication." This tendency toward "psychologism," basing explanation on the aggregation of facts about individuals, assumed the institutional structure of society could be understood through that kind of data (Mills, 1963). To this tendency he contrasted a more macroscopic perspective, oriented toward the European critical tradition of Max Weber and Karl Marx, who dealt with "total social structures in a comparative way . . . to connect the various institutional spheres of a society, and then relate them to prevailing types of men and women" (Mills, 1963, p. 554). The media sociology perspective combines not only both molecular and macroscopic perspectives, but also an awareness that the individualistic bias in communication research alerts us to a common ecological fallacy: *Because we can and do measure the behavior of individuals, we must not conclude that individual level factors are the sole causes of behavior.*

THE SEARCH FOR THEORY

The field's audience and effects emphasis also can be understood as a product of the quest for academic knowledge and prestige. Delia (1987) argues that disciplines like sociology and psychology, although pursuing questions with funding appeal to corporate and government, still value theory development as a professional imperative. Investigators sought to accommodate their disciplinary requirements for theory building, a more prestigious activity than their more pragmatically necessary practice of administrative research. In this respect, we can see that the practical questions of Lazarsfeld formed a viable model for future research only by being infused with theory by Robert Merton. Merton had status as a theorist, well respected by the university administration, and drew overflow crowds to his lectures. Lazarsfeld's leadership, on the other hand, came through the quantity of research he produced through his Bureau. Coleman (1990) notes that the applied research conducted by Lazarsfeld in mass communication did not have much prestige within the university, but his collaboration with Merton protected him and gave legitimacy to his enterprise. Merton's prestige and his "theories of the midrange" added respectability to the more opportunistic mass communication studies of his colleague and friend Lazarsfeld. Had it not been for this partnership, the early studies of media effects may not have been nearly as influential in providing a template for the larger field.

Where was this theory to be found? In large part, a change in accepted methodology changed the places where studies would look. Columbia's ascendance over Chicago privileged the search for transcendent laws of behavior and theory within large-scale patterns of observations over the more "subjective," less representative, naturalistic (even journalistic) style. The preference for standardized methods, an effort to avoid bias and build objective knowledge, devalued the more interpretive and creative elements in the Chicago research. In effect, this shift defined away the theoretical potential for media sociology, given that the study of media institutions and organizations is almost by definition less given to the study of representative samples. Instead, one or a few settings are typically explored in depth, and the work that goes on there interpreted within the social and cultural context. The interpretive and participant observation style of Herbert Gans in his newsroom studies, for example, would have been greatly out of place in this audience-centered and quantitative approach. In fact, the continuing quantitative domination of sociology makes Gans still unusual within his field, although he has become well known within the media studies area just because he offers a different perspective.

The Engineering Models

One crucial theoretical context was provided by the broader model of the communication process itself. Nowhere can communication's break with the Chicago tradition be seen more clearly than in the rise of models proposed by Claude Shannon and Norbert Wiener, whom Rogers called "the engineers of communication" (1986, p. 82). Their approach to the communication process stemmed not from the broad humanistic and social science tradition of the Chicago School, but from the field of applied science, directing communication research toward a pre-occupation with linear, one-way effects. A closer look at these models shows how they effectively defined out of consideration the broader concerns of media sociology.

Shannon's original information theory was published in the *Bell System Technical Journal*, but was later extended and applied to human communication by Warren Weaver, with the combined work published as *The Mathematical Theory of Communication* (Shannon & Weaver, 1949). Rogers calls the Shannon and Weaver paradigm "the most important single turning point in the history of communication science" (1986, p. 85). Their theory treated information as a general concept that could be expressed mathematically and, thus, could unify questions in human communication, computers, biology, spanning across mass and interpersonal communication, regardless of "channel." The widely adopted Shannon and Weaver model depicts communication as a linear transmission of a "signal" from the source-transmitter to the receiver-destination. The model, in effect, takes the messages being transmitted as a given, as the starting place of the process. When applied to media as the "source" and "transmitter," only the efficiency of its signal remains to be evaluated.

The other "engineer of communication" was a mathematician at the Massachusetts Institute of Technology, Norbert Wiener. His theory of cybernetics examined how a system maintains order through a process of information feedback (Weiner, 1948). Both models have important implications for media research, for rendering information into a mathematical concept obscures the question of values within the larger message. Reducing communication to its smallest, universal components, as an engineering problem of signal and noise, limits close questioning of its larger symbolic and cultural structure. The same could be said for the cybernetic approach to system-maintenance, allowing the media to be pictured as part of a largely stable and functional system. This view would reach its full flower with the social engineering approach to communication encouraged by US wartime objectives, which Schramm and many other social scientists helped by mounting a number of government-sponsored studies involving propaganda and persuasion. This model, using communication and improving its efficiency to accomplish social objectives, did not end with the war but has continued to profoundly influence research. The consensus, however, as to what constitutes worthy social objectives has eroded considerably since then. We can see how this merger of human and machine communication, reducing social communication to the language of formulas, glosses over precisely those questions posed by media sociology: Whose order is being maintained? What feedback channels act to impose some forms of order and suppress others?

The engineering models have been influential precisely because they are helpful in describing a complex process, isolating important features of that process and clearly expressing relationships between them. But like any useful model, the simplification of reality creates its own distortion. The more compelling and "self-evident" a model appears, the more difficult it is to be mindful that other important features have been omitted. Through the reduction of communication to a simple linear process, the larger cultural formations are smoothed over or rendered invisible. If the media are plugged into the sender–receiver model and seen as carrying discrete messages—which may or may not punch through audience filters—then no theory is to be found in looking for the forces underlying those messages.

The quest for mathematical modeling in the social sciences fits this approach with its search for quantitative regularities within the boundaries of existing systems. Understanding those processes is valuable, but to the extent that we take political, economic, and media structures for granted, the structures themselves fail to come under scrutiny. In line with the mathematical models, for example, Katz and Lazarsfeld assume the comparability of media and personal influence, that one competes with the other. However, as Gitlin (1978, p. 81) argues, "Everyone has the opportunity to exercise 'personal influence' directly on someone else, albeit informally, and generally the relation is reciprocal, whereas the direct influence of mass media belongs routinely and professionally to the hierarchically organized handful who have access to it." Thus, the prevailing model of the mass communication process conspired to locate theory at the level of audience response, with a selected unitary message of interest conceived as producing a varied pattern of responses in an audience.

The Received History

As the postwar roots of communication research began to congeal into something akin to an academic "field," we can point to one final set of pressures constraining the lines of research—the politics of the field itself, the way it sets boundaries and tells an accepted narrative about its origins and special trajectory. Peters (2008) has argued that in striving to lay claim to institutional legitimacy as a self-sustaining academic field, communication gave up on a wider intellectual sweep from which it could have drawn. Indeed, decisions to formalize certain programs of study into "fields" must be understood for their political implications, the way they stem from and reinforce the system of societal power. Understanding how powerfully the "definition" of a field acts to encourage some questions while defining others away requires recognizing its "received" history, with its implicit assumptions and their larger implications. A "paradigm," or model for doing research, is enshrined in the "received history" that defines the normal and the marginal by telling stories about who was important, what they did, and what it signified.

As the typically recited story goes in textbooks and other accounts, the field began in the concerns over the potential for media manipulation on a massive scale, exemplified by such notorious events as Orson Welles's *War of the Worlds* radio show of 1938 and the ensuing panic among listeners. Subsequent large-scale empirical studies of the audience produced a more "limited effects" perspective, by identifying the social and psychological "filters" used by the audience to limit media impact. The early political campaign studies, for example, concluded that "reinforcement" of preexisting views was the predominant effect. In Klapper's influential summary of the field (1960), *The Effects of Mass Communication*, media were said *not* to be necessary and sufficient causes effects, but rather operated through a nexus of mediating factors and influences. Much attention since then was devoted to finding a message capable of blasting through these seemingly dense audience filters or to determine which personal characteristics were most important in this mediation.

As Carey (1996) reminds us, the narrative of the history of mass communication research is a self-conscious creation that serves a definite set of purposes. Most importantly, casting such a history firmly within the existing institutional framework of the US commercial mass media effectively neutralized the broader critique of modern society by the critical scholars of the Frankfurt School. By creating a story of the field, we can see how effectively questions not fitting the script were screened from view. Empirical studies of media themselves, or "communicator" studies, although perhaps not extensive, had been around a long time. Leo Rosten's 1937 book *The Washington Correspondents* was among those largely excluded from narratives of the field's history. And until recently the broader contributions of the Chicago School were not considered part of the field's history. We can only speculate, of course, that had its approach remained dominant, the questions of media sociology would have been more central to the social sciences and communication.

THE ROOTS OF A SOCIOLOGY OF NEWS

To show how powerfully the field's prevailing paradigm shaped research, Reese and Ballinger (2001) looked closely at two particularly important studies in the media sociology tradition—projects that represented a break with the dominant paradigm.

These studies are important precursors to the later newsroom studies: David Manning White's *The "Gatekeeper": A Case Study in the Selection of News* and Warren Breed's *Social Control in the Newsroom*. White's article appeared in *Journalism Quarterly* in 1950 and examined the personal reasons given by a newspaper editor for rejecting potential news items. Breed's work appeared in *Social Forces* in 1955 and considered the broader process of how news organizations socialized reporters to follow policy, even if doing so meant distorting what they might otherwise have written as "objective" first-hand observers. Both have been cited and reprinted numerous times (Berkowitz, 1997) and were both linked to the early leaders of communication research. For White it was to social psychologist Kurt Lewin, with whom White studied at Iowa (Shoemaker, 1991; Shoemaker et al., 2009), while for Breed, it was Paul Lazarsfeld and Robert Merton, whom he encountered as a graduate student at Columbia.

The irony is that both studies were potentially subversive in challenging the taken for granted prevailing media systems. They called into question the assumption that media are a natural and benign mirror on society—and instead showed that media content is constructed. By identifying gatekeepers, White brought into focus the intuitive notion that not all that happens in the world gets into the news, and that gatekeeper decisions are influenced by their own subjectivity. If news is what gatekeepers say it is, how can it be an unproblematic reflection of reality? Breed questioned how journalists could be "objective" when they were targets of social control and obliged to follow publisher policy, set before events actually happened.

Although both studies departed from the prevailing concern with audience and effects, they were still arguably at home in the "limited effects" reinforcement approach of Lazarsfeld and colored by the functional tradition of Merton (1949), with its emphasis on how social stability is maintained. White justified the editor's subjectivity within a context of reinforcement: "all of the wire editor's standards of taste should refer back to an audience who must be served and pleased" (1950, p. 389). Thus, White argues, an editor "sees to it (even though he may never be consciously aware of it) that the community shall hear as a fact only those events which the newsman, as the representative of his culture, believes to be true" (1950, p. 390). These questions, however, of "culture" and what he "believes to be true" are the critical concerns of media sociology, but they were put aside for a later day. White's focus on gatekeeper news "selection" implied that proper operation of these gates yields unbiased news. Having enough space would lessen the need to make choices and thus render news more objective (as some suggest for online journalism). Of course, this "in or out" focus overlooks message structure, or framing, and doesn't consider whether gatekeepers' choices constitute a systematic pattern across media. Instead the gatekeeper's available messages are presumed to flow from the environment, keeping the community in a relatively harmonious balance. Indeed, in later writing, White argued that mass culture "follows the needs of the people rather than fashioning them" (Rosenberg & White, 1971, p. 19). Ironically, White's mentor Kurt Lewin (1947a, 1947b) introduced gatekeeping theory (and its prede-cessor field theory) as a way to achieve social change (Shoemaker & Vos, 2009). Un-fortunately, White's work was atheoretical, as were the many studies that followed. Gatekeeping theory could have been adopted as a way to study change in social structures and even how to change them, but White took gatekeeping in an applied direction that emphasized news decisions at the individual level.

Breed presented arguably a more critical voice in trying to reconcile how con-servative publishers were able to successfully control the more liberal journalists in their organization, such that "the existing system of power relationships is main-tained" (Breed, 1955, p. 193). His wider framework, however, shows that he con-siders this to be a potentially correctable flaw in an otherwise satisfactory system for newsgathering. By locating the source of bias squarely with the publisher, he implied that were it not for their policies, journalistic norms would be sufficient to produce objective reporting. In the "received history" of the field, White and Breed were often relegated in textbooks to a small section representing "communi-cator" studies. Their potentially troublesome findings were "repaired," interpreted and integrated into the larger field, reinforcing the prevailing functional view of media and society. For example, the early standard text, *The Process and Effects of Mass Communication* by Schramm and Roberts (1971), absorbed both the White and Breed studies into the limited effects tradition as agents of reinforcement rather than social change.

> the individual reporter or editor views and interprets the world in terms of his own image of reality—his own beliefs, values and norms. Thus, *to the extent that his image reflects existing norms and values,* he is likely to overlook or ignore new ways of perceiving the world or approaching problems.
>
> (p. 382; emphasis added)

The Breed study of newsroom policy is similarly domesticated: "To the extent that media policy reflects the norms of a given culture or subculture, so too will the information they transmit" (Breed, 1955, p. 382). In both cases newsroom policy and practices are deemed unproblematic to the extent that they are in harmony with prevailing "norms and values" (with the assumption that they largely do). Received history directed attention away from the key question: How does news get made? If media themselves are not thought to constitute a social problem, then the forces controlling those media and shaping their symbolic fare, including the news con-struction process, are equally unproblematic. Any problems to be found are rooted at the individual and not systemic level.

SUMMARY

Historically, a number of factors moved communication research toward an individ-ual or micro-level (or "molecular") approach, toward questions of media audiences and effects, and away from questions of production and control. In this chapter, we have provided a framework for understanding this state of affairs and for providing the larger historical context within a broader sociology of knowledge. Theories and research, after all, do not exist in a vacuum; they are human activities, shaped by the same cultural forces as our lives.

We have shown how a field's history reflects the prevailing paradigm, with the limited effects, reinforcement perspective of the postwar era being particularly influential. Of course, this benign view of a functionally organic news media is still on display in such places as the Freedom Forum's museum of news in Washington, DC, the "Newseum," which celebrates the profession (Reese, 2001a). The paradigm was broadly influenced by the "engineering" models of Shannon and Weaver, which focused on information at the expense of culture and social structure. The way the field has been defined has powerful implications for shaping the kinds of questions asked about media. If media are not thought to constitute a social problem, then the forces controlling those media and shaping its symbolic fare are equally unproblematic. To the extent that the field defined media effects narrowly, with focus on specific, short-term measurable effects, the dominant paradigm has excluded the long-term, more pervasive effects produced by the media through their patterned, routinized, presentation of particular symbolic frames.

Regarding media impact as "limited," mediated by a nexus of mediating influences, rendered the control and nature of the media themselves unproblematic and not worthy of study in their own right. If the media provide merely a nervous system for society, or fodder for individual conversations, then it is of little interest who makes news and what goes on behind the scenes. But far from dismissing "mere reinforcement" as evidence of media impotence, it should be recognized as a profound impact on the field that requires appreciating the larger cultural significance of the media beyond specific measurable results. Accepting their power in this broader sense makes them objects worthy of study in their own right.

Some time went by before the key questions posed by the early roots of media sociology were taken up by others, but since the late 1960s there has been a steady rise of interest in such questions. Following the benign functionalism of the postwar era, the field changed in response to the breakdown in social consensus. Social conflicts over war and civil rights made media representation problematic and no longer taken for granted as a mere reflection of culture. A particular wealth of newsroom ethnographies emerged around 1970, including most prominently the work of the sociologists Herbert Gans, Gaye Tuchman, Mark Fishman, Todd Gitlin, Edward Epstein, and Harvey Molotch (who we will take up in later chapters). It is noteworthy that these scholars, who knew and were influenced by each other, came to media research as "outsiders," from outside of the communication field, allowing them to expand on the provocative insights of White and Breed. Now a sizable body of research has developed in this area, addressing the forces behind the media message. Within the communication field, we can see how the expansion of its boundaries has helped pose the critical question at a broader macro, institutional level: How does it work—and in whose interest?

In some respects, the field we map out in this book, with its concern for the broader cultural context of mass communication, represents a return to the concerns that characterized the University of Chicago in the first half of the century—reincorporating it within the "received history" of the field. There has been a shift toward a more critical examination of the power behind societal institutions, a more macro approach that emphasizes viewing media as a cultural form, in an historical and philosophical context, with specific ties to economic and political power. The Marxists, for example, had always considered the media a symbolic environment for its ideological implications, as a superstructure built on an economic base, and more recent studies of media, whether from radical or more traditional democratic pluralist perspectives, have tackled such issues. The publication of the "Ferment in the Field" volume of *Journal of Communication* in 1983 was a visible certification of the growing importance of a more critical approach beyond a strictly positivist, behaviorist perspective. This has meant a greater acceptance of more qualitative, open-ended, and interpretive research methods in the communication disciplines, including journalism and mass communication programs (Parisi, 1992).

Of course, media sociology does not automatically dictate a method. Early large-scale quantitative surveys, for example, were conducted of news workers (for example, Johnstone, Slawski, & Bowman, 1972), and conversely critical and qualitative methods can be applied to studies of audience reception in the cultural studies tradition. But at the cultural, institutional, and organizational levels a greater assortment of methods has been employed. More recently, studies of the online public sphere—whether blogosphere, Twittersphere, or larger networked public sphere—have adopted more macro-oriented methods of network analysis that specifically examine relationships *among* units of analysis, as they combine into clusters and other kinds of structures that suggest the larger sociological context. These methods naturally lend themselves to the study of the "network society" and the hyperlinked interconnections of the media ecosystem. These networks can be seen not just as pathways through which information is transmitted but as themselves embedded collectivities of social capital, community "in" communication—a very Chicago-style concern. All this is to say that these approaches have invigorated communication research, strengthening the importance within it of media sociology by raising the issues of content, and its cultural and institutional roots.

In the remaining chapters, we will turn to the questions that interest us—and that have traditionally been underrepresented. We present this increasingly substantial body of research, with influences from individual, organizational, social, economic, and cultural factors (the lower left quadrant of our matrix in Figure 2.2). Although we shift attention to the communicator and issues of production and control, we do so within an organized theoretical framework, the Hierarchical Model. This hierarchy of influences is ultimately important in understanding the audience and effects, because they determine the available information from which audiences must choose, and they are thereby indirectly responsible for the entire range of effects that have traditionally fascinated communication scholars.

CHAPTER 3

Mediating Reality

In 1951, two young scholars set out to compare what people thought about a parade. It was an important parade, celebrating the return to the USA of World War II hero General Douglas MacArthur, whom President Harry Truman had just dismissed as head of the United Nations Command in the Korean War. The dismissal was unpopular with many Americans, and he was honored across the country, resulting in MacArthur Day being declared that spring in Chicago.[1] Kurt and Gladys Lang were interested in the latest communication technology—television—and they asked a question: Would people who saw the MacArthur parade in person, standing there on the curb, take away the same impressions of it as those who watched the parade on television?

The simple answer is no. Imagine standing on a parade route. Waiting for a celebrity to come along is boring. When the celebrity gets to you, you and those around you cheer for a while and then stop when he's gone. It was a fleeting experience: The celebrity passed by all too quickly, and you are disappointed that you didn't see him long enough or get a close enough view. Now imagine watching a televised parade. The camera and announcer focus on the most important part of the parade—the celebrity. You see close-ups of the celebrity and hear the announcer's descriptions. All along the parade route, people cheer. The parade is exciting. The celebrity is impressive. The crowd loves him.

By *mediated reality*, we mean the view of the world that the media portray, a view that is influenced by a myriad of factors on at least five levels of analysis. We believe that media content does not mirror reality and that the world according to the media differs in important ways from other representations of reality, such as presidential speeches or political group pronouncements. Producers of news and entertainment content mediate reality through the mere process of doing their work, but also because of their relationships with culture, power, and ideology.

In Lang and Lang's study, which perspective was the real one—from the curb or from the television? Does personal observation give you a more or less realistic representation of the event than a mediated version? Answering this question is the purpose of this chapter and requires some understanding of what we mean by reality. Setting up comparisons between mediated and direct, personal observation, along with other forms of social reality has been an important analytical strategy in understanding how the media message is shaped, and how it takes on certain predictable and structured tendencies. In Chapter 1 we introduced some of these issues of content, the possibility of an external reality and the social construction of that reality, but here we explore them more deeply.

PATTERNS OF MEDIATED REALITY

Media sociology scholarship has grown tremendously since the 1991 and 1996 editions of *Mediating the Message*, especially studies that analyze the patterns of reality conveyed by media content. We now know much more about how the world is portrayed in media such as newspapers, television, radio, television, blogs, and computerized virtual reality programs. As a result, scholars can more accurately assess the extent to which these patterns of media content distort or mirror other representations of social reality (which Fishman [1980] defines as those things that society knows about itself). Do the media show a world of racism and sexism? And, if so, how does that amplify existing patterns in the larger society? Does the news portray events as they really are? Who is in the news? Who are the characters in television, film, and video games? What behaviors do they exhibit? Where do they come from in the social system? How are they presented in relation to others in society? The studies we include here address these questions and help us better understand the symbolic environment created for us by the media. When we examine studies of media content, we see patterns of the people represented and how their environment is portrayed. Communication research has produced a vast number of content studies, and we identify some of them below that have a particular bearing on mediated realities.

The Media Environment

As we write this, there are more sources of news and entertainment content than at any time, with the media expansion accelerating in the late 20th century. The advent of the Internet created many new types of media, which largely amplify and redistribute the messages of the older media. We struggle with language to adequately describe what is today a combination of what we sometimes call traditional media (such as television networks, the news agencies, and printed newspapers), online media (including traditional media that have migrated to the internet platform), and social media (such as blogs, YouTube, Facebook, and Twitter). The study of mediated communication is an etymological mess: Should we call it mass, social, or online? Is it interpersonal, social networking, computer-mediated communication, or something else? The definition of mass medium traditionally included the idea of one sender (a media organization) transmitting information to many receivers (the public). Today the communication architecture consists of many senders and many receivers.

Many people hoped that the subsequent increase in the flow of information around the planet, itself an enormous public sphere, would improve people's quality of life, especially for the oppressed (Jönsson & Örnebring, 2011). Activist networks are using the Internet to convey anti-corporate globalization messages in the Infospace. Twiki software and the decentralization of the Internet can help mobilize millions of people worldwide (Juris, 2005, p. 205). Douglas Kellner and Gooyong Kim (2010), however, conclude that although more people now have access to counter-hegemonic information, "they also face the risks of ensnaring established social constituencies in the tentacles of the dominant culture and ideology" (p. 6). The most popular YouTube videos are entertaining, some mashed from existing corporate content, showing the influence of existing social institutions even in this new public space. Although YouTube itself does not become involved in social issues through centralized organizational decisions, Kellner and Kim argue that its content amounts to "corporate media spectacles" that ultimately reinforce the status quo. Not everyone has the access, talent, or motivation to create and post videos on YouTube, and those who do so are primarily white, male, and work in English. This mirrors what we know about the Internet, that it is primarily "occupied by the dominant class in society" (Kellner & Kim, 2010, pp. 25–8).

Jönsson and Örnebring (2011) concur, having studied user-generated content in Swedish and UK online newspapers. They categorized information and popular culture content about people, with the first primarily political and the latter addressing the cultural sphere, and private content documenting individuals' lives. User-generated news contributions were "virtually non-existent" in online newspapers. Commenting and participating in discussion forums were common, but the authors considered these to be "parasitical" ways of adding to existing content. The newspapers invited contributions of articles and photos for their travel and health sections, whereas blogs contained mostly private content, oriented toward personal or everyday life (Jönsson & Örnebring, 2011, pp. 133–9). Jönsson and Örnebring conclude that user-generated content is not the same as journalism or even participatory journalism, and it does not compete with online mainstream news media over control of news content. Although users are participating and interacting more, their role in the political sphere is weak. Their value-added contributions not only help legitimize the media's news function, but also help maintain the same relationship with the audience. Although users are invited to contribute in their role as citizens, newspapers see users as being consumers, people to sell to advertisers: "Participation (irrespective of its level) does not automatically equal either production or power" (Jönsson & Örnebring, 2011, p. 141). The authors conclude that the empowerment of citizens is difficult within the structure of traditional media organizations. This empowerment faces further impediments in countries like China, where the government battles internet users over what content is allowed. The country's most negative news often appears on web portals first and then may diffuse to the news media, depending on government reaction (Xu, 2012, p. 42). Jane Singer's (2005) analysis of political blogs associated with US newspapers showed that journalists are maintaining control over their blogs' content, acting as gatekeepers. Although they link to many sites, most go back to mainstream media sites (Singer, 2005, p. 173).

Hopes that the Internet would equalize the flow of information around the globe, increase the diversity of information available, and improve the quality of oppressed people's lives have yet to be fulfilled (as we consider in the next chapter). So in spite of the vast changes in the technological environment, which we acknowledge and take into account, there continue to be deeply structured and powerful roles for media systems. The "mass" media of previous editions of this volume have given way to a reconstituted media space, but these new media still amplify and redistribute messages of the "traditional" media—reproducing existing hierarchies (international, corporate, state, professional, and institutional) as seen above, although in important new ways. Thus we continue to examine these structured tendencies, which manifest themselves in a variety of mediated "realities," and find explanation in different levels of influence.

Politics

The mainstream news media's mission is covering social institutions at the nation's ideological center and pointing out threats near the boundary between normal and deviant. For example, the 4thEstate.net's analysis of VoiceShare (the proportion of citizen sources to elite sources) in the summer of the 2012 US presidential election showed that no more than one-third of statements in major US newspapers were by individuals not representing any social institution (Citizens Lack Voice Among Top Newspapers, 2012), with the remaining statements made by political organizations and their candidates. Still, the ability of internet users to customize their news pages and to search for specific information has been of concern to politicians since 2000. Partisan selective exposure occurs when people seek only information that reinforces their existing political predispositions. Natalia Stroud (2010, p. 557) posits that there may be a downward circular spiral between partisan exposure and the polarization of political attitudes, but found that communication with people of different political opinions could moderate the process. Exposure to media content that uniformly supports one side of the political spectrum may encourage extremist political participation. Tim Groeling (2008) looked at whether television networks' political coverage was biased in favor of one candidate in early 2008, analyzing content surrounding political polls from Fox's Special Report, ABC's World News, the CBS Evening News, and NBC's Nightly News. He found that Fox aired more positive content about George W. Bush.

In his analysis of how the news media covered the 2004 US presidential election, Lance Bennett (2005) reports that pseudo-events (see Chapter 7) have been replaced with the creation of *reality television news reporting*, the use of dramatic narrative and visuals to present a mediated event that becomes more real than the event itself. Like pseudo-events, reality television news reporting begins with an event organized for the sole purpose of getting media coverage—a presidential candidate arriving in a city to make a speech, for example. For those at the speech, it is the real event; however, for people who see coverage only on television, the televised event is the real event. News takes information out of one context and repackages the event to apply the frame wanted by journalists. As a result, reality "blurs," because the televised event becomes the real event, even if it is different from the original event in important ways (Bennett, 2005, pp. 370–1). Bennett concludes that political news emphasizes drama over factual information, especially information that conforms to the dramatic script. When candidates charge that their opponents communicate false information, many journalists, editors, or producers find it difficult to question the lie. In contrast, journalists who do recognize the dangers of allowing lies to be communicated over and over again find it difficult to get their stories on the front page. Correcting the lie lacks the drama of the original, false claim (Bennett, 2005, p. 367).

Journalists also fit their existing schemas to reality-defining events, as Inka Salovaara-Moring (2009) reports from an interview with Lana Ghvinjilia of the Open Society Georgia Foundation:

> When an American armed military ship, Dallas, pulled up to Georgian port of Batumi the first thing that they started to carry out was mineral water bottles— and all their big TV networks were filming that. US is on humanitarian mission! Mineral water for Georgians! That is something we certainly don't need. Georgia has been famous for its mineral water for hundreds of years.
>
> (Salovaara-Moring, 2009, p. 364)

One of the most spectacular reality news events occurred in 2003, when US President George W. Bush made a jet landing aboard the aircraft carrier *Abraham Lincoln*, announcing that his mission in Iraq was accomplished. Bennett (2005, p. 371) points out the back story of information that journalists could have covered, but didn't so as to not detract from the dramatic moment. First, rehearsing the Bush landing delayed the *Abraham Lincoln*'s trip from war to its home at San Diego. Bush made sailors wait to see their families. Second, the rationale given to the media for the jet landing was that the carrier was beyond helicopter range of land but in fact it was circling just out of sight of the mainland.

Although many journalists knew the back story, they left it out of their stories, instead focusing on the reality-defining event itself and commenting on its usefulness in the upcoming political campaign (Bennett, 2005, p. 371). The reality-creating event was successful because the news media filtered out information that contradicted it. A reporter from the *Washington Post* wrote: "Bush emerged from the cockpit in a full olive flight suit and combat boots, his helmet tucked jauntily under his left arm. As he exchanged salutes with the sailors, his ejection harness, hugging him tightly between the legs, gave him the bowlegged swagger of a top gun" (Milibank, 2004, p. A24; cited from Bennett, 2005, pp. 371–2).

The ability of such dramatic news events to shape people's social reality creates a demand for even more drama from journalists and campaign managers—"the truth versus drama." If one candidate is better at creating news realities, then viewers' own reality becomes skewed, constructed by the distorted information. Bennett concluded that these reality frames work against people's ability to critically engage the complexities and veracity of election information (2005, pp. 372–4).

Geography

Mosco (2004, p. 85) rejects the belief that the Internet is "ending" geographic constraints on information flow. The vast majority of media are physically tied to one geographic location, which attaches them to a defined community of audience members and a specific audience-driven market for advertisers. This is particularly true of media that are printed or distributed by satellite or cable, but there is evidence that it is only partially true of online news media. Mike Gasher and Reisa Klein (2008, p. 194) studied the news geography of three newspapers that have both print and online editions, with that geography calculated by studying a medium's content, audience, and advertisers. This seems clear enough for print newspapers, which have historically helped develop their physical communities and also have been shaped by them. As early as the 19th century, journalists were taught that proximity to an event increased its newsworthiness, and even today most news articles are driven by the occurrence of local events. Although the Internet has changed our conception of distance—whether in physical or virtual units—it has not evenly distributed the flow of information around the world. Countries in parts of the world that have the most power tend to send and receive the most information, but primarily about each other. The other parts of the world can be invisible to the news media, because their lower power and fewer economic resources make them less newsworthy (Salovaara-Moring 2009, p. 198).

Salovaara-Moring (2009) calls these areas *geographic dead ground*, "spaces that are outside the cultural understanding of the scopic regime of an observer. Thus they are cognitively distant spaces where things and issues do not appear as meaningful or relevant" (p. 351). When journalists cover events in other countries—especially those that are culturally distant—they often have only "thin" information about the context of those events. Therefore their reports are generally about the drama of the most current events and tend to frame their stories dualistically—us versus them, good versus evil. Such reporting lacks a narrative that could support the most current facts with an understanding of history and culture. Instead, reporters use their own culture as a referent, thus making everything else relative to it by using analogies to give their stories color. "Historical analogies make international relations intriguing, interesting, worth watching, and participating in without which foreign news might lack drama-producing imagery . . . It put things and relations, as it were, into perspective and make them tastier, less boring, and more purposeful" (Salovaara-Moring, 2009, pp. 360–1).

Salovaara-Moring distinguishes between news and cultural narratives (2009, p. 362). For example, news narratives include information about international power relationships and unanticipated conflict, and creates an us–them cultural dichotomy. If the media instead used a cultural narrative, they would include more information about the area's history, putting the current news event into a temporal-spatial context, with information about the complexities of international relations and potential solutions about solving the problem. When news coverage is solution free, she writes, it gives the impression that violence and conflict are inevitable and causes people to think about war instead of peace. The media map of the world is a simple one that focuses on few locations, thus reinforcing existing hegemonic power structures (Salovaara-Moring, 2009, pp. 362–4).

Gasher and Klein (2008) came to similar conclusions, having analyzed content from *The Times* (London), *Libération* (Paris), and *Ha'aretz* (Tel Aviv). Although the three newspapers covered 67 locations around the world, most of their online stories were filed in their home countries (Gasher & Klein, 2008, p. 201). The authors observed that the topics sports, business, entertainment, and lifestyle are less spatially bound than most hard news and therefore "have more international mobility" (Gasher & Klein, 2008, p. 201). Advertisers are more interested in supporting media that cover these topics. Sports was the most-covered topic in a study of ten countries (Shoemaker & Cohen, 2006). Gasher and Klein note that successful online news publications may change their staffing to concentrate on editing news agency copy over creating staff-produced stories, because the more general agency content appeals to people in diverse locations. "News flows are determined less by ideals of equity, fairness, and balance in international-news exchanges than by the political, economic, and military power of the nations who make news" (Gasher & Klein, 2008, pp. 206–8).

Wilke, Heimprecht, and Cohen (2012) compared the televised foreign news coverage, or the *news geography*, of 17 countries during 2008, concluding that the flow of information around the world is skewed and some countries do not appear in foreign news at all (p. 302). The USA was the most-covered country, but its media ran only a small number of stories about the other countries. In most continents, countries covered their neighboring countries more than those farther away. In the case of North America, however, the USA comprised more than half of all foreign news in Canadian television, whereas Canada was rarely covered in the USA. The authors speculate that US dominance of world news may have been due to the 2008 presidential election and its important economic, political, and cultural ties to other countries.

Crime and Violence

Crime has always been a staple of news coverage, possibly because it represents environmental threats that need correction (Grabe, 1999; Shoemaker, 1996). In a study of news magazine content in 1994 and 1995, Maria Grabe (1999) found that crime was the topic of the first news story three-quarters of the time, and that the placement of crime stories mirrored an inverted pyramid—the most crime stories were at the beginning of the magazine and the fewest at the end. Grabe uses *functional theory* to explain this: If the news media help the status quo maintain the existing social structures, then crime in the news helps warn social institutions of potential threats (1999, p. 162). Although the amount of crime news supports a functionalist perspective, the content of crime news also is important. Grabe described crime news as the forces of good fighting the forces of evil, with victims depicted as prey. Most crime news appeared before the accused party goes to court, and the news media portrayed the accused as guilty in these stories. Grabe showed the "inevitability of a criminal's arrest" in 86 percent of all program cases (1999, p. 165). The news magazines' story template encouraged the audience to define crime as existing because of individuals' failings, not because of societal issues such as poverty (Grabe, 1999, p. 163). Their moral was that "crime doesn't pay." Most criminals in news magazines' crime stories were adult males, and around half were African Americans. Portrayals of crime in the media shape the audience's *social realities*, their personal views of the world. In Gerbner's terms (1988), the media "cultivate" personal beliefs about the world.

In the television reality show *Cops*, minorities were usually suspected of drug-related crimes, whereas whites were involved in domestic disputes (Cotter, de Lint, & O'Connor, 2008). The police and victims were both usually white: White suspects accosted white victims, and black suspects accosted black victims. This world of crime favored specific problems and solutions that could be shown within the constraints of the dramatic narrative (Cotter et al., 2008, pp. 283–5).

What happens when the forces of evil are natural? Tierney, Bevc, and Kuligowski (2006) suggest that the media also frame disasters as mythic struggles between good and evil. When Hurricane Katrina destroyed much of New Orleans, the news media used a civil unrest frame in most news about victims, emphasizing them as either out of control bad guys or as ineffectual and deserving of charity. As the event evolved, the news media exaggerated looting and other crimes, giving the sense that the people were at war with one another (Tierney et al., 2006, p. 57). Those who could not leave New Orleans before the storm hit were depicted as being irrational and out of control. These media frames encouraged authorities to focus on law and order, instead of encouraging and helping people help themselves (Tierney et al., 2006, pp. 74–5).

Violence in time of war is not labeled crime but rather as terrorism or as just evil. Aday, Livingston, and Hebert's (2005) study of the 2003 Iraq War looked at media coverage of five US networks and Al Jazeera, finding that the stories were overwhelmingly neutral and mostly about the "whiz-bang aspects at the expense of other important story lines" (p. 16). Half of the CNN and Fox stories were about the battles. Whereas all American networks ignored domestic protest against the war, Al Jazeera covered the battles plus information about protests and discussions between countries. In addition, the authors found no support for the idea that stories from journalists embedded with US troops were more positive toward the war than independent journalists. In all, content of war coverage de-emphasized blood, morbidity, and mortality and instead emphasized heroism and new weapons (Aday et al., 2005, pp. 16–18).

People

People in the media world differ from those in, what we call for now, the real world. Some groups are underrepresented or portrayed in negative ways or both. The majority of studies involve ethnicity and gender, but we also include recent studies that concentrate on age and sexual identification. We find that the portrayal of most people is stereotyped, a shorthand way of generalizing what we know and feel about a few people to others like them. Stereotypes emphasize the variance between categories of people and de-emphasize the variance within each category.

Ethnicity

In the world of the news media, the category *white* is not used as an ethnicity; it is the default option against which all other people are compared. White people's race is never mentioned in the news media, whereas the labels Latino- and African American are routinely applied, whether the individuals are criminals or political candidates. Yet in the USA, white is the most important ethnicity of all, in the sense of privilege, because whites benefit from the best education and jobs and have the most money and power—not only in the media world but also in actuality. This is found in other countries as well. For example, in Australia, the news represents the majority of people as Anglo, despite the presence of multiple ethnic groups (Phillips, 2011, p. 23). In Belgium, a 2003 government-mandated Charter of Diversity was aimed at increasing ethnic diversity in many areas of Flemish life, including media content. A study of television news programs, however, found no significant change in media coverage of ethnicities (Bulck & Broos, 2011, pp. 211–12).

Studies of ethnicity have generally found that media practitioners use a deviance frame, us versus them (Bai, 2010, p. 406; Zhao & Postiglione, 2010). The tendency of stereotypes to be based on categorical in-group and out-group identifications results in much error in identifying the groups and behavior toward them; there may be as much variance within out-groups (and within in-groups) as between in- and out-groups. Stereotyping people according to their physical characteristics is dysfunctional, leading to cultural stereotyping and prejudices that define who has power in society and who is powerless.

In the news media, journalists—who as children were taught the same cultural lessons as their peers—distribute stereotypes through their words and images. Because stereotypes can be activated without conscious thought (Lasorsa & Dai, 2007, pp. 282–3), journalists need both to be motivated and have the ability to question and overcome a lifelong set of schemas. Distinguishing between deceptive (inaccurate and plagiarized information) and authentic (fair and accurate) news stories, the scholars found that stereotypes are more likely in deceptive stories, which are also more negative in tone (Lasorsa & Dai, 2007, pp. 287–8).

Stereotypes about ethnic groups are based on trivialities such as darker skin or body structure judged to be different from "typical" white American features

(Dixon, 2006). But is there a typical white American? The historic intermixing of many races in the USA has resulted in a people who may identify with one ethnicity or another but who are often physically descended from more than one race. As such, ethnicity is not always identified by one's physical characteristics, but also by people's intertwined cognitive and emotional relationships. Dixon has investigated *skin tone bias*, finding that people who watch a lot of television news use skin color to decide the guilt of accused criminals: Those with any range of dark skin are judged to be more culpable than white-skinned individuals, but only among those who watch a lot of television news (Dixon, 2006, p. 141). Dixon points out that stereotypes *prime* people's creation of later images, such that racial cues affect judgments, especially in ambiguous situations. In a later study, Dixon (2008) found that watching television network news made viewers more likely to endorse negative African American stereotypes, such as being physically intimidating.

Ethnic blame discourse in the news reveals how juveniles charged with crimes are portrayed in Los Angeles local television news. Both African- and Latino-American young people were shown as perpetrators of crime more often than white youths. Fewer Latino-American youths were shown in the news than were actually charged by the police (Dixon & Azocar, 2006, pp. 152–4). Gant and Dimmick (2000, pp. 201–2) suggest that such differences may be due to routines associated with constructing local television news stories: Television reporters discover crime events by listening to police scanners, which biases their universe of crime news stories toward individuals' crimes of passion rather than more complex crimes. Lynn Owens (2008, p. 365) studied ABC, CBS, and NBC network news coverage of Hurricane Katrina in 2005, finding that African American reporters were more likely than white reporters to use minority sources.

An analysis of network prime-time programs between 2000 and 2008 (Signorielli, 2009a) showed that the proportion of African American to white characters decreased over time. African American actors were cast primarily in situation comedies written to emphasize minorities (Signorielli, 2009a, pp. 323–33). African Americans are typecast as either educated and in the middle class or as lower class, uneducated, and criminal (Dates & Stroman, 2001).

This is also true for other ethnic and racial groups. Angie Chuang (2012) compared two events in which Asian men shot and killed people. In 2009, 42-year-old Jiverly Wong killed 13 people, then himself, at an upstate New York immigrant services center. The *New York Times* said that it was the USA's "worst mass shooting" since the 2007 shooting at Virginia Tech University, where Seung-Hui Cho killed 32 people, then himself (Chuang, 2012, p. 245). The news media used the two men's South Korean ethnicity to explain their violent behavior but did not reveal that one man had been in the USA since 1990 and became a US citizen in 1995, and the other had been in the USA since he was eight years old (Chuang, 2012, p. 251). Chuang concludes "the actuality of a perpetrator's Americanness was overshadowed by racialized and stereotypical notions of foreignness. Hence, mainstream newspapers appeared to have conflated ethnic with foreign" (2012, p. 251), ignoring their

Americanness and concentrating on their foreignness. Both men were presented as "other" to the predominantly white media audience (Chuang, 2012, pp. 255–6).

The *diasporic media*—those that represent immigrant groups—help immigrants succeed in their new society, offsetting negative images of their ethnic group in the mainstream media and strengthening their communities (Bai, 2010, p. 408). In Sang Bai's study (2010) of the newspaper *Korean Daily*, Korean Americans were shown as victims of crimes by African Americans and as victims of discrimination by white Americans (p. 385). The diaspora of immigrants to, for example, the USA puts them at the mercy of the new country's cultural forces, including advertising. Yet the commercialization of ethnicity by American advertisers has included far more positive images of ethnic groups than are found in their news and entertainment portrayals (La Ferle & Lee, 2005, p. 151).

Historically, mid 20th century media portrayed all nonwhite people with grossly oversimplified stereotypes: Native Americans as primitive and savage, Asians as corrupt and violent, Latinos as hot tempered and lazy, and African Americans as shiftless and easily frightened (Wilson & Gutierrez, 1985). From virtual invisibility in the 1950s, the proportion of African American television characters increased from the mid 1960s to the 1990s, but the portrayal of African Americans has been primarily negative on television (Atkin, Greenberg, & McDermott, 1983). Even newspaper comics underrepresented African Americans (Atkin, 1992). The number of shows centered on minority characters increased dramatically between the 1960s and 1980s, but then fell off dramatically (Atkin, 1992, p. 344). The 1970s national news featured less affluent blacks as "protesters, criminals, and victims" (Gans, 1979, p. 23). Police brutality was generally presented as a "black-white" problem, ignoring abuses of Latinos (Jordan, 1992).

Jack Shaheen (2003) analyzes how Arabs and Muslims have been portrayed in some 900 Hollywood films produced since 1896. He observes that Hollywood Arabs have been treated as the "other" consistently over the past century, whether they are presented as Arab Americans or as Arabs from other countries: "From 1896 until today, filmmakers have collectively indicted all Arabs as Public Enemy #1—brutal, heartless, uncivilized religious fanatics and money-mad cultural 'others' bent on terrorizing civilized Westerners, especially Christians and Jews" (Shaheen, 2003, p. 172).

Portrayals of Arabs in the news have been as stereotypical as those in the movies. Mary Ann Weston (2003) analyzed newspaper coverage of Arab Americans pre- and post-destruction of the World Trade Center and the Pentagon attack in 2001. During the six months before the attacks, stories portrayed Arab Americans as citizens who were active in American society, both complaining of ethnic profiling and supporting political candidates (Weston, 2003, p. 97). Immediately after the attacks, newspapers portrayed Arab Americans as "double victims," who had both lost loved ones in the attacks and had been discriminated against. Newspapers portrayed Arab Americans as "bewildered and victimized" (Weston, 2003, pp. 97–8), failing to describe the diversity of the Arab American community, more than half of whom were Christian.

According to Lynn Owens (2008), *incognizant racism* is reflected in network news: "The patterns of racial inclusion and exclusion could reinforce an image [among viewers] of minorities as a group whose identity, knowledge, and interests are both narrower and different from Whites" (Owens, 2008, p. 367). After their study of more than 2,000 characters in US prime-time television commercials, Mastro and Stern (2003) proposed that ethnic viewers' self perceptions could be influenced by the ways in which ethnics are portrayed in advertising. Most characters in the study were African Americans and whites, being presented roughly in proportion to the population. Latinos, however, were drastically underrepresented and were often portrayed in sexual frames (Mastro and Stern, 2003, p. 645).

Gender

Although women are a majority of the US population, in the media world they are underrepresented and devalued. As news sources, women are often absent, even in media coverage of issues that involve women, such as abortion, birth control, Planned Parenthood, and women's rights (4thestate, 2012a). During the early part of the 2012 presidential election, women comprised only about 20 percent of top journalists' sources (4thestate, 2012c), and this pattern is not new. In the late 20st century, when women entered politics they got less news coverage than their male opponents, and women candidates' news coverage was more about questioning whether they were viable candidates than about their issues (Kahn & Goldenberg, 1991, p. 180). Caryl Rivers (1993) noted several themes that dominated news about women: their frailty, hormonal imbalances, their "genetic" lack of math skills, and their inability to marry after they became 30 years old (Rivers, 1993, p. 3).

Robinson and Powell (1996) looked at news coverage at the intersection of race and gender, as two prominent African Americans were depicted in the 1991 televised US Senate confirmation hearings of Supreme Court nominee. The event turned into a "political spectacle" when Anita Hill testified that Clarence Thomas had sexually harassed her during the time he was her supervisor at the Equal Employment Opportunity Commission. Two frames summarized the discourse: gender-based for Hill and race-based for Thomas. Although Thomas was confirmed as a justice, Hill's messages "resonated with women's latent fears of being subjugated and harassed in the workplace" (Robinson & Powell, 1996, p. 298). Thomas's messages re-legitimized male dominance and successfully played the race frame, such that a vote against him would be a racist vote (Robinson & Powell, 1996, p. 298). Robinson and Powell conclude that "postmodern political struggles increasingly assume the form of multifaceted, sensationalistic battles of surface impressions orchestrated via mass electronic media" (1996, p. 296).

Historically scholars have found that there have been about twice as many male as female characters in television programs (Tuchman, 1981), and in 1952 men were 60 percent of prime-time characters compared with 74 percent 20 years later, and 80 percent of employed characters were male. In the 1970s and 1980s, the typical prime-time television character was a white man between 40 and 50 years old (Greenberg, 1980), with minority characters being underrepresented (Signorielli, 1983). Women characters were shown as young, in low-level jobs, and in family roles. Women were even stereotyped in television commercials, where men were seen as more authoritative and provided more voice-overs, even for women's products (Signorielli, 1985; Greenberg, 1980, pp. 44–5).

More recently, a longitudinal study of US and Canadian G-rated movies—those most likely to draw audiences with children—found that females were fewer and composed only 28 percent of all speaking characters (Smith, Pieper, Granados, & Choueiti, 2010, p. 780), a stable figure over the 15 years studied (p. 784). The authors concluded that the films "may subtly perpetuate the status quo and reinforce a hegemonic view of girls and women" (Smith et al., 2010, pp. 782–4). The more realistic video games showed women with smaller waists and hips than the average American woman (Martins, Williams, Harrison, & Ratan, 2009). The thinnest female characters appeared in games rated for children (Martins et al., 2009, pp. 831–2).

In the 1950s and 1960s Betty Freidan's research portrayed working women as primarily absent from magazine pages; instead they were portrayed as wives and mothers (1963). Later studies (such as Douglas & Michaels, 2004) showed that the mother role was dominant. Popular women's magazines in the 1970s depicted women in terms of the presence or absence of men in their lives, furthering a dependent and passive stereotype. Women's work was secondary to their home life and even undesirable (Franzwa, 1974). Helen Butcher and her colleagues (1981) noted a consistent image across media outlets: women as mothers, wives, and sex objects.

The coming-of-age white male was the focus of Lesley Speed's (2010) study of "vulgar" teen movies over three decades, including the iconic 1970s film *Animal House*, *Porky's* in the 1980s, and *American Pie* in the 1990s (Speed, 2010, p. 821). Speed speculated that the vulgarity of the 1970s was a reaction to the 1960s credo of questioning authority, with *Animal House* satirizing politics during the Nixon administration and the Watergate scandal. The very popular *Porky's* represented a detachment from social change during the more conservative 1980s, leading Speed to speculate that film studios increased production of vulgar movies as an attempt to attract teen audiences and to increase profits. *Porky's* portrayal of a brothel as part of the characters' transition into "real men" reveals "a crisis of masculine identity . . . and the failure of male sexual mastery in apolitical ways" (Speed, 2010, pp. 827–8). The films "allude to the waning of middle class privilege and to contemporary youth's lack of insight into its social positioning" (Speed, 2010, p. 837).

Age

From her study of television characters between 1993 and 2002, Signorielli (2004) suggests that the television world is made up disproportionately of young characters, especially young females. Yet as female characters age, they become less central to stories' plot lines, and this is also true of minority male characters. Minority women are less likely to be cast in the older roles. Middle-aged television women are portrayed as younger than their male cohort, whereas elderly women appear to be slightly older than men of the same age. Men are shown as vital and making the most out of life, whereas women are portrayed as being able to do less and less. Notably, for those characters of 16 to 21 years of age, whites are more likely to be portrayed in adult roles, but similarly aged minorities are portrayed as children (Signorielli, 2004, p. 296). In the television world, jobs are mostly given to those who are young or in middle age, although older white males have the most prestigious jobs. Because there are few older role models among television's characters, children may perceive that they have a limited range of jobs in their lifetimes. In addition, older viewers may believe that they are devalued and should retire earlier than necessary (Signorielli, 2004, pp. 295–7). The age of television production staff may influence the age and stereotyping of characters in their television programs (Healey & Ross, 2002).

Greenberg (1980, p. 27) found a similar imbalance in the early world of television: People from 20 to 49 years of age represented two-thirds of television characters but were only one-third of the census population at the time. Signorielli (1985) noted that both very young and very old were underrepresented and negatively stereotyped on television. Older men were treated more favorably than older women. Cultivation theory predicts that, when older people spend a lot of time watching television, they may assume that television's stereotypes depict what their own lives will be like: fewer job opportunities, less prestige, and less ability to enjoy themselves (Signorielli, 2004, p. 241). Thus, ultimately the media world may help construct and reproduce the "real" world in a self-fulfilling prophecy.

Sexual Identification

There are many stereotypes of gay men and lesbian women in the media. In a study of newspaper stories about same-sex marriage in 2003 and 2004, two-thirds of the more than one thousand sources were gay males. Among heterosexuals, the most negative comments came from men. The male sources had higher power jobs, and female sources were of less value in public affairs (Schwartz, 2010). A more recent (2004–5) analysis of newspaper and magazine coverage of gay and lesbian parents and their children found that media stories imply that the children grow up to be heterosexual. Landau (2009, p. 96) found that same-sex parents and children are shown as having families and lives much like those of heterosexual parents and children, thus reinforcing heterosexual norms. For many years, there were no regularly appearing gay, lesbian, bisexual, or transsexual characters on US television programs. Amber Raley and Jennifer Lucas (2006) found that in the 2001 television season, gay men and lesbian women had frequent interactions with children and made about the same number of affectionate gestures (nonsexual) toward children. None of the eight programs studied included more than two gay or lesbian characters. Nearly twice as many gay or lesbian jokes were told by gays or lesbians than by heterosexual characters (Raley & Lucas, 2006, pp. 30–1).

There have been many media devoted specifically to gay and lesbian consumers—on and offline, national and local. Some have been fighting for their economic lives, because they compete for gay and lesbian consumers with the more general media. Gay and lesbian consumers spend $845 billion per year, according to Prime Access, but their use of gay media is primarily local (Pardee, 2012). Faced with falling profits, national television networks such as Logo and Fab eventually widened their programming schedule to appeal more to heterosexual consumers. Gays and lesbians are as likely to access relevant information in the mainstream media as in gay media, leading Pardee to conclude that gays and lesbians do not want to be isolated and are interested in buying the same products as the general public.

Barbara Freeman (2006) writes about market forces on the appearance of articles about lesbianism in the mainstream Canadian magazine *Chatelaine*, from 1966 to 2004, a leader in writing about feminism and sexual identity: "The magazine's treatment shifted cautiously over almost four decades in accordance with both heterosexual social norms and the market values of the Canadian magazine market" (Freeman, 2006, p. 816). Although the number of articles increased over the years, the magazine moved away from social issues and toward individuals' needs, including beauty and fashion, but at the loss of their sexual identity. Lesbians were repackaged as consumers, a result of lower profitability for general-interest magazines and a movement toward niche publications.

Bad News

Most news seems to be bad news—crime, war, suffering, stealing, shooting, scandal, death, and more. The news world includes genocide, slavery, and psychosis; it emphasizes illness, conflict, and controversy. Bad news includes mistakes, prejudice, disasters, stupidity, and evil. The melodramas around hurricanes, tornadoes, and earthquakes feature the best and worst of people, but often tend to dwell on the latter. More positive events can become news, but Weiner (2005, p. 173) complains about one positive event that was virtually ignored by the mainstream news media: The mapping of the human genome showed that the genes of any two people on Earth are 99.9 percent alike. All humans are "equal in origin, except for the miniscule differences between us as individuals" (Weiner, 2005, p. 175). Although some results of the Human Genome Project were covered in the media, no newspaper ran a headline such as "all humans are genetically equal" (Weiner, 2005, p. 175).

When focus group participants had to summarize the US news media in one word, they came up with labels such as sensationalist, bad, aggressive, deceptive, manipulative, vicious, negative, exploitive. Television news got the worst bashing. So why do people watch it? "It's truth, it's reality." "It's primal." "I don't want to see it. I don't want to know . . . But I'll watch it. I don't know what makes me do it" (Luntz, 2000, p. 70). Bad news is an unstated news value: Television news directors in one study said that they don't try to depict the world as negative; they try to show what happens each day (Galician & Pasternack, 1987, p. 88). Still, television's lead story is usually bad news, as are the first five stories (Johnson, 1996, p. 207).

This bad news tendency is not uniquely American, but the amount of bad news varies among countries (Shoemaker & Cohen, 2006). Shahira Fahmy and Mohammed Al-Emad (2011) found that both the Arab- and English-language versions of the online network Al Jazeera presented similar views of the Middle Eastern conflicts. Contrary to accusations that the English version is sanitized, Fahmy and Al-Emad found that neither network placed much emphasis on the conflicts—15 percent of stories on the Arabic site and 13 percent on the English site—and that most of the stories were not prominently placed. In addition, "the vast majority of those involved in the conflict were framed negatively, with Al Qaeda agents portrayed more negatively than any other agent involved in the conflict" (Fahmy and Al-Emad, 2011, p. 228). There was no evidence that one site was more negative than the other.

The preference for certain kinds of news in the mediated world—variously termed bad, negative, atypical, discrepant, compelling, or deviant—appears to be deeply rooted in psychology. Experiments, beginning in the mid 20th century (such as Levine & Murphy, 1943), have shown that bad news is longer remembered than good news and that it inhibits memory both for the stories preceding and following it (see, for example, Shapiro & Fox, 2002; Wicks, 1995; Newhagen & Reeves, 1992; Mundorf, Drew, Zillman, & Weaver, 1990; Graesser, Woll, Kowalski, & Smith, 1980). Bad news communicated visually is remembered longer than if it is presented verbally. "Photographic images are explicit indicators of the objects they depict, . . . while words must be elaborated to extract their symbolic meaning" (Newhagen & Reeves, 1992, p. 38). Bad news is forgotten at a slower pace (Levine & Murphy, 1943, p. 513), and forgotten bad news can be quickly retrieved from memory when a similar event re-occurs (Wicks, 1995, p. 676).

Like the body's autonomic system, most of the systems that run our communities and nations operate unnoticed. Is it good news to know that your heart is still beating, that you are still breathing? Undoubtedly, but who wants a television news program devoted to everything that's working okay? We expect things to work properly, but when the levees are about to break, we want to know about it. Journalists' anticipation of problems—worrying about the worst that could happen—may help by gaining the attention of those who can fix problems (Martin, 2008, p. 180).

Brown and Kulik (1977, pp. 96–7) suggest that bad news events activate an innate mechanism in the brain that gets our attention, a result of biological evolution.[2] Shoemaker (1996) proposes a hard wired theory to explain why human societies have news, especially bad news. Assessing an event's newsworthiness is an innate process among all humans as a result of both biological and cultural evolution. Our tendency to look out for deviant events kept our long-ago ancestors alive, with biological evolution occurring over hundreds of thousands of years.

Today, this tendency manifests itself in the emotions and cognitions of media consumers. For example, Maria Grabe and Rasha Kamhawi (2006) found several differences between women's and men's responses to both positive and negative news: women were more aroused by positive news; men were more aroused by negative news. Women recognized more and recalled more information from positive news; for men, this was true of negative news (Grabe & Kamhawi, 2006, p. 359). Grabe and Kamhawi conclude that, instead of there being an overall memory difference between men and women, any gender differences observed "boil down to message valence" (2006, p. 363). As far as learning from the news, "positive framing benefits women, negative framing benefits men." This study helps explain why most news is negative: Journalism was established by men, was run by men, and is still mostly carried out by men. If men prefer bad news, then it is hardly surprising that most of our news is bad. If the news media want to educate citizens about important issues, the journalistic status quo will not favor women. Put succinctly, the male response to a negative environment (non-life threatening levels) serves a defensive survival function: detecting, investigating, and protecting offspring from potential danger. Because the lives of offspring are more closely linked to the survival of mothers than fathers, females are predisposed to an avoidance response to negative stimuli, steering themselves and their young clear of potential danger (Grabe & Kamhawi, 2006, pp. 363–4).

Most bad news research has studied its cognitive impacts, primarily attention, learning, and memory. LeDoux (2000) points out that the wave of cognitive psychology in the mid 20th century put the study of emotion aside. Emotion's subjectivity made it more difficult to study, whereas attention, knowledge, and memory could be more objectively quantified (LeDoux, 2000, p. 2). However, there is evidence that emotional reactions to news events are as likely as cognitions. For example, news about a shocking event can create a flashbulb memory, such as the assassination of a country's head of state, the explosion of a space shuttle, a revolution, or a sudden personal tragedy. Such events are both intensely surprising and emotionally arousing, creating a mental "picture" of the circumstances you were in when you got the information: where you were, what you were doing, how you felt, and how others felt. John Bohannon's (1988, p. 192) study of people's memories of the space shuttle Challenger explosion revealed that these personal circumstances are better remembered than facts about the event itself.

The effect of emotionally arousing messages on information processing depends on whether the emotion is positive or negative: Emotionally negative messages reduce the amount of cognitive processing allocated, resulting in less memory (Lang, Dhillon, & Dong, 1995, p. 324). In addition, emotionally negative content is remembered better if it is presented visually. Greater verbal memory is associated with positive, less emotional messages (Lang & Friestad, 1993, p. 666). Thorson and Friestad (1989) found that the more emotionally intense advertisements are, the more they are remembered. Information from "an emotional commercial can be stored very strongly in the stream of television viewing episodes, but searching semantic storage for information about heavy-duty laundry detergents would not access it" (Thorson & Friestad, 1989, pp. 320–1).

SOCIAL REALITY

We can look at social reality in two ways: First, we all have individual perceptions about what the world is like, but, second, some of those perceptions are based on cultural knowledge rather than personal experiences. Myths, for example, are stories about our culture, and their messages shape the reality of everyone in the culture. Social cognition is the intersection between people and the world, the study of how people make sense of the world by comparing the information they acquire from people and direct experience with information from other sources, such as the media. The knowledge that we acquire defines our understanding of the world. Although a person may develop an isolated view of the world, social cognition makes it more likely that we incorporate information and emotions from people around us. In the end, however, your personal social reality is the sum of your own experiences plus the values and information shared with those around you.

The Construction and Reconstruction of Reality

In building their social realities, people use both construction and reconstruction mental processes (Shapiro & McDonald, 1995). Watching television, for example, requires the intake and evaluation of information; this is construction, an ongoing process. If information is remembered, these memories are used to reconstruct our thoughts and feelings about the television show, and this reconstruction process guides what we think, feel, and do in the future. Shapiro and McDonald find that people have an emotional threshold at which an object becomes real (1995, p. 335). Both cognition and emotion help people figure out what the world is like. They can learn not only from the plot of a television show, but also from the characters' social relationships involving gender, race, and other human characteristics (Shapiro & McDonald, 1995, p. 331). Social reality is strongly influenced by the media, especially when it is emotional or exciting. Not only is currently constructed information available, but the reconstruction of information is gradually stored over time.

The visual representation of still images and television appears real, but photographs or videos do not mirror reality. Instead, our perceptions of objects are derived from our brains, with the world of color and shape we see around us being a property of the brain and not of the physical world. For example, humans' perceptions of color are formed by how the brain combines the wavelengths of light. We perceive things within a small part of the electromagnetic range, largely centered on green, possibly because it is the result of reflections from the leaves of plants, a primary food source for our long-ago ancestors (Johnston, 1999, pp. 14–15). We are surrounded by changes in electromagnetic radiation, air pressure, and chemicals, "but that nonbiological world is pitch dark, silent, tasteless, and odorless. All conscious experiences are emergent properties of biological brains, and they do not exist outside of those brains" (Johnston, 1999, p. 182).

Jane Raymond (2003) points out that constructed and reconstructed representations are the result of the brain analyzing and integrating sensory information. The representations are

> the result of much editing, some biophysical censorship (e.g., we cannot see infrared light), and a significant amount of cognitive and emotional spin doctoring. Although these persuasive mental inventions sensibly guide our actions in response to physical objects most of the time, they can also misinform, leading to inappropriate actions (e.g., accidents) and simple failures to perceive that which may be obvious to others.
>
> (Raymond, 2003, p. 60)

For example, watching a parade involves complex operations. Not only does the parade move through space and time, but our eyes and heads are also moving and we have our own perceptions of time. Some human actions preclude others (such as not being able to look right while looking left), and our brains must organize input from our senses by deciding which stimuli to pay attention to and which to ignore. (Ignoring does not imply no processing, since limited processing is essential to making the "ignore" decision.) Our brains must construct and reconstruct representations of the parade. Perception, attention, and memory interact to determine mental representations of the visual information we receive. Because of variations in people's experiences, their interpretations of visual information also vary (Raymond, 2003, p. 63). The parade we see is not what others see.

In addition to the physical world of chemicals, radiation, and air, human judgment is also influenced by inputs from the people around us. Social reasoning is a complex process. In trying to understand other people, we approximate mental representations of their cognitions and emotions, even if we have never shared their experiences. We know that other people are difficult to understand (Johnston, 1999, p. 164). "The evolution of social reasoning skills may have been the major impetus for the rapid evolutionary expansion of the human brain. That is, our big brain may have evolved, not as a tool for conducting differential calculus, but as a tool for coping with the complexities of social decision-making" (Johnston, 1999, p. 165).

Thus, our social reality is the sum of the physical forces in our environment, what we personally experience, plus what we understand about other people. Based on such complexity, it is no surprise that no two people share the same social reality.

REALITY

Since the first humans looked at the stars, they have wondered about the stars, sun, and moon and how they got there. Are they a manifestation from God, defined by God, and monitored by God? Are they just matter—what we can sense—or do they only exist in our thoughts? When we use language to describe the stars, does language change reality?

We have a commonsense understanding of what is real (your broken leg) and not real (monsters under a child's bed). Is realness confined to things we can experience directly? We have not seen Jupiter's moon Europa, but we are taught that scientists have observed it, a form of scientific realism. If we state that love is real, we acknowledge that reality includes the mind in addition to what we can touch or observe (Stewart, Blocker, & Petrik, 2013). Our day-to-day lives do not require careful consideration of abstractions such as reality, real, and realism, largely because of shared assumptions with other people: We agree that a chair has four legs. Yet from philosophy to neuroscience, scholars are interested in how we perceive the external world. Is what we perceive as the physical world merely the pictures in our brains? Does the physical world exist only as radio waves, chemicals, and electromagnetic energy, with our conscious brains bringing it to life with colors, sounds, and tastes?

Philosophy

As the oldest of the social sciences, philosophy uses logical thinking and the interaction of ideas to consider reality, with knowledge built over centuries. Metaphysics is the oldest philosophical tradition, dating from the sixth century bce.[3] When you gaze at the stars and wonder how the universe came to be—created by God or the Big Bang?—you are engaging in metaphysical thought, but which option is real and which illusion? Plato (427–347 bce) wrote about realism and illusion using the metaphor of people chained in a cave all of their lives, believing that their world was the real world. Hallman (2012) provides a modern interpretation:

> Imagine that you have spent your entire life in a movie theater, chained to your seat so that you are able to see only the images projected on the screen in front of you. Wouldn't you . . . assume that the images on the screen were real? However, if you were able to break the chains and turn toward the light of the projector, . . . [and] your eyes became accustomed to the . . . light, you would realize that what you are now seeing is the source of the projected shadows, and that it is more real than [the images on the screen]. And, if you . . . found your way out of the theater, . . . you would discover a world outside that differed radically.

> (p. 189)

The Buddhist philosopher Nagarjuna (c.150–250 ce) taught that all objects and phenomena are empty of essential reality. Nagarjuna doesn't mean that nothing exists, but rather that a thing comes into existence only by depending on other objects and phenomena. They affect one other, and through this process an object becomes real (Stewart et al., 2013, p. 507). Tenzin Gyatso, the 14th Dalai Lama, writes: "This suggests that things exist, but not intrinsically so; existence can only be understood in terms of dependent origination" (2005, p. 112), which can be the words used to designate the object or phenomenon or a mediated description of it.

Modern philosophy began with René Descartes (1596–1650), who believed that reality was a continuum and that a thing's realness is measured by its closeness to perfection. Hence a human is more real than an animal, because of a human's ability to reason. An animal is more real than a rock, because the animal is alive (Stewart et al., 2013, p. 180). Isaac Newton (1642–1727) showed by his discovery of gravity that a phenomenon could be real even if, although its effect could be observed, the phenomenon (gravity) was not itself visible (Rosenberg, 2012, p. 154). Immanuel Kant (1724–1804) believed that reality was discoverable through a person's senses, but that things not experienced were not real (Stewart et al., 2013, p. 83).

The theory of evolution by Charles Darwin (1809–82) was a dramatic shift in the definition of reality, in showing that random variations in the environment caused biological organisms to adapt, creating new biological structures. Darwin's theory showed that no metaphysical powers are necessary to create the many designs and functions in the world, that such mystical notions are illusion (Rosenberg, 2012, p. 107). This led to 20th-century philosophy, which was dominated by positivism and scientific realism. Positivism held that there are only two kinds of statements: those manifestly true, such as a dog is a mammal with four legs, and those that can be tested to be true or false, such as large dogs live for fewer years than small dogs. Logical positivists begin defining reality with a theory, whereas scientific realists begin by accumulating the results of many studies, giving them predictive power and bringing them closer to defining reality (Rosenberg, 2012, p. 150).

Science's certainty about the power of logic and mathematics led a group of French philosophers, including Michel Foucault (1926–84), to reject the idea that we can fully understand anything and to argue that science shows us only illusions (Stewart et al., 2013, pp. 334–5). Postmodernists reject the idea of an objective reality, arguing instead that the "deconstruction of language shows that the relationship between all objects, language, and reality illustrates that reality is created by language" (Stewart et al., 2013, pp. 334–5). Deconstruction exposes the myths of "linguistic descriptions masquerading as reality" (Stewart et al., 2013, p. 235).

Other scholars have looked at the relationship between language and reality. For example, Benjamin Whorf (1956) studied languages in many cultures and concluded that, although the structure of language is not uniform across cultures, the structure of language within a specific culture affects how native speakers understand reality. Noam Chomsky (1957) had a different view of language structure, postulating that there is an innate human grammar. Jean-Paul Sartre (1905–80) believed that to appreciate fictional media, including novels, art, and (today) television shows, one must suspend the belief that the experience is real. The audience must be trained to separate reality from fiction (cited in Stewart et al., 2013, p. 391).

Science

Our conscious thoughts direct our emotions and behaviors, even when sleeping. But what is consciousness and how does it integrate into the brain? Thagard (2005, pp. 179–82) defines consciousness inductively: There is a complete lack of consciousness in the dead, and therefore consciousness must require life and certain biological processes. Studying comas, concussions, syncope (fainting), and sleep led him to the conclusion that consciousness is a function of biological, neural, electrical, and chemical causes. Without all of these, consciousness is not possible.

Neuroscientists have two general conceptions of how the brain works (Thagard, 2005, p. 170). Some use the analogy of mind-as-computer to create mathematical simulations of the brain. Others conduct experiments on the brain itself (Johnston 1999, p. 3). If brains are like computers, they continually scan and acquire information, with nerve cells helping to construct a cognitive representation of an object (Johnston, 1999). When encountering a green leaf, our eye gathers information about the attributes of the leaf and this manifests into a pattern of nerve impulses. "The neural pattern simply represents the attributes of the object in the outside world, while the cognitive processes, like seeing or thinking, are the equivalent of computational procedures that manipulate these symbolic representations" (Johnston, 1999, p. 4). The brain is compared to a computer, whose hardware and software control all mental processes, including perceptions of reality. Constructs such as cognitive representation are the product of cognitive psychology, a field that has little interest in studying emotion, but Joseph LeDoux (2000, pp. 3–4) notes that "minds are not either cognitive or emotional, they are both, and more."

But brains are not merely computers; they are biological entities that change in response to external stimuli. Brain processes are "electricity in a neuron that travels to the synapse, releases a chemical, and then turns into electricity again in the next neuron. So the brain action is electricity-chemicals-electricity-chemicals, and so on" (Weiner, 2005, p. 37). Because consciousness can be changed by disease, neurochemistry, and electrical stimulation, we know that all conscious thoughts and feelings are properties of the brain, "and they can arise without any input from the outside world" (Johnston, 1999, p. 6). The brain manufactures its own reality, but we are unaware of it.

> The illusion of naïve realism is so powerful and ubiquitous that we come to believe that objects really are red, or hot, or bitter, or sweet, or beautiful, and . . . we talk about the world around us as if it is full of light and sounds and tastes and smells. The physical world certainly contains electromagnetic radiation, air pressure waves, and chemicals dissolved in air or water, but not a single light or sound or smell or taste exists without the emergent properties of a conscious brain. Our conscious world is a grand illusion!
>
> (Johnston, 1999, p. 13)

The processing of external stimuli by the brain is now understood to begin with the intake of information through our senses. If you hear gunshots and screams nearby, these sounds travel through your auditory system to the auditory thalamus, the medial geniculate body (MGB), and then to the amygdala and the auditory cortex (LeDoux, 1996, p. 1230). The amygdala tells the brain that you are in a dangerous situation. Its messages go first to the brain stem, causing epinephrine (also known as adrenaline) to be released. This causes changes throughout the body, including increases in heart and breathing rates and the tightening of muscles. Subsequent inputs from the cortex help the amygdala determine whether the danger is real. Emotions are the result of these interactions. The conscious feeling of fear and of other emotions is the interaction of current experiences, activity by the amygdala, and long-term memories (LeDoux, 2000, p. 17).

Media Content and the Brain

When watching a horror movie, you expect to be frightened, but it is your brain that determines when fright begins and whether you are personally being threatened. The amygdala notifies the brain stem and the cortex that a threat has been detected. The brain stem increases heart rate and the release of hormones such as epinephrine, and the cortex analyzes the reality of the threat. This process occurs over and over again in the movie, resulting in your still being excited when you leave the theater. Your brain makes all of this happen in response to inputs from the movie, and indeed most people go to see horror movies specifically for this effect, to be frightened. Less dramatic effects result from viewing less horrific movies, but three-dimensional movies intentionally startle people by programming characters that leap from the screen. The movie industry wants to make the movie more realistic for the audience, possibly because the more realistic a stimulus is, the more emotion is created by the brain.

Whether the news media elicit this startle reflex depends on the topic and its presentation. Boring topics and dull presentations don't activate the amygdala, but the news is sometimes astonishing. Coverage of the September 11, 2001, attacks on the World Trade Center and the Pentagon was that and more. People saw an airplane fly through the south tower of the World Trade Center and hit the Pentagon. They saw people jump from the top of towers and watched both towers collapse. Many viewers saw the disasters on live television news, showing rescuers struggling to evacuate the two towers, but many people watched these events occur again and again for hours. Eventually the networks decided that images of the planes hitting the towers and people jumping from skyscrapers were just too graphic, too horrible for the audience to see. They shifted to news of the recovery.

Judging whether images are too graphic for viewers is a common media practice, including among newspaper photographers' still images. Killing, dying, and their aftermath are rarely shown in the news; in fact, the sight of American coffins being returned to the USA from Iraq and Afghanistan has been politically sensitive. The term too graphic, in neuroscientific terms, indicates that the activated amygdala causes an unacceptably large increase in negative emotion.

We wrote earlier in this chapter that the television world is not the real world, but nonetheless, what we see on television and other media can have a profound effect. On 9/11, what we saw was more horrific than any horror movie—not only were our amygdalas on high alert, but also our brain's cortex advised us that it was actually happening. We know that live television news gives us only a few windows on an event, but in this case it was more than sufficient. Although mediated reality is thought not to be as horrible as the reality of personal experience, its effects have their own powerful significance.

We conclude that news content can activate the amygdala in the same way as entertainment content, but boring news topics and ordinary television productions are not likely to activate it (or lead to high television ratings). Everything we experience through our senses, everything we do or say is determined by our brain's inputs and outputs, both cognitive and emotional. The real world is the picture in our heads, making the media role in creating these pictures correspondingly significant.

SUMMARY

In this chapter we describe the reality conveyed by media representations, but knowing what the media world is like, even knowing that it reinforces hegemonic systems of control by those who have power, is not in itself a sufficient end. We study mediated reality because of its critical relationship with the individual's social reality. Indeed, the impact of media content on the social system begins with impacts on individuals, but the social system cannot be understood as just an aggregate of individuals; it also incorporates the role of the media in elaborating the relationship of individuals to those in power.

Digital television images are not real; they are code—ones and zeroes—organized to represent people and objects (Weiner, 2005, p. 29). So how do we live our lives, knowing that the images we see in the media and in our everyday world are merely patterns of electricity, chemicals, and neurons in our brains? How can we consume news, knowing that stereotypes abound and that the news reinforces powerful people and institutions? As we watch increasing violent crime in fictional television and reports of lowering crime in the news, we wonder what the truth is, whether we can walk in our neighborhood at night.

As for Lang and Lang's (1953) parade study, discussed at the beginning of this chapter, viewers of the televised parade were much more excited than those standing by the curb, and they also thought that the general looked more noble. The camera lens revealed only a small part of the parade, creating an illusion that the crowd was wild about MacArthur, whereas on-scene observers understood that many people were cheering because they were on television for the first time.

Our larger discussion of reality reminds us that mediated objects—whether portrayed as fiction or news—are not the objects themselves. News realities can be manipulated by both sources and practitioners, resulting in news reports that differ in important ways from other information about the world. The media world amounts to the brain's biological operations and cognitive representations in reaction to sound waves and electromagnetic emissions. Some representations are more accurate than others, but we are entertained and taught by the media to think in specific ways about our lives, people, and places, and to appropriately respond to emotional images, sights, and sounds. The symbolic environment built by our brains is problematic, because we know it contains inaccuracies and incorrect assumptions, yet it effectively defines our social realities and our daily lives.

The following chapters look closely at how media reality is shaped. Media content is not a natural product of our world, nor is it a complete or accurate description of it, but rather media content is limited by our culture and social system. We now know that our mediated realities—from any medium, social or mass—are not real in the sense of mirroring some objective, externally discernable reality, but that they have a profound impact on individuals, social collectives, and the world. To understand how those realities are shaped we turn now to the heart of the book in the next five chapters, which outline the hierarchy of influences on the mediated message.

NOTES

1   In 1951, General MacArthur arrived at Midway Airport in downtown Chicago, dedicated a bridge, was honored with a parade, and gave a speech that evening (Lang & Lang, 1953, p. 3).
2   It would have been functional (or adaptive, in Darwin's theory) for early humans to attend and quickly react to unexpected events, giving them an adaptive advantage.
3   Its etymology comes from the Greek word for nature, which Aristotle called "physics," the subject of many of his books. The term "metaphysics" was invented after Aristotle's death by his book editor, who while organizing notes saw that the first section was called "Physics," but there was no heading for the second section, and "so he invented a word—'After Physics' (meta meaning 'after,' and physica meaning 'physics'). So the exalted inquiry into the nature of reality forever after has been known as metaphysics—and all due to an editorial mistake" (Stewart et al., 2013, p. 75).

CHAPTER 4

Social Systems

In this chapter, we look at forces that can influence media content starting at the social system level of analysis. The macro, most encompassing level is a broad and complex one that incorporates insights from all the other perspectives, asking in effect what they all "add up to." This question, broadly speaking, involves exploring "meaning in the support of power," ideas in the service of interests, and indeed we labeled this chapter in the 1991 and 1996 editions of *Mediating the Message* the "ideological" level for that reason. We broaden this perspective to the social system more generally, although ideology is still an important way of understanding its inner workings. In this book we treat the social system level as the structure of relationships among people and the institutions they create. When dealing with how such structures relate to media, a number of perspectives have been used, and inevitably they connect with larger theories of society. A comprehensive treatment is beyond our scope, but we introduce how these larger systems have been examined, the special issues that this level of analysis addresses, and review some of the major studies that have taken up these questions. Taking up the larger society, itself a system, we must first distinguish among the more important subsystems that constitute it—ideological, economic, political, and cultural—before taking up the conceptual issues of power and control that directly involve media.

Social systems have been defined a number of ways in communication research. Tichenor, Donohue, Olien, and Clarke (1980) target the "community," and how conflict within it affected the knowledge gap between people who are more or less well educated.[1] Shoemaker and Cohen (2006) compared news values among ten countries, suggesting the national system is the essential focus. Others think of social systems as the interaction between social institutions or actors, such as Barbara Pfetsch's (2004) definition of a political communication system "as the integration of two functionally differentiated subsystems. In other words, the political communication system regulates cross-border communication between politics and the media" (p. 350). This perspective views a social system as an *aggregation of subsystems*, such as political, economic, cultural, and mass communication. In the next chapter we discuss the closely related influences on content from social *institutions*, such as government, financial, and religion, which are the structural manifestations of political, economic, and cultural subsystems, but here we look at the broader systemic context.

How can something so complex be investigated? Media systems are often studied *comparatively* by looking at two or more countries, as is the case in Daniel Hallin
and Paolo Mancini's book *Comparing Media Systems* (2004) and in *Comparing Political Communication*, edited by Frank Esser and Barbara Pfetsch (2004). Even here, as
globalization has complicated the authority of the nation-state, these comparisons
are no longer as clear; so, we consider taking up the larger planet as a social system.
This gives us an opportunity to consider the implications of globalization for the
transformation of these macro-level systems. Other research approaches in the critical, Marxian tradition don't rely on the empirical cause-and-effect analysis of variables and comparison, and we address how the internal working of a system can be
examined through critical and interpretive approaches to how power is expressed
through media in ways that work to sustain that system.

SOCIAL SYSTEMS AS LEVEL OF ANALYSIS

The social system level is the base on which the other levels of analysis rest. Studies
on this level focus on the larger social structure and how it becomes cohesive, rather
than separately focusing on the operation of its component parts. Indeed, in the
Marxist tradition, it is an object of faith that no aspect of society can be understood
apart from its social and historical context. So because we ask in whose interests
social institutions, media organizations, media routines, and individuals ultimately
work, we cannot avoid questions of value, interests, and ultimately power. The studies discussed in this chapter provide an important, overarching context for studies
at the lower levels. In Chapter 3 we discussed how media content portrays a map of
power relationships in society, with power defined as "the structural capacity of a
social actor to impose its will over other social actors" (Castells, 2007, p. 239). Here
we look at the powerful in society and at how that power is played out through the
media. We assume that ideas have links to interests and power and that the power
to create symbols in media content is not a neutral force. Not only is news about
the powerful, but also the news paradigm structures stories so that events are interpreted from the perspective of powerful interests. Castells (2007) notes "throughout
history communication and information have been fundamental sources of power
and counter-power, of domination and social change. This is because the fundamental battle being fought in society is the battle over the minds of the people"
(p. 238).

Theories of communication are often revealed to be theories of social systems,
where we look specifically at how the media function as extensions of powerful interests in society. In a classic early example of linking news coverage, the Glasgow
University Media Group (1976) compiled extensive documentation of media content
in the book *Bad News* that shows how labor unions, rather than corporate management, were blamed for industrial disputes in Ireland: Labor positions were "demands," whereas management positions were "offers." Individuals, the routines of
media work, media organizations, and other societal structures combine to maintain

a system of control and reproduction of the dominant ideology. Thus, we examine how powerful sources act in their own interests, not as individuals, but as a class that transcends any one organization, industry, or place. From this perspective we can see, for example, that the actions of US advertisers arise not just from the interests of a single firm, but are a systematic and structural result of a capitalist advertiser-supported media system.

MEDIA AND GLOBALIZATION: THE PLANET AS SOCIAL SYSTEM

As a growing global communication system weakens the power of individual countries, some scholars contend that media studies have focused too much on the country or nation-state and its political system as a unit of analysis (Esser & Pfetsch, 2004), Indeed, the simultaneous transmission of information to large parts of the world is often called "global" (e.g., CNN as "global" news leader), but this definition refers more to the size of the potential audience and less to the social system from which the information is sent. The reason for scholars' interest in globalization "has to do with increased emphasis on the general awareness of other parts of the world as a basic feature of today's 'post-modern' society" (Nohrstedt & Ottosen, 2000, p. 26). Although often equated with globalization, the idea of *cultural imperialism* was suggested in the mid 20th century to describe an increasing diffusion and adoption of American (or Western) ideas and media products around the world (Crane, 2002). According to Elasmar and Bennett (2003, p. 2), those interested in studying cultural imperialism combined the political, economic, and cultural subsystems to gather information "about the contemporary international intentions and behaviors of states, using conspiracy theory as their premise" (pp. 2–3).

Today the term *globalization* is more likely to be used, even considering that the term is "poorly defined and difficult to research systematically" (Hallin & Mancini, 2004; Crane, 2002, p. 1). Anthony Giddens' (1997; from 1990) definition of globalization recognizes its complexity:

> The intensification of world-wide social relations which link distant localities in such a way that local happenings are shaped by events occurring many miles away and vice versa. This is a dialectical process because such local happenings may move in an obverse direction from the very distanciated relations that shape them.
>
> (p. 64)

Giddens uses the term *local transformation* to explain the process in which foreign media, products, and ideas interact with those in other parts of the world. "The increasing prosperity of an urban area in Singapore might be causally related, via a complicated network of global economic ties, to the impoverishment of a neighborhood in Pittsburgh whose local products are uncompetitive in world markets" (1997, pp. 19–20).

The global media system is clearly more complicated than the tendency toward cultural, political, and economic globalization once suggested by the 20th century metaphors of McLuhan (global village, 1962) and Luhmann (world society, 1997). Diana Crane reflects this complexity, preferring the term *cultural globalization*, which is "the transmission or diffusion across national borders of various forms of media and the arts" (2002, p. 1). Instead of homogenization, she conceptualizes globalization as the product of diverse cultures from various parts of the globe, the parts not always equating with nations. Other scholars have also suggested that globalization does not equal planet-wide homogenization. For example, Richard Hawkins argues that any blending of cultures is happening around "regional power centres," and that globalization should be defined as relationships between regions, rather than between nations (1997, p. 178). Joseph Straubhaar also describes the "'regionalization' of television into multi-country markets linked by geography, language and culture" (1997, p. 285). These *cultural regions* are not necessarily based on proximity (Crane, 2002).

A somewhat different approach is proposed by Anne-Marie Slaughter (2004), who argues for the study of an interlacing web of *government networks* "composed of national government officials" (2004, p. 4), which are already fulfilling many of the functions that would be required by a world government without the difficulties of establishing it. Nation states are "disaggregated," but still important in government networks, because they give officials the power to interact globally, forming both horizontal and vertical relationships among nations. Existing alliances such as the British Commonwealth, the Nordic System, Asia-Pacific Economic Cooperation, and the Organization for Economic Cooperation and Development are *horizontal* in that they are official relationships among nation states. Government networks, in contrast, are *vertical* relationships within which work can be conducted without the formal requirements of international alliance. These vertical networks incorporate aspects both of nations and of supranational entities: Government officials both represent the power of their nation states and are the key ingredient of something larger. For example, a supranational world court could interact with domestic courts, thus harnessing the power of domestic judiciaries (Slaughter, 2004, pp. 137–44).

Some scholars use the term *globalization* when referring to worrisome effects of 21st century media content, perhaps because it puts less blame on specific countries for "exporting and imposing a single social imagery" (Hallin & Mancini, 2004, p. 27) and more on the process of communicating in the age of the Internet. For example, Thussu (2007) says that scholars should consider the idea of how a global "infotainment" system is created. From this perspective, *infotainment* becomes the "discourse of diversion," taking the audience's attention away from important problems and to the capitalist lifestyle (Thussu, 2007, p. 9). Castells proposes that technological innovations such as the Internet bring into question the validity of defining public spaces as nation states, because "human communication, especially through social networking sites, has created 'communal identities'" (2007, p. 258) that obscure national citizenship. Geography is still an important determinant of belief systems, and these structures are closely related to the differential flow of information among nations (Barnett, Chon, & Rosen, 2001; Barnett & Sung, 2005). The technology necessary to participate in a global communication system has itself not diffused equally across the globe, as can be seen in unequal patterns of internet use (Google Trends, 2012). Some governments, such as China and North Korea, have tried to control the flow of information into and out of their borders (Shoemaker et al., 2011), but control is never absolute. Information flows from and about an event in a complex web of networks, some personal but most mediated. Particularly newsworthy information about an event moves in a circuitous path from local to international and back again (Shoemaker & Vos, 2009).

As a network itself, the Internet corresponds to Castells' (2008) definition of globalization as the "networking of networks." Certainly digital technologies are a necessary but not sufficient condition for global communication. In identifying cross-border communication as the "core phenomenon" of globalization, Kai Hafez (2007) takes a skeptical look at what he calls the "myth of media globalization." He argues that it fails to produce true transnational media platforms, or dialogs across boundaries—rather a combination of linguistic and digital divides, along with enduring regional preferences, has served to reinforce those boundaries. International reporting, a key component of the would be global public sphere, flunks Hafez's "global test," incurring the same criticisms others have leveled for years at national journalism: elite-focused, conflictual, and sensational, with a narrow, parochial emphasis.

Tsan-Kuo Chang, Itai Himelboim, and Dong Dong (2009) studied the extent to which news travels freely around the world by randomly selecting five countries from each of the core, semi-periphery, and periphery categories. They describe the Internet as an open global network that serves as a platform for media organizations, with content that can be characterized by *open media code*, meaning that hyperlinks within one story can make it easy for readers to follow their interests anywhere in the world regardless of space or time. Their findings show, however, that most internet content does not contain links to websites in other countries: "The offline world of foreign news reporting is somehow reproduced in the online environment" (Chang et al., 2009, p. 155).

In addition, in some countries the political subsystem tries to control the foreign websites that people can access (Chang et al., 2009). China, for example, battled Google in 2010 on issues of citizen access and government monitoring. The result is that a censored version of Google is available from the government's internet provider within the Chinese mainland, whereas the full Google service is available to those on the mainland through a provider in Hong Kong (Hleft & Barboza, 2010). The government there offers the uncensored search engine, but has a record of who uses it. This sort of closed system and the tendency for the USA to cite largely domestic websites work against the development of a truly global network.

Although much media globalization discussion overstates the potential of a unitary, one-world system of international dialog (Hafez, 2007), concerns remain about the tendency for communication technology to be concentrated in a few hands. For example, information is sent by worldwide satellite broadcasting networks, including CNN International, BBC World, and Al-Jazeera (Shoemaker et al., 2011). In addition, there is an oligopoly of news agencies that send information among nations, such as the Associated Press, Reuters, and Agence France Presse. They were the "first transnational media systems," and their work helped create "a modern global consciousness" (Boyd-Barrett, 1997, p. 132). Within the tendency to homogenize cultures, the news agencies also increase the diversity of texts available, because clients send information about their locations to the news agencies, thus influencing this consciousness (Boyd-Barrett, 1997, p. 143).

Giddens (1997) takes the position that studying nations as social actors can be appropriate, but that most scholars don't provide theoretical arguments to support this decision. In fact, when studying international relationships among nations, it is apparent that over time the transfer of autonomy and power from one nation to another has changed many times. Something between the rigidity of nation states from earlier centuries and a worldwide society is emerging, and a movement toward and development of some supranational social structures is sensible for studying media content. On the other hand, we must be careful not to obscure important differences in ideology, politics, economy, culture, and media content among nations. Media and globalization are tightly intertwined, one supporting the other to yield—if not a one-world "monoculture"—at least what Reese (2010, p. 348) in his review of this area calls a "global news arena"

> supported by an interlocking cross-national awareness of events, in a world further connected by networks of transnational elites, media professionals among them, who engage each other through mutually shared understandings . . . The globalized practices of media and communication, the expectations citizens have of them, the way officials and elites interact with them within and across national boundaries, provide a synchronized set of pathways through which global influence works and new geometries defined.
> (Reese, 2010, p. 348)

SOCIAL SYSTEMS AS SUBSYSTEMS

A number of *subsystems* compose the social system. For example, the *ideological subsystem* is not an alien belief system imposed on an inhospitable host culture, but instead works through existing values. Communication connects the ideological subsystem to the *cultural subsystem* by transmitting familiar cultural themes that resonate with audiences. These themes or *frames* are selectively chosen and constructed into a coherent whole. Although both culture and ideology are concerned with meaning, ideology is tied more closely to interests: class and otherwise. Together we introduce four subsystems that relate to the content of the mass media: ideological, cultural, economic, and political that interact in many ways (Hawkins,

1997; Elasmar, 2003). We recognize that these systems are closely interrelated, but take it as a matter of emphasis, much as Appadurai (1990) used the idea of five "scapes" to describe the dimensions of global flow that represent the building blocks of larger social formations: ethno, media, techno, finance, and ideoscapes. His perspective underscores the complexity of the national and globalized social systems, through which we view media sociology.

The Ideological Subsystem

Perhaps the most important is the ideological subsystem. In the USA, scholars have often regarded ideology as an individual belief system (Chapter 8), but here we use the term *ideology* to represent a societal-level phenomenon. This is in keeping with the European tradition of media studies, in which ideology is considered a total structure within a social system. We assume that all processes occurring on the other levels of analysis work toward a pattern of messages that in some way reflects the characteristics of the total social system.

A significant body of system level analysis has taken a Marxist perspective, sometimes termed *critical* or *radical*, which has emphasized general and abstract theorizing more than hypothesis testing. By *ideology* we mean a symbolic mechanism that serves as a cohesive and integrating force in society. Raymond Williams defines ideology as "a relatively formal and articulated system of meanings, values, and beliefs, of a kind that can be abstracted as a 'world view' or as a 'class outlook'" (1977, p. 109). According to Samuel Becker, ideology "governs the way we perceive our world and ourselves, it controls what we see as 'natural' or 'obvious' . . . An ideology is an integrated set of frames of reference through which each of us sees the world and to which all of us adjust our actions" (1984, p. 69).

Questions of ideology often center on how diverse groups with conflicting interests work together in a society. As Alvin Gouldner (1976, pp. 230–1) put it, "ideology assumes special importance as a symbolic mechanism through which interests of these diverse social strata may be integrated; through the sharing of it the several dominant strata are enabled to make compatible responses to changing social conditions." Stuart Hall argues that studying ideology allows scholars to recognize the media's ability to "define situations and label groups and individuals as deviant" (1989, p. 309). This aspect of ideology became more popular among communication scholars after the 1960s and 1970s, when the breakdown of the social consensus enhanced polarization and focused attention on the media's exercise of societal control. Ideology also focuses our attention on the symbolic influence of media on audiences, the "definition" that prevails, and the legitimation and exercise of symbolic power (Hall, 1989, p. 309). Lee Artz (2007) acknowledges that class isn't everything, but:

> Recognizing the class character of media practices, processes, and structures cannot explain why *Betty La Fea* became a success in Colombia in 1999–2000,

nor predict if it will be a hit for ABC in the United States in 2006. However, media practices, processes and structures, in general, make no sense without understanding the social class relations of production.

(p. 147)

Fundamental to the US social system is belief in the value of the capitalistic economic system, private ownership, pursuit of profit by self-interested entrepreneurs, and free markets, a system intertwined with the Protestant ethic and an emphasis on individual achievement. The companion political values center around liberal democracy, a system in which all people are presumed to have equal worth and a right to share in their own governance, making decisions based on rational self-interest. These values are articulated and reaffirmed in the media (Exoo, 1987). However, Herbert Altschull notes that the word *ideology* "has a somewhat sinister connotation in the United States," and it is more narrowly understood as relating to "ideas about the role of the press in public affairs" (1995, p. 58):

> American practitioners and scholars often disagree about the role of the press . . . Still there does exist an ideology composed of four articles of faith: (1) The press is free of outside interference, be it from the government or from advertisers or even from the public; (2) the press serves "the public's right to know"; (3) the press seeks to learn and present the truth; and (4) the press reports facts objectively and fairly . . . [T]hey might also be construed as moral imperatives—that is to say, instead of characterizing what the press *is*, they might declare what the press *should* be.

(p. 59)

The idea of ideology as a normative construct continues throughout this chapter, although usually more subtly than for Altschull (1995). Whether ideological influences on the mass media are judged to be good or bad, positive or negative, functional or dysfunctional, depends largely on point of view. We can see in social system theories that when it is described as the tool used for control by the powerful, ideology seems undesirable and something we might want to change. When described as a tool for social change, we might endorse it if we are in favor of the changes. When ideology is seen as the product of accumulated forces that shape our social realities, then it may seem inevitable or invisible. But if we become aware that our social realities are being manipulated, then ideology seems less benign.

The Economic Subsystem

At the macro level, the economic system has been an important component of communication research, especially in the field of "development" communication. In 1958 Daniel Lerner hypothesized that the growth of a country's economic subsystem is a function of its urbanization and the literacy of its population, which in turn was tied to media growth; so a country's communication infrastructure has been closely tied to its economy. Following the vast social instability in two world wars, Western social scientists wanted to build communication infrastructure as a precursor to economic development, using Harry Oshima's idea that a good communication system can act as a "multiplier" on economic growth (1967, p. 17). Since this postwar consensus period, development studies no longer have a coherent theoretical identity, according to Ankie Hoogvelt (2001), and as a theoretical construct *the third world* no longer has the same meaning in the 21st century, although the economic system continues be the most important lens for understanding international communication.

As its most important economic organizing principle, capitalism does not necessarily mandate any particular communication structure; in fact, there is substantial diversity in media formations among capitalist countries (Artz, 2007). Indeed, the economic cooperation of media across these countries has resulted in transnational media, which Artz defines as "enterprises that produce within one nation but are jointly owned by multiple corporations from multiple nations" (2007, p. 141). He contrasts them conceptually with two similar terms: *International media* are those that produce content in one country and distribute it to others; whereas *multinational media* are based in one country, but produce content with foreign media companies, distributing it in many countries (Artz, 2007, p. 148). The transnational media join with other coordinating social structures, creating "new transnational class institutions," such as the World Trade Organization, the International Monetary Fund, the World Economic Forum, and the International Telecommunications Union. At its most basic level, according to Artz, these emerging media are determined directly by their economic underpinnings: "The transnational media represent the class interests, class perspectives, and class ideology of the transnational capitalist class, albeit smoothly marketed in a diversity of cultural forms" (2007, pp. 150–1).

The Political Subsystem

Like economics, the political system both constrains and is conditioned by the media of communication. Given the importance of news to democratic functioning, the political system has been a key component, even if implicitly, of communication research. The theories of George Herbert Mead (1934), C. Wright Mills (1959), and Jürgen Habermas (1962) are said to draw direct links between communication and politics, and "set out the provocative thesis that the very basic presuppositions of language—equality, reciprocity, sincerity and truth—are also the basic presuppositions of democracy" (Winseck & Cuthbert, 1997, p. 165). From the perspective of Habermas (1962), public communication directs the nature of the political system when communication spheres can be open and "driven by the force of argumentation, not power." This "*communicative* dimension of democracy . . . is not only crucial to the legitimation of power and authority, but, as Mead and Mills have pointed out, to the cultivation of 'democratic minds'" (Winseck & Cuthbert, 1997, p. 165). Early in the development of the communication field, Siebert et al.

argued in their classic *Four Theories of the Press* that "the press always takes on the form and coloration of the social and political structures within which it operates" (1956, pp. 1–2), a relationship that Barbara Pfetsch (2004) describes as mutual. That media–political system connection has been the basis for the tradition of cross-national comparative research that followed. Hallin and Mancini (2004), for example, distinguish between three major models of political system development: "polarized pluralist, Mediterranean" (including France and Spain), "democratic corporatist, Northern European" (including Germany and the Netherlands), and "liberal or North Atlantic" (including the USA). Beyond these broad system categories, we take up in greater detail the relative influence of the political system when we reach the social institutional level (Chapter 5) where it has been most often addressed. Practically speaking, it is often difficult to meaningfully separate the political and economic systems, leading to a *political economic* perspective that we consider later in this chapter.

The Cultural Subsystem

Anthropologists define culture as "the pattern of meaning embroiled in symbolic forms, including utterances and meaningful objects of various kinds, by virtue of which individuals communicate with one another and share their experience, conceptions and beliefs" (Thompson, 1990, p. 132). Thus the process of communication is central in the development and evolution of culture, as the media help constitute how people think of themselves and how they construct values and norms. Some have taken this to mean that the ability of new communication technologies to cross time and space easily has the potential to facilitate a " 'universal' democratic culture," which Dwayne Winseck and Marlene Cuthbert (1997, p. 156) say is an oversimplification. That a region or country's culture is fragile and easily replaced by a dominant foreign culture is basic to early discussions of cultural imperialism. The entry of foreign products and ideas into a social system was assumed to destroy and replace the local culture, but as we discuss below, the fears inherent in the cultural imperialism version of globalization have not been realized. More recent, less deterministic thinking treats cultural transmission as a two-way process and recognizes that local culture can be stronger than was originally thought and need not succumb to a global "mono-culture."

Immanuel Wallerstein's (1997) *world system theory* suggests that countries in the "core," essentially Westernized nations, transmit an homogenized global culture to nations in the "periphery," in the process of cultural imperialism. Concerns over this process caused some governments to restrict foreign media, especially television programming and films from the USA (Elasmar, 2003, p. 157). But others suggest that these fears are exaggerated. Martin Shaw (1997, p. 30; from 1994) prefers to visualize the globe as a place where there is much diversity in cultures and warns that global audiences may not equally understand the symbols transmitted.

With the emergence of competing international television satellite services, including BBC World Service and Al-Jazeera International (Paterson, 1997), debates about cultural imperialism have given way to concerns about globalization. Much of the scholarly discussion of globalization includes television news as part of the process without considering the meaning inherent in foreign television's content: the "particularities of such global media products, are all but ignored" (Elasmar, 2003, p. 145). Ignoring the meaning of foreign content and how audience members interpret and react to it is a result of how scholars think of their own cultures. Our national identities affect our assumptions concerning both the effects of foreign media content on our culture and the effects of culture on our media.

> By and large, Americans may not expect that the meanings and the cultural forms they invent are only for themselves; possibly because they have seen at home over the years that practically anybody can become an American . . . The Japanese, on the other hand, —so it is said—find it a strange notion that anyone can "become Japanese," and they put Japanese culture on exhibit, in the framework of organized international contacts, as a way of displaying irreducible distinctiveness rather than in order to make it spread.
>
> (Hannerz, 1997, p. 12)

The movement of cultural products around the world should be regarded as the action of transnational entities rather than as the action of discrete nation states, according to Hannerz (1997).

> As long as there is room for local cultural production as well, this may in itself be helped in its development by the availability of a wider range of models . . . [T]here is perhaps only a thin line between a defense of authenticity and an antiquarianism . . . The more realistic hope for continued cultural diversity in the world, with some linkage to local heritage, would rather seem to be for a diversity in motion, one of coexistence as well as creative interaction between the transnational and the indigenous.
>
> (Hannerz, 1997, pp. 14–16)

Crane (2002, p. 18) points out that the development of a global culture is a dynamic process, with the relative dominance of cultures constantly shifting. The early online dominance of the USA is diminishing as other countries develop their own internet-based communication systems. US cultural products are only one set of many on the Internet.

SOCIAL SYSTEM AS CONCEPTUAL MODEL

The media operate with each of these subsystems in the process of system maintenance, and more specifically as agents of social control. Here we must understand the exercise of power, which has been a crucial concept at this level particularly in the critical tradition of media research. Before reviewing some of the theoretical perspectives, we consider this dynamic of control, because the idea of setting boundaries is an accessible and intuitively observable media function.

Media and Social Control

The concept of deviance has long been of interest to social scientists. As Stuart Hall (1997) puts it, the media's ability to define an event gives them power within a social system. One of the key functions of the media is to maintain the boundaries within society, to define ideas and actions as either within the bounds of acceptability or as deviant and not politically legitimate. Outsiders may be shown as crazy, as having ideas and taking actions that no sensible person would adopt. From a symbolic interactionist perspective (Blumer, 1969) we assume that deviance is continually being defined and renegotiated as the participants interact with each other symbolically. The media continually cope with new ideas, reaffirm social norms, and redraw or define boundaries. Daniel Hallin (1993), helping to understand how the news media maintain these social boundaries, divided the journalistic world into three spheres: consensus, legitimate controversy, and deviance (Figure 4.1) The "mother and apple pie" domain is the consensus of American ideology: "Within this region journalists do not feel compelled to present opposing views or to remain disinterested observers. On the contrary, the journalists' role is to serve as an advocate or celebrant of consensus values" (Hallin, 1993, pp. 116–17). The ideas of journalistic objectivity and balance are relevant to the sphere of legitimate controversy: "This is the region of electoral contests and legislative debates, of issues recognized as such by the major established actors of the American political process" (Hallin, 1993, p. 116). People and ideas outside of the mainstream of society are in the sphere of deviance. Here, says Hallin, journalists cast off their aura of neutrality, playing "the role of exposing, condemning or excluding from the public agenda those who violate or challenge the political consensus" (1993, p. 117).

But who decides where the line between deviant and not deviant lies? And how is this made to look natural? Shoemaker's (1996) hard wired theory of news proposes that human beings' innate interest in deviance is the result of biological evolution, whereas the specific definitions of deviance vary among cultures and over time. In their study of news in 10 countries, Shoemaker and Cohen (2006) supported these ideas: More than three-quarters of the 36,000 newspaper, television, and radio news items that they studied included some element of deviance.

The concept *deviance* can be defined in several ways (Shoemaker, 1996). An early definition of deviance as pathology was consistent with the 19th century understanding of society as an organism not unlike the human body. Thus, for example, homosexuality was conceived as an illness in the body of society and therefore something that could be "cured." Today, most people perceive deviance as something negative and regard information about the violation of social norms, such as crime, as "*bad news.*" In either case, media coverage of deviance alerts powerful social actors about people and ideas that may threaten the status quo. According

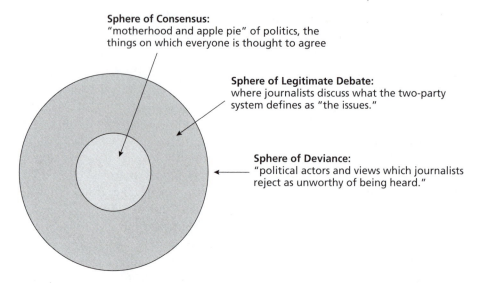

Sphere of Consensus:
"motherhood and apple pie" of politics, the
things on which everyone is thought to agree

Sphere of Legitimate Debate:
where journalists discuss what the two-party
system defines as "the issues."

Sphere of Deviance:
"political actors and views which journalists
reject as unworthy of being heard."

FIGURE 4.1   *Spheres of consensus, controversy, and deviance (based on Hallin, 1993)*

to the interests of their owners, who themselves are powerful elites, media are also understood to label ideas, people, and groups as deviant causing them to become less legitimate in the eyes of the audience (Shoemaker, 1982).

Deviant labels can be self-reinforcing and self-fulfilling. In his now classic work, Todd Gitlin (1980) argued that the transformation of the 1960s political group Students for a Democratic Society (SDS) from visionaries to primarily protestors was a function of the news media's labeling of the group as being involved in violent social change. Media emphasis on violence attracted those who were more interested in violent action than ideas, and thus the composition of SDS membership changed over time to become more consistent with the media's deviant labels.

Studies of social protest highlight this dynamic of media boundary maintenance. For example, Luther and Miller (2005) studied the words that journalists used to describe pro- and antiwar demonstrators before and during the 2003 US-led Iraq War. Negative words such as *violence, unpatriotic, disorderly*, and *arrest* were more likely to be used to describe antiwar demonstrators, thus cuing the audience that the group should be seen as disruptive. By contrast, pro-war demonstrators were described more positively, with words such as *freedom, peaceful, patriotic, love, religious*, and "the portrait of God-fearing and caring Americans come to light" (Luther & Miller, 2005, p. 90). Thus, the media work to legitimate elite positions and de-legitimate those outside of the consensus.

In their analysis of radical protest, Doug McLeod and James Hertog have carried out an extensive program of research. In one of their early works, they examined how Minneapolis's local media covered marches in that city by anarchists between 1986 and 1988. Media cues de-legitimized the group: for example, the newspaper headline "Anarchists Organize to Wreak Havoc Downtown." At one demonstration the anarchists burned three flags—from the USA (representing capitalism), the USSR (representing communism), and McDonald's (representing corporations)—but the news only showed the burning of the American flag, completely changing the meaning of the event and rendering it instantly unpatriotic. In addition, statements from official sources emphasized the deviance of the anarchists, and news cameras positioned themselves behind police barricades, visually placing the media in opposition to the anarchists (McLeod & Hertog, 1992; also in Hertog & McLeod, 1988). Although anarchists admittedly fall far outside the typical two-party political discourse, the way the media cover such groups creates and rigidly perpetuates that political boundary.

THEORIES OF POWER AND IDEOLOGY

Extreme ideas test boundaries, but how are they set and linked to larger systemic structures? At the social system level of analysis, the central questions include: Who has power? On what is it based? How is it exercised? To what extent does the media's symbolic content systematically serve to further the interest and power of certain groups, through representation of class, gender, or race? The theories of media as shaped by social systems are closely derived from theories of society. The following brief descriptions of several of these perspectives show how these questions can be addressed.

Structural Functionalism

Structural functionalism explains how a social system can be maintained by the actions of a social structure and how a threat or tension within the social system can threaten its stability and result in change. A *homeostatic* structure is one that acts to maintain social order, much as a thermostat regulates temperature in a home. The term *function* can be defined in several ways: as something usual or natural (the function of situation comedies is to entertain people), as one thing that depends on another thing (the number of pages in a paper-platform newspaper is a function of the number of advertising pages), and, as a verb, to operate as expected (the news routines function to minimize the effects of journalists' political beliefs on the stories they write). The communication literature is replete with discussions of how media function to maintain existing political, economic, cultural, and/or ideological subsystems. The media are assumed to alert elites when the degree of social tension about an issue becomes dangerous to the status quo, and when a new idea (or person, group, event) enters the social system. In some situations, the media increase the amount of attention to the threat as a way of alerting elites that action must be taken and/or to suggest that the public should not take the threat seriously, or the media "symbolically annihilate" the threat (in Gerbner's [1972] phrase) by ignoring it, effectively eliminating it from public discourse.

The idea that the media function to maintain the social system, as a relatively benign force, emerges naturally from functional theory, but its imagery has permeated the communication research literature (as we discussed in Chapter 2). Critics of functional theory, however, suggest that it predicts lack of change and therefore cannot be falsified. The fact that a social system is stable for decades does not guarantee that it will be stable in the future; for example, a charismatic leader can challenge the existing power structure and mount a successful revolution. Of course, most changes in a social structure are smaller: For example, what effect did the 2008 worldwide recession have on the US political subsystem? What function did the news media play in either stabilizing or changing the political subsystem? Functionalism describes conditions best during times of social consensus, stability, and relative harmony.

Democratic Pluralism

In the USA, the dominant political theory of social systems is democratic pluralism, a model that values and assumes diversity in society and is heavily influenced by two 18th-century philosophers: John Locke, with his "marketplace of ideas" and Adam Smith's "invisible hand" of the market. In a liberal democratic social system, power is understood to be distributed across many competing interests, which creates a more or less stable, self-maintaining, and balanced political subsystem. Even elites are viewed as sufficiently divided so as to make unlikely any undue concentration of power (Rose, 1967). Thus, questions of power and ideology typically have not been as central in the USA, because power is not considered problematic. As Denis McQuail states, a pluralistic model asks "whether media offer opportunities for politically diverse audiences and/or audience interests to flourish" (1986, p. 143). The competitive nature of liberal democracy is assumed to be healthy for the system and not interpreted as social conflict unless deviant ideas become too powerful.

Thussu (2007) suggests that *free-market neo-liberalism* best characterizes the post-Cold War philosophical successor to pluralism:

> Dismantling barriers to the free flow of information was seen as essential to growth, and significant trade in goods and services would not be possible without a free trade in information. The globalizing ideology of these multilateral organizations drove the establishment of a pro-market television and telecommunication infrastructure.
>
> (Thussu, 2007, p. 43)

Thus the whole world became a market, increasingly so in the early 21st century, as internet-based media offered enhanced accessibility to products and services, with advertising and public relations companies carrying the democratic ideas that drove the expansion of corporations.

Marxism

In a radical departure from the pluralist view, Karl Marx proposed a competing theoretical approach in describing a society characterized better as tension than equilibrium, rooted in conflict along class lines, with power being fought over by dominant and subordinate groups. Marx and Engels (1970) directly link ideology to the ruling class, which derives its power from its control of capital.

> The ideas of the ruling class are in every epoch the ruling ideas; i.e., the class which is the ruling material force in society is at the same time its ruling intellectual force. The class which has the means of material production at its disposal has control at the same time over the means of mental production, so that thereby, generally speaking, the ideas of those who lack the means of mental production are subject to it.
>
> (Marx and Engels, 1970, p. 64)

There are clashes, however, within the Marxist perspective over how completely economics determines ideology, as we show in the following sections. On the one hand, political economists assume that the link between economic conditions and ideology is fairly direct, and they regard media content as ultimately determined by the economic relations in society. Therefore, they are less apt to examine the specific practices or mechanisms through which economic relations become manifest in media content. On the other hand, the cultural studies approach considers the ruling class ideology to be much less monolithic and automatically determined. Rather, it assumes that the media have more autonomy in crafting their messages and takes the meanings of those messages more seriously. Media content is viewed as being *polysemic* (subject to different interpretations) and as containing many contradictory elements, a result of the ruling ideas struggling to domesticate subversive ideas and retain their privileged status.

Political Economy

The term *political economy* was first used in 1615 to describe "the science of wealth acquisition common to the State as well as the Family" (Hoogvelt, 2001, pp. 3). For the mercantiles who dominated the following century, wealth was not a goal in itself; it was a means to achieve political power, such as using wealth to support large armies. In 1776 Adam Smith reintroduced the term political economy as a conceptual break with the mercantiles. Instead of wealth being accumulated to enhance political power, his *liberal economics* theory saw "the invisible hand of the market as the best regulator of the economy" (Hoogvelt, 2001, p. 5). Marx offered a third view of political economy. His theory of class struggle outlined in *Capital* (1938) was a critique of liberal economics, suggesting that when individuals work to better themselves the result is *not* the betterment of the public, but instead a series of crises that would ultimately destroy capitalism (Hoogvelt, 2001). The crises were the result of the differentiation of labor between owners and workers. When political economists adopt a traditional Marxist approach, they use the base/superstructure metaphor to depict ideology (superstructure) determined by a material base of economic relations. Curran, Gurevitch, and Woollacott argue that "the role of the media here is that of legitimation through the production of false consciousness, in the interests of the class which owns and controls the media" (1982, p. 26). Changes in media ownership do not greatly alter power relations, because each owner acts in a manner consistent with the interests of capital.

In their often cited work, Murdock and Golding (1977) argue that a proper analysis of news production must focus on the economic context of control, as well as its class base. Media content is a cultural commodity within a capitalist system, a process of commodification that has "colonized" cultural domains from the Status of Liberty to the Berlin Wall. Capitalism is understood to have a generalized, abstracting drive to reduce everything to the equivalence of exchange value (Garnham, 1979). Capital in the culture industry seeks the most lucrative markets, which results in the most resources going to the gathering of more lucrative, non-news information. Nicholas Garnham (1979) observed that the industrialization of culture is characterized by a sharpening struggle to increase productivity, with high-profile buyouts of media firms by non-media corporations (see Chapter 6), staff layoffs, and the erosion of the lines between the business and news departments in many newspapers and television stations understandable within this framework.

Within this tradition, Kellner charges the control of information around the globe by a small number of large conglomerates with surrendering "the lively critical media necessary to ensure a vital democracy" (2004, p. 31). Power has been consolidated within these conglomerates, such that they now control all aspects of the communications industry from the news to entertainment in all sorts of platforms, including books, music, broadcasting, and the online entities of all of these. But the political economy approach does not assume that the media simply reproduce the prevailing ideas of their owners. More recent scholars reject the orthodox "vulgar" Marxist view of the media as mere channels of dominant ideology, arguing that the media are sites of struggle between rival ideologies. Curran (1990) argues that this represents a retreat from former positions:

> During the 1980s, even researchers in the political economy tradition began to back off. Thus, Peter Golding, a leading political economist, stressed the importance of ideological management and the individualist values of reporters rather than economic ownership of the press in accounting for the tabloid crusade against "scrounging" welfare claimants.
>
> (p. 143)

This view suggests a number of questions that can draw on the media sociology research we introduce in the following chapters, with special attention given to media ownership.

Instrumentalism

Mosco and Herman (1981) introduced *instrumentalism* as a variation of political economy theory, exploring in greater detail the media as an important "elite power group." Media ownership has become more and more concentrated, allowing the industry to successfully resist obstacles to greater profit and exert increasing control over its own scrutiny, especially through regulatory bodies such as the US Federal Communication Commission (Akhavan-Majid & Wolf, 1991). Domhoff (1967, 1970, 1979) regards the media as organically inseparable from elites and thus far from autonomous. Although conflicts among elites are played out through the news media, the media are seen as far more instrumental for elites than they are antagonistic to their interests. Domhoff focuses from a sociological perspective on the means by which the ruling class exerts this control and develops a common outlook, rejecting the economic as the only basis for ruling class power.

Control by the ruling class can be achieved by means other than purely economic. For example, members of the ruling class regularly come in contact with one another (such as in preparatory schools, universities, clubs, and boards of directors), giving them opportunities to influence policy (stock holding, policy groups, funding of institutes and think tanks, political action committees, and so on). In 1956 C. Wright Mills traced the pervasive control exerted by the ruling class on the social structure in his book *The Power Elite* and proposed that the convergent interests of business, economic, and military elites form an apex at the top of the social structure. The upper class is more cohesive than the lower class, assisted by connections and exchange of personnel between these sectors, and thus can focus its power more effectively.

Hegemony

Antonio Gramsci (1927) proposed the idea of a powerful hegemonic force as an extension of Marxism, to help explain the power of ideas in helping forestall revolutionary pressures, and this theory is often cited in critical analyses of the media. The term *hegemony* refers to the means by which the ruling order maintains its dominance, and Gitlin defines it as the "systematic (but not necessarily or even usually deliberate) engineering of mass consent to the established order" (1980, p. 253). The mass media are understood to be an important cultural apparatus, but one that has relative autonomy; therefore the ruling powers cannot directly supervise all aspects of the day-to-day production of content. Media institutions serve a hegemonic function by continually producing a cohesive ideology as a unifying force, a set of commonsense values and norms that reproduce and legitimate the social system structure through which the subordinate classes ultimately participate in their own domination (Gitlin, 1980).

Gramsci's theory emphasizes the role of ideology, giving it greater autonomy than in traditional Marxism, but still linking it to the dominant structure. Control of the mass media must be maintained without sacrificing legitimacy, which helps those in power maintain their authority, yet this control is regarded as a conflicted and dynamic process, which must continually absorb and incorporate disparate values (Gitlin, 1980, p. 51). In Raymond Williams' words, hegemony "does not passively exist as a form of dominance. It has continually to be renewed, recreated, defended, and modified" (1977, pp. 112–13). Hegemonic values in news are said to be particularly effective in permeating the common sense of a society, because they are made to appear natural. These values are not imposed through coercion; instead they indirectly become part of the normal workings of media routines and the interconnections between the media and other power centers. In fact, the relative autonomy of the mass media gives their content more legitimacy and credibility than if their messages were directly controlled. With control all the more effective by being invisible, the media "certify the limits within which all competing definitions of reality will contend" (Gitlin, 1980, p. 254). They do this in practice largely by, for example, accepting the frames imposed on events by officials and by marginalizing and de-legitimating voices that fall outside the dominant elite circles—a process that also falls with the routines level, to be explored later in Chapter 7.

Within this hegemonic tradition, radical critics argue that when pluralists focus on those issues that do make the media agenda, they overlook the concentrated operations of powerful institutions. Lukes (1974), for example, observes that the most effective power prevents conflict from arising in the first place. The critical approach to studying media content embraces this broader, multi-dimensional view of media power: the ability to shape perceptions that make the existing order appear natural and unchanging, with alternatives that are hard to imagine. This, according to Hall, is an ideological model of power, "shaping of the whole ideological environment—a way of representing the order of things which endowed its limiting perspectives with that natural or divine inevitability, which makes them appear universal, natural and coterminous with 'reality' itself" (1982, p. 65).

Hall's cultural studies approach combines aspects of political economy and the Marxist structuralist perspective with a more literary approach that concentrates on media texts, but which rejects the simple base/superstructure connection. Cultural studies scholars look more closely at the connections between society and media and place them in a broader cultural context. Samuel Becker, for example, notes that one of the key questions asked in the British Marxist school of media studies is how the dominant ideology is linked to the norms and practices or "occupational ideology" of media workers (1984, p. 73). Murdock and Golding (1977, p. 35) argue that scholars must analyze the "link between the general set of values in that culture and the ruling ideology and occupational ideologies." This has direct relevance to how we will more closely examine the journalistic occupational ideology in later chapters.

World Systems

Global perspectives on systems have become increasingly relevant to understanding media. Immanuel Wallerstein's world system theory (1993), for example, understands the world as being divided artificially into economic and political segments that have been gradually combined into a global social system driven by capitalism and with its roots in the economic relationships among imperial states, the former colonial powers. In world system theory, however, political power is less important than commercial connections, because capitalism has always been a transnational economic phenomenon. With its components shifting over time, within the historical dynamics of capitalism, the fortunes of one part of the world may wane while others wax: "It has been based . . . on a pattern of cyclical swings wherein the 'animal spirits' of the entrepreneurial classes, in pursuing their own interests, regularly and inevitably create mini-crises of overproduction which lead to downturns or stagnations in the world-economy" (Wallerstein, 1993, p. 3).

The decline of the liberal democracies' wealth has caused a loss of hope and optimism that had stabilized their political subsystems during the expansion of capitalism, leading Wallerstein to predict major upcoming instability in the world, that nations such as Iran, which are "in the periphery of total otherness," would assert their power, flaunting geocultural norms (Wallerstein, 1993, p. 4). This "is a picture of world turmoil, but it is not necessarily a pessimistic one" (Wallerstein, 1993, p. 5). The first half of the 21st century would create, in his view, a "situation of 'free will,'" meaning that the world system would be a creation begun by late 20th century politicians (Wallerstein, 1993, p. 5).

Giddens (1997; from 1991) faults world system theory for concentrating so heavily on economics, and questions the core, semi-periphery, and periphery categories, because this process does not take into account "political or military concentrations of power which do not align in an exact way to economic differentiations" (p. 22). Thus, Giddens suggests that "world society seems likely in the foreseeable future (centuries as well as decades) to remain divided between highly differentiated segments" and that the process of global integration will instead accentuate differences between states (1997, p. 30). With respect to media, he argues that existing global institutions would not be possible without "the pooling of knowledge which is represented by the 'news'" (1997, p. 24).

INFLUENCES ON CONTENT FROM SOCIAL SYSTEMS

All of these perspectives guide our thinking about the role that the media play within social systems. These systems provide the larger macro context that, in turn, guides the processes at the other levels of our hierarchy as they work to yield predictable patterns of content. As we view media sociology through a systemic, often ideological perspective, we might best put the question: How does it work? More specifically, how does the relationship between media and power play out in actual practice?

The News Paradigm

One useful example of these workings is the case of journalistic occupational ideology as seen through the process of "paradigmatic repair." Closely related to the dynamic of hegemony, Thomas Kuhn (1962, p. 23) introduced the notion of *paradigm*, "an accepted model or pattern," that helps people make sense out of the world. A paradigm is valuable as long as it provides a useful guide for practitioners who share its underlying assumptions. Although Kuhn spoke of scientific paradigms, this concept has also been applied to journalism.

The journalistic paradigm, like others, is validated by consensus, as it focuses most attention on certain problems, but necessarily excludes from view other questions that cannot be easily fitted into its framework. That the way information for media content is gathered, written, and transmitted seems so natural suggests hegemony at work. One learns the paradigm mostly by engaging in the discipline, rather than by memorizing rules; the most important rules are often not written (Kuhn, 1962). The routines that journalists engage in (Chapter 7) give us valuable clues about the contours of the guiding paradigm, and a violation of these routines becomes a threat to the news paradigm itself and must be defended. The borders of a paradigm are revealed by "anomalies" that do not fit comfortably into the defining characteristics of the paradigm; they threaten the paradigm by calling into question its limitations and, in turn, the ultimate credibility of media and therefore must be repaired.

A key feature of the US news paradigm has been the notion of *objectivity*, which is discussed further in Chapter 7. Journalists have found it increasingly hard to maintain that they are wholly objective and have fallen back on more defensible standards such as accuracy, balance, and fairness. Even if the world has changed, media workers act as though it hasn't, and the underlying principle of reporter detachment remains firmly entrenched. As Hackett (1984) observed, the paradigmatic opposite of objectivity is bias, and the fault is assumed to lie with the individual reporter or editor. That's why journalists operating within the news paradigm have not found personal values to be occupationally useful, and their values are usually not obvious, being safely within the range of core societal values.

Thus, journalists have been understood to be objective when they let prominent sources dictate the news, but they were considered biased when they used their own expertise to draw conclusions. Hallin (1986), for example, showed that the media did not become strongly critical of the war in Vietnam until President Lyndon Johnson's elite council of advisors, the "wisemen," changed their opinions, a pattern of deference to insider critics that still operates. Giving serious attention to non-official sources is discouraged as not newsworthy. By accepting valueless reporting as the norm, the media accept the boundaries, values, and ideological rules of the game established and interpreted by elite sources. The editing process is also compatible with hegemonic requirements. Editors rise to their positions only after fully internalizing the norms of the journalistic paradigm. Although reporters are presumably in closer contact with reality, editors are considered less apt to succumb to bias than reporters, who may get wrapped up in a story and be blinded to the big picture.

Case Study: A Socialist at the Wall Street Journal

Violations of the *news paradigm* call for repairs, or normalization, particularly when the violations strike at hegemonically sensitive borders of the paradigm. Reese (1990) presented a case study of one such violation involving a journalist at a prominent news organization. When A. Kent MacDougall, who had more than 20 years of reporting experience, said that he had written under an alias for radical publications while at the *Wall Street Journal* and had selected story topics based on his radical beliefs, there was a strong response from the news industry implying that MacDougall had used the uneasy relationship between professional routines and personal values to his advantage. Acknowledging paradigmatic ambiguity, he said he learned that "editors would support a reporter against charges . . . that the reporter's story was biased or had some other major defect as long as the reporter had gotten all the minor facts right" (MacDougall, 1988a, p. 19). Knowing that reporters must speak through sources, he said, "I made sure to seek out experts whose opinions I knew in advance would support my thesis . . . Conversely, I sought out mainstream authorities to confer recognition and respectability on radical views I sought to popularize" (MacDougall, 1988a, p. 23).

Dow, Jones & Company, at that time the parent company of the *Wall Street Journal*, issued a strongly worded reaction:

> We are offended and outraged that a former *Wall Street Journal* reporter now claims he tried to pursue a hidden ideological agenda within the pages of the *Journal* . . . We have reviewed articles he wrote while at the *Journal* and we believe our editing process succeeded in making sure that what appeared in print under his byline met *Journal* standards of accuracy, newsworthiness and fairness.
>
> (Austin, 1989)

The MacDougall case provides a rare glimpse of the fuzzy lines between right and wrong in journalism, where there is often no rulebook or final arbiter. The conservative attack on him was particularly forceful given his value system and zeroed in on the idea of violated boundaries, with the group Accuracy in Media predictably raising concerns "about the ability of Marxist agents to penetrate the mainstream media" (Kincaid, 1988, p. 4).

After MacDougall's violation the repair process was revealed by examining the discourse surrounding the case. Since the stories he wrote were in the past and could not be revised, several post-hoc repair strategies were followed: First, the owners disengaged and distanced the threatening values from the reporter's work, claiming that his values were one thing and his professional work another; second, they reassured readers that journalistic routines would prevent threatening values from distorting the news ("the system worked"); and, third, they marginalized the man and his message, making both appear ineffective. The case illustrated how professional-level routines are engaged to protect ideological boundaries within the US press, showing that boundaries are not a fixed given but must be continually nego-tiated and defended. Since this study, others have found the idea of paradigmatic repair to be helpful in identifying the boundaries at work from a macro perspective (e.g., Berkowitz & Eko, 2007; Carlson, 2012; Meyers, 2011).

One of the biggest threats to the traditional news paradigm is from online media, which give more people easier access to national and local political dis-course. Carlson (2007) interviewed political reporters to find out what role they saw blogs playing in the 2004 US presidential election, whether they should be consid-ered within the context of the news paradigm, with its legitimacy and credibility, or as part of the attack- and counter-attack forces that are part of a liberal democracy (Carlson, 2007, p. 264)? Journalists who were interviewed called on their profes-sionalism to give themselves authority, but they feared that blogs could threaten the hegemony of "offline" news media. Although these journalists thought that blogs were held to different standards and operated under different social constraints, they realized that blogs and the internet platform offered them "an enticing anti-dote" to their traditional limitations and encouraged "greater transparency" (Carl-son, 2007, p. 274).

The Propaganda Model

To understand how elite power operates through media, Herman and Chomsky (1988, p. 2) proposed the now widely known propaganda model, which combines elements of political economy and instrumental perspectives. Beginning with the assumption that media serve the dominant elite, and that this is as true when the media are privately owned without formal censorship of content as when they are directly controlled by the state, their model contains five news "filters":

1. concentrated ownership of the mass media, owner wealth, and profit orien-tation of the dominant mass media firms;

2. advertising as the primary income source of the mass media;

3. media's reliance on information provided by government, business, and experts funded and approved by agents of power;

4. "flak," the regular attacks on media, used as a means of disciplining the media within acceptable bounds;

5. "anti-communism" as national religion.

In ensuring serviceable news coverage, the ownership and advertising filters link media organizations to economic power and make it difficult for alternative media organizations to be heard. Media routines cause reporters to rely on government and corporate executives as sources of media content, both of which have strategic news-making advantages compared to individuals and citizen groups. The government produces authoritative news through its vast information staff, and corporations have large budgets for public relations efforts that effectively subsidize the cost of information gathering for the media (Gandy, 1982). Herman and Chomsky (1988) define *flak* as negative responses to the media, including complaints, threats, petitions, letters, and articles, which they say originate mainly from the political right, which is most likely to have the resources to fund it. Accuracy in Media, one of the original such monitoring groups, worked within the propaganda model to harass, intimidate, discipline, and generally keep the media from straying too far from acceptable elite viewpoints (Chapter 5). McChesney (1992) has argued that if right-wing criticism did not exist, journalists would have to create it: "The alternative of a press corps being roundly praised by conservatives for their subservience to the powers-that-be would hardly meet even the rudimentary standards for a profession, and would cast the legitimacy of the entire media structure into doubt" (p. 12).

The anti-communism filter is considered a political control mechanism because communist philosophy threatens the basis of the propertied class and is firmly fixed in the sphere of deviance. Anti-communism historically has had an instrumental value for elites, who have used it to justify military action to suppress it and support fascist governments to oppose it, and to keep domestic left-wing and labor movements off balance and fragmented. After the post-1989 fall of communism, this filter may seem out of date, but the term "socialism" is frequently invoked with the same intent, and "terrorism" has taken on much of the same ideological dynamic, as the authors noted after 9/11. In their review of this model, Lang and Lang (2004) fault it for conceding no legitimacy to the state, with its one-directional flow depicting media organizations as largely passive. Although criticized as overly deterministic, the filters provide a way of integrating a number of structural tendencies, relevant to different levels of our hierarchy, into a large systemic (and critical) view of press performance.

The products of these filters are deployed beyond national boundaries through global news work. Thussu (2007) provides an example of how national propaganda machines provide content competing for the same audience in the Middle East:

> In 2002, an Arabic language popular music and news radio station, Radio Sawa, aimed at a younger Arab audience, was launched and Radio Free Farda began transmitting into Iran. In 2004, Al-Hurra started broadcasting, funded by the Broadcasting Board of Governors (BBG), a US federal agency that supervises all non-military international broadcasting. The Pentagon, too, established a propaganda network: Al-Iraqiya, a radio and television station run by the California based Science Applications International Corporation, one of the largest US companies providing surveillance services for US intelligence agencies.
>
> (p. 137)

Within the political economy tradition, the propaganda model puts particular emphasis on ownership structures, and one need not be a Marxist to attribute great importance to these influences. Herbert Altschull (1984), for example, proposed four patterns of ownership at the social system level: First, in the *official* pattern media are controlled by the state (such as in a communist country); second, in the *commer-cial* pattern media reflect the ideology of advertisers and their media-owning allies; third, in the *interest* pattern media content reflects the ideology of the financing group, such as a political party or religious group; fourth, in the *informal* pattern content reflects the goals of individual contributors who want to promote their own views. The mix of these financing patterns varies from country to country and over time within countries in dictating how—whether called free or state controlled—the media reflect their financial base. Variations in ideology can be introduced through the interest and informal funding patterns, but these make up a small percentage of the available content, and their messages must contend on a playing field structured by the dominant ideology transmitted through the commercial media.

In contrast, in China the government officially owns all domestic mass media, whether funding comes mostly from advertising and subscriptions or from the Communist Party, and each media firm has an official censor who must approve all content before transmission. At CCTV, for example, even hour-long programs could be pulled at the last minute, when all production had been completed. Chinese journalists often self-censor as they try to negotiate the delicate balance between the demands of the consumer-oriented audience and advertisers and the demands of the central government for content that follows the country's core values. Self-censorship is not unique to Chinese journalists, of course, but is a part of the news culture in the soft-authoritarian system of Singapore and even the relatively liberal monarchies of the Persian Gulf states.

All journalists, in their desire to learn the "rules," whether written or not, must figure out what can and cannot be included in their reports. If they want to advance in the organization, they learn to constrain the universe of which events should be covered, which sources are to be interviewed, and which ideas included in their stories.

The Control of Information in Time of War

Military conflict highlights the media control exercised by national and political systems. During the Vietnam War of the 1960s and 1970s, reporters went wherever they wanted to go and made graphic images showing the horror of war that shocked the American public and ultimately helped turn them against the war. In contrast, when the USA invaded Iraq in 1990, military personnel (including those who were young officers during the Vietnam War) established what has become an increas-ingly extensive and rigid set of rules concerning where war reporters can go and what they can report, to ultimately control the flow of information and hence pub-lic opinion about war. By the time the USA invaded Iraq again in 2003, the military had perfected their control of the media (Luther & Miller, 2005).

From an ideological perspective, the entire structure and pattern of reporting is important, not just whether specific stories are censored or whether some war zones are placed off limits to journalists. The natural working of the media system yields predictable patterns of content, and the government does not have to censor programming in order to enjoy highly supportive news for its foreign policy. Routines usually work to the advantage of the dominant ideology. In his study of news coverage of Vietnam, Hallin (1986) observed that reporters shared the Cold War consensus prevalent in the early years of the war, a consensus reinforced by their routines and reliance on military officials for information and transportation. They became close to the soldiers as they shared hardships and faced risks together. Defending one unit's search and destroy mission, an NBC reporter said in his story: "There was no discriminating one house from another. There couldn't be and there did not need to be. The whole village had turned on the Americans, so the whole village was being destroyed" (Hallin, 1986, p. 140).

Media Militarism

Local television in particular provides ideological guidance by helping structure a way of thinking about government policy that is all the more persuasive for being based on familiar local people and organizations. In local television news the media's cultural and economic imperatives of audience appeal are amplified. The interlocking and reinforcing triangle of government, news media, and corporate needs works together to further a culture that is supportive of military action.

Reese and Buckalew (1995) examined how one local television news organization covered both pro- and antiwar demonstrations after the first President Bush's Gulf policy. After the air war began in 1991, they showed that local news produced an ideologically coherent body of reporting that supported the government's actions. Local reporters easily neutralized antiwar protest by placing it at odds with more "authentic" patriotic sentiment of the pro-war demonstrators. At one demonstration, there were ten times as many people in the antiwar group as at the pro-war rally, but this story was framed to present the form of balance required by the journalistic paradigm while finding a consensual middle ground. The national anthem was shown being sung to the American flag, positioning the antiwar group favorably in relation to the pro-war side. In addition, many news reports symbolically linked the pro-war position to a cluster of positive elements that included *the troops*, *the troops' families*, *patriotism*, and *protecting the country's interests* (Reese & Buckalew, 1995, p. 52). One typical report included a news anchor talking over images of a veterans' rally: "The US must show 100 percent support for our troops in the Middle East. That's the message from veterans who say they are upset over the number of antiwar protests. They say it sends a bad message to the troops in the Middle East, that we don't support them" (Reese & Buckalew, 1995, p. 52).

Indeed, supporting the troops was one of the most effective means of managing opposition to Gulf policy, by establishing a clear consensual foundation for community solidarity. The patriotic impulse allowed local television to restore a sense of community that was threatened by divided opinion over policy. According to Ravi (2005), public emotions and patriotism always play a role in determining media content in wartime: "Even those who oppose the war mute their voices once it starts lest they should be accused of giving comfort to the enemy. In the case of the US news media, this also translates into some measure of deference to the president as the commander in chief" (p. 59).

Ravi's study of content in five newspapers from the USA, the UK, Pakistan, and India during the Iraq War showed little to no information about civilian casualties in the newspapers of countries that were at war, which would have portrayed the home country's soldiers as callous and as outside of their country's sphere of social consensus (2005, p. 59).

Outside of the USA, large amounts of information about the first war against Iraq were transmitted to nearly all parts of the world, to governments and audiences alike, by the American satellite network CNN. It was a global media event (Nohrstedt & Ottosen, 2000). The outcome of the war was presented by the mass media as a triumph for the Allies. Kuwait was returned to sovereignty, although not to democracy, but Saddam Hussein was still in power. Western media ignored the realities of the war, instead concentrating on technologies instead of on victims in the Arab world (Nohrstedt & Ottosen, 2000, pp. 12–13).

In the 2003 war against Iraq, satellite networks from other regions brought more diverse coverage to the international audience, although few Americans could access these networks (Reese, 2004). When US President George W. Bush decided to invade Iraq, the government launched "a propaganda campaign to depict Saddam Hussein as an imminent threat to the United States and to insinuate that he was responsible for the 9–11 atrocities and was planning others" (Chomsky, 2003, p. 3). Kumar (2006) attributed the military control of media to two factors, their 30 years of practice since Vietnam and, from a political economic perspective, the interests of giant media conglomerates generating war propaganda that served both political and economic interests:

> In order for US based media conglomerates such as AOL-Time Warner, Disney, Viacom, etc. to continue to be profitable and to extend their reach, they rely on the government to protect their interests domestically, policies like the Telecommunications Act of 1996 that have allowed for unprecedented media concentration. Internationally, the US government, through institutions like the WTO, pries open foreign governments for US media investments. In the case of Iraq, the conquest for that country and the strengthening of US control in the region allowed US based media conglomerates and telecommunication giants to be better positioned to dominate the Middle East markets.
>
> (Kumar, 2006, p. 51)

The War on Terror

The destruction of the World Trade Center in New York City and the attack on the Pentagon on September 11, 2001, were watershed events in American history. Journalists were not immune from the public's strong emotions stirred by the attacks, with many expressing sadness and anger that week. But when they returned to a more professional distance, including questioning the actions of government, some were fired. When some television journalists refused to wear the ubiquitous American flag as a lapel pen, there was an outcry from the public. McChesney (2002) observed that during this time debate was absent and the decision to go to war almost automatic:

> The picture conveyed by the media was as follows: a benevolent, democratic, peace-loving nation was brutally attacked by insane evil terrorists who hated the United States for its freedoms and affluent way of life. The United States needed immediately to increase its military and covert forces, locate the surviving culprits and exterminate them; prepare for a long term war to root out global terrorist cancer and destroy it.
>
> (p. 93)

Patriotism was *de rigueur* for journalists in the months following the attacks, especially for television journalists. Konner called it "a curtain of prescribed patriotism" (2002; cited in McChesney, 2002, p. 88). Many engaged in self-censorship, and even using antiwar sources in news stories was discouraged—not only by media owners or politicians, but also by audience members. The *Phil Donohue* show was canceled because Donohue was said "to delight in presenting guests who are antiwar, anti-Bush, and skeptical of the administration's motives," despite the fact that it was the top-rated show on MSNBC (Kumar, 2006, p. 60).

Media scholar James Carey agreed that a major effect of 9/11 on the US media "was to draw journalists back within the body politic" (2002, p. 87), making them less the watchdogs and more the supporters of government:

> Cosmopolitanism and ironic distance from society along with independence from the institutions of democracy were exposed as unsustainable fraud. Mutual dependence and solidarity, not altogether salutary, became the order of the day. The press was re-nationalized, global corporations found they needed the protection of democratic practice, and journalists experienced the vulnerability that is at the root of patriotism and nationalism.
>
> (Carey, 2002, p. 87)

According to McChesney (2002), this shift in journalistic ideology had occurred previously when the US went to war; 9/11 "merely highlighted the antidemocratic tendencies already in existence" (p. 92). Analyzing US media coverage of other wars, he notes:

> Despite all the talk about being a feisty Fourth Estate, the media system in every one of those cases proved to be a superior propaganda organ for militarism and war . . . This is the context for understanding the media coverage since September 11. The historical record suggests that we should expect an avalanche of lies and half truths in the service of power.
>
> (McChesney, 2002, p. 93)

As the 9/11 story developed on television news programs, the policies of the Bush administration were encapsulated as "the war on terror." This phrase had the ideological advantage of naming no nation as the enemy, but potentially making every nation suspicious. Downing (2007) writes that: "After 9/11, 'terrorism'—meaning non-state violence against civilians—has become the pre-eminent evil . . . 'Terrorism's' conspicuous utility lies in its open-endedness: no state can be negotiated with to end this war, no one can finally assert with total confidence that there are no terrorists left" (p. 65).

In their interviews with US journalists, Lewis and Reese (2009) found a similar effect, that the phrase "war on terror" had "emerged as a powerful ideological frame . . . a socially shared organizing principle." The frame provided "linguistic cover for widespread political change in the name of national security" (Lewis and Reese, 2009, p. 85).

As time passed, however, the phrase moved from being "Bush's war on terror" to "America's war on terror": "The US news media not only transmitted President Bush's preferred phraseology, but also reified and naturalized the policy, making it an uncontested and unproblematic 'thing'" (Lewis and Reese, 2009, p. 90).

As a frame for media content, the War on Terror was expanded to shape both foreign and domestic policies (Reese & Lewis, 2009), including in the terror story the stereotyping of terrorists and "journalistic narratives on 'Muslim terrorism'" (Karim, 2002, p. 102). Altheide (2003, p. 37) argues that the fear frame, so prevalent in media content after 9/11, was used to introduce social control where previously there had been acceptable levels of dissent and differences of opinion: "The politics of fear is buffered by news and popular culture, stressing fear and threat as features of entertainment that, increasingly, are shaping public and private life as mass-mediated experience and has become a standard frame of reference for audiences, claims-makers, and individual actors" (Altheide, 2003, p. 38).

Wagner (2008) shows how an emphasis on fear by the media was used to broaden the definition of the word *terror* to include ecological sabotage (ecotage), criminal acts meant to help protect the environment but not harm humans. Combining terrorism and ecotage has created "ecoterrorism" (Wagner, 2008, p. 25). Because the Earth Liberation Front, for example, expressed its ideological environmental positions against ownership by damaging property, the FBI labeled it a domestic terrorism threat in February 2002 (Wagner, 2008, p. 26). By labeling the group as ecoterrorists, the media conveyed to the public that the group is to "be feared, and by extension, stopped, controlled and prosecuted" (Wagner, 2008, p. 36).

The Media and Elites

In the instrumental tradition, research has examined how elite control is exercised at the system level. Dreier (1982a) exemplifies this approach in his examination of the interconnections between the membership of top media boards of directors and the membership of other boards, finding that owners and top executives of the most prominent elite media companies (publishers of the *New York Times*, *Wall Street Journal*, and

Washington Post) were among the most strongly interconnected with other power centers, including elite universities and Fortune 500 corporations. Dreier suggests that this commanding vantage point within the inner circle of the capitalist structure led these media owners and executives to adopt a liberal corporate philosophy. Conservative critics have said that top journalists are a new social elite, arguing that as such they are hostile to American society and government (Corry, 1986; Rusher, 1988)—an argument we'll examine further in Chapter 8. But far from making journalists hostile to American values, social elite status strongly links journalists to those who hold power within the social system. When the content of these elite media adopts an adversarial tone, it does so only as a corrective action to preserve the capitalist system. We can regard the actions of elite interests at the social system, ideological level, because they transcend the interests of any single business or industry, addressing instead the needs of the business class as a whole.

Source selections by news producers mark the boundaries of political debate and give important insights into the ideological assumptions behind their news judgments. Reese et al. (1994) used network analysis to show how sources are combined and arranged within and across news programs and stories on television. Their analysis showed that sources formed a cohesive insiders group that cut across issues and programs. The insiders group consisted largely of government officials and former officials, but also included top journalists and experts from think tanks. As Reese and his colleagues concluded:

> The media restrict debate by organizing it primarily in relation to the government process, especially in the narrow political range defined by the two-party system. Establishing the middle ground with centrist or conservative experts and "objective" insider journalists further anchors the "conventional wisdom" in a format easily applied across many issues.
>
> (1994, p. 104)

SUMMARY

The social system is the foundation from which all media content is constructed, the macro-level base upon which influences from other levels rest. The characteristics of the social systems affect the interactions of social institutions, the existence and makeup of media organizations, the types of routines adopted, and the values of individuals. Although we've chosen to take up the system level prior to the others in the Hierarchy of Influences, we shouldn't regard those other levels of analysis as secondary or automatically dictated by the social system level. We are not social system determinists, such that factors on other levels of analysis are unimportant. As we will see in Chapters 5 through 8, social systems are large and complex and it is impossible for forces at the social system level to determine the exact nature of media content. In the stream of mediated reality, to become news an event must also traverse the wide river of routines of media work and survive policies of media organizations, and even then the event elicits reactions from social institutions.

Getting information about even one event transmitted to the audience is a complex process, and although social system forces are powerful, they are not uniformly strong at every moment. There is substantial variance in news topics, and the way topics are treated is not always in the direction preferred by media owners or other powerful elites. The levels interact with and condition each other, constraining and enabling, but are not directly "caused" by each other. It's tempting to ask which level is most important in the overall model, but answering that question is more a matter of emphasis, an empirical question that depends on the circumstances.

Social systems can be difficult to fully comprehend, especially to the extent that they have become naturalized and hegemonic. They may become taken for granted and the society difficult to imagine were they to be absent or significantly changed; the researcher must take a step back with a critical distance, while being mindful of the larger web of global connections. The interpretive critical tradition has brought important insights to this level, helping to understand how structures give rise to meanings that work in favor of certain interests. Macro systems don't lend themselves to direct observation and laboratory manipulation; they must be examined as they are, imagining what meanings could have been produced but weren't and what alternative systems might have developed but didn't.

One's own social system is inevitably seen as natural but comparative research in the empirical tradition. Such research can help assess the importance to the media of macro variables such as culture and political system. Comparing social systems cross-nationally, a mainstay of international communication research, now risks overlooking important features, with globalization bringing a host of supranational entities and cultural linkages that transcend traditional political boundaries. Nation-based social systems must adapt or give way to more integrated transnational, global systems, but the idea of the planet Earth as a unitary social system is neither empirically accurate nor theoretically helpful. The Internet brought hopes for more global exchanges of media content, but although such flows are important they are still constrained by the various economic, political, cultural, and ideological factors we've discussed in this chapter. And although the evolving world system feeds on such information flows, some nations still jealously guard their citizens' exposure to foreign ideas while others lack the technological infrastructure to connect their citizens to the world.

Having laid out the theories of society and macro perspectives underlying the social system level, we now take up the next level of analysis—social institutions. As we proceed through the Hierarchy of Influences, we continue to be mindful of the questions posed at the system level: What do they add up to?

NOTE

1   The knowledge gap hypothesis proposes that, as the amount of information about a topic grows within a community, people who are well educated will acquire the information at a faster rate than those less well educated (Tichenor et al., 1980).

CHAPTER 5

Social Institutions

After the social system—but before the organizational—level of analysis lie many forces outside of the formal media structures themselves. Clearly, the media exist in relationship with other institutional power centers in society, relationships that can be coercive or collusive and can shape media content. The more powerful the parties involved, the more likely they are to enter into a collaborative symbiotic relationship. Theorists such as Castells (2007) conceive of the media as a generalized institutionalized space, with its logic and organization that structures politics. Gamson similarly regards media as a site and "master forum," on which politics is played out (Ferree, Gamson, Gerhards, & Rucht 2002). As Benson (2004) notes, this media space in these discussions is overly broad, undertheorized, and the variables comprising it not specified as to their interrelationships. This social institutional (formerly extra-media) level of the Hierarchy of Influences helps understand the factors affecting that master forum, particularly when directed at the practice of journalism, leading us to understand it as a relatively homogenous social practice, with similar concerns over legitimacy and commercial success.

Certainly, the political and media institutions have grown more interdependent. The idea of mediatization describes a distinctive stage in the long-term development of contemporary mass democracies in which many political processes have grown more or less dependent on mass media. These issues transition into questions of ideology, asking on behalf of what trans-sector interests does the arrangement work? Media power at this level resides not in the action of specific individuals or organizations but in a larger institutional sweep, where perspective shifts to see organizational structure as an inter-organizational field, the outcome of institutional forces.

In this chapter we review a number of issues relevant to this level and some of the directions research has taken. Many things have changed, especially given the crisis in the US newspaper industry, the globalization of media, and the rapid innovations brought about by technology. We can't do justice to all of these developments but instead present a more theoretical context within which to understand media in a context of institutional upheaval. We preface this chapter with a more extended discussion of the shifting media-society institutional context, particularly in the political communication realm. Much has been done in the last several years to examine this context, and some of the most interesting and exciting research pertains to this level.

In the 1991 and 1996 editions of *Mediating the Message* these issues were extrinsic to or "extra-" media factors, and—after accounting for all the factors intrinsic to media organizations—served as a theoretical cluster of everything left over, such as advertising, government, technology, public relations, media watchdog groups, and audiences. This encompassing of a host of different factors, having in common only that they were outside organizational boundaries, was not a particularly elegant conceptualization. Benson (2004) notes that we gave short shrift to government or political constraints on media and suggest no theories of statist influence. He correctly pointed out that more theorizing was needed as to how these elements fit together at the meso level of analysis and how they were related to specific political and economic factors. Although it may still make sense to regard these factors as having this level in common, we should consider more specifically how they represent an *institutional* level of influence. There's been a resurgence of attention in recent years to the sociology of news *within* the institution and the organization, particularly concerning ethnographic studies of the online newsrooms (Paterson & Domingo, 2008), but the shifts in new media also give increasingly greater importance to understanding the boundaries *between* journalism and other social institutions. The new media lead to cultural tensions in institutions, whether with the Chinese government trying repeatedly to control communication online or the US military struggling to find policies for soldiers using social media. We are witnessing an expanding media space, while ironically witnessing in the US context the contracting and more precarious journalistic employment within traditional institutions.

INSTITUTIONAL TRANSFORMATION

As such we have made significant changes in this renamed social institutional level of the Hierarchy of Influences since our original 1991 volume: the media, the profession, the technology, and the external influences that, under global networks, now include so many more factors operating at a distance. Indeed, the biggest challenge at the social institutional level is to actually define the boundaries of those institutions, given that their borders are now more fluid and their relationships more complex and multi-layered. Control is no longer situated in well-defined and easily identifiable institutional containers. Even if those organized containers still exist in recognizable form, they don't have the same influence as before.

Gatekeeping power is neither the sole province of professional decision makers, nor determined by the audience users, but results from the interaction between them—an interaction harnessed and most visibly indicated by the algorithms of selection used by online news aggregation sites such as Google News. News values are embedded now in networks, and within those networks each of us has a unique configuration of structured relationships with news sources, either directly or through our social contacts. With social media each of us can have a unique information "board of directors" that we have appointed to monitor the world and alert us to items of interest.

THE NETWORKED MEDIA SPACE

From a *normative* standpoint, we ask what relationships produce the best quality of news coverage, particularly regarding issues of autonomy and dependence on the state. The USA, for example, has a long tradition of prizing journalistic independence, even if it has been more of an ideal than an always accurate description of reality. This norm of journalistic independence encourages the conceptual separation, drawing distinct boundaries between journalism and other social institutions. Considering this arena of press–state relations more closely helps illustrate some of these changes. The two-by-two model of press–state actors in Figure 5.1 illustrates the increasingly fluid and integrated relationships among media and other social actors within an institutional context. This model reflects some simple relationships and areas of emphasis in understanding the nature of news, particularly in the arena of politics and public affairs.

Taking the top level row, we note that most research attention has been devoted to the *institutional* level, with political scientists typically favoring the state side as the more determinative and influential side of the relationship and one more worthy of study (Entman, 1993). Journalism and media studies researchers have obviously taken the more media-centric, left side of this relationship. Only recently, have we begun to take more seriously the non-institutional or citizen level, manifested as the non-professional, citizen bloggers who have taken on a larger part of the journalistic task. In the bottom right-hand corner, non-institutionalized social movements have received some attention, but there has been little attention at all to the influential and growing work of non-governmental organizations (NGOs), many of which are institutionalized but tend to encompass citizen efforts across a wide range of interests (Waisbord, 2011). The mobilizing of grassroots efforts around moral issues, such as human rights, gives them a special standing and influence.

From an institutional perspective, these entities in the four cells traditionally have been compartmentalized separately in our theorizing, but boundaries between them now seem more arbitrary. Of course, there are still formal news organizations,

Arena	Journalistic	Political
Institutional Level	News professionals	State, officials
Citizen Level	Bloggers	NGOs, social movements

FIGURE 5.1 *Typology of press–state actors*

and their unique influence can be observed (as in Chapter 6). The traditional norm of journalistic independence encourages the separation, and it's been helpful conceptually to draw distinct boundaries between journalism and other social institutions. And in spite of globalization, there are still unique news and political cultures that affect news values, but the relationships are less tidy than before. Increasingly we must look at those boundaries more closely and consider networks of influence that combine elements of all four quadrants, interpenetrating and mutually influential. The 2012 Occupy Wall Street movement that expanded from the USA to around the world is an example of the integration of journalistic work with social movements, as these participants exploit social media, even printing their own newspaper to develop and share their message. In another kind of boundary work, citizen news bloggers have linked online to professional news sources as a matter of course, but professional news organizations once were determined not to link to information sources outside their own online sites for fear of losing audience attention outside their cyber-boundaries. In time, though, journalists working for these media have begun to link out themselves, to participate in the larger online conversation—a response to norms that emerged in a community larger than professional news sites but encompassing them, creating a broader institutional context.

Research has begun to examine the citizen journalist/blogger level of the journalistic column, but often this has pitted the traditional against online media in a competitive relationship, asking which is more influential. But of course professional journalists themselves now take on aspects of individual citizen bloggers, and the latter are often invited into more traditional media platforms or hired directly. The *New York Times*, for example, hired as a media writer Brian Stelter, a few years after he gained an audience while still a college student with his website tracking the television news industry. So the relationship is complementary, and different news platforms now combine to create what Benkler (n.d.) calls the "networked public sphere." Anderson (2010) has examined the news ecology of Philadelphia to trace the emergence and lifespan of a specific issue, a task that required taking both the institutional and citizen levels into account to describe a larger journalistic structure—one that included bloggers and the traditional press at both the local and national level.

And the outcomes of this *networked public sphere* are less predictable. Sociologists Molotch and Lester (Molotch & Lester, 1974) considered how news was constructed, as happenings were promoted into events. The occurrences underlying this process could be intentional or not and promoted by either the instigator of the occurrence or an informant. Beyond the more institutionally constituted news—characterized as routinized and purposive work—the changes in the news system have provided more opportunities for non-routine events of what the authors called accident, scandal, and serendipity. These categories have new relevance online, where story appeal cannot be planned in advance. Web metrics now include measures such as most-emailed stories and are available for news organizations to measure the unpredictable appeal of various stories to audiences, shifting the character of news values away from professional norms and toward audience interests. In explaining the operations of the online American gossip media organization Gawker, one of the editors emphasized that "serendipity is an important part of the operation . . . The job of journalism is to provide surprise" (Fallows, 2011)—and to surprise even the gate-keepers themselves.

SOCIAL INSTITUTIONS AS LEVEL OF ANALYSIS

The social institutional level of the Hierarchy of Influences leads to an understanding of journalism as a relatively homogenous social practice, with similar concerns over legitimacy and commercial success, glossing over organizational differences in favor of making broader statements about the media in general, considering how journalistic practices are more alike than different. The idea of *media work* promoted by Deuze (2007) reflects this perspective, allowing him to group journalists along with advertising/public relations professionals, game designers, and filmmakers as a class of *creatives* for study, with organizational differences receding into the background.

Two major approaches have been helpful in conceptualizing the news media as a new unit of analysis placed in relationship with other institutions in the larger social system. Indeed, we assume media cannot be understood except in relation to other fields. Advocating a sociology of media for political communication problematizes their level between the organizational and the societal. Benson (2004, p. 280) argues that the "social organization of newswork is the outcome of the news media's relationship, as a relatively homogeneous institution, to political and economic power." He suggests that "national culture" is too broad to be useful and should rather be theorized in terms of its institutional parts. The relatively greater prominence of cross-national research in media sociology has supported this perspective by allowing us to consider variations in key relationships between political, economic, and media institutions—and how they contribute to democratic outcomes. Theorizing at this level has developed through two important and related lines of thought: new institutionalism and Bourdieu's field theory. Both take a more historical perspective to understanding the dynamics of social relationships that operate between specific media organizations and the society as a whole. Both are valuable in helping to understand the shifts in the position of media in a period of technological upheaval.

Institutionalist Theory

The *new institutionalist* perspective asks whether it makes sense to regard journalism as a relatively homogenous institutional actor. Beyond the formal organizations labeled institutions by political scientists (e.g., Congress), this concept has a broader sociological meaning in the sense of rules, routines, scripts, and other practices that reproduce themselves over time in an equilibrium, punctuated by shocks at critical junctures. All news organizations face similar challenges, economic, professional, and informational, involving making a profit, legitimation, and access to timely information. This gives institutionalism much in common with the routines and organizational level perspective, which we take up in the next chapter. We are alerted to those practical means of solving organizational "uncertainties." To the extent that these problems are shared across an inter-organizational field, then institutions can be said to cohere. As Ryfe (2006, p. 137) summarizes the key principles in this perspective: "Institutions mediate the impact of macro-level forces on micro-level action," and "institutions evolve in a path-dependent pattern," making it important to examine the historical path of a given institution, particularly the timing and sequence of key moments that become determinative in shaping an institution and its tendency to remain as it is.

Giving the media status as an institutional actor allows us to take it seriously in relation to other key political institutions. For political scientists, who are not as likely to cite communication research than vice versa, this point seems counter-intuitive but helpful in justifying the study of media. Yet the power of media, particularly manifested in the mediatization of politics, long has been a general premise for communication scholars. Furthermore, the political "homogeneous media" assumption underlies a tradition of effects research connecting news media use to various audience outcomes. When people are asked how often they pay attention to "the news," then it has in a sense become institutionalized.

The institutionalist approach to news media was spurred by the publication of related volumes by Timothy Cook (1998) and Bartholomew Sparrow (1999), who both advocate treating the media as a political actor. In his more historical approach, Cook argues that news practices evolved at the beginning of the 20th century to resolve "uncertainties," leading organizations to take on a particular shape. Sparrow takes a more ethnographic perspective and, rather than assuming they always do work together, explaining *how* the "different rules, norms, and practices" of news-work manage to "interact and coexist" (Sparrow, 2006, p. 148). Ryfe summarizes the evidence for this institutionalist view found in the "extraordinarily homogenous" pattern of news across organizational, geographic, and other differences (2006, p. 135). Journalistic practices of objectivity, balance, and detachment, for example, are "taken for granted assumptions and behaviors that have become deeply embedded within the transorganizational field of journalism" (Ryfe, 2006, p. 138), at least in the USA. News has, in this sense, become "institutionalized," and for certain areas (such as financial news) this has happened on a global level.

Sparrow argues that reporters are "company men" who go along to get along, a tendency that reproduces the status quo. The institutionalist perspective provides a way of more explicitly theorizing the hegemonic status quo, but in emphasizing equilibrium it also has the spirit of functionalism. In posing the question "to what extent does the US have an institutional media?" Sparrow (2006) acknowledges that they are not completely internally homogenous, that splits are occurring along the lines of geography (national vs. local), partisanship, and style (entertainment-oriented news or conventional). Nevertheless, the news media are an institution in the sense of being a significant political and governmental actor.

Clearly, journalism practices are no longer taken for granted. Given the upheavals in recent years and challenge to traditional "objective" forms by more opinionated channels, we are now at a critical juncture for the news institution, which is far from a state of equilibrium. Institutionalism helps explain stability, but Ryfe notes that in its concern with critical junctures institutionalism may be more helpful in explaining shifts from one stable form to another. What institutional form is journalism on its way to becoming? The 9/11 attacks arguably represent such a critical institutional juncture, given the psychological trauma to the USA and the proximity to the headquarters of many elite news organizations. During the aftermath of the terrorist attacks, unfolding real-time events were emphasized, with journalists blurring the lines between reporting and patriotic expression. Veteran CBS News anchor at the time Dan Rather became emotional when he appeared on David Letterman's *Late Night* show a week after the attacks, professing his allegiance to his commander in chief: "George Bush is the President, he makes the decisions, and, you know, as just one American, wherever he wants me to line up, just tell me where."[1]

By taking homogeneity as a benchmark, analyses of national news coverage gauge under what circumstances news becomes more internally diverse: homogenous in the case of the American attack on Fallujah in Iraq and less uniform in the case of the Abu Ghraib prison scandal (Entman, 2006). The challenge then is to explain the "shock to the system" that might be underway in affecting this change, whether involving primarily political, economic, or professional factors.

Technology has certainly contributed to these shifts. In a study of online news videos on YouTube, Peer and Ksiazek (2011) found that they shared traditional television production values, but the most popular ones, including those originating from traditional broadcast platforms, differed in content standards regarding fairness, detachment, and objectivity. The authors suggest that this relaxing of traditional objective standards in the more biased world of online news represents a shock to the system of mainstream news and signals a change in institutionalized practices.

Field Theory

Institutionalists establish the presence of various orders within societies but have less to say about the relations among them. That is where the *field theory* approach of Pierre Bourdieu comes in, as advocated particularly by Rodney Benson (2006; Benson & Neveu, 2005). Modern societies, through the interplay of economic and cultural capital as forms of power, develop specialized spheres of action, or *fields*, which have their own relative autonomy and power dynamics among them. Like institutions they develop their own internal homogeneity and have their own rules, arising from contingent historical "path dependency." That is, to understand a field one has to consider how it got there, a location contingent on past moments that in turn govern the future direction. If rolled back and started over, a different path would likely result. These fields have their own internal logics and tend to persist even when historical circumstances change.

Applying this perspective in journalism is complicated by the increasingly fluid boundaries between the journalistic field and others. This approach goes beyond simple measures of ownership and other financial factors to consider cultural factors. In facilitating the analysis of multiple factors simultaneously, Benson suggests how this model helps account for the economic and cultural tensions that play out within various media: "between culturally rich, but often economically starved, alternative or literary journalism (*The Nation*, *Mother Jones*) and culturally poor but economically rich market journalism (commercial television news)," with news organizations like the *New York Times* and *Wall Street Journal* able to accumulate both forms of capital and thereby exercise leadership over the entire field (Benson, 2006, p. 190).

Fields exercise their own conditioning power on the individuals that embody them. In terms of *structuration theory* they are constraining and enabling, not determinative. Individuals have their own complex historical trajectory, or habitus, that brings them to their position within a field. Thus, to understand the actions of social actors, Bourdieu brings the time line of history, the unique path that brings each of us to the present moment. If we are tempted to minimize the power of individuals, located as they are within a web of larger macro forces, Bourdieu grants them more of it to the extent that they are located within a profession that seeks to differentiate itself from other power centers and exercise its own autonomous influence, including on other fields of cultural production.

Field theory perspectives have spurred new interest in cross-national research, which helps to disentangle the relationships among commercial, political, and media factors as they vary across national cultures. For example, although the American and French media have many similarities, their respective "objective/informational" and "political/literary" traditions represent a field variable, leading the French national elite press to present stories with a mix of facts and opinions while being more ideologically diverse, more critical of the government than the *New York Times* (Benson, 2010). Other cross-national analysis has included consideration of the effect of privacy laws (Esser, 1999) and government intervention (see Benson 2004 for review). Thus journalism in a particular national context is not a single thing, naturally determined by the political structure (Hallin & Mancini, 2004), but rather an outcome undergirded by a complex interaction of economic, political, and media fields.

Institutional Realignment

Institutional level influence also can be seen during historical intra-national transitions, in those settings where there has been a realignment of forces, including the explosive growth of media in the developing world. China, for example, presented such an opportunity when market forces were allowed greater latitude in the late 1980s, without fundamental change in the political system, causing journalism practices to shift in order to exploit these changes. Pan (2000) examined this macro-level change in the mid 1990s when China was accelerating its media commercialization process, with correspondingly rapid growth in the advertising industry. Asking the question "how does a journalism institution change itself?" (Pan, 2000, p. 276), he used in this case not a "field," as such, but another spatial metaphor to explore how journalists seek *maneuvering room* as they negotiate and exploit the tensions created by realignments of political and economic forces.

In this study, the more distant a newspaper was from the ideological center, the more commercially appealing it was; although the higher a news organization was in the political hierarchy, the more it enjoyed access to news sources. The *spatial reconfiguration* that resulted obliged journalists to become entrepreneurial actors, seeking market success without challenging party ideology. They pushed into non-routine activities as opportunities to find those areas of reporting beyond political controls. His case shows that hierarchical levels of media influence are not always necessarily in harmony (peaceful evolution via marketization); when the economic basis for media changes but authoritarian power of the political field remains intact, institutions must adapt to create space and creatively incorporate old and new values.

Whether we call journalism an institution or a field, its boundaries have become more porous. Where does the journalistic field end and others begin? How are various participants adapting to the "rules of the game"? Given the increasing diversity of the journalistic field, including the rise of opinion-driven journalism of news organizations like Fox and other cable news shows or the vast range of sites on the Internet, it's harder now to argue that it does represent a single institution. We now have to understand better how the journalistic components at both the professional and citizen level have reconstituted themselves in a networked public sphere, one that is in the process of reaching a new equilibrium. The institutional boundaries are where these interesting developments are taking place.

SOCIAL INSTITUTIONS AS CONCEPTUAL MODEL

The complexity of the institutional level cannot be easily addressed with the kind of cause-and-effect empirical analysis of specific variables. The shifting institutional boundaries are best seen in case studies of a number of recent high-profile developments, where we can see the transformations underway. We include here such vantage points on the journalistic field provided by the process of news innovation, the professional response to boundary challenges, and how these shifts are being played out within the university arena in journalism education.

Innovation and the Profession

The professional logic of journalism has been important in advocating ethical practice, truth-seeking, fairness, and quality, but the part of that logic emphasizing control lacked self-reflection and a meaningful relationship with its citizen audience.

Now often romanticized, the old journalism used control to slip into practices that didn't always serve democracy. Professional boundaries are under special assault from technology-enabled citizen journalism. Given the digital network that facilitates citizen production and dissemination of news, the core question as posed by Seth Lewis is "how does journalism become a shared practice in a shared media space without losing the professional core that gives it authority and power to work on society's behalf" (2011, p. 1626). This question is played out in the process of news innovation, in which philanthropic leaders have become key catalysts for change.

Historically, journalism foundations have worked to uphold and strengthen professional boundaries. The Newseum in Washington, DC, funded by the newspaper-based foundation Freedom Forum, is a good example of the profession's tribute to itself. The Knight Foundation, another advocate with roots in the newspaper industry and today the most important philanthropic force in journalism, reflects the shifting professional boundaries in its innovation competition. Formerly an aggressive defender of the profession, Lewis notes that Knight has moved the rhetorical field in its programs from "journalism" to "information," from the "news industry" to a greater concern for "news and information," opening journalism to a wider set of fields, interests, and actors. The Knight News Challenge begun in 2006 is one of the most important initiatives intended to encourage innovation in this area, offering millions of dollars to support "innovative ideas that develop platforms, tools and services to inform and transform community news, conversations, and information distribution." Lewis examined the applications to the funding competition, which were to be digital, open source, innovative, focused on the local community, emphasizing democratic engagement, and replicable (2011, 2012). The initiative did not favor legacy institutional media and received only a few applications from professional journalists or newspapers. In that respect the News Challenge has helped opened significant space for contributors from other fields, such as computer programmers and media activists, to bring new ideas into journalism.

Lewis examined the factors identified in the proposal submissions that predicted a successful Knight Challenge grant, among the most prominent of which included use of crowd-sourcing and user participation. Thus, Knight has moved away from its historic emphasis on strengthening the profession as it was and moved toward a broader sense of journalism involving open, more broadly flowing channels of civic information and user engagement. Along with an emphasis on software, Lewis notes that these are features not traditionally associated with institutionalized journalism, and through them the news innovators of the Knight Challenge are developing an "ethic of participation" that has potential for advancing transparency and democratic quality.

WikiLeaks and the New York Times

In another important case, the recent controversy over WikiLeaks illustrates the shifting boundaries of the journalistic field as it struggles to adapt to new players.

The transparency activist organization worked in partnership with the *New York Times* and two European news organizations in 2010 to release a massive and unprecedented amount of US military documents to the public. In spite of the partnering relationship, many in the professional press were highly critical of WikiLeaks' leader Julian Assange, including the executive editor of the *Times* itself, Bill Keller. Clearly, WikiLeaks has many characteristics of journalism, winning Amnesty International's new media award 2009 and regarded as "journalistic" even by Pentagon critics. From a legal perspective, journalists are those with the intent to obtain information for public dissemination, and Assange himself has laid claim to being a journalist—although it's still being worked out how constitutional protections such as those enjoyed by the *New York Times* would be extended to entities like WikiLeaks. Legality is only part of institutionality.

The controversy over WikiLeaks reveals a struggle not just over the propriety of releasing sensitive documents to public view but an attempt by the traditional media to preserve their identity over threats perceived from the *networked public sphere*. In considering the vitriol leveled at Julian Assange, creator of WikiLeaks, Coddington (2012) identifies this case as a key example of paradigmatic repair. The professional news media were obliged to distance themselves from WikiLeaks in order to repair the breach of the threatened paradigmatic boundaries and preserve their own professional legitimacy. Coddington argues that the *Times*, particularly via Bill Keller, engaged in this repair process through its discourse about WikiLeaks and Julian Assange: It upheld its own institutionality by contrasting itself with what it regarded as a more unstable entity, one which lacked a place of operation, accountability, and identity beyond that of Assange himself; the *Times*'s response compared its own socially approved, routinized, and mutually respectful relationships with sources to WikiLeaks' more distant and antagonistic relationship. And, finally, Coddington describes how the *Times*'s opinion of its own objectivity was contrasted with Assange, who was said to be an advocate for an "agenda" and a foe of the USA. The repair process shows the institutional distinctions are not clear cut, favoring some alignments over others. How does one, for example, distinguish between the objectivity of Fox News and Assange: Both have agendas, Fox with a partisan agenda and Assange with a value-based transparency point of view. Yet of the two, Fox is regarded as part of the professional media and thus within the paradigm.

In its emerging combination of professional and other media forms, the networked public sphere challenges the routine and traditional institutionalized relationship between state and press. The government had become accustomed to managing that relationship during the period Hallin (1992) has called the *high modernism* of American journalism. Journalists in effect made a Faustian bargain with government: They would get access in exchange for not questioning the inner workings of power. *New York Times* reporter Judith Miller was a prime example of that prior comfortable arrangement, trading access for control and predictability. Miller had been critical of Assange for not being "professional" in trying to verify his sources, but she famously had defended her reporting on non-existent weapons programs in Iraq via her source Ahmad Chalabi: "[M]y job isn't to assess the government's information and be an independent intelligence analyst myself. My job is to tell readers of the *New York Times* what the government thought" (Massing, 2004). Both Assange and Miller helped the public know what American leaders and allies were thinking; the difference was that Miller and official sources could use each other in a more predictable, symbiotic, and institutionalized relationship compatible with the interests of the National Security State.

According to legal scholar Yochai Benkler (n.d.), the response of the professional wing of the journalistic field, denying Assange membership in its club, ironically threatens the very press freedom from which it has benefited. In Benkler's view, it would be unfortunate to pit the emerging platforms of news against the traditional—as though to label one responsible and the other not—because the combined emergent networked version of these forms is critical for democratic functioning. Traditional journalism institutions ultimately have no choice but to adapt to open source networks in a "mutualistic interaction." In striving to differentiate themselves from groups like WikiLeaks, Benkler argues that the traditional media serve to leave these parts of the networked public sphere vulnerable to government extra-legal suppression and control (something the institutional press has been able to resist with their historical constitutional protections). As with the Knight initiative, the WikiLeaks case shows professional boundaries in flux. Drawing them too narrowly only prolongs the inevitable institutional adaptation and the integration of the professional and citizen sectors of the public sphere.

Journalism Education at Colorado

As the journalistic field has become more porous, it has been just a matter of time before it was reflected in journalism education at the university level. A case has been made in recent years for distributing the components of journalism more widely on campus—and all kinds of hybrids in between. The continued existence of academic programs that once were taken for granted is now in doubt. Before the media disruption of the last decade, the existence of the journalism profession and media institutions had been assumed, and journalism education had grown steadily (even as a global phenomenon), accompanied by a sharpening of its professional mission (and the desire of the profession to be involved in it). Journalism as an academic enterprise has a number of tensions and fault lines, but the balances previously in place have been disrupted even more by the disarray of the institutional media and professional community.

At the University of Colorado, for example, there were calls in 2010 for the "discontinuance" and "strategic realignment" of its long-standing school of journalism, which is now no longer a free-standing unit on campus. As a backdrop of this decision, opposed by many within the school, one must consider how universities pursue their own institutional imperatives, including the drive for prestige, as signified for example by membership in the American Association of Universities. Noting that only a few of the most prestigious research universities in this group, in the Ivy League and elsewhere, teach journalism, campus leaders talked of reorganizing the school within a larger unit combining computer science and information studies, to take advantage of their common domains and exploit Colorado's research expertise in the technology oriented fields. Thus, professional schools of journalism face their own issues with boundaries and turf within the university—signified as in the Knight News Challenge by the changing rhetorical ground of information and communication.

In response to the Colorado actions, some defenders from within the academy argue essentially "we need journalism more than ever and just as it is." And, indeed, journalism education has had a number of strong advocates over the years, justifying it as an academic discipline devoted to developing the liberal arts (reading, thinking, civic participation) in a context of application. Wisconsin's Willard Bleyer said, "No other profession has a more vital relation to the welfare of society or to the success of democratic government" (quoted in Bronstein & Vaughan, 1998, pp. 16–17). Communication institution builder Wilbur Schramm wanted journalism to be as strong as the university, not as weak as itself, and Carnegie Foundation leader Vartan Gregorian calls journalists the sense-makers of society. As a result, many have advocated that journalism be central to universities (quoted in Reese, 1999).

Journalism, however, has not had a tradition of critical self-reflection, one of the hallmarks of a profession. But that didn't stop groups such as the Freedom Forum from trying in the 1990s to enforce the proper disciplinary boundaries and approach within the academy. The Forum, through its *Winds of Change* report, was a powerful advocate at that time for the practical side of the theory/practice debate, pitting one against the other. Robert Giles, later head of the Nieman Foundation for Journalism at Harvard, urged that journalism students take courses in the mainstream departments from the "real scholars." The *Winds* report complained that journalism professors were "anti-professional" and too critical of the profession. Reese (1999) argued during that period that media concentration and associated philanthropic power had increased the industry voice in the academy, in an often self-congratulatory, self-reinforcing pattern—arguably a response at the institutional level to declining professional legitimacy in seeking greater control within the academy where it could recoup prestige (or in field theory terms, converting economic into cultural capital).

Now we see a different kind of pull. Without a robust, unified, and confident profession as ballast, the "set of skills approach" to journalism training was left with a weakened champion and partially discredited—and the gravitational power of the research university ethos began to exert its own influence. In years past, leaders of groups such as the Freedom Forum served as advocates for journalism's field status on campus, warning that journalism must not be swallowed up by "communication"—not unlike Zelizer's (2011) recent concern for the larger research field. As the Forum's leader Charles Overby once said, "I don't care where journalism is taught as long as it's taught" (personal communication). But it's been remarkable how little the foundations have had to say about events at the University of Colorado.

INFLUENCES ON CONTENT FROM SOCIAL INSTITUTIONS

In the 1991 and 1996 editions of *Mediating the Message* we reviewed a number of specific influences at this level of analysis, including a number of research studies. Many of them merge into issues of legal constraints, ethics, and policy, beyond the scope of our focus. Where appropriate we continue to cite early studies as a way of showing the kinds of changes afoot. Many of these insights remain on track, while others must be reassessed in view of these changes. In regarding those forces emanating from outside the media, extra-media, we can see that it could include just about anything. We touch on some of the major components that are particularly influential without claiming to provide an exhaustive list.

Media Sources

At the extra-media level, sources of content wield important influence. We also can regard sources as a routines-level influence to the extent that the relationships have been routinized, but here we place the emphasis on the systematic influence of sources, considering in particular who has the resources to access media. For journalists, news sources certainly lie outside the organization's boundaries and exert a powerful influence on shaping the message. In attributing to them significant influence, Gans (1979, p. 80) defines sources as "the actors whom journalists observe or interview, including interviewees who appear on the air or who are quoted in . . . articles, and those who only supply background information or story suggestions." Of course, official sources have long been relied on, a pattern noted in our discussion of news routines (Chapter 7). To the extent that they are relied on in certain predictable ways, we can say this relationship has become routinized, but at this level their influence has also become institutionalized. The difference lies in the power these sources are thought to exemplify. Fishman (1980) elevates this relationship to a more institutional basis by noting how journalism and government represent bureaucratic machines engaged with each other to produce news.

Sources obviously have a significant impact on media content because they are the origin for much of what journalists know. The most intentional influence occurs when sources withhold information or lie; but they may also influence the news in more subtle ways, by providing the context within which all other information is evaluated, by providing usable information that is easier and cheaper to use than that from other sources, and by monopolizing the journalists' time so that they don't have an opportunity to seek out sources with alternative views. In Gandy's (1982) enduring notion of information subsidies, which fits this institutional perspective, these sources represent investments by powerful social actors in promoting their views and perspectives into the public arena.

Official Sources

US presidents have a strategic advantage in making news and work an institution-ally predictable media system. Presidential influence has only grown since entering the modern media age with Richard Nixon, and extending to Barack Obama, an innovator in using social media effectively to amplify his campaign and govern-ing message. Notwithstanding First Amendment freedom, presidents have histori-cally sought to direct the news media in support of national policy. In 1961, the enemy was communism and President John Kennedy spoke directly to a meeting of the American Newspaper Publishers Association.

> In time of war, the government and the press have customarily joined in an effort, based largely on self-discipline, to *prevent* unauthorized disclosures to the enemy. In time of "clear and present danger," the courts have held that even the privileged rights of the First Amendment must yield to the public's *need* for national security . . . I do ask every publisher, every editor, and every newsman in the nation to reexamine his own standards and to recognize the nature of our country's peril. Every newspaper now asks itself, with respect to every story: "Is it news?" All that I suggest is that you add the question: "Is it in the national interest?"
>
> (Reeves, 1993, pp. 108–9)

The publishers did not appreciate Kennedy questioning their professional prerogatives, but in the years after 9/11, presidents have not needed to be so explicit and heavy handed. The news media have engaged with the president under a similar outlook, for example, on the "war on terrorism." NBC's *Meet the Press* host Tim Russert, one of the most reputed national journalists, said in the weeks following 9/11:

> Covering the war on terrorism is not like covering politics, a presidential im-peachment or a missing intern. In times of war, the media should lower our voices, modulate our tone. "Yes, we are journalists, but we are also Americans," Russert said in a speech Friday to the Congressional Medal of Honor Society. "We are at war, and all of us must come together as never before," Russert said. "Simply put: There are those who want to destroy us, our people—men, women and children—our institutions, our way of life, our freedom. This presents some interesting issues for the media."
>
> (Johnson, 2001, p. D4)

Institutionalized Source Power

Official sources, such as government figures or police, are often preferred by jour-nalists, not only because they are more easily available for an interview but also because journalists and their editors believe that official sources have important things to say. They accept the things official sources say as factual. Entman (2003) has updated this relationship in his *cascading activation* model of political influence, from the powerful political actors to the media in a cascading process of influence. He argues that their institutional resources and position allow the administration to influence other elites, who in turn affect the media, which guide the public, with each lower level receiving a mix of influence from the levels above:

> As is true of actual waterfalls also, moving downward in a cascade is relatively easy, but spreading ideas higher, from lower levels to upper, requires extra energy—a pumping mechanism, so to speak. Ideas that start at the top level, the administration, possess the greatest strength. The president and top advisors enjoy the most independent ability to decide which mental associations to activate and the highest probability of moving their own thoughts into general circulation.
>
> (Entman, 2003, p. 420)

In his analysis of news frames after 9/11, Entman shows that the media were not entirely passive as receptacles of government propaganda but contributed counter-frames through prominent writers like Thomas Friedman and Seymour Hersch. This institutional struggle is signified by the pattern of source selection visible in media content, with organized voices having a greater likelihood of gaining visibility. Reese, Grant, and Danielian (1994) illustrated this pattern in a network analysis of news sources on television, showing how official sources and their think-tank allies occupy a privileged position of centrality in the structure of relationships exemplified by the news content in which they were featured.

As agents of social control, law enforcement agencies have a significant institutional role in projecting their workings into the news, a relationship of long-standing interest in media sociology. As Sherizen (1978) points out in his early study of crime news, the police (who are by far the most often used source of information about crimes) "supply reporters with a constant stream of usable crime, and this information, fitting into the work requirements of the reporters, becomes the raw material from which crime news is written" (Sherizen, 1978, p. 222). "The police have a vested interest in crime news appearing in newspapers and other media . . . The more crimes which become known, the more aid the police may be able to gain in seeking increases in departmental budgets" (Sherizen, 1978, p. 212).

The police are only one of many institutions vying for strategic advantage by using the media as a site of promotion. In their analysis of police media units in Australia through interviews and content analysis, McGovern and Lee (2010) underscore the finding that the police are "pivotal" in shaping the construction of crime news and its own image. That power has grown over the last 20 years through the professionalization of law enforcement, risk, and image management, and as news organizations have cut back their own resources:

> The danger in this climate is that with a largely compliant and uncritical media, and the capacity of policing organizations to control much of the flow of

information, police organizations have the ability to frame a great percentage of narratives about law and order and policing. Policing organizations can thus "mediate" the landscape upon which crime stories speak themselves.

(McGovern & Lee, 2010, p. 459)

Although news organizations and law enforcement have different institutional goals, they have grown in symbiosis to create an influence beyond just restricting access to information. In her analysis of coverage of police in the *Los Angeles Times* and *New York Times*, Lawrence (2000) supports the tendency for the press to report narrowly when covering issues of police brutality, supporting law enforcement as "primary definers." In the periodic scandals involving use-of-force, however—such as the 1991 Rodney King police beating in Los Angeles—media become a "site of struggle," more open to other voices and perspectives.

The reality television show *Cops*, although not produced by a news organization, shows the effect of this institutional embeddedness. The camera takes the police perspective (as news crews often do) as they make arrests, break into houses, or chase down fleeing drivers. *Dateline NBC* takes the relationship even farther with its "To catch a predator" series, a hidden-camera investigation. The series crew works with a private cyber-watch organization to entrap sexual predators and lure them to a home with a purported under-age child. The anchor ultimately reveals himself as a *Dateline* reporter and stands by as law enforcement officials are on hand to arrest the fleeing alleged predator. In addition to investigating, the media themselves have become the "enforcer."

Interest Groups

Interest groups communicate their stance on issues through the media to influence legislation and public opinion and behaviors. The National Rifle Association lobbies the US Congress against gun control, and the National Organization for Women advocates for an Equal Rights Amendment to the US Constitution. The influence of interest groups has been tracked using the traditional agenda-setting model. Tracking the issues promoted by the right-wing Christian Coalition, for example, Huckins (1999) found a significant causal influence on the agenda of major US newspapers. Others have tracked the transmission of frames from interest groups to media, finding that for the abortion issue, the pro-life groups were more successful in having their rhetoric adopted by six major newspapers (Andsager, 2000).

One way interest groups get their message across is by designing and holding events that the news media will cover, such as demonstrations and protests (Wolfsfeld, 1984). In his famous term, Daniel Boorstin (1971) calls such occasions "pseudoevents," suggesting that they are somehow fraudulent and inferior to "real" events. With reality becoming a much more slippery concept in recent years, these events have become the kind of subsidy Gandy wrote about, a way that sources have of "underwriting" or subsidizing the cost of information-gathering. Media, like other institutions, have "resource dependencies" and have come to rely on this structuring of "event-reality." We could argue that the very idea of manufactured events has now become commonplace, with the public largely accepting that things don't just "happen" anymore (except for perhaps the weather and crimes), but rather are planned with the intention of their being covered. Even on reality television shows, the extent to which things happen spontaneously is suspect. Does anyone believe that the cast members of MTV's reality hit series *Jersey Shore* were behaving naturally when they knew they were being recorded throughout the day?

Media Watchdog Groups

In some instances, changing media content directly is the interest group's goal. The media watch function has become a critical part of many interest groups, to maintain a constant awareness of how their image is being represented to the public. The Israeli–Palestinian conflict has generated a particularly heated sensitivity to the favorability of coverage received in the US press. In forming Palestine Media Watch following the 2000 Intifada, activists monitored coverage and encouraged journalists to cover the conflict using an international law framework. Handley's (2011) research showed that systematic monitoring could be effective if criticisms based on that tracking were deemed by news workers to be "journalistically useful."

This monitoring function is particularly valued by large corporations in evaluating the success of their public relations campaigns, plus managing their reputation and risk to their brand. Firms such as the German-based Media Tenor, which also works with academic researchers, provides what it calls "strategic media intelligence" by conducting content analyses of media using accepted social science procedures. Other groups are more politically motivated with their own axe to grind, and their "monitoring" may be more designed to exert pressure based on anecdotal evidence. Conservatives have adopted belief in liberal mainstream media bias as a tenet of their ideology, but liberal groups are also part of the media watch landscape.

Among the early "bias-watch" groups was the conservative Accuracy in Media, founded by Reed Irvine in 1969 to, according to its website, "promote accuracy, fairness and balance in news reporting," with an emphasis on what it regarded as liberal distortions in "the media." The Media Research Center was launched in 1987 to "educate the public and media on bias in the media," but more pointedly to "prove . . . that liberal bias in the media does exist and undermines traditional American values."[2] Left-leaning organizations include Fairness and Accuracy in Reporting, which advocates for structural media reform to address corporate influence on the news: "challenging media bias and censorship since 1986."[3] The magazine *Adbusters* and its related organization are "a global network of culture jammers and creatives working to change the way information flows," gaining prominence through its leadership in the Occupy Wall Street movement.[4] And Media Matters bills itself as a progressive group, in its website mission, "dedicated to comprehensively monitoring, analyzing, and correcting conservative misinformation in the US media."[5]

This bias-watch mentality has penetrated deeply within media institutions. When Kenneth Tomlinson, former editor of *Reader's Digest*, was appointed to head the Corporation for Public Broadcasting in 2004, he quickly caused controversy when he hired a conservative consultant to monitor the "bias" of one of its programs (*Now* with Bill Moyers). Critics said his actions threatened public broadcasting's professional independence from the inside, instead of helping the Corporation for Public Broadcasting insulate it from political considerations as it was intended.

Other groups include Project Censored, the Global Media Monitoring Project, and the Center for Media and Democracy and its PR Watch. Beyond the watchdog function, some are more directly involved in efforts to reform the media. Billing itself as the "largest media reform organization" in the USA, Free Press says, "through education, organizing and advocacy, we promote diverse and independent media ownership, strong public media, quality journalism and universal access to communications."[6] In this respect, the media monitors have moved beyond simply calling attention to press distortions—in hopes of "policing" the boundaries of the media conversation, holding the press to agreed-upon norms—and instead have recognized that institutional change will be needed to affect the kind of changes they seek.

Testing the specific impact of these groups on media is difficult, with the evidence of their influence usually relying on anecdotal accounts. Their effectiveness can be seen indirectly, however, in the rising percentage of the audience that believes the media are politically biased: A 2009 survey by the Pew Research Center, for example, found that 74 percent thought the press tended "to favor one side." Audience polarization is found in the partisan difference in those regarding Fox News favorably: 72 percent of Republicans vs. 43 percent of Democrats. Rather than proving a point, the media monitoring efforts feed and reinforce beliefs already entrenched and contribute to the larger debate about the proper institutional role of the media. Media monitors have also paid attention to entertainment programs, which feed into the larger culture wars. It appears that, with the proliferation of entertainment options on cable and the Internet, the traditional national commercial networks have become smaller targets for their critics. Nevertheless, advertising-reliant television producers are still sensitive to criticism from even small groups. In 2011, for example, a political activist David Caton and his personal organization, the Florida Family Association, received attention for condemning the cable channel the Learning Channel for its reality-series program, *All-American Muslim*. His charge that the program was unduly favorable toward Muslims led the home-improvement chain Lowe's and the online travel company Kayak.com to regard it as too controversial for their tastes and pull advertising from the show (Editorial, 2011).

Inter-Media Influence

To a certain extent, each news organization acts as a source for the others, helping knit together and provide cohesion for the institutional field—something we later address as a routines and organizational level phenomenon. Journalists read, watch, and listen to news, from their own and from competing organizations; and when a story breaks first in one medium, it may quickly be picked up by others. This process has been of interest for media sociology since Warren Breed (1952) wrote of "dendritic" influence in the 1950s, flowing out from influential news organizations to lesser ones in a pattern resembling the branches on a tree. Some media have established themselves in their own sphere of influence. For example, the weekly *New England Journal of Medicine* has been an often-quoted source of medical news: "From an editor's point of view, the Journal may be an ideal source of medical news because the publication often reflects the conflict and controversy within the medical profession" (Caudill & Ashdown, 1989, p. 458). For general news, however, the final arbiter of quality and professionalism has historically been the *New York Times*. An elaborate longitudinal study in Belgium, for example, showed how this inter-media influence works, as a short-term effect, mitigated by language difference and stronger for newspapers than television (Vliegenthart & Walgrave, 2008).

The extent to which elite media transmit influence to other media is no longer as clear. Boczkowski (2004, 2009), for example, has contributed important news ethnographies, particularly showing how the online social media environment has affected media production. If inter-media monitoring has always been a factor (from the interpersonal, individual reporter level on up), Boczkowski shows how it has become more pervasive and embedded in the process through technology (including instant messaging and other digital communication tools), which also provides decision makers with real-time field outputs rated for newsworthiness based on computer algorithms. This awareness of the "journalistic field," he says, "enables the actors, situated in localized newsrooms, to capture distributed information flows they would have missed otherwise" (Boczkowski, 2009, p. 51). In an environment of media abundance, this leads to a paradoxical increase in imitation and field-wide conformity. He provides an account of Argentinean journalists' "spontaneous, mindless and matter-of-fact" monitoring and imitation of other news sources in lieu of the actual gathering of news. This news-life is so enveloping that one journalist reported spending her day tracking online news sources, and at night keeping CNN on in the bedroom while she slept (Boczkowski, 2010). Recalling the early days of reporters looking over each other's shoulders (Sigal, 1973), the question remains: Do they imitate because of commercial pressures, or in a common (more routines-level) desire to receive mutual reinforcement for their news judgments?

The media also rely on each other for institutional guidance when they occupy the same partisan space. The rise of the conservative movement in the post-Watergate era has led to a "counter-establishment," a self-referential nexus of influential book publishers, news media, radio programs, think tanks, and foundations. In their book *Echo Chamber*, Jamieson and Capella (2008) examined three components of that chamber: the *Wall Street Journal*, Rush Limbaugh's syndicated radio program, and Fox News television. They find consistent themes and frames across these platforms, showing that this subset of the journalistic field, at least, maintains a remarkable homogeneity. The "enemy" is a unifying source, whether characterized as "liberal," "communism" (now socialism), or the "cultural elite"; the legacy of Ronald Reagan is a common theme, hailing him as ending the Cold War, reviving the economy, and opposed at every turn by the "liberal" media. And, of course, the mainstream media are constantly monitored for bias, featuring their errors, reframing the mainstream as liberal, and singling out reporters who praise Democrats as proof of that bias. The success of this media space is seen in the ratings success of Fox News, and their unity can be attributed in part to their monitoring each other to reinforce audience expectations. The head of the conservative Media Research Center, for example, appears regularly on Sean Hannity's Fox program to review examples of perceived bias in the "mainstream media."

A similar interlocking influence is found within the international elite sphere, where the *Financial Times* is the undeniable leader when it comes to European Union news and policy. The *Financial Times* serves a critical need for its audience, linking elite sphere members and gaining it privileged access to those sources, thereby reinforcing its role as the "sun" around which other related media revolve (Corcoran & Fahy, 2009).

Advertisers and Audiences

To the extent that the media are supported by advertising, their funding sources will invariably help determine media content. Altschull (1984, p. 256) takes a one-directional deterministic view: "The content of the press is directly correlated with the interests of those who finance the press. The press is the piper, and the tune the piper plays is composed by those who pay the piper." Even public broadcasting, which is technically noncommercial, has not been immune. Its programs have come to rely on "enhanced underwriting" from corporate and foundation sponsors as a significant revenue source, including news programs on National Public Radio's All Things Considered and Morning Edition. But this reliance has made it just as ratings-conscious in some ways as the commercial networks, and critics charge that it has encouraged a similar institutional focus in its news reporting (Reporting, 2004).

Magazines became the first national advertising medium following their "reinvention" by Samuel S. McClure, Frank Munsey, and Cyrus Curtis in the early 1890s. Magazines were to be a medium for the middle class, who were (not coincidentally) also the target for consumer goods advertisers (Peterson, 1981). These magazine entrepreneurs found that by refocusing magazine content on stories popular with the middle class and selling subscriptions at a price below the cost of producing and distributing a subscription, the size of the magazine could be dramatically increased, making magazines a desirable advertising medium. This pattern was quickly repeated in newspapers; when the broadcast media came along, they took this to its extreme—giving away their content to anyone with the equipment to receive the signal. The mass media became an "adjunct of the marketing system." The subscription charge for print media and ultimately for cable and pay-TV channels "became essentially a fee to qualify the reader (or viewer) for the advertiser's interest" (Peterson, 1981, p. 20).

Modern multinational manufacturers and advertising agencies therefore have considerable power to dictate favorable public messages. Various scholars have shown how advertising support serves to reduce, for example, critical reporting on business (Davis, 2002). This control can be explicit in the form of direct "censorship," but more often it is expressed systemically; the advertising and media institutions are dependent on each other and adapt accordingly. Media research has often focused, however, on the more explicit side of this relationship. In the news media, where the dividing line between the business and editorial sides was supposed to protect professional judgment from undue influence, advertisers were never afraid to "use their financial muscle to protest what they perceive as unfair treatment" (Jamieson & Campbell, 1983, p. 97).

Advertising and Big Tobacco

At one time, the tobacco companies provided one of the richest sources of media advertising in the USA and provided historical textbook cases of media influence. In 1957, *Reader's Digest* published a landmark article about the health effects of smoking; ads were subsequently withdrawn by the American Tobacco Company (Weis & Burke, 1986). In 1959, the powerful industry lobby group, the Tobacco Institute, threatened to withdraw ads from publications that advertised a competing product, "tobaccoless smoke." The Institute also "convinced the New York Transit System not to place rail commuter ads promoting an upcoming story on lung cancer in *Reader's Digest*" (Weis & Burke, 1986, p. 60). Bagdikian reported that in 1988 Saatchi and Saatchi—"the world's biggest advertising conglomerate"—bought a small agency servicing an antismoking campaign for the Minnesota Department of Health. To avoid angering the Brown & Williamson Tobacco Company, which was spending $35 million with Saatchi for the Kool cigarette campaign, Saatchi ordered its new acquisition to drop the Minnesota account before Brown & Williamson dropped Saatchi. There was good reason for such fear. Only three months earlier, R.J. Reynolds Tobacco, one of the world's largest advertisers, had dropped Saatchi because "it had created a Northwest Airlines television commercial showing passengers applauding the airline's No Smoking policy" (Bagdikian, 1989, pp. 819–20).

Kessler (1989) investigated the editorial and advertising content of six major women's magazines (e.g., *Cosmopolitan* and *Good Housekeeping*) to see whether the presence or absence of tobacco advertising was related to the amount of editorial content about the health hazards of smoking—"the number one cancer killer of women" (p. 319). Although women's health was a major topic in the magazines, there was almost no editorial content about any health hazards of smoking, even in *Good Housekeeping*, which did not accept tobacco advertising. The *GH* health editor told Kessler that plans to do a major story on the health hazards of smoking had been "cut down time and time again by people who make the big decisions," because the link between lung cancer and smoking is "not very appealing" and "too controversial" (1989, p. 322). As Kessler pointed out, even though *GH* can't lose tobacco advertising income, it might lose advertising revenue from non-tobacco subsidiaries of the tobacco conglomerates. Even movies were affected, with stories required to depict smoking favorably in exchange for helping to underwrite production costs (Weis & Burke, 1986).

Early Network Television Advertising

Network television was totally dependent in the early days on advertising revenues, and advertisers didn't hesitate to give feedback to the young networks. In the 1950s, according to Gitlin's history,

> advertisers and their agencies . . . regularly read scripts a day or two in advance of shooting . . . Sponsors who bought whole shows, or major portions, didn't shrink from direct censorship . . . At the behest of an ad agency for a gas company sponsor, CBS took out half a dozen instances of the word "gas" referring to gas chambers in a "Playhouse 90" drama on the Nuremberg trials. After the quiz show scandals of 1958, CBS President Frank Stanton "set down an explicit rule: Advertisers would no longer be permitted to read scripts in advance and intervene if they thought their corporate images at risk. Instead, they would be permitted to screen the filmed episodes, and, if they wanted to beg off a particular one, the network would excuse them."
>
> (Gitlin, 1985, pp. 255–6)

As television grew in commercial success and desirability as an advertising platform, key clients were no longer able to wield the kind of veto power they did in the earlier years. From time to time, however, scandal would render news organizations more vulnerable to attack. General Motors, for example, said in 1992 that it would pull advertising from all NBC News programs (although not from entertainment or sports programs) as the result of a *Dateline NBC* segment, "Waiting to Explode," the segment showing how certain General Motors (GM) trucks could catch fire if hit by another vehicle. To film a sequence in which the truck was hit, NBC hired an outside contractor, who rigged the truck with an explosive device so that it would catch fire more easily during the filming. GM dropped a lawsuit against NBC in exchange for a 3¼-minute apology on a *Dateline* show and an agreement that NBC would pay General Motors nearly $2 million ("GM suspends ads on NBC's news programs," 1993, p. 3a). Although this kind of high-visibility concession forced by advertisers is rare, the media do respond to advertisers in the aggregate, to their perceptions of what advertisers will tolerate. Audience tracking methods, especially for online media, have become more sophisticated, making it easier to determine precisely who is watching and reading.

Advertiser-Created Programming

Over the years, the effects of commercial support on media content have become ingrained. They were effectively satirized by documentary filmmaker Morgan Spurlock, in his 2011 production *The Greatest Movie Ever Sold*, about the process of film advertising and marketing. In the movie industry, product placements have become an expected and important source of production support, in which the sponsor pays to have its product featured in the movie. BMW, for example, paid handsomely to have its cars featured in the James Bond series of films as a way of accentuating the kind of sophisticated, high-tech, and upscale image it hopes to associate with its products. The cars are expected to perform well and look good in the film, so presumably the scriptwriter would be constrained in the story from showing the car breaking down or being criticized by the driver. Spurlock turns this creative constraint on its head in his film, making the entire production about his pursuing a multitude of sponsors for his production: He agreed to sign "non-disparagement" contracts while retaining final-script approval. POM Wonderful, a pomegranate product company, agreed to pay $1 million to have the film itself called *POM Wonderful Presents: The Greatest Movie Ever Sold*. Thus, the seeking of the product placements and the related negotiations with sponsors about the context of their product appearances becomes the content of the movie itself. Through that inversion, Spurlock raised the important cautionary question of how much of producers' creativity is affected by these relationships (also an organizational issue we return to in the next chapter).

The Traditional Newspaper "Firewall"

The impact of advertising on newspapers has been a particular concern for research. Newspapers represent a mature institutional presence in the media landscape with supposedly clear demarcation lines within the organization and a robust professional culture intended to minimize commercial intrusion into professional judgment. Violations of this protection have been of great interest. With daily newspapers pressure often came from their major advertisers, particularly real-estate and auto dealers. In a survey of 41 newspapers' real-estate news staff, for example, more than three-quarters of editors said that advertisers had threatened to pull ads in response to unfavorable coverage. More than one-third said that ads had actually been pulled (Williams, 1992, p. 167). The corporatization of the newsroom and ongoing economic stress have made business considerations even more acute, causing news companies to adopt creative strategies in adapting to advertisers.

American newspapers early on had structured a firewall between the business and editorial departments, bridged by the publisher, but that wall was dramatically breached in a high-profile case of the *Los Angeles Times* and its CEO hired in 1995, Mark Willes. His selection had not come from journalism and was soundly decried by traditionalists such as Max Frankel (2000), former editor of the *New York Times*, who recounted the story.

The tendency of media companies to confuse their editorial and sales missions was already widely apparent when Willes was recruited from the packaged-food business five years ago to reverse the economic fortunes of the *Los Angeles Times*. But he chose to make himself the embodiment of the trend, loudly scoffing at the idea that reporters and editors needed to be insulated from commercial plans and pressures. He vowed to "use a bazooka, if necessary" to blow up the wall that most good newspapers tried to maintain between their news and business departments. To the dismay of journalists everywhere, Willes ordered a paperwide collaboration in the design of corporate strategies. He wanted not just his top editors and executives to plan together but also their staffs many levels down. He pushed different news desks and sections to develop their own business plans. He asked reporters and editors to propose ideas for selling more papers and ads, and he expected the business staffs to shower the newsroom with moneymaking ideas for coverage.

(Frankel, 2000)

Proving his critics correct, it was revealed in 1999 that the *Times* had agreed to share profits from a special magazine it would publish on the Staples sports arena in the city with the management of that arena. The deal raised serious questions about how impartial the coverage in the magazine would be given the financial conflicts of interest, leading to a lengthy internal investigation by the paper's media writer, David Shaw (1999):

That arrangement constituted a conflict of interest and violation of the journalistic principle of editorial independence so flagrant that more than 300 *Times* reporters and editors had signed a petition demanding that their publisher, Kathryn Downing, apologize and undertake "a thorough review of all other financial relationships that may compromise" *The Times*'s editorial heritage.

(Shaw 1999)

Since then, of course, newspaper circulation and revenue at the *Times* and elsewhere have continued their decline, putting pressure on news organizations to find new revenue through creative relationships with advertisers.

Public Relations

The public relations sector has grown rapidly, especially in the corporate and governmental realm where it plays a major role in managing the media. The term *public relations* encompasses an enormous range of activities, from "the simple mailing of press releases plugging orchestras and activist groups to giant campaigns that generate ink and air time for celebrities, products, and political positions" (Bleifuss, 1994, p. 72). Now, of course, public relations experts help manage the entire range of media platforms, including Twitter, Facebook, and search engine optimization strategies. How directly influential are public relations campaigns in affecting media coverage? The evidence is mixed. In her study of government public information officers (PIOs) in Louisiana, Turk (1986) found that not only was half the PIO-provided information used by daily newspapers, but the newspapers also gave issues the same emphasis that the PIOs did. On the other hand, she also found that of all stories about the state agencies being studied, fewer than half included PIO-provided information. Whereas Albritton and Manheim (1983) found that a public relations campaign improved Rhodesia's image in the US press, Stocking (1985) claimed that public relations activities have no effect on media content beyond the intrinsic news value of the organizations being promoted. Interest groups also conduct public relations campaigns that target journalists and use the media to focus public attention. Not every organization can afford to buy advertising, however; but getting coverage in the media can be an especially cost-effective method of reaching the public for resource-poor interest groups.

The effects of public relations have not been vigorously pursued by empirical, non-proprietary research, perhaps because its influence as a growing institution sector has been taken for granted. We can assume significant systemic impact given, like advertising, the vast resources devoted to public relations, with information management employment growing far more rapidly than journalists (especially in recent years). Pinpointing specific success stories empirically is more difficult. Zoch and Molleda (2006) are among those advocating a more theoretical approach to the influence of public relations, tracking its information subsidies and agenda building efforts. Cross-national research has shown that countries receiving public relations efforts improve their image in the US media (Zhang & Cameron, 2003). More recently, Kiousis and Wu (2008) observe that those countries retaining US public relations counsel were able to improve the tone of their US news coverage. Berger (2001) found success for the Business Roundtable, a major lobbying association for large American firms, in its efforts to put its issues on the public agenda.

From a critical perspective, public relations reinforces the power of elites as primary definers of social reality. Public relations professionals outnumber journalists in the USA and UK, helping to form interlocking, often cozy networks among government, media, and law enforcement. When Rupert Murdoch's tabloid London editors were charged with hacking into phone voicemails for story details, the high-profile scandal revealed the prominent public relations operatives for both the government and police who had once worked for Murdoch. In an ethnographic approach, Davis (2007) examined the networks of contact among elites and journalists in Britain—where these relationships are tighter and more geographically focused—to discover how media management efforts are directed beyond just shaping public opinion to helping manage inter-elite conflict. Instead of dispersing power among elites, he argues that this pattern of media management "leads to public exclusion as the parameters for debate and negotiation become narrower" (Davis, 2007, p. 55). Journalists, "captured" by their "policy communities," join with corporate and governmental actors within this micro-sphere to form "elite discourse networks" or "iron triangles." Using interviews and ethnography, Davis takes an institutional focus to identify sites of political, corporate, and military power and their corresponding communication and discourse environments. This approach helps "describe the formation of elite, self-referencing networks, made up of journalists/ editors, political elites, professional communication staff and other interest group representatives" (Davis, 2007, p. 73), with the ironic result in his insight on public relations that the public "is either simply imagined or excluded from consideration altogether" (p. 73).

State Control of Media

There is little doubt that governments of all countries exert control over the media. Perhaps the most visible form of social institutional influence is direct regulation and other constraints placed on media by the state. This influence can be expressed not only through violence and coercion but also through more subtle and less visible means. In countries where the media are largely privately owned, controls are exerted through laws, regulations, licenses, and taxes. Where they are primarily government owned, control is exerted through media financing (Janus, 1984). Press freedom is located not only within the US constitutional context but internationally within the Universal Declaration of Human Rights, Article 19, which states: "Everyone has the right to freedom of opinion and expression; this right includes freedom to hold opinions without interference and to seek, receive, and impart information and ideas through any media regardless of frontiers."

Based on that premise, the Freedom House organization conducts a regular ranking of press freedom around the world, considering each country either "free," "partly free," or "not free," based on the legal, political, and economic environment. A three-color world map of press freedom using the survey is prominently displayed and regularly updated at the Newseum in Washington, DC. Although many discussions of press freedom begin with the legal framework's restrictions of guarantees and editorial independence from political power, the Freedom House index does recognize also that the concentration of media ownership and transparency of economic subsidies to media has an effect on press freedom. Its 2010 survey showed that according to these criteria, only 15 percent of the world's population lived in countries with press freedom, 42 percent were in partly free countries, and 43 percent in not free countries. The countries themselves were evenly distributed across these three categories, signifying an overall decline in press freedom since 2005. The USA, although designated free, is ranked well below the top, with the Scandinavian countries scoring highest.

The global extension of press freedom issues has important implications for the kind of media environment required. When all speech may effectively be global, it is difficult for one country to impose censorship on speech originating elsewhere. Recognizing that information is no respecter of national boundaries, Bollinger (2011) has argued that Article 19 should become the 1st Amendment of the *global public forum*. He argues that the USA needs to make significant investment in global news reporting, perhaps through existing public broadcasting such as National Public

Radio and the Public Broadcasting System, to create a credible institutional force for global newsgathering on the order of the British Broadcasting Corporation.

The effects of the US government do not necessarily operate through the enforcement of specific policy. They arise out of a broader institutional adaptation to US policy. Chang (1989), for example, found in his study of US policy and coverage of China in the *New York Times* and *Washington Post* between 1950 and 1984 that "the more the government favored US–China relations, the more the newspapers preferred better relations between the two countries" (p. 504). His analysis suggested that newspaper coverage changed in response to government policy shifts.

Debate over the public's right to know versus the government's need to maintain national security is heightened during wartime. During the Persian Gulf War of 1991 the US military effectively controlled information about the war to the greatest extent up until that time, leaving the world's news media to use pool footage in most cases. The public knew what the Pentagon wanted it to know (Lee & Devitt, 1991). Journalists had to sign agreements that they would obey press restrictions before they received visas for Saudi Arabia, and all photographs, video, and battlefield dispatches had to be cleared by military censors. Reporters were allowed only to travel in predesignated "pools" with US military escorts always at their side. Those who attempted to cover the war independently were sometimes detained and threatened by US soldiers. Twenty years later the Pentagon had developed its press relations to a high degree of sophistication, inviting select reporters to be "embedded" with military units when the USA invaded Iraq in 2003. Analyzing the reporting of those embedded journalists compared to "independents" showed that the embeds were more likely to favor in their reporting a "liberation" than an "invasion" frame (Sivek, 2004).

The intersection of the military–industrial media complex can be seen in the tendency of television networks to use retired military officers as sources and on-air commentators. An extensive report published by the *New York Times* illustrated this practice with a retired general turned lobbyist, turned favored media consultant for NBC News and talking head: General Barry McCaffrey. Although arguing he was objective given his criticism of the execution of policy in Iraq, the general nevertheless advocated views in line with his business interests (Barstow, 2008). These sources were doubly compromised, earning money from defense contractors and privately briefed by the Pentagon in an effort to shape coverage, leading the *Times* to conclude that "[r]ecords and interviews show how the Bush administration has used its control over access and information in an effort to transform the analysts into a kind of media Trojan horse—an instrument intended to shape terrorism coverage from inside the major TV and radio networks" (Barstow, 2008).

The Media Marketplace

Compared to other advanced democracies, the USA has pursued a more purely market-based commercial media system in which each medium must compete with the others for audience and advertiser attention. Although there has been much concern in recent years about its future commercial viability, the news business in much of the world, including China and Brazil, is more robust. Concerns loom larger in the USA where much of the prognosticating and research has been taking place. There is a tendency to romanticize the press performance of the past, but a healthy financial picture did not guarantee distinguished journalism. Indeed, observers have called it a fortuitous historical intersection that professionalism intersected with profitability for so many years, allowing advertising profits to provide a necessary (if not sufficient) condition for accountability journalism and contribution to democracy. Now, given the trends in press performance, McChesney and Nichols (2010) argue that the market alone has not proven adequate to support the kind of journalism required by local communities. Noting that the USA provides far less of that kind of support for its media than other countries, they recommend that greater subsidies will be needed to produce the kind of journalism needed for democratic functioning.

This competitive environment has shifted dramatically in the past 20 years. For newspapers, of course, competition with other papers was not uncommon, but now even some large communities may be without a newspaper altogether. Hundreds of cable and satellite television channels and content on internet platforms mean the competition has shifted from local to global platforms. The animating principle in media market studies has been diversity—the variety in the content that is offered the audience—because competition is assumed to create a "marketplace of ideas" that facilitates the free discussion of important issues. When one of the two or more newspapers in a city goes out of business, is the audience left with poorer coverage of the diverse concerns in the community? A number of studies have shown little or no support for such a hypothesis. Entman (1985) compared the content of 91 newspapers from communities with two competing newspapers, two papers with a single owner, or only one newspaper. He found little evidence to suggest that competition encourages diversity. In another study of four Canadian newspapers, Mc-Combs (1988) found that the surviving newspaper may actually improve its content following the death of its competitor. In a similar study in Cleveland, McCombs (1987) found only random differences between the surviving *Plain Dealer*'s content before and after the *Press* folded. But this conclusion has been harder to support as the resources for conducting local journalism have been hollowed out overall. These kinds of studies are less feasible today given the shifting terrain; it is difficult to find comparable news organizations in the same community to compare.

The struggle for institutional influence among media, state, and commercial sectors raises the question globally concerning the greater threat, whether it comes from government or concentrated media conglomerate power. In cases such as Rupert Murdoch's news complex in the UK with its close ties to government, and Italy's leader Silvio Berlusconi with his media empire, the overlap between government and media power has grown greater, making it harder to keep them analytically distinct. In any case, the economics of the media marketplace are an ongoing concern for research.

Market Characteristics

At a macro level we can see that emerging media compete with each other for a slice of the consumer pie. This kind of economic analysis can provide a sense of how new media are affecting old ones. McCombs (1972) carried market influence beyond the community level to the social system as a whole, arguing in his *constancy hypothesis* that the amount of economic support available in the USA is a major constraint on the growth of the mass media. In other words, "the media will grow and expand at a rate dictated by the general economy" (McCombs, 1972, pp. 5–6). McCombs shows that over time spending in new media comes at the expense of the old, such that the proportion devoted to all media remains the same. Son and McCombs (1993), in their follow-up study, however, found that consumers appeared to be paying more for both traditional and new media, and Dupagne (1997) further argued that there is no theoretical basis for relative constancy. Indeed, it's becoming more diffi-cult to argue that the newer media are direct functional equivalents of the old. The smartphone, for example, not only acts as a phone and displays news but allows the user to plug into social networks. Which previous medium has it displaced? In-deed, rather than displacing, it has enabled the performing of new and overlapping functions.

Media Policy

American ideology historically feared having any state involvement with media, which raised the specter of propaganda under authoritarian control. Policy debates about the media industry often proceed with the sense that a press independent of government involvement is a pre-ordained natural state for the USA. Particu-larly with the early days of broadcasting, however, historical accounts have shown that turning the radio spectrum, a public resource, over to commercial interests was a policy decision strongly influenced by business lobbying (McChesney, 1993). With the collapse of the traditional US newspaper industry, there has been much discussion about new business models other than the advertising-supported press. In essence, the news has become decoupled from its traditional base of advertising support. Will the traditional market-based news media, on which the USA has relied more than other democracies, be sufficiently robust to support community health and democracy? Nonprofit online news publications have begun, most visibly *Pro-Publica*, and university programs in journalism are also contributing reporting to professional outlets. Others have advocated more vigorous government investment in newsgathering as a critical component, although it runs counter to the tradi-tional concerns that state involvement may threaten journalistic independence. As Benson and Powers (2011) point out, "Government has always and will always influence how our media system functions, from the early newspaper postal subsi-dies to handing out broadcast licenses and subsidizing broadband deployment. The question is not if government should be involved, but how" (p. 1).

In their review of 14 nations' experience with public broadcasting, the authors point out a number of ways that the undue influence of the state may be managed:

- First, in several countries, funding is established for multiyear periods, thus lessening the capacity of the government to directly link funding to either approval or disapproval of programming.

- Second, public media seem to be strongest when citizens feel that media are responsive to them rather than to politicians or advertisers (i.e. when they are truly "public"). Funding structures and oversight organizations that create a direct link between public media and their audiences foster citizen engagement, involvement and accountability.

- Third, the legal and administrative charters establishing public broadcasters work to assure that public funds are spent in the public interest—providing diverse, high-quality news and other content. At the same time, these charters and related media laws restrict the capacity of governments to exert influence over content in a partisan direction.

- Fourth, public agencies, administrative boards, and/or trusts of one type or another exist in all countries to serve as a buffer between the broadcasters and the government in power. The independence of such agencies, boards, and trusts is bolstered through a variety of means and by creating an "arms-length" institutional relationship between the public broadcaster and partisan political interference or meddling.

(Benson and Powers 2011, p. 4)

Benson and Powers argue that publicly subsidized media produce better, more diverse public affairs programming that is more critical of government than their commercial counterparts. Western Europe has a tradition of mixed public and private media, providing an opportunity to test their performance. Comparing England, France, and Germany, Esser (2008) shows that public media covered elections more extensively than commercial channels. Similarly, public media provide more extensive public affairs content and international news (leading to important enhancements in citizen knowledge) (Curran et al., 2009). Benson (2010) himself has done extensive cross-national work, showing that publicly supported newspapers provide better coverage—more critical of government, more depth, and with greater diversity of perspective.

Tracking Institutional Relationships

Institutional relationships can be tracked at the system level in the pattern of interconnections, a relatively uncommon type of media research. Studies like this, influenced by C. Wright Mills (1956) and the community power tradition in sociology, have shown how strongly US media are linked to the centers of society.

In an often-cited study by Dreier (1983), for example, directors of the 24 largest newspaper-owning companies in the USA shared a "web of affiliations" with those in the US power structure. Such institutional affiliations are accomplished through membership in business and trade associations, activities in nonprofit groups and social clubs, and corporate directorships. Dreier found that large and influential newspapers, such as the *New York Times*, *Washington Post*, *Wall Street Journal*, and *Los Angeles Times*, were the most heavily interlocked with other elite institutions, and therefore, he argued, have a common ideology with other large corporations.

This ideology—*corporate liberalism*—is used by those in the capitalist power structure to "forestall changes from below and stabilize the long-term foundations of capitalism by implementing strategic reforms to co-opt dissent" (Dreier, 1983, p. 447). Large corporation leaders, with a greater interest in the welfare of the system as a whole, differ from those in small and medium-sized companies, who by contrast have a greater parochial outlook and concern with a single company's short-term interests. The corporate ideological outlook (at the time) supported unions, social welfare, foreign aid, and government regulations; and news organizations owned by such corporations tended to reflect a more liberal ideology in their content. Some, such as the *Chicago Tribune* and *Los Angeles Times*, had changed from extreme conservatism to a liberal outlook (Dreier, 1983, p. 447).

In his study of 50 publicly held media corporations, Han (1988) found that media corporations' boards of directors were interlocked with boards of directors from non-media corporations: that is, the boards of directors shared members. Most of the 300 directors of the 25 largest newspapers also served as directors of leading businesses, banks, and law firms (Dreier & Weinberg, 1979). Akhavan-Majid's (1991) study of leading newspapers and television stations in Japan similarly showed many interlocking directorships and overlapping social club memberships. Journalists and industrial leaders there tended to have similar educational backgrounds and belonged to the same professional clubs.

Media corporations are most often interlocked with financial institutions, and this may have serious consequences for media corporations that are bought out with the cooperation of financial institutions. By varying their stock ownership, financial institutions can control the basic decisions in media corporations: "Interlocking directorate ties with major advertisers, financial houses, law firms, competing firms, and other elite social institutions thus can raise a question of the autonomy of media firms" (Han, 1988, p. 182). Large media organizations are dependent on resources controlled by these elite social institutions, rendering media more vulnerable to the control of giant corporations: "The greater the dependency of a media firm on the elite institutions, the greater the chance for their control over mass media" (Han, 1988, p. 183). In a more recent study, An and Jin (2004) examined the boards of directors of 13 publicly traded newspaper companies from a resource-dependency perspective, viewing the selection of outside directors as co-opting environmental uncertainty, facilitating inter-firm collusion, and monitoring potential threats. Over time, as predicted, greater financial independence (news organization strength) led to less reliance on interlocks with financial institutions and leading advertisers.

In Dreier's (1983) analysis it was precisely the need of these media organizations, acting on behalf of the deeper societal interests, to protect the best long-term interests of the US government (not acting on momentary partisan motives), explaining their actions in challenging the government with reporting on, for example, the Pentagon Papers and Watergate. It was necessary to the overall national interest. Big insurance companies once played such a role, as the most central entities in the network of corporate structure. They were central because they necessarily took the decades-long view of the best core interests of the capitalist system. The failure of insurance giant American International Group in 2008 suggests that something has changed. Rising debt (and foreign borrowing) brought on by politically popular tax cuts coupled with stable social costs, along with the impersonal drive for larger and larger profits, has yielded riskier unregulated markets. The current crisis drives home the need for someone to help mind the core preservation role of protecting the system from itself. We can only speculate that the weakened legitimacy of key elite media institutions such as the *Times* and *Post* has made it more difficult to reach consensus from within the inner core of the system.

SUMMARY

In this chapter, we have reviewed a wide variety of influences on media content that operate outside of the media organization. Media rely on a variety of sources for content, ranging from government officials to interest groups, who can be shown to exert influence. Advertising and public relations represent massive investment in directing the shape of media discourse and institutional advantage, and their influence can be isolated and measured in specific instances. Government policy and control exert direct and obvious effects on media, both restrictive in the case of censorship and enabling in the case of the media subsidies more common in other advanced democracies. The shifting commercial marketplace for media is the host environment and a critical influence, particularly for the rapidly changing news business, leading to a heightened concern over finding new business models that will ensure media quality. But our understanding of this level goes beyond the relative profitability of one sector of the economy.

Given the eclectic list of factors associated with this level of analysis, the question could easily be asked: What influence does it not contain? We can isolate specific institutional agents, such as advertisers, officials, and sources, but we must analyze their influence more broadly flowing from larger power dynamics. In considering these influences, we remember that media are institutions and part of a web of institutional relationships. This structure is most clearly exemplified in the research on media company boards of directors that shows their web of interlocking connections with other major firms. The social institutional level helps us think more clearly about the way media practices are situated in relation to other centers of social power. We need to understand how those relationships have developed historically and how institutions like journalism are shifting into new forms of equilibrium. The three case studies presented earlier—of Knight's innovation challenge, WikiLeaks, and the Colorado journalism school—are another window on this dynamic. We see individual behavior and organizational response within the context of larger pressures on the journalistic field leading to the large macro-level adaptations.

Unit vs. Level of Analysis

Some studies guided by this level of the hierarchy don't necessarily have a specifically institutional focus as such. West (2011), for example, locates the impact of television news consultants at the extra-media level. Since the days of the Eyewitness News model, consultants have made recommendations tending to exert a homogenizing effect on broadcast news, and they technically can be placed outside the media organization's boundaries. Consultants report a picture of the audience in terms of market research, but television news journalists, more so than managers with a more direct business stake, caution against it determining content. Those with a greater business interest in local station success support the advice of consultants, while journalists are more critical (Allen, 2007). Thus, what is directly measured here is how individual professionals *perceive* influences exerted on them from outside the organization. From a broader perspective, however, the institutional level alerts us in such studies to consider how consultants serve to respond to and rationalize market pressures already in place. In that respect, consultants are the embodiment of the drives for efficiency and profitability that help reduce "uncertainties."

The institutional fields have been dramatically altered by technology. Previously we had regarded technology as an influence from outside media, and undoubtedly the digitization of communication has been transformative since the Hierarchy of Influences was introduced. But it is perhaps more appropriate to regard technology as changing the resources and conditions to which institutions must adapt, it is the changing atmosphere in which media reside and makes possible new "assemblages" that are available for study. One of the most sweeping technology-led changes is toward media "convergence." Klinenberg (2005), in his local news ethnography, looks at the journalistic field as shaped by changing technology and corporate integration, observing the now familiar demands on journalists to be flexible and fast. This pressure toward ever-greater efficiency takes place within the overall intrusion of marketing principles, so technology works to facilitate and accentuate larger power dynamics. As Klinenberg notes, "The political economy, cultural conventions, and regulatory restrictions governing the news industry will play powerful roles in determining how advanced communications technologies enter the matrix of journalistic production, just as they did before the digital age" (2005, p. 62).

Institutions and Networks

Based on these technological changes, some media futurists are fond of proclaiming that networks and citizens have rendered institutions obsolete, that vertical hierarchy has given way to horizontal network, and that somehow information-creation and journalism will be carried out for free. But institutions aren't dead yet, and it's difficult to see how citizens can contribute to media content without the institutional work on which they depend (for the "future of news" debate, see Starkman, 2011). When the Knight Foundation partnered with Mozilla to create a news–technology partnership, their goal was to encourage journalists, programmers, and developers to create innovative news ideas—working to move the journalistic and computer software fields closer together in the "open source" ethic, making information accessible, verifiable, and sharable. As Usher and Lewis (n.d.) point out in the Nieman Journalism Lab Blog: "Open source requires some form of leadership. Either you have someone at the top making all the decisions, or you have some distributed hierarchy." They echo the words of a newspaper editor in adding the caveat: "Someone's gotta be in control here."

It's true that institutions are becoming more porous, with new ecosystems for networked news that knit them together in different ways, so it's important not to compartmentalize these institutional actors too rigidly. Research will be guided by methods that are sensitive to this new reality. Latour's actor-network theory, for example, advocates "following the actors" without worrying so much about membership in discrete institutional containers (reviewed in Turner, 2005). Howard (2002), for example, introduces a network ethnography methodology to track members of a more distributed community of practice, an e-politics community that "extends from the major political parties to activist networks, telecommunications and computing professionals, and journalists" (p. 562). As the case examples show, the most interesting phenomena lie in how the boundaries between institutions are shifting, how they are recombining into new and complicated interrelated forms—with the gatekeeping process and emergent news values embedded in these networks. We next turn to the specific media organizations that constitute the media institution and consider how their internal structure and workings exert a particular level of influence.

NOTES

1 See www.onthemedia.org/2011/sep/09/complaisant-media-after-911/transcript. (Accessed April 28, 2013.)
2 See http://archive.mrc.org/about/aboutwelcome.asp.
3 See FAIR website, http://fair.org/about-fair.
4 Adbusters website, http://www.adbusters.org.
5 Media Matters website, http://mediamatters.org/about.
6 Free Press website, www.freepress.net.

CHAPTER 6

Organizations

In this chapter we turn from larger institutional issues to those influences tied more directly to specific media organizations. When we think about the "media," it is often in terms of the "organized" work carried out by identifiable and prominent firms, whether news or entertainment. We want to understand the questions beyond the "trans-organizational" media institution as a whole to those pertaining to the organizational level of analysis, introduce a conceptual model for thinking about organizations, and review some of the studies tackling organizational impact on media content. As with so many other areas, technology has changed the nature of media organizations, restructuring existing ones and making possible new configurations, so we first consider those changes before proceeding to what researchers have found.

An *organization* is a collective of individuals and/or groups whose members work toward common goals, giving the organization an identity. An organization distinguishes itself from others based on its ownership, goals, actions, rules, and membership, establishing boundaries to the extent that we can distinguish organizational members from outsiders and that we can see its members performing specialized functions in roles that are usually standard to the organization and other organizations with which it affiliates. Some members, called boundary spanners, are directed to interact with nonmembers and other organizations (Jemsion, 2007; Marchington & Vincent, 2004). Organizations are goal directed, often composed of interdependent parts that are bureaucratically structured. They also compete with other organizations for resources, which in the case of media organizations are primarily audiences and advertising revenue (Turow, 1984, 1997).

A media organization creates, modifies, produces, and distributes content to many receivers. Thus we can look at influences on content from variables such as the ownership of the organization, policies, goals, actions, rules, membership, interactions with other organizations, bureaucratic structure, economic viability, and its stability. If we use these as benchmarks, we must conclude that the characteristics of many media organizations have changed over the past two decades. Although these changes in many cases have taken place over an even longer period of time, sometimes crossing the century mark, it is convenient to think of media organizations of the 21st century as fundamentally different from those of the previous century.

In the 20th century, the US mass media industry experienced many technological changes. Each technological shift left its mark on content, often because new media organizations were created, distributing new and different content to the audience. Many established media not only survived technological change, but also flourished as a result: Newspapers survived the invention of radio, and radio survived the invention of television, as did magazines, film, and music. For example, a small number of radio networks and large-circulation magazines became thousands of local radio stations and smaller-circulation magazines that were targeted at specific audiences. A small number of broadcast network organizations became a large number of cable network organizations. The film production and distribution system expanded with the invention of digital media (such as VHS tapes and DVDs, both now largely replaced by next-generation technologies).

The mass media industry was organized along familiar lines, such as newspaper companies, broadcast television and radio networks and affiliates, magazine and book publishers, music producers, film production companies, video game producers, as well as affiliated organizations that carried out advertising and public relations. Media distribution organizations included book and music stores, movie theaters, as well as theaters that present opera, ballet, and music of many genres.

Most media content made its way to the audience from an organization with a brick-and-mortar address in the physical world. Newspaper companies often delivered daily or weekly newspapers to the home. Television and radio organizations were allocated specific frequencies in the radio spectrum and used these to broadcast programming for reception on home television and radio equipment. Later television programs and films were delivered on digital media, either purchased or rented. Cable television organizations and their satellite equivalents created and distributed the bulk of television shows and became alternative media for the creation and distribution of content. In other cases (such as to see a film or buy a book), the audience went to a content distribution site (such as a theater or bookstore) to receive mass media content. At the close of the 20th century, the invention and application of internet technology and software began the transformation of content creation, production, and distribution.

The diffusion of media content over the Internet has changed both media organizations and their content. The Internet communication platform carries information developed by many types of organizations, including the mass media, social media, and those that offer other products and services. Some media exist in both the physical and virtual worlds, and others exist only in a virtual online form. Some online media organizations are familiar (newspapers and television networks) and some are newer (blogs and social media).[1] Quickly advancing technology in both computer hardware and software has made it easier for businesses to develop online media organizations and for audiences to receive their content.

Even so, the movement of media content from familiar platforms, such as paper and cable, to the Internet platform was not an easy one for media organizations. The importance of their economic goals—to make a profit—pushed them toward innovation, even in the face of strong uncertainty about advertising support. Many media organizations have revised their business models to include an online presence (Bagdikian, 2004, p. 145), because of declining or stagnant revenue: Newspapers are struggling and television networks, although still the audience's top news source, are facing an uncertain profit stream. Both types of media organizations realize the need to keep up with technological innovations and to bring in more readers, viewers, and listeners.

The incorporation of online divisions into existing media and the creation of new media fed the digital generation's desire for more online content (Stelter, 2009). Keeping up was expensive, because it required experiments and innovations, many of which were not successful. Advertisers were slow to migrate online, but eventually advertisers began following audiences and some online media became viable economic entities (Bagdikian, 2004).

For example, CNN is one of the most successful media companies, because it has integrated its television and internet divisions—each helps make the other better (Stelter, 2009). Showing that online media organizations could be profitable requires a reliable and valid way of measuring audience exposure to the Internet. The Nielsen organization, which had tracked audience support of traditional mass media content for decades, uses the number of people who view a web page as one measure that can be compared across websites. Nielsen reports that in 2008 CNN.com was the top news website by a significant margin: It captured an average of 1.7 billion page views a month, about half a billion more than the second most popular site MSNBC.com (Stelter, 2009, p. 2).

The movement of media content to the Internet has changed not only media organizations, but also whole industries. The music industry has undergone dramatic changes with Apple's introduction of the iTunes online store, which unbundled songs from their albums and distributes them individually at a smaller cost. Audience members download songs to their computers and to portable electronic music players, causing many brick-and-mortar music and booksellers to go out of business or to drastically cut their offerings and services. Many books no longer under copyright were electronically scanned and are made available for downloading at no cost, and online media organizations distribute books in both paper and in digital forms for e-book readers. Some radio organizations also created content for the Internet, which in the case of National Public Radio (NPR) meant teaching the staff "digital storytelling skills" (Dorroh, 2008, p. 26). In 2008 the radio network began training 450 editorial staff, using a $1.5 million grant from the Knight Foundation. NPR developed a new business model that allowed them to add visual content to what had been purely audio.

Driven by decades of declining circulations, newspapers began the migration to the Internet in the mid to late 1990s (Scott, 2005), but some found it difficult to maintain both paper and internet editions. The US stock market crash of October 2008 and the subsequent worldwide recession severely reduced newspapers' advertising revenue and led to severe staff layoffs. Some newspapers went out of business (such as the *Rocky Mountain News* from Denver, Colorado, and *The Sentinel* from Portland, Oregon) (LedeObserver, 2009), and others became smaller versions of themselves online (e.g., the *Tucson Citizen*). Major city newspapers were somewhat more secure, but some (e.g., the *Chicago Tribune* and the *Detroit Free Press*) survived by drastically cutting the size of their paper editions and expanding their online editions (Dumpala, 2009). The *New York Times* has both paper and online editions, resulting in two related organizations, one to create the paper edition and the other to create the online version.

The "New" Media Organizations

New organizations arose from emerging digital platforms. New forms of online media were invented and evolved quickly, beginning in the 1980s, and were referred to collectively as the new media, but this term is no longer appropriate, given the age of many such organizations. The blog is an online media form that can fulfill many organizational goals. Some blogs house the password-protected ruminations of individuals, while others convey the public communications of media organizations, the whole of which is the blogosphere. The growing importance of the blogosphere has changed the jobs of some communication workers, such as reporters who must now contribute to a daily blog in addition to preparing their usual news messages.

Social networking sites, such as Facebook and Twitter, invite individuals to put personal information on the Internet so it can be accessed by others. Although many individuals apparently thought that the information they put on Facebook went only to their "friends," Facebook and other sites such as MySpace sent their members' personal data to advertising companies (Steel & Vascellaro, 2010). Pandora makes personalized radio stations viewable to anyone on the Internet who knows a person's email address (Singel, 2009). Although Facebook users wrongly assumed their information was private—Facebook has since taken steps to give users more control over a complex set of privacy settings—this demonstrates the increasingly meaningless difference between mass and interpersonal communication on the Internet: Am I showing this funny photo only to my friends and family, or am I making it available for worldwide distribution? Once on the Internet, all information, including images, is vulnerable to being used by anyone. These practices allow citizens to engage in "organized" media work and also have been incorporated into the work of established media organizations.

The most ambitious of the new online organizations is Wikipedia. This online communication organization's content is written and edited by more than 15 million people, with thousands of new articles created each day. Wikipedia has become an important research tool, whether for a quick fact or a detailed explication of a concept, but the very openness of its content results in uneven accuracy and completeness.

The information conglomerate Google owns several media organizations, such as YouTube, a leading website for posting videos, and Blogger, a service that makes it easy for people to create their own blogs. Although Google may not have initially thought of itself as a media organization, its expansions into news aggregation, photo archiving, scholarly research, and mapping street by street have made a powerful communications firm.

Media Organizations and Change

The constantly changing media landscape has resulted in several types of media organizations, all of which can deliver information about the world to audiences. Although technological changes can affect our understanding of what media content is and of the types of organizations that produce content, the media of the 20th century still have a strong presence. Although most media organizations now have internet editions, some have not changed. We can still buy news on paper, in broadsheet, tabloid, or magazine form; watch broadcast or cable television and listen to broadcast and satellite radio; buy a book printed on paper or a music album on a disk; see movies in theaters or on DVDs and Blu-Ray at home; and enjoy a season's subscription to the opera.

The development of media organizations on the internet platform not only has extended the 20th century media's core purposes, but it has also changed the way in which people interact with media content. Perhaps most importantly, receivers of online media content can also be its producers and senders. Thus the world is now described by millions more reporters, and it is created and represented by an equivalent number of authors, photo- and videographers, film producers, and musicians. Online media content is accessed on many types of home and business computers, on game consoles, on computer-ready televisions, and on handheld computers.

Because online media organizations have access to more and different tools for gathering, processing, presenting, and delivering information, the content they offer is more extensive and often quite different from the older offline organizations. Most significantly, interactive media allow the audience member to participate in the creation of content, changing people's expectations of the media, and offer new views of the world.

THE ORGANIZATION AS LEVEL OF ANALYSIS

Our decision to treat media organizations as a level of analysis between the social institutional and routines levels does not indicate that we believe the three are independent domains. To the contrary, the levels are conceptually related, but we also believe that there are sufficient unique attributes of each level to justify studying them separately. On the one hand, routine practices of communication work are often the same across producers of similar content. For example, both bloggers and film producers have their own ways of working as groups, but their respective routines are quite different. Similarly, if we look at organizations as themselves being part of a larger interaction with other social players, we expect that different types of media organizations will interact in varying ways.

Parsing the distinct influences attributable to the characteristics of media organizations is the goal of this chapter. Placing the organizational level in the middle of our Hierarchical Model allows us both to investigate influences on content that cannot be attributed to individual workers or the routine practices of their work and to recognize that media organizations are entities whose actions are not completely dependent on the way they work, or their relations with other social institutions. Considering an entire organization reveals how role perspectives change depending on the individual's position in the hierarchy. At times the different routines and requirements of media workers, though they may work in the same organization, bring them into conflict. For example, an editor may need more reporters to adequately cover a community, but the publisher may not be able to justify the added expense. Similarly, the routines of editors and reporters, who often have different agendas, must be reconciled. Editors tend to be more audience-related than reporters, who are more source related (Gans, 1979). The editor is not tied to a beat and thus can help reporters avoid being co-opted by their sources. When push comes to shove, individual workers and their routines must be subordinated to the larger organization and its goals.

This approach has much in common with the routines perspective introduced in the next chapter. Both levels stress that media content is produced in an organizational and bureaucratic setting, but the more macro organizational focus shows the points at which routines run counter to organizational logic, and it reveals internal tensions not indicated by an emphasis solely on routines or individuals. The routines of media work form the immediate context for the individual worker, whereas the organization is a more complex system with many specialized parts, each having its own routines. Any one person cannot have direct contact with them all. Specific policies issued from the top of the organization can overrule lower-level routines. Although organizational leaders are individuals, and as such have their own routines, top executives actually make and enforce policy on behalf of the organization in the service of organization level goals.

To fully understand the organizational nature of media, however, we must consider the entire structure. Ultimately all members of an organization must answer to the owners and top management, who coordinate the entire enterprise. The increasing complexity of the corporate ownership structure makes this coordination process difficult. This is especially true when media organizations are themselves owned by conglomerates, whose main mission might be selling non-media consumer products or services. Even independently owned media organizations can form important "interlocks" with other types of companies, both through stock ownership and by sharing members on their boards of directors (see Chapter 6). Thus, deciding where organizational boundaries lie in a complex network of interlocking interests can be difficult, but these broad connections have an important impact on content and must be considered.

The Characteristics of Organizations

By characteristics, we mean the organization's traits or properties. Although to some extent all media organizations are similar in that their purpose is to produce words and images for audiences to see and hear, there are many important differences among them. Organizational influences on media content can be studied both across organizations within one industry and among different industries. It is logical that organizations that produce blogs should be different from those that produce films, but such lines became blurred in the late 20th century, when many media organizations went online to supplement their usual content.

In addition—beyond the obvious technical differences—an organization that produces news on a paper platform may not have the same organizational structure as a firm that produces news for the internet platform. For example, although the paper and internet divisions of the parent company may share content, the online edition can have more content in many different formats, including interactive features that are impossible to convey on paper. The online edition can also include a searchable archive, which in the case of the *New York Times* includes a searchable archive of both paper and internet editions from 1851 to the present. How does the online organization accomplish its goals, and do differences in organizational structure result in different content?

Other characteristics of media organizations include ownership, roles, structure, profitability, platform, target audience, influence from advertisers, and market competition. Of course, to describe the characteristics of an organization is not the same as demonstrating that those characteristics significantly influence its content in a causal manner. Sometimes organizations are small and stretch the very definition of "organization" in consisting of one person who creates a blog, gathers information, posts it, and transmits it from home, perhaps after working at another job.

Other organizations, such as television networks, are large formal structures with physical and/or virtual locations and paid employees who work on assigned tasks. This range of size and formality describes the continuum of media organizations—most are in between these extremes. It may seem logical that large organizations can accomplish more than an individual, but that one person can go online to create and transmit messages to audiences anywhere in the world. Although technology has leveled the playing field, there is no doubt that an organization's staff and other resources make information gathering and distribution easier when compared to the solo practitioner.

The Disaggregation of Organizations

Sometimes the organizational collective is ephemeral, such as the people and companies that come together for the purpose of producing one film and then disperse to work in other combinations. This is particularly likely in industries that require intense levels of technology (McGarty, 2004). Disaggregation theory predicts that technologically driven industries can purchase the functions they require by contracting with third parties, "each of whom can deliver their element of the functionality in a minimal marginal cost manner" (McGarty, 2004, p. 23). The essentially virtual company coordinates the work of the third-party vendors to minimize overhead and maximize profits. Film producers create virtual organizations to accomplish specific goals, then the parts disband and reconfigure into something different, based on the characteristics of the next film. The film production organization combines actors, special effects experts, writers, film editors, directors, and other creative people, as well as distribution services. If one part of a virtual organization is not satisfactorily performing, it can generally be replaced without recreating the entire organization.

Online Media Organizations

Perhaps the most prolific of the online media forms is the blog, which is in many ways different from traditional media. With as few as one or two people gathering information and writing the content, there is little overhead—a computer, software, and internet access at minimum. For a blog to become a media organization, however, it must take on the formal features of an organization, such as having a name or title, a public address in cyberspace, one or more goals, and publication to an audience. Whether one or many people produce the content is often irrelevant, because bloggers glean their material by searching the web for information that has already been gathered, processed, and distributed by other organizations and individuals. These become the blog's shadow staff. Some bloggers are political, while others offer guides on how to build something (for example, Problogger teaches people how to blog; Engadget and Mashable are popular technology blogs).

The characteristics of media organizations are evolving in reaction to changes in the environment, both financial and technological. That many daily newspapers would go out of business in the early 21st century was considered highly unlikely in the early 1990s (Newspaperdeathwatch.com, 2010), as was the movement of news to the Internet. We can't easily predict what media organizations will look like a decade from now, but we can develop some conceptual frameworks to help track those changes.

THE ORGANIZATION AS CONCEPTUAL MODEL

To better understand the influence of organizations on content, we turn to gatekeeping theory (Shoemaker & Vos, 2009). The gatekeeper interacts with the organization, whose components must work together. The first gatekeeping study (White, 1950) looked at how and why the gatekeeper selected news items from three wire services. In this study, selection of content was a process flowing through the decisions by one person, which might lead one to think of the overall gatekeeping process as a series of linear decisions even if made by multiple individuals. A better understanding of the gatekeeping process, however, considers news item selection to be a complex series of interrelated decisions made at all five levels of the Hierarchical Model. Rather than think of news items as being selected by a series of gatekeepers, each bounded by his or her routines, in this chapter we look more broadly at the organization as gatekeeper.

A classic case study makes this point: Bailey and Lichty (1972) studied the process through which NBC News personnel came to a decision about how to use one of the most visually dramatic news stories of the Vietnam or any other war. While on camera, a South Vietnamese general calmly shot a prisoner in the head and blew his brains out. The NBC correspondent and camera crew filmed the execution, but they were uncertain about how to package the execution when they sent it up to the next level in the organization. That afternoon the crew met with the Saigon bureau chief to discuss the best way to organize the execution with other events of the day. A telex was sent to New York with information about all of their available stories.

When Robert Northshield, executive producer of the Huntley-Brinkley Report, arrived for work the next day, he read that film of the execution was available. He also realized that a photograph of the shooting had been already widely publicized by Associated Press photographer Eddie Adams, who captured the moment that the bullet hit the prisoner's head. Northshield called the Tokyo bureau, where the film had been sent for satellite transmission, and expressed his reservations about whether showing the filmed execution would be in good taste. The Tokyo producer assured him that the film was "quite remarkable," and so Northshield authorized the satellite transmission to New York so he could view it. But by the time he saw the film, there was little time left to decide.

Bailey and Lichty (1972) studied the process through which the information about the execution traveled from person to person throughout the organization, as facts were understood and new information surfaced. There were many gates in the organization, all interrelating, with the New York staff being involved in the decision-making process all along. "Reporters, editors, producers, others know which stories are most likely to be broadcast. Each 'gatekeeper' has to estimate how the program's executive producer—and even his superiors—will receive the story" (Bailey & Lichty, 1972, p. 229). Northshield cut the film at the point where the prisoner fell to the ground, rather than show the corpse with blood spurting from its head, a scene he thought was "awful rough." This was not completely a personal decision, because Northshield made decisions on behalf of NBC News. In this case the executive producer intervened more than was usual, because the film stretched the boundaries of perceived audience taste. Yet the story had strong news value, having earlier in the day been certified as culturally acceptable news when the print media published Adams' still photo. Since NBC was the only television network to have filmed it, there was competitive pressure to use the film.

This case shows how the decision process engaged the organization at its many levels. The very fact that the story was not "routine" made the upper-level network's control more visible. Many NBC News personnel worked on the story, and ultimately their selection criteria interacted, resulting in a decision and a story that was broadcast under the organizational banner. Bailey and Lichty (1972, p. 229) regard the news organization as an entity with a complex central nervous system and many interdependent parts, an approach suggesting that the organization's decisions may differ from the aggregation of its individual employees' decisions or from the simple routines of their communication work.

The Primacy of Economics

For most organizations, the primary goal is economic, to make a profit. Secondary goals built into this overarching objective include producing a quality product, serving the public, and achieving professional recognition. In unusual cases, the owner of an organization may choose to make the economic goal secondary. For example, the *Washington Times* was owned by News World Communications, an arm of the business empire controlled by Rev. Sun Myung Moon, until the corporation sold it in 2010. Even with its economic losses, it gained significant influence inside the Beltway (Sperry, 1995). Rupert Murdoch lost billions when he sought to acquire in 2007 the prestige and influence associated with the *Wall Street Journal*. Yet if professional goals are to be met, an organization obviously cannot afford to ignore the economic goal indefinitely.

The economic goals of media organizations have had a particularly important effect on content at the turn of the century (Bagdikian, 2004). The revenue of most media organizations fell from 2008 to 2010 (Pew State of the News Media, 2009), but many were in trouble far before that. In 2008 the [Chicago] Tribune Company, being $13 billion in debt as a result of Sam Zell's purchase of a sports franchise, filed for bankruptcy reorganization in December. The *Minneapolis Star-Tribune* and Philadelphia Newspapers filed for bankruptcy early in 2009. Other newspapers redefined their business plan. For example, in 2008 the Detroit Free Press (in a joint operating agreement with the Detroit News) tried to save on printing and distribution costs by cutting the paper back to several days a week (Pew State of the News Media, 2009).

When a company is privately owned, management can operate the business as they see fit, but stockholders own most larger media firms. This form of ownership intensifies the purely economic objectives of the company, since the stock market cares little for public service if it means sacrificing profitability. In publicly traded organizations, shareholders may hire and fire corporate officers as stock prices rise or fall. Managers of publicly traded companies are replaced if they fail in their responsibility to maximize profits for the stockholders. If any part of an organization lacks economic viability, then the company can be reorganized into an organization that is technically different but functionally equivalent. The alternative is redefining the organization's mission, which could lead to the deletion of some parts and/ or the addition of others. Today the Internet figures prominently in media organizations' business plans and is changing how the organizations produce content. Online news sites increasingly depend more on advertising for revenue and less on funding from their parent companies (Bagdikian, 2004, p. 145). Although television news still gets a larger audience than newspapers, there is a strong trend in both types of organizations creating and maintaining websites.

The Bottom Line

Herbert Gans and Leon Sigal, the authors of classic media sociology books, typically viewed economic considerations as "constraints" on news work, having an indirect influence on editorial decisions (Sigal, 1973; Gans, 1979). Why indirect? Because classic 20th century news organizations put up a structural barrier between employees responsible for content and those responsible for profitability. For example, Sigal found that the *New York Times* and the *Washington Post* had decentralized their budgets, giving each news desk control over its share of resources within which news decisions are made, with relatively little concern for cost-effectiveness. Sigal (1973) concluded that the need to maximize profits in news organizations did not facilitate news work. Instead it acted only as a constraint, establishing the parameters within which gatekeepers must contend for scarce resources, an interaction that is bureaucratically structured.

The professional instincts of news managers, rather than any hope of direct commercial payoff, required them to go over budget if they were to cover unexpected newsworthy events. In the late 1980s, Gordon Manning, former CBS news executive, told his staff "don't ever let me catch you missing a story because you wanted to save money" (Boyer, 1988, p. 89). This is in stark contrast to the 2010 budget-cutting memorandum to employees by ABC News President David Westin: "We will rely upon our program staff through the day and night to cover unexpected events and marshal personnel from across the division to cover scheduled events" (Krakauer, 2010), meaning that fewer people must accomplish the same amount of work.

Unlike the more buffered media economic picture studied by Gans and Sigal, media personnel are now more likely to evaluate each news item in terms of how it will affect circulation and/or ratings. Television networks compare the profitability of news programming divisions with those responsible for sports or entertainment content and make budget decisions based on the size of each division's audience. Unprofitable divisions of an organization receive lower budgets, suggesting that whether professional goals usurp economic ones is dependent on the organization bringing in enough money to survive (Sigal, 1973)—and this has become less and less feasible since the mid 20th century.

The national newspapers, newsmagazines, and television networks studied by Sigal and Gans were relatively flush with money in the late 1960s and early 1970s. From all accounts the profit motive has become increasingly more important since then, transforming economic constraints into dictates and weakening the insulation of the news department from the larger firm. We should ask to what extent these economic dictates, as they became more severe, affect the media's content.

Organizations can do two things in response to negative budget forecasts—sell more of their product to the right people, thus increasing revenue, or reduce the costs of production.

In the rush of daily journalism, most stories cannot with any precision be weighted based on their economic payoff, but all news items are evaluated for their audience appeal, which can translate into higher circulations and ratings, thus producing greater advertising revenue. As competition for audience attention grows, newspapers do more research to discover their readers' wants and needs. Most papers of at least 100,000 had research capabilities in the late 1980s (Veronis, 1989).

At profit-driven local television news stations around the USA, a look at coverage during ratings sweeps periods shows that producers are well aware of the economic payoff of violence and to a lesser extent sex, which grab attention in news just as they do in prime-time entertainment shows. Prime-time documentaries now deal less with serious issues and more with celebrity interviews. It seems that US commercial television, given its weaker and briefer tradition of public and community service, is more susceptible to economic influences than newspapers. The skyrocketing salaries paid to star news anchors and correspondents, designed to increase product appeal to the audience, have left fewer resources available for news gathering. News directors argue that these cuts do not affect news judgments, but clearly economic considerations have reduced the traditional core of local news reporting (Standish, 1989). McManus (1994) calls broadcast news "market-driven journalism," showing at the newsroom level how the desire to optimize profits dictates story selection and production standards, overriding professional values.

Expenses

The work of media organizations can be expensive. Films can cost millions of dollars to produce, betting on big box-office revenues to offset the expenses. Occasionally films with much lower budgets are successful, but these are exceptions rather than the rule. In television programming, reality television shows are less expensive to produce than dramas or situation comedies. Advertisers find that audiences like them, and so the cost-effective reality programs have become numerous.

In contrast, the 30 or 60 minutes devoted to a televised news program can be less cost-effective than entertainment programming. Although most Americans say they rely on television news, the size of news audiences is generally smaller and thus advertising supports less of the expense of producing the shows. It is expensive to gather information from local, state, regional, national, and international venues; create news messages from it; check facts; add visuals; edit and produce it; and transmit it to an audience, day by day. This is as true for print media as it is for televised news. In light of decreasing revenue, some news media constrain expenses by decreasing the size of their geographic area of interest or rely entirely on news agencies for information about the larger world. Some media organizations reduce the frequency of their publication, from daily to weekly, or from 12 months a year to 10.

In 2012 the New Orleans *Times-Picayune* reduced the number of printed newspapers to three a week. Other news organizations cut their staffs and rely on information from other sources. For example, public relations agencies count on some news media following up on their stories or even using the information in news releases verbatim. Television news programs receive video news releases from public relations agencies, produced in a news format that the organization can use as its own.

For the most part, the commercial mass media make money by delivering audiences to advertisers. To the extent that the desired target audience consumes the media products, content is then deemed attractive to advertisers. In the logic of media economics, it is less expensive—and therefore hopefully more profitable—to imitate a popular film or television show than to develop something new and untested. The fads and cycles in entertainment media content are largely a function of this. A popular police drama is followed by other police dramas, whereas a popular reality show is imitated by other versions. In films, a box-office hit often follows itself with one or more follow-up films, such as the Toy Story franchise. Media organizations also provide messages compatible with advertisements (such as putting a magazine ad for shampoo opposite a story about hair products), and advertisers pay to place their products in prominent positions in television shows and films.

Economics exerts an equally powerful effect on television (broadcast, cable, and satellite) news programs, because the length of any given news show is fixed. In a 30-minute news program, about 10 minutes is routinely devoted to advertising. If additional time is needed to cover unexpected events, such as terrorism, this reduces the amount of time left for entertainment programming. The economic influence on television news began to be seen in the lower number of discretionary news programs, such as documentaries. The small audiences for serious documentaries made them unprofitable in a period when no major network can afford to write off a block of time to low revenue-producing programming, and they have now found a home on HBO or other niche channels, such as the History Channel.

In the print media, a formula determines the number of pages that can be devoted to editorial content (news or features) as a function of the number of advertising pages sold for each day, week, or month in a publication's cycle: Fewer ad pages means less space available for news or features. As a result, the number of pages of a print publication varies across time. For example, magazines directed at young women generally have special bridal issues early in the year, because these attract not only many readers, but also companies that would not advertise otherwise. In newspapers, the Sunday edition is generally large, due to the many ads and advertising inserts from local businesses.

This economic logic is less important for online media, since the incremental cost of adding each story is far less than in the printed media. Therefore, many articles can run longer than in the paper edition. In fact, the printed media often provide links to websites to help the reader who wants more information on a topic; the printed and online editions may complement each other. Still, information has to come from somewhere, with accompanying costs, even for bloggers with few expenses. Reposted information has been gathered and produced by someone, and therefore cost someone something. When the blogger uses information from another website, the information comes with a financial subsidy from the organization that created it. News portals such as Google News and Yahoo! News have been criticized for selling advertising alongside links to news stories whose expenses were born by other organizations.

Revenue

Most cable and satellite television networks receive revenue both from advertising and from fees paid by cable and satellite companies to access their shows. Many cable providers carry local broadcast television stations as a public service. Local television stations compete head to head with each other because they offer a similar product, whether entertainment or news. For television the fixed time available for advertising makes every programming decision an economic trade-off, especially so under conditions of broadcast scarcity.

A famous news example from the early years of commercial television news makes this point: When Senator J. William Fulbright's Foreign Relations Committee was holding hearings on the Vietnam War in early 1966, Fred Friendly was the head of CBS News. CBS's morning shows drew the most viewers, and therefore preempting scheduled entertainment programs to cover the unusual hearings would be costly. Nevertheless Friendly had been given permission to do so for two full days of testimony, although not without resistance from his superiors. When Friendly asked for three more days of preemption to stay with the continuing hearings, the request was rejected. In a comment quaintly anachronistic in today's context, Friendly replied: "I find this situation untenable. You are making a news judgment but basing it on business criteria, and I can't do this job under these circumstances" (Friendly, 1967, p. 233). Epstein concluded from this incident that "even the president of a network news division cannot consistently buck the economic logic under which the network operates and survives" (1974, p. 123). The secondary goals of divisions within a media firm must ultimately be compatible with the goals of the larger organization. This calculus had been further refined by the 1980s, when the golden era of network news began to close.

When General Electric bought NBC in 1986, the chairman Jack Welsh asked the news department for a cost–benefit analysis of the news product: "How much does it cost NBC News per story covered? How many stories that are covered actually get on the air? (Auletta, 1991, p. 38).

Advertising

Newspaper content is also shaped by major advertisers affecting internal organizational relationships. The real-estate industry, for example, represents a major portion of newspaper advertising revenue in most communities. Consequently, some newspapers turn the real-estate section over to the advertising department. One Florida real-estate editor considered the newspaper as an "agent of prosperity . . . There is a much closer interaction between ads and news than [there] used to be" (Lesly, 1991, p. 22).

All media organizations have struggled to find an economically successful business model that would support content on the internet platform. As of 2008, most companies offered free content with the expectation that advertising dollars would follow. When advertising budgets were cut as a result of the recession that began that year, some organizations concluded that advertising revenue would not be enough (Perez-Pena & Arango, 2009).

Subscriptions

The business strategy for most online media has been to offer free content to draw in large audiences and hence advertisers, but some newspapers found that readers gave up paying for subscriptions to the printed newspaper because they could read the online version for free. Producing media content, whether printed or online, is expensive. Should the audience get it for free? Will advertising revenue be sufficient, or must the audience pay for access (Robertson, 2006; Perez-Peno & Arango, 2009)?

A growing number of media organizations have begun selling subscriptions to their online customers. If the customer has a print subscription, the online medium can be bundled with it at a lower cost. Subscriptions began experimentally, with varying results. In 2004 the daily newspaper in Spokane, Washington, set a subscription rate of seven dollars a month for access to the online newspaper, but the online newspaper was free to paid subscribers to the printed newspaper (Robertson, 2006). The fee slowed traffic at the online site for several months, but a year later traffic had increased by 50 percent. Besides affecting traffic, charging for online content focused their audience to primarily local people, which pleased the primarily local advertisers.

Some content is deemed more valuable to the audience and hence more likely to generate subscription income, such as pornography, financial information, and some local news. The "disaggregation" of subscription content from free content gives online media organizations a better chance to generate subscription revenue. The daily newspapers *Tulsa World* and *Albuquerque Journal* have successfully changed their websites as a subscription service, as have the weeklies *Chicago Reader*, *Detroit Metro Times*, and *The Village Voice*. Each provides a unique local service, especially in classified advertising and entertainment content (Scott, 2005, p. 98).

Other online media are also charging readers for access, including the *Wall Street Journal* and most online media owned by Rupert Murdoch, of the News Corporation. In 2010, facing huge financial losses from his media around the world, Murdoch reversed his vow to let people read the online *Wall Street Journal* for free and announced that his online newspapers would begin charging for access (Perez-Pena & Arango, 2009). A commentator from the online version of the *Independent on Sunday* wrote that charging for online news is actually good for democracy, because the fees support good journalism, with dependable content. She noted: "If you want bad information, that can be had for free online. Good journalism, on the other hand, is expensive: Journalists are trained professionals, and news gathering is an expensive business" (Smith, 2010).

Cable and satellite television services have always charged subscribers, based on the type of content subscribers want to receive, but free streaming online services such as Hulu have encouraged people to trim or eliminate their cable and satellite subscriptions. This has encouraged cable industry experimentation with other types of services. Time Warner's CEO Jeffrey L. Bewkes, for example, proposed "TV Everywhere" as a strategy to keep regular subscribers, by giving them free access to many online networks (Perez-Pena & Arango, 2009). In the summer of 2010, Hulu followed with its own premium online service HuluPlus for both new and older television series (HuluPlus, 2010). Both programs compete with Netflix's instant streaming video service for movies and television shows, and Amazon has started its own streaming video service (Amazon Video on Demand, 2010; Netflix, 2010).

Ownership

When a media organization is privately owned, it can follow the owner's interests and engage in behavior that might be considered inappropriate or risky for a corporation. When owned by a large corporation, however, the media organization might engage only in behaviors that already have been shown to be profitable, becoming more risk-adverse.

Multiple Media Ownership

Media scholars have paid particularly close attention to those corporations that own more than one media organization. Absentee owners are thought to be less inclined to adopt a vigorous editorial policy and aggressive news coverage. The greater the physical distance of the owners from the community being served, the more local community interests take a backseat to corporate and economic pressures. Bagdikian (2004) contends that when chains take over a newspaper, they typically increase ad and subscription rates, reduce serious news—which is more expensive to gather—and hire less qualified journalists.

The debate over newspaper chain ownership increased in the 20th century as the number of independently owned newspapers declined. Fewer concerns have been raised over broadcast ownership, given the restrictions on the number of stations that can be owned by one company and the weaker public service tradition of local broadcasting. Is there a meaningful organizational difference between chain and independent newspapers? This question was more important in the 1980s than now, when independent newspapers are rare. Whereas the employee of the independent newspaper is socialized to the single local organization, the chain newspaper employee must be socialized additionally (or instead) to the larger chain, an effect that transcends the local community. Thus the organizational role may take precedence over the chain employee's role as a member of the community. They form weaker community attachments due to the job mobility necessary to rise within the larger firm, something particularly true for broadcast journalists.

However, scholars have found both positive and negative effects of chain ownership (Hale, 1988). Some studies from the 1980s showed that chain ownership did not necessarily diminish a newspaper's performance. Indeed, chains can bring acquisitions more in line with industry standards for the proportion of space devoted to news, editorial, and feature selections, and they can infuse new capital and vigor. In 1988 a group of scholars concluded that there was no direct evidence of chain owners interfering in local newspapers (Picard, Winter, McCombs, & Lacy, 1988, p. 204).

More recently, Dunaway (2008) studied how corporate media ownership and market contexts affected coverage of the 2004 US Senate race in Colorado and, in the same year, the coverage of the gubernatorial race in the state of Washington. Dunaway found that corporate-owned newspapers produced 16 percent less issue coverage about the two elections than did large, privately owned newspapers. An even stronger effect was observed in local television coverage: Television stations owned by large corporations were 23 percent less likely to cover the issues (Dunaway, 2008, pp. 1198–200).

Scott, Gobetz, and Chanslor (2008) studied local television news content produced by stations in a small media group and by those that were part of a large chain organization. Compared to television stations in the small group, chain-owned stations produced less local news overall, used less locally produced video, and fewer on-air reporters:

> The results of this research offer support to critics who voice concern over the effects of increased concentration of ownership. In this case, the effects of large-corporate ownership on local news detrimentally impact the US Federal Communications Commission's public policy goal of localism, news that is part of the vital function of the press.
>
> (Scott et al., 2008, p. 95)

Cross-Ownership

Other patterns of ownership that have concerned scholars involve corporations that own both newspapers and broadcast organizations in the same community, generally called cross-ownership. Of particular interest is how the merging of the two media, with their different organizational requirements and structure, affects the news product in both. Cross-ownership has been criticized for constraining the diversity of media content, because only one company controls the voice of both television and newspaper outlets in the community.

Studies from the 1970s have shown that cross-owned television stations and newspapers transmitted just as much if not more news and public affairs information than media that were not cross-owned (Wirth & Wollert, 1976; Wollert, 1978). This suggests that a company's newspaper, with its primary orientation toward news, may help its television counterpart by infusing the newspaper's news values into the more entertainment-oriented broadcast organization. In 1973 Stempel found that media news was less comprehensive in towns in which one company owned all media, but a follow-up study (Pritchard, Terry, & Brewer, 2008) found no support for this. In their project, a corporation that owned newspapers in Milwaukee, Wisconsin, and Dayton, Ohio, and which endorsed John Kerry in the 2004 presidential election, did not limit coverage of George Bush in their talk/radio stations. In fact, Bush received much more radio time (Pritchard et al., 2008, p. 22). Furthermore, in their analysis of clusters of newspapers, television, and radio stations in Chicago, "the proprietors of the cross-ownerships . . . permitted their media outlets to publish and broadcast a diversity of view points . . . The slant of news and opinion in the non-cross-owned media was not significantly different from that of cross-owned media" (Pritchard et al., 2008, p. 23). Scholars have not addressed this issue recently, possibly because cross-ownership is more common now, with the Internet opening up the competitive environment far beyond the local community.

Another factor to consider is that many news media now use more than one platform for their products. When both newspapers and television stations have complementary internet sites, they can use each other's formats. Newspapers can supplement text and still images with recorded video clips of news events and with live streaming video. Television stations can supplement their video format with text and still photos. This cross-pollination of formats may ultimately have more of an effect on news content than cross-ownership.

Ownership and Innovation

The ownership of media organizations has generally become larger and more centralized over time, with one corporation owning many organizations that produce content. Although the number of publications, networks, and other media products make it appear that there are many companies that own mass media, in truth most media organizations are owned by a handful of corporate media giants. In the fourth edition of his book, *The Media Monopoly* (2004), Ben Bagdikian reports that a small number of corporations control most of the media business in the USA; this is down from 50 corporations when the book was first published in 1982.

For example, the Walt Disney Company owns Walt Disney Pictures, as well as the film companies Pixar, Touchstone, and Miramax. Disney also owns several television networks, including ABC, ESPN, ABC Family, Lifetime, and A&E. Clear Channel Communications owns radio stations in all 50 of the United States and has a partial interest in SiriusXM satellite radio. Based in Germany, Bertelsmann AG has an interest in many book, magazine, and music companies, such as Random House,

Bantam, Doubleday, Alfred A. Knopf, Princeton Review, Cosmopolitan, National Geographic, Men's Health, Sony BMG, Arista, Columbia, Epic, and RCA (Columbia Journalism Review, 2010). Sometimes the parent organization is not directly involved in producing media content; for example, General Electric owns NBC and its affiliates Telemundo and Universal Pictures.

These conglomerates take fewer risks than smaller companies do, because the priority is to obtain economic and political advantage. Their corporate goals can permeate the entire firm—as media firms become more diversified and complex, the economic goal is the only thing the many parts of the corporation have in common. Major expansions or contractions of organizational functions occur only after financial analysts predict (or announce after the fact) the news about the changes' effect on the bottom line. Small changes occur as budgets are nudged up or down, but the need to stay within budgeted limits affects all media organizations, even those that are owned by governments. Whether expenditures fall within the budgeted amount is studied in detail each month, quarter, and year, often acting as a stimulus for change. Whether the change is toward innovation or conservation is controlled by many factors, including ownership of the organization and its ongoing economic health. Scholars have been particularly interested in how these economic goals affect the media product.

Stepp's interviews (2008) with US newspaper journalists revealed the journalists' beliefs that trying to do more work with lower budgets will sacrifice quality, and that profitability and public service are becoming incompatible (Stepp, 2008, p. 22). When media organizations had greater control over the flow of information, making a profit was easier. With the advent of the Internet and associated technologies, audiences have many more sources of information, and revenues are distributed across all information organizations. In Stepp's conclusion, "The mainstream media have proved sadly slow in corralling their share. Why didn't they capture the market in online classifieds long before Craigslist? Why didn't they become the home base for local video long before YouTube? Why didn't they recognize the power of social connections, long before Facebook?" (2008, p. 25).

The Organization's Economic Health

As the economics of media content production became less and less stable toward the end of the 20th century, most news organizations cut resources available to create content, including both the number of staff members and the amount of news that could be transmitted (Stepp, 2008, p. 25). Predatory owners in leveraged buyouts saddled many otherwise profitable newspaper companies with large debt they were not able to sustain. Within a year after William Dean Singleton's Media News Group bought the San Jose Mercury News, the number of staff was cut by 22 percent (Farhi, 2007, p. 24). "Some parts of the paper's newsroom have simply just disappeared, among them a five-member projects team that included a 40-year Merc veteran Pete Carey, who was part of a group that won a Pulitzer for foreign reporting in 1986. Carey is now a business reporter" (Farhi, 2007, p. 24). Perhaps more than anything else, this demonstrates the primacy of the organization's economic goals over all others. By the beginning of the 21st century, unprofitable media divisions were often completely restructured by their corporate owners, resulting in fewer services, the merger of previously distinct functions, and a reduction in the number of personnel.

"The digital age makes our business more competitive than ever before," wrote David Westin, president of ABC News in a 2010 memo announcing the Walt Disney Company's "fundamental transformation" of its news division "to ensure that ABC News has a sound journalistic and financial footing . . . We will do it with a business model that ensures we will be here for our audiences for many years" (Westin, 2010). Westin said that ABC News was moving "boldly and promptly. In the past we've sought out less expensive ways to replicate what we've always done. The time has come to re-think how we do what we are doing" (Westin, 2010). In fact, by 2010 there was little doubt that if most media organizations had planned downsizing and restructuring earlier, they would have been in better economic shape (Doctor, 2008).

Covering International News

News organizations' need to make a profit was once judged to be less important than the excellence of its news coverage, which was rarely profitable. In the mid 20th century ABC, CBS, and NBC sent reporters and camera personnel around the world, wherever events were most newsworthy. Both television networks and newspapers established news bureaus in major capitals, headed by US reporters, with local personnel providing translation and transportation. To the extent that the reporters did not speak the local language, they had to rely on the veracity and talent of the translator. In the 1990–1 Persian Gulf War, reporters became famous for reporting from their hotels, rarely seeing events at first hand.

Recent budget cuts have had perhaps the largest impact on the coverage of news in other countries. Today's news organizations rarely can afford the high costs of sending Americans to other countries as foreign correspondents. For example, in late 2008, none of the "big three" television networks had full-time correspondents in Iraq, a country with which the USA was officially at war and had 130,000 troops stationed there. Many newspapers also closed their foreign bureaus, including the *Boston Globe* and the *Philadelphia Inquirer* (Hamilton, 2009, pp. 51–2).

Instead of relying on American reporters to analyze a situation at first hand, when a newsworthy event occurs, journalists and camera crew local to the country are hired as freelancers to report on it by the US organization. This costs the organization less, because the freelancer works less than full-time and also doesn't receive benefits such as medical insurance, which can add 40 percent or more to the full-time journalist's salary. Scholars need to investigate how hiring local journalists can change the perspective of the news, and whether it is for better or worse. There may be other effects on international news content. Previously news media relied on one or two reporters to cover one country or even a region such as the Middle East, whereas now it is more likely for the home office to synthesize the views of multiple local journalists. Using local journalists can provide more cultural context for news reports, allowing editors or network producers to choose among several perspectives, but the disadvantage may be that it is difficult for them to judge the validity of individual reports.

Another accommodation to the economic downturn is that organizations now tend to rely on a smaller number of international news services for information about an event. For example, the UK's Reuters news service emphasizes financial news, with 200 news bureaus world wide and 2,800 journalists and a reach of 1 billion people a day (Reuters, 2010). Established in the mid 19th century in the USA, the Associated Press is a nonprofit cooperative organization with about 1,500 newspaper members and 5,000 radio and television members in the USA, as well as members in many other countries. Its reach can extend to more than half of the world's population (Associated Press, 2010).

When considering changes in how the news media cover events in other countries, it is important to evaluate not only the benefits and costs of relying on local journalists and large international newsgathering agencies but also the extent to which these entities control the flow of information and its diversity. Paterson conducted an ethnography of the key television news agencies in London, showing how by controlling the visuals distributed to news organizations around the world they effectively dictate the way stories are framed (Paterson, 2011).

With so many news media cutting their foreign bureaus, it is notable that *Wall Street Journal* content has become more international. After Rupert Murdoch's News Corporation purchased the newspaper in 2007, the *Journal* invested $6 million to upgrade its coverage of other countries, perhaps reflecting News Corporation's interests in many countries. The newspaper used its upgraded coverage of other countries to attract new readers (Featherstone, 2009, p. 32).

The Organization's Architecture

There are many variations in how organizations' roles can be combined and structured. The power associated with the sections of an organization and the relationships between them vary both across and within media. Organizational structure has a pervasive, if not readily identifiable effect on media content. Charts are often used to illustrate an organization's architecture, with boxes representing organizational roles and lines the paths of authority. At the top is the owner (sometimes a person, at other times a board of trustees), the most powerful entity in the organization. Under the owner are various departments, each headed by an executive or supervisor who maintains the organizational roles carried out by employees within the departments. Such charts help organizational employees answer four questions:

1. What are the organizational roles?

2. How is the organization structured?

3. What are the organization's policies and how are they implemented?

4. How are the policies enforced?

For all media, the ultimate power lies in ownership. In most companies stock ownership entitles the shareholder to vote for directors on the board that runs the company. Top management is either part of the board or accountable to it. The stock may be broadly owned or controlled by one family or a few large investors. The *New York Times* is a good example of how ownership can be structured to ensure the autonomy and control of a media organization. The *Times* is part of the New York Times Company enterprise, which also owns other newspapers, magazines, and broadcasting companies. The paper has remained in the hands of descendants of Adolph S. Ochs, who purchased the paper in 1891 and earned a reputation as an independent and leading voice among the news media. Recognizing the importance of ownership, Ochs distributed company stock such that voting rights and control remain within the family (now the Sulzbergers). Thus the newspaper's executives are not subject to pressures from outside stockholders. Furthermore, a stockholders' agreement among the trustees prevents them from selling, merging, or giving up the control of the company. Such a move could be taken only if they unanimously agree that it would best serve the primary objective of the trust: "To maintain the editorial independence and integrity of the *New York Times* and to continue it as an independent newspaper, entirely fearless, free of ulterior influence and unselfishly devoted to the public welfare" ("Notice of 1989 Annual Meeting and Proxy Statement," 1989, p. 3).

Organizational Roles

Organizational charts also show the titles of people who perform each function—or at least suggest who is supposed to carry out these functions. As individuals are hired or promoted into these roles, they take on the duties and authority associated with the positions. The number and type of roles in the organization show how specialized or differentiated positions are. Depending on the power and personality of the employee, the organizational role may change to fit the person rather than the person fitting the job, which can result in relationships with other positions that are not reflected on the chart. People's views of their jobs are largely determined by the roles they fill in the organization. Roles shape their orientation toward organizational issues by providing a distinct vantage point on and stake in decisions. Recruitment patterns help reproduce and maintain the views associated with these roles.

Organizational Structures

Although lines in an organizational chart show how organizational roles are connected, they rarely convey how complex the organization is. Charts do not show the varying amount of power distributed along each line—each is the same width. Generally, however, the lines at the top of the organizational chart represent more authority than those lower down, with organizational roles being more powerful at the top. Another measure of authority could be the number of people each role supervises.

Google's organizational structure begins with the chief executive officer, who is also the chair of the board of directors, which in 2010 consisted of nine people. Below the board, the company is divided into 16 operating committees, each with multiple senior staff who supervise many others. As with most large organizations, the Google architecture is largely vertical, meaning that Google's organizational roles look like a wide triangle—small at the top and increasingly wide toward the bottom (Google, 2012).

In a vertically organized architecture, power flows from top to bottom, with little exchange between people in the top and bottom roles; if roles appear side by side this may connote similar amounts of power, although this is not always the case. Although a person's position within the organizational structure greatly determines the power invested in a role, power does not entirely stem from one's position in the organization chart. Lower-ranking employees may have special expertise or other means to thwart directives from the top, requiring negotiation and compromise. Corporate and top-level executives set organizational policies, set budgets, make important personnel decisions, project the commercial and political interests of the company, and when necessary defend the organization's employees from outside pressures. Below the executive level are middle managers responsible for editing, producing, coordinating the process, and mediating communication between the bottom and top of the organization. Front-line employees are at the bottom of the chart: writers, reporters, videographers, programmers, and other creative staff who gather and package the raw material that constitute the organization's product. In a horizontally structured organization, power flows from one person (or a small group of people) to others who have specialized roles, but who share similar power. Communication among the organization's roles is regular and multi-directional. Creating the organization's product can happen only if all roles work together, often on the same content at the same time.

Reflecting the changed media landscape, many organizations reorganized to produce content on new platforms and/or with fewer financial resources. The *Atlanta Journal Constitution* newspaper had a typical vertical structure prior to its reorganization in 2007. The owner Cox Media Group owns many media organizations, each of which has a corporate executive (Stepp, 2007). The newspaper reorganized into a more horizontal structure: Its 12 traditional editorial roles were abolished in favor of four departments: (1) news and information, (2) enterprise, (3) digital, and (4) print. The first two departments create content that is presented on either one or both platforms represented by the latter two departments: the news on paper and the online news site ajc.com (Stepp, 2007). As Editor Julia Wallace describes the change:

> We had a newsroom built for the old world. In the old world, the content people had control of the print [edition] but not online, and I thought that was an

unwinnable situation. We can't just be a newspaper anymore. We need to be a news and information company. Online will become the new mass medium, and print will be aimed at settled adults.

(Stepp, 2007, p. 16)

The simplified structure supports only about three-quarters of the previous staff members, with some beats being dropped and others combined, and the delivery reduced.

Television networks are also generally complex, vertically structured organizations, with news divisions that are now less structurally insulated from the larger enterprise. Reporters, writers, producers, and videographers may report to the executive producer, who reports to the head of the news division or, if the network distributes only news, the president of the network. The news head is often one of several presidents who report to the president of the network, who then reports to the parent company. Television networks often had news bureaus in major US cities, as well as in foreign capitals, but reorganization has reduced much of this complexity.

Organizational Processes

The term *process* refers to how the work of the organization is accomplished, given its structure. For example, newspaper structures were once intentionally separated, to make news coverage of people and companies independent of their political or advertising support of the newspaper. This resulted in two parallel processes, one to sell advertising and the other to produce the news and feature content that went around it. Communication between the two sides of the structure was intentionally limited. As the profitability of news organizations decreased, however, the two processes increasingly overlapped. Business managers now routinely meet with editors as they plan the day's or week's content, and individual journalists work with advertising representatives when events have both newsworthiness and the potential to sell advertising (Hart, 2009, p. 11).

This integration of the news and business sides of newspapers accelerated during the overall restructuring that many newspapers experienced after the mid 1990s, from primarily vertical to a more horizontal architecture on each side of the organizations. The changes occurred in two ways: the integration of news and business processes and the substitution of a team-based routine of news gathering and processing for the traditional beat system routine. Instead of assigning a reporter to cover a specific content area, such as the police or education beat, the editor assigns teams of reporters to collaborate on an assignment (Gade, 2008, pp. 371–2). These new processes are based on a conceptual understanding of the newspaper as a whole, whose staff members interact in a process that best accomplishes the entire work of the organization. Roles are less specialized, with news and business personnel working together to generate the day's newspaper, and this new process redefines the term content to include everything that appears in the newspaper—news, features, opinions, obituaries, crossword puzzles and comics, classifieds, stock prices, and advertising.

This organizational restructuring and recreating the process of news work has fundamentally changed the routines of producing a daily newspaper and the role of editors in it. Gade's survey (2008, pp. 371–2) of US newspaper editors found that their understanding of their own influence in their restructuring organizations depends largely on their perceptions of profitability as an organizational goal. The more important editors believe profitability is to their organizations, the less influence they see themselves as having within the organizations. Editors may understand their organizations' profitability as something over which they have little control, in the same way that they have limited influence when it comes to cutting resources. They do not see resource efficiencies in substituting the team-based horizontal organizational structure for what had been an editor-controlled vertical structure, because both reporters and editors must spend more time coordinating and planning the work of teams. Because this additional administrative burden is understood as directly decreasing resources for gathering information and for writing and editing stories, editors perceive increasing control from outside forces, resulting in a lower-quality news product (Gade, 2008, pp. 383–4). Lee and Hwang (2004, p. 195) describe this corporate "synergy" as a buzzword for the suppression of journalistic autonomy and professional values to the corporation's need to make a profit for its owner.

Organizational Policies and Power

Although the connections among roles in an organizational chart show how power is in principle exercised, the chart can convey neither the type of policies owners create nor the actual ways in which owners carry them out. An organization's policies are sometimes written, but more often are understood by its employees through a process of socialization to the norms of the organization. In his 1955 study of newspaper policies, Warren Breed referred to this as "social control in the newsroom" (p. 327), revealing that the exercise of power by owners is not a phenomenon new to the 21st century.

ORGANIZATIONAL INFLUENCES ON CONTENT

Having established the key components of organizational structure, we ask: How do these structures affect media content? How is media content shaped by organizational roles and by the power relations among them? In one sense, the structure simply reflects an organization's allocation of resources, how it adapts to the environment, and how it plans to accomplish its work. For example, the maintenance of a news bureau in Washington, DC, reflects a decision that news from the capital has value to the organization, increasing the likelihood that government events will routinely become news. Such effects are obvious, a consequence of the beat system and newsworthiness that we cover next in Chapter 7, the routine practices of media work.

In this chapter on media organizations, however, we must also consider more subtle effects on media content—factors that result from content being produced in an organizational setting as such. Each organizational structure gives rise to a distinct occupational culture. For example, an extra layer of bureaucracy between the *New York Times*'s Washington bureau and its home office resulted in a perception by the capital press corps that the *Times* was more an editor's paper and the *Washington Post* more a reporter's paper (Sigal, 1973).

To better see the effects of organization variables, we can contrast a political blog produced by one person with a city newspaper or local television news program. On the one hand, the blog is seemingly accomplished outside of an organization, yet it is more productive theoretically to think of it as a minimalist organization: It has a name, a published web address, and an employee whose role is to gather and synthesize information; write and post messages; communicate with readers and vendors; and solve technical problems. The blogger must organize the resources and tasks necessary to accomplish the work, however informal that organization is. On the other hand, covering a city's news on a daily basis requires a more formal allocation of resources distributed across multiple employees whose work days tend to be scripted by the roles they play in gathering information, writing, editing, supervising, and in performing executive functions such as payroll or negotiating contracts with vendors.

In one sense, the organization exists to formalize conflict, first, among employees who accomplish the work of the organization by negotiating and revising their scripted power relationships and, second, between its members and those outside of the organization. The larger the organization, the more conflict becomes an inevitable part of operations; it is no coincidence that larger organizations have formal charts that effectively reify this conflict and power. Organizational structure is the playing field on which employees compete for scarce resources. News gathering is an expensive process and not always predictable: Events don't always occur during normal working hours. Even when they do, such as from regular city council meetings, the nature of such routine events can make them boring and not worthy of coverage. This uncertainty leaves considerable room for the influence of organizational factors (Sigal, 1973).

Conflicts also occur laterally between departments. News editors must balance the needs of two constituencies—their reporting staffs and the larger organization. They compete for resources but ultimately must reach an accommodation, especially for space in the publication. Conflict is particularly seen in turf struggles over events that have overlapping jurisdictions within the newspaper (Sigal, 1973, p. 21). For example, if a Japanese conglomerate purchases a US film company, then the conglomerate's newspapers, entertainment, and foreign sections could all legitimately cover the story.

The Exercise of Power in Media Structures

From the organizational perspective, we may ask how the producers of content are affected by other parts of the organization. How does the business department of a newspaper, for example, affect the editorial side? How do other subsidiaries of a conglomerate affect media content? The recent wave of media mergers, take-overs, and closings can help us focus attention on how changing an organizational structure can impact the media product. When revenue shrinks in a bad economy, expenses must also decline, putting increasing pressures on those who create content (Hart, 2009). Emerging partisan-oriented news organizations like Fox bring their own new intra-organizational disputes over boundaries. A video highly critical of the Obama administration, for example, was broadcast during the *Fox and Friends* program, which is billed as an entertainment program. The video, supplied by a Fox News associate producer, was roundly criticized as extreme propaganda and a virtual attack ad for the Republican Party, obliging a news division leader to repudiate the video. This blurring of the lines within the larger Fox corporation was problematic for the news side, which lays claim to being a legitimate news organization.[2]

Decades earlier, William Randolph Hearst used newspapers to manipulate social policy. In the 1950s, he put his *New York Journal-American* to work on behalf of Senator Joseph McCarthy and his hunt for communists in government and the mass media. In the 1970s, Henry Luce promoted the political virtues of Richard Nixon in the pages of his news magazine *Time*. Nixon was eminently compatible with Luce's staunch anti-communism (Halberstam, 1979). Media owners may use their partisanship to curry political advantage for their enterprises.

Few media owners maintain as high a profile. They are not crusaders but instead prefer to acquire or sell their holdings as their economic goals dictate. Recent studies by Pollock (2007) and Beam (2003) reveal how the priorities of owners translate into news coverage. The controversial North American Free Trade Agreement (NAFTA) of 1995 bifurcated the interests of business on the one hand with the interests of labor unions and environmentalists on the other, and coverage of the treaty more closely reflected the interests of owners than of laborers (Pollock, 2007, p. 169). Beam (2003) compared newspapers with stronger and weaker market orientations, finding that an organization's emphasis on profitability is related to how closely content follows the demands of audiences and advertisers: The stronger the market orientation, the less information the newspaper contained about the routine workings of government, including politics (the making and administration of laws), crime and the justice system, and news about international diplomacy and the military (Beam, 2003, p. 382). Instead, newspapers with strong market orientations are more likely to cover entertainment, sports, and the private lives of individuals (Beam, 2003, p. 380), presumably because audiences (and hence advertisers) are more interested in lighter fare.

Autonomy

The larger and more complex a media organization is, the more likely it is that organizational factors prevail over influences from the individual and routine levels of analysis. Organizational influences may distort journalists' ability to objectively describe the world, and a fiercely independent journalistic culture may be inconsistent with corporate goals. When organizational structures kept the news department autonomous and buffered from influences by the business side of the company, such effects were less likely. Now that news and business functions are integrated in the restructured news organizations of the 21st century, we have to ask whether journalistic autonomy is sacrificed for profitability. In today's news organization, a business executive has replaced the editor as the person in charge of the overall company. When news departments work closely with business departments, daily news meetings routinely include personnel from both sides of the organization (Squires, 1993, p. 20).

Concerns about journalistic autonomy have increased as the structures of media organizations have become more complex. Previously, the primary organizational threat to journalistic objectivity was an overeager publisher who wanted to slant news content in favor of a local business. Today, the threat is more abstract. As media organizations have become more complex, multiple levels of bureaucracy have been inserted between front-line media workers and top management. The more levels there are in an organization's structure, the less top management worries about news workers' autonomy and their other professional values, such as ethics. Although this distance tends to prevent top executives from routinely trying to influence the coverage of specific events, they may still do so under pressure from owners or from leaders of other powerful social institutions. As organizations increase in complexity, their boards of directors create interconnections between media executives and those in other industries. Although reporters are advised against being politically active for fear it will impede their objectivity, no such restrictions are placed on top media executives. The directors of large media firms often sit on the boards of other institutions, including banks, universities, and large corporations that rely heavily on media advertising. Influences from social institutions are covered in the previous chapter.

Analyzing the changing roles within media organizations helps us evaluate the autonomy and relative power of those responsible for content and of those whose job it is to concentrate on profits. The blurring of these responsibilities resulted in Fox News Channel host Bill O'Reilly playing both news and advertising roles (Hart, 2009) by positively introducing a company's commercial and then following it with the statement: "For encouraging kindness and generosity in America, the Liberty Mutual people are patriots" (Hart, 2009, p. 10).

Editors, producers, and others who supervise the employees who create media content are increasingly drawn into greater marketing schemes that concentrate on research about what the audience wants, and this is as true of entertainment content as news. In corporate synergies, books become films that have closely tied product placements from other organizations in the conglomerate. Music in a film is released by another arm of the conglomerate, which is played in the radio stations it owns. The film is released on digital media and shortly after that it is advertised around similar television programming in affiliated networks (Bagdikian, 2004).

For example, Micro-Games America (MGA) Entertainment owns the license for a line of Bratz dolls marketed to pre-teen girls. The dolls are marketing vehicles for a line of Bratz media products, including television, books, DVDs, and magazine articles:

> The names of specific Bratz products are integrated through out Bratz media content in a children's media version of 'plugola, ' where media content promotes subsidiary licenses of the same media owner. Here, the connection is the license and its corporate owner MGA, with Bratz media involving various media companies (News Corp, Titan Publishing, Grosset & Dunlap).
>
> (McCallister, 2007, p. 252)

Cinematic narrative is subject to many influences, some subtle and others glaring, especially when the needs of CEOs and advertisers predominate over the needs (and routines) of filmmakers. We might expect a corporation's products to be placed in a story that is affirmative and upbeat, avoiding anything that would reflect negatively on the company's products, but there are exceptions. In the long-running series of James Bond films, violence has apparently appealed to audience members who can afford expensive and powerful sports cars. There will always be concern when messages are selected not for their importance to the audience, their newsworthiness, or their artistic significance, but instead for how they fit into a larger organizational marketing scheme.

Policy

How does an organization see to it that its members conform to its policies? How does the organization exert control over its members in the production of content? Supervisors (such as editors) must control those who create content and managers (such as publishers or producers) must control supervisors, whereas the owner(s) must control the managers. Control is essential, given the inherent conflict within levels of an organization, and so the most important question is not whether employees are controlled, but rather who does the controlling and what are their agendas (Hirsch, 1977, p. 26)? New employees must be socialized to organizations' routines, and routines must be enforced. At the same time, there must be a way to handle situations that are not covered by routine procedures. Most control is straightforward and accomplished through a reward system. Promotions and salary increases go to the workers who perform their jobs well, from the standpoint of their supervisors. Other control is equally powerful because it is subtle and unquestioned.

In 1956 scholars Nixon and Jones concluded that differences in quality within the newspaper industry appeared to hinge on the social responsibility and competence of the owners and operators of a newspaper. We are now less concerned with overt propaganda-style messages promoted by ideological publishers such as Robert McCormick of the *Chicago Tribune*, known for his ultraconservative editorial policies until his death in 1955. His opinions often ran counter to both public opinion and his own journalists (Windhauser, Norton, & Rhodes, 1983). Scholars should explore questions of news quality, quantity, and emphasis on the local community. If otherwise similar media with different owners vary in their content, we presume an organizational influence that supersedes whatever routines may be held in common.

The question of control in the news business becomes particularly problematic, where journalists often assert their own autonomy against what they may consider management interference in their professional turf. Nevertheless, as we have seen, organizational leaders can dictate content directly with explicit policy guidelines. For example, in the late 1980s, one newspaper put forth an overt policy in response to its coverage of a rally for gay rights. A memo urged news staffers to "never forget that we are putting out family newspapers in conservative communities. We must never forget that this should be a prime consideration in story and photo selection, in editing, and in cutline and headline writing" (Document, 1989). Studies of newsrooms have shown that overt conflicts over stories don't come up very often, because publishers cannot exert overt power on a day-to-day basis (Gans, 1979; Sigal, 1973). Obviously the multitude of daily news decisions makes closer supervision impossible. Instead, the organization sets the boundaries and guidelines to direct these decisions. Tunstall (1971) has argued that most organizational policy is traditional and relatively fixed. Journalists learn unwritten policies through experience and by observing the kinds of stories used by the organization. Top management gets involved when the stakes are high, setting specific policies, and this intervention itself has the effect of letting news workers know that the boundaries have been reached. Relations between reporters and editors cannot be too heavy handed. Reporters can counterbalance the power of the editor to the extent that they have the support of their peers and greater first hand knowledge of the subject matter. They must rely on each other if they are to fulfill the inexorable demands of daily news gathering.

The absence of visible attempts at control doesn't mean that there is no control. Whenever media workers deduce what their supervisors want and give it to them, de-facto control has been exercised. Although the predictable routines of news gathering may prevent many policy conflicts, these routines are part of and meet larger organizational requirements, which establish the boundaries of acceptability. Outside of the boundaries of acceptable conduct (and content) lies the realm of deviance, of actions that are assumed to conflict with the policies of higher-ups. Whether policies are overt or covert, if employees do not come to an understanding of acceptable and deviant behaviors, they are either fired or leave for a more palatable organization.

Gans (1979) found an interesting mix of power relationships between editors and reporters. Reporters objected more to having an editor change their stories than having them killed altogether. Gans reasoned that writing is considered the reporter's job, whereas editors decide what makes it into a publication. By killing one story, however, the editor indirectly communicates the boundaries of acceptable content and can cause a reporter to self-censor when preparing subsequent stories. Because reporters strive to be taken seriously, they are vulnerable to pressures to conform, especially if they begin writing things that diverge from the common wisdom of the newsroom. Editors may doubt reporters' credibility and wonder if they can be trusted. From the standpoint of reporters, it is safer to hew to the common wisdom and avoid straying outside the boundaries of acceptability.

Breed's classic study of newsroom socialization shows how news rooms enforced written policies—the covert and "consistent orientation" of a paper's news and editorials toward issues and events, revolving primarily around partisan, class, and racial divisions (1955, p. 327). Breed asked, "How is policy maintained, despite the fact that it often contravenes journalistic norms, that staffers often personally disagree with it and that executives cannot legitimately command that it be followed" (1955, p. 330). He concluded that control would not be as important, if the job of the organization was only to report the news as objectively as possible, but then of course being objective was not a news organization's only goal. Overriding objectivity, said Breed, is the primary objective "to get the news" (1955, p. 342). As Breed put it: "News comes first, and there is always news to get" (1955, p. 342), precluding fiddling too much with any single story.

Common ways of exerting control include the editing process, in which reporters quickly learn which are objectionable phrases and facts. In fact, the editorial process is so effective at teaching reporters the unwritten policies of the newsroom, that executives rarely reprimand or make explicit policy decisions. Breed said that "in the infrequent case that an anti-policy story reaches the city desk, the story is changed; extraneous reasons, such as the pressure of time and space, are given for the change . . . Thus the policy remains not only covert but undiscussed and therefore unchanged" (1955, p. 339).

Forty years later, Elbot (1992) confirmed Breed's idea of social control, arguing that reporters feel the "invisible hand" if they threaten institutional interests—which include promoting organizational growth. Self-regulation and self-censorship, however, mean that this hand is rarely needed. Reporters who follow the organization's policies are rewarded with special assignments and recognition, whereas "those reporters who most threaten institutional interests are the . . . independent, curious, unafraid investigators who are constantly looking for stories behind the story which may identify the real institutional interests and their activities" (Elbot, 1992, p. 6). The sacrifices these reporters make to get the story may also play out in having to move from one organization to another and in risking the stability of their non-work lives.

News organizations have sought out African American, Latino, and other ethnic media workers as a way of making their reporting staffs closer to their minority communities (see Chapter 8). Their apparent assumption was that, for example, being African American would make a reporter understand the black community and report better on it than the previously all-white editorial staff. Unfortunately this attempt to ethnically diversify news staffs often did not have the desired effect. African American and Latino reporters understood the same reporting routines because they went to the same journalism schools as the white reporters did. Their backgrounds had more in common with the white reporters than with the ethnic communities they were supposed to cover. In addition, once hired, they were subject to the same organizational socialization processes. If minority journalists worked against changing the routines of news coverage, then they risked being told that they lacked professional competence. Wilson and Gutierrez (1985) noted that such unwritten policies were stronger than formal ones, which usually came with procedures for changing them. In their study, they found that minority reporters were told their stories lacked newsworthiness or that there was no space or time to include them.

Thinking about the ethnicity of reporters on the individual level of analysis leads one to conclude that a more diverse workforce will improve the media's ability to reflect a multicultural society. But even when minority journalists reach the top of their profession and presumably have the most influence on content, their influence has been mediated by how and whether they adapted to their organization's culture. *Washington Post* reporter Jill Nelson (1993), for example, writes, "For many of the black folks there, the *Washington Post* is neither heaven nor hell, but some weird, journalistic purgatory, a seemingly endless proving ground on which, just when you think you've won the game, the rules are changed" (p. 85). She also observed that the more successful a minority journalist was, the more the journalist has fashioned him- or herself in the image of the dominant white and male organizational culture. A familiar socializing technique, she argued, is for an African American reporter to be assigned to write a front-page story exposing in vivid detail some aspect of pathology in the black community. Thus, in view of organizational policy, even minority employees may not be able to change the way media portray minority issues. Policy perpetuates the majority cultural viewpoint, as institutionalized in the views of the organization. Clearly, at the organization level of analysis, we must question the extent to which organizational values predominate, and how individuals adapt to the controls imposed on them by others.

Bias

In mass media content, bias can result when factors intentionally favor or disfavor a person, thing, or topic, but bias in favor of large-scale corporate interests is largely invisible to the audience. The issue emerges only when owners express strongly held political views, as was the case when Murdoch, Hearst, and Luce each exerted their political influence (Bagdikian, 2004; Halberstam, 1979). This is of particular concern in the news media, where the goal of objective news reporting can be easily manipulated.

When Rupert Murdoch bought the *Wall Street Journal*, there were fears that his political views would be reflected in the news pages, but that has not occurred (Featherstone, 2009). Instead, he and his executives "have displayed barely disguised contempt for [the newspaper's] core strengths" and have changed the culture of the newsroom, moving the newspaper away from in-depth reporting and "decisively toward a more terse, scope-oriented form of journalism that they believe is more in keeping with the information age" (Featherstone, 2009, p. 31).

Newspapers sometimes endorse political candidates, which might provide a direct measure of political attitudes held by corporate leaders. The more important question, however, is to what extent do these attitudes find their way into news pages, which in the USA are supposed to reflect the objectivity of the organization and its employees. Gilens and Hertzman (2000) analyzed newspaper coverage of a proposed change in the 1996 Telecommunications Act that would loosen restrictions on television station ownership, finding that owners who thought they would gain from the new policy ran twice as many positive comments as negative. The reverse was true of newspapers whose owners had nothing to gain, with negative comments being three times more likely than positive (Gilens & Hertzman, 2000, p. 384).

Between 1940 and 1964, US newspapers showed an overwhelming tendency to endorse Republican candidates. In 1964, the Democratic candidate Lyndon Johnson was endorsed more than his Republican rival Barry Goldwater. Between that race and 1992, Republicans were again endorsed most. But in 1992, when Democrat Bill Clinton ran against the incumbent president, Republican George Bush, Clinton was endorsed more. Many newspapers now decline to endorse a candidate at all, rising from 13.4 percent uncommitted newspapers in 1940 to 62.8 percent in 1992 ("Clinton's the Choice," 1992).

This depoliticization of newspaper endorsements matches the corporate trend away from overt partisan or personal bias in the mainstream press. In general, newspapers have rarely been blatant about systematically favoring in news articles the candidates endorsed in their editorials, but there was early evidence that newspapers biased their reporting of public opinion campaign polls: Poll coverage in elections up to 1972 favored those candidates that newspapers endorsed, unless a nearby competitor had endorsed someone else, in which case coverage was more evenhanded (Wilhoit & Auh, 1974). Of course, now that it is rare that daily newspapers have a competitor in the same city, newspapers have more latitude in covering political candidates. In another early study, Donohew (1967) found a positive relationship between a publisher's attitude toward an issue and the newspaper's treatment of the issue. More specifically, Mann (1984) found that in reporting anti-Vietnam War demonstrations in the mid 1960s, pro-war papers gave smaller crowd estimates than did antiwar papers. News coverage of the same rally differed dramatically between the *Charlotte Observer*, which called demonstrators "honorable Americans," and the *Atlanta Constitution*, which disparaged marchers as "vile-mouthed anti-American extremists" (Mann, 1984, p. 282).

Thus, we can see that the religious, political, and other idiosyncratic personal bias raises greater alarm about owner influence than the much more fundamental corporate economic bias. By establishing corporate policies in line with their own interests, owners can have an unmistakable impact on media content.

SUMMARY

Organization level factors have a critical impact on media content. When we look at these organizations, we question the roles performed, the way they are structured, the policies flowing through the structure, and the methods used to enforce those policies. The primary goal sought by most media organizations is economic profit. News organizations, in particular, have faced highly visible economic pressures in recent years that now play a greater role in dictating journalistic decisions. Organizational structure influences content by affecting the occupational culture and by determining the degree of independence media organizations have from the larger corporate enterprises, of which so many are now a part. The growing complexity of media conglomerates means that the smaller organizations composing them must now be more mindful of their effect on each other, and therefore news organizations may now encounter many more potential conflicts of interest. As we discussed earlier, the Internet has changed the media landscape, leading us to revisit the question of what constitutes an organization. Earlier questions of organizing for news have broadened as the boundaries have shifted, blurring the distinctions between news, information, and entertainment. Yet many of the organization level questions remain the same.

Of course, the ultimate organizational level power lies with media owners, who set policy and enforce it, and their influence has been an important concern in the news media. When news departments were buffered from the larger firm, content was controlled indirectly through hiring and promotion practices and through self-censorship. This organizational perspective reveals the context within which the routines of media work are carried out. These organizations themselves are subject to their own limits imposed by their environments. It is to these routine influences that we turn next.

NOTES

1 It is rare for a mass media organization to exist completely "offline." In fact, most organizations have some sort of web presence.

2 See www.huffingtonpost.com/2012/05/30/fox-and-friends-anti-obama-video_n_1556557.html. (Accessed June 1, 2012.)

CHAPTER 7

Routines

In this chapter we explore the ways media workers do their jobs, what they think about them, and what rules the organization imposes on them. We call these the *routine practices* of communication work, rules—mostly unwritten—that give the media worker guidance. What can or should be done? What will lead to criticism? We open the chapter with a discussion of routines as a conceptual model. We ask where do routines come from? How do they come about? These are not insignificant questions, because they address the very process through which information about events becomes stories about events. Much content is shaped by the routinized production of news and entertainment. And of course there are the social media: Do they have different routine practices? How do the routines of the older media interact with the routines of online media?

There are three sources of routines: audiences, organizations, and suppliers of content. For example, what audiences want may or may not be known to the journalist. When the marketing and editorial sides of news production were firmly ensconced on the far sides of organizations' buildings, marketing information about audience content preferences was used to sell advertising but not to shape content. A few letters from audience members came to editors, but they had limited influence. But as newspaper circulation gradually declined, editorial and marketing personnel worked together to help keep the organization afloat. What the audience wants becomes critical, and content more likely to follow the results of focus groups and surveys.

Organizations want to increase income and decrease expenses—to make a profit. This leads them to create processes that make the work of the organization more efficient. Thus there is gatekeeping, ways of making decisions, and the centralization of work around events. And then there are the external suppliers of content—sources who control the information given to the media. They either facilitate or constrain the flow of information, a description that fits the public relations industry. Because most news comes from the government and other complex organizations, journalists arrange their work around bureaucratic schedules, with officials and experts making up the majority of people talked about.

We look next at studies of media routines, including how the media make decisions, how content is shaped, how stories are written, and the mediation of content by people who have a lot to gain from their successful influence. We review a range of both old and newer research studies. We also offer a case study of the first Persian Gulf War—how journalists interact with military officials and the latter attempt to control the face of war.

Wilbur Schramm, a "founding father" of our field, wrote in 1949 of "*the cues, the processes, the relationships* which enter into the encoding, transmitting, receiving, decoding, and ultimate disposal of the message" (Schramm, 1960, p. 175, emphasis ours). As we will see, these cues, processes, and relations of the news production business are what we today call routine practices. In addition, Schramm could have been writing about the social media in this passage: "And beyond the message and the chain there are great communication networks and organizations of human society. But the network is merely a set of interlocking chains, and the communication organizations . . . are merely networks with a specific communication purpose" (1960, p. 175). Schramm could be describing the 21st century relationships among the original news organizations, online news media, the social media, and the social institutions with which the media interact. In describing communication as interlocking chains, he says that when people begin to doubt the media, such as may occur in dictatorial governments, the people will develop "very long and important interpersonal chains [which] tend to develop side by side with the mass media" (Schramm, 1960, pp. 175–6). As the social media and blogs work side by side with traditional journalism, our analysis of routines must be expanded accordingly.

Journalists' Work

As individuals in groups, journalists have developed styles of thought from an endless pattern of norms in response to common situations. We refer to these as routines, those patterned, repeated practices, forms, and rules that media workers use to do their jobs. Routines represent a set of constraints on the individual worker and form the immediate context, both within and through which these individuals do their jobs. Computers now act at the direction of individuals to perform many of the same routines of news shaping, presentation, and delivery. Although both journalists and programmers can customize news content for specific communities, traditional news organizations' communities have been geographically defined. News content created for physical and virtual communities share some but not all routines.

The gatekeeper—as individual—decides which information is selected to become news, how it is produced, and on which platform it is delivered, thus bridging the inner core and the outer ring of our model in Figure 4.1 (see Shoemaker & Vos, 2009). This reminds us that the individual—whether journalist or computer programmer—fills a role and serves a function within a larger system. Whether in news or entertainment industries, the media gatekeeper must winnow a larger number of potential messages to select only a few. The book publisher chooses from many possible titles. The television network programmer selects from among several situation comedies and dramas for the upcoming season, the newspaper editor selects a handful of stories from among hundreds for the front page, and the Facebook user decides what to add to her own page and what to post on others' pages. Yahoo aggregates news products created by other organizations, using computer algorithms to make decisions.

Decisions are not only made at the whim of the individuals.[1] Gatekeepers also represent their professions, organizations, and the occupational settings that limit their decisions. To understand these limits we must take into account the organizational system in which people work, including the routines and craft norms that are a part of systematic information gathering. The idea of norms addresses whether behaviors are considered right or wrong (Jackson, 1966, p. 113). The standardized, recurring patterns of news, social media, and entertainment content largely result from these routine practices, which ensure that the media system will respond in predictable ways and that its core practices cannot be easily violated. Routines form a cohesive set of rules that become integrated to define a media professional. Tuchman (1977a) describes the routines of workers in the traditional media. She notes that reporters who have mastered the routine modes of processing news are valued for their professionalism (what questions to ask, how to handle hard and soft stories, what techniques are appropriate to each).

Wilson Lowrey (2006) suggests that routines, or as he calls them "professional processes," are constantly changing (p. 482). Hallin (1992) observed that over time journalists have accepted the bureaucratic structure of the newsroom and the corresponding professional routines. He notes "contemporary journalists have internalized the constraints of professionalism far more than the 1930s writers had done, and are also far less politicized than their predecessors. They are committed more strongly to the norms of the profession than to political ideas" (Hallin, 1992, p. 15). Svennik Høyer (2005) notes that, as the routines of journalism have changed since the 1860s, "basic forms of journalism have been shared among journalists of different nationalities. Over time the technology, the techniques, the thinking and the ways of presenting news has crossed borders" (Høyer, 2005, p. 9).

Organization Work

The study of media routines is linked to an organizational perspective. Organizations create different routines to accomplish their work, creating tensions between the worker and the needs of the organization. Although the media may serve different functions, they share many organizational similarities that outweigh the differences. Thus whether news or entertainment, online or offline, from the social media or printed media, we ask: What are the stable, patterned sets of expectations and constraints that are common to most media organizations, and how do they change over time? News messages are symbolic content, produced according to practical considerations. Routines develop in response to these considerations and help organizations cope with the tasks at hand (Hirsch, 1977, p. 15).

Although entertainment and news organizations may be thought of in much the same way, we focus primarily on news, largely because there is less research on entertainment media routines. Much news research has been directed to the day-to-day activities of lower-level media workers: reporters, editors, and writers. The routines of media practice constitute the immediate environment of these media workers. Although publishers and others in the bureaucratic structure are also bound by routines, higher-level media workers are given greater range of movement.

Although we don't normally think of news work as a blue-collar occupation, the production of news is in many respects organized like a factory. All organizations try to routinize their work to improve efficiency, but some companies require it more than others. In observing a local television news station, Charles Bantz and his colleagues found that several factors produce routinization in television news. They found that television news people changed jobs more often than those in the print media, creating a continual turnover in personnel. Easily learned routines were essential for smooth organizational continuity, because television news required careful coordination of complex technologies that required specialized roles, scheduling, and other routinized procedures to put a news show together smoothly. In addition, competition for readers and advertisers led stations to hire news consultants who prescribed formulaic guidelines for the number of stories and their length. These factors led to "technically uniform, visually sophisticated, easy to understand, fast-paced, people-oriented stories that are produced in a minimum amount of time" (Bantz, McCorkle, & Baade, 1981, p. 371).

Bantz argued that the "television news factory" divides tasks into chunks at different stages along the assembly line—from generating story ideas to presenting the newscast. This highly routinized structure often lacks flexibility, and the highly specialized factory structure lowers news workers' investment in and control over the final news product. In addition, the factory structure fails to encourage professional values espoused by news workers. Instead workers are evaluated on their productivity—doing the assignment on time rather than well—not their time spent on trying to improve the system. Organizations' routines don't always mesh with the individual-level professional goals.

Routines as Level of Analysis

It is clear that the routines and organizational levels overlap conceptually. After all, organizations, most of which want to make a profit, design their architecture to accomplish their work efficiently. Media organizations establish rules within which individuals must work. If all news media had the same routines, then there would be little motivation to study them. But we find that routines within a type of medium (such as among television and news networks) are similar, whereas routines between media types (for example, television news with online news aggregators) are substantially different. These similarities within and differences between the ways media organizations work can be looked at separately to take a different perspective on the industry. Thus we treat media routines as a separate level of analysis from the organizational. Ultimately, routines are most important because they affect the social reality portrayed in media content. As Altheide (1976, p. 24) says, "the organizational, practical, and other mundane features of newswork promote a way of looking at events which fundamentally distorts them."

ROUTINES AS CONCEPTUAL MODEL

The study of routines has few theoretical underpinnings. Basic political and cultural theories shaped the development of the media, as did gatekeeping theory of the mid 20th century. More recently, a news paradigm has evolved to explain the shared thinking of news content production. Svennik Høyer (2005) summarizes the news paradigm as including five routines: (1) the event, (2) news values, (3) interviewing, (4) the inverted pyramid, and (5) objectivity: "Journalism is culturally and socially dependent. News must be adapted to cultural forms to be easy to understand, while journalists must operate according to professional norms, in order to make their routines socially acceptable" (Høyer, 2005, p. 14). Høyer proposes that the news paradigm doesn't fit every part of the social environment: The news paradigm is not used by all journalists; there are cultural influences and conditions through which information passes differently. This would be especially true under autocratic regimes and when highly polarized conflicts make it impossible to apply these routines (Høyer, 2005, p. 16). Geiß (2011) says that if a story attracts too much media attention and causes a news wave, the news media can be distracted from covering other important stories.

Media routines do not develop randomly. Given finite organizational resources and an infinite supply of potential raw material, routines are practical responses to the needs of media organizations and workers. Media organizations must efficiently deliver, within time and space limitations, a product that is acceptable to the consumer. Profit-making media strive to make a product that can be sold for more than it cost to produce. Thus, a media organization can be described much like any other business that strives to find a market for its product. The organization must adapt to constraints and must create routines that optimize the relationships between an organization and its environment.

As we suggested earlier, media routines stem from three domains: audiences, organizations, and suppliers of content. A demand from audiences for certain technologies (such as cable television or broadband for internet users) influences how sources make information available to organizations. A routine located in the middle of the triangle in Figure 7.1 would serve all the audience, organizational, and source domains equally. For example:

- When audience members use social media to reach people, they acquire information that can ultimately influence a media organization's production of the day's events. The information feeds back to consumers in the audience.

- The organization creates routine practices to handle the material that it must process and produce.

- What raw product is available from suppliers (sources) of information?

In Figure 7.1 we show the relationships among these domains. Each media routine can be placed within the triangle formed by the domains. For example, the long established inverted pyramid routine lies between production and consumption—organizations arrange information in decreasing order of importance, a pattern expected by consumers. Access to visual information increases the likelihood that an event will become suitable for television news. Each routine must strike a balance within the three constraints, none of which can be completely ignored.

Audiences as Consumers of Information

The media spend a lot of money studying their audiences. Newspapers keep a close watch on circulation figures. Broadcasters rely on companies such as Nielsen and Arbitron to give them the ratings and audience shares of their programs. The media are keenly interested in the size and demographic characteristics of their audiences, primarily because advertisers must know how to reach their target audiences. Audience data help gauge public acceptance after the fact but are not of direct help in guiding the countless choices that are involved in producing media messages.

Given the nature of the product, the question "What's news?" is inherently more difficult than "What sells?" Perhaps that is why we puzzle more over defining news than entertainment; entertainment producers have a more direct link to the audience than do their news counterparts. By watching the bestseller lists, the top grossing movies, and the highest-rated television programs, entertainment producers know what sells. Unlike news producers, movie studios can even try out different

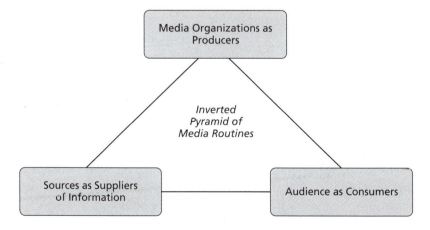

FIGURE 7.1 *Routines are shown inside of the triangle that shows relationships among sources/suppliers, organizations as producers, and content consumers*

endings with preview audiences; an editor, however, cannot consult audience members before making news selections. Audience research may give media workers ideas about the general interests of viewers, listeners, and readers, but it cannot help much in their daily choices.

For pre-internet media organizations, direct feedback from audience members was minimal. Few letters were received by news organizations and even fewer were published, after being cut and edited. Much has changed. The interactivity inherent in internet-based media organizations allows audience members to purposively comment on content or to email content links to others (Shoemaker, Johnson, Seo, & Wang, 2010). By studying comments and types of articles emailed, both editorial and marketing departments receive a richer data set about what the audience wants than they could ever get from a survey or focus group.

Internet technology also allows media organizations and advertisers to unobtrusively capture information about the audience's use of news, entertainment content, and advertising. Time spent, number of clicks, and page views allow organizations to directly measure several dimensions of audience interest in content and advertisements. More importantly, a news organization can as a result of this information customize its content for its user, or customer:

> by focusing customer's attention to a selected subset of news stories, or by augmenting selected news with related material or illustrative comparisons. Focusing can include filtering, which means showing only the stories that are assumed to be most relevant to the customer, or prioritization, meaning highlighting and emphasizing these stories. The goal of customized news augmentation is to relate the news stories better to what the user already knows. Augmentation combines continuous news streams with automatically selected personal or communal contextual information from heterogeneous sources.
>
> (Turpeinen, 2000, p. i)

News Values

News judgment is the ability to evaluate stories based on agreed-on news values, which provide yardsticks of newsworthiness and constitute an audience-oriented routine. That is, they predict what an audience will find appealing and important, and in practice they direct gatekeepers to make consistent event selections. Certainly 20th century news media technology—although it evolved quickly—did not encourage two-way communication. The organization delivered news to the audience, who received it. Two-way communication required special work on the part of audience members, in writing letters or visiting news offices, and therefore was rare in comparison to the interactivity the Internet makes possible.

Media organizations, in trying to figure out what sort of news the audience wants, have incorporated their production procedures into stable and enduring craft norms. For example, in 1925, Charles Merz wrote that the most newsworthy stories include fights "between well-identified antagonists which involves the element of suspense" and those that emphasize sex and crime (p. 158). Not a bad description of 21st century news, but what routines result in news about fights, sex, and crime? In 1978, Philip Schlesinger studied the BBC and concluded that journalists base some routines on assumptions about the nature of the audience and what journalists think news audiences want to receive (pp. 115–16).

Over the years, news values have become predictable; they have long been included at the beginning of most journalism textbooks. In one way or another, these news values have for many decades guided what people will find interesting and important to know about (from Stephens, 1980; but also see Baskette, Sissors, & Brooks, 1982; Dennis & Ismach, 1981):

- *Prominence and importance.* The importance of an event is measured in its impact; how many lives it affects. Fatalities are more important than property damage. Actions of the powerful are newsworthy, because they have more ability to affect the general public.

- *Conflict and controversy.* Controversy and conflict alert us to important issues that one of our social institutions should address. Conflict is inherently more interesting than harmony.

- *The unusual.* Oddity also interests us. We assume that the events of one day will be similar to the next inherently boring. When we read or view stories about unusual events, we are merely attending to the exceptions that create this routine.

- *Human interest.* People are interested in lots of things that have no direct effect on their lives, including celebrities, political gossip and human dramas. Interest is based on the fact that the subject's life is so different from our own.

- *Timeliness.* News is by definition timely, about new events that are close to us in time. People have limited attention spans and want to know what is happening now. Timely events may also more likely to require action to repair them.

- *Proximity.* Events that happen nearby are sometimes more newsworthy than distant ones, and local events may be more interesting to the audience than distant ones. Community media seek local angles of national stories so as to better interest the audience. As we are regularly exposed to news from all over the world, proximity may be less important.

(Lee, Han, Shoemaker, & Cohen, 2005)

The limited attention and interest of the audience is important in creating these news values. Even if the media could transmit everything that occurred in a day, the news content would not be useful or interesting.

News and Newsworthiness

Long-standing professional news values have led people to equate the construct of *news* with that of *newsworthiness*: If it's in the news, it must be newsworthy, meaning that it has one or more of the above characteristics. In fact, newsworthiness is only one of many influences that result in the social artifact *news*. There are many influences that decide not only which of the day's events become news, but also how information about them is molded into the news product. Influences from all levels of analysis determine the day's news; they are not as visible a target.

The confusion lies in the definitions of news and newsworthiness (Shoemaker, 2006). News is a thing, a social artifact that can be read, viewed, or interacted with. Deciding what's newsworthy, on the other hand, is a cognitive exercise, a judgment that any person can make. Shoemaker's hard wired theory of news (1996) suggests that humans are innately interested in threats and the unusual, because of a biological imperative to attend to deviance: conflict, controversy, sensationalism, celebrity and prominence, and the unusual. Surveillance of the environment is an evolutionary, adaptive activity (Darwin, 1936) that enhances our quality of life and affects whether we live or die: Our ancestors looked out for threats, thereby enhancing the probability that they would live, procreate, and pass their genetic inheritance down to the next generation. Over the generations, attendance to deviance has become hard wired in the brains of all humans and has manifested itself in the surveillance function of the news media.

Of course, people communicated about interesting events before the printing press. Travelers brought news of the last village to the next. Taliesin, chief bard of Britain during the sixth century, described the minstrels and their news: "Strolling minstrels are addicted to evil habits. Immoral songs are their delight. In a tasteless manner they rehearse the praise of heroes. Falsehood at all times they use" (Hartley, 2009, pp. 17–18; translated from the Welsh). Bad news and deviance has long been what people want to know about.

In 1940, Robert Park (reprinted in Tumbler, 1999, p. 13) compared news to history as two different ways of knowing. Park says:

> news is always or mainly concerned with the unusual and the unexpected. Even the most trivial happening, it seems, provided it represents a departure from the customary ritual and routine of daily life is likely to be reported in the press . . . It is not the intrinsic importance of an event that makes it newsworthy. It is rather the fact that the event is so unusual that if published it will either startle, amuse, or otherwise excite the reader so that it will be remembered and repeated.
>
> (Tumbler, 1999, p. 12)

Galician and Pasternak's (1987) survey of national television news directors revealed that scheduling good or bad news was not a conscious decision for most newscasters; none had a policy about the proportion of good and bad news stories. Still, most of these gatekeepers opened their news programs with a bad news story, believing it more newsworthy. They agree that showing bad news is "not an attempt to present the world negatively but an accurate reflection of the world" (Galician & Pasternak, 1987, pp. 87–8). Shoemaker and Cohen (2005) asked focus group participants from ten countries about bad news in the media. Although people longed for more good news, they understood why bad news was most of their local media menu: They believed that bad news was often more important and that people wanted to know about bad news (Shoemaker & Cohen, 2005, p. 89).

Bad news often signals a problem that needs attention (Grabe, 1999). We can easily see that covering bad news is more efficient for the audience than if the media dwelled only on what was going right. In totalitarian regimes, newspapers have been published that reported only good news. In the former Soviet Union, for example, the media were used to spread positive messages, such as a farm collective that exceeded its harvest projection, or the opening of a new tractor plant. Such announcements were designed to meet the state's needs, not those of the audience. Glasnost brought openness and a removal of some constraints on the media (Schillinger & Porter, 1991), but subsequent changes in Russian government have swung toward more routine government control of the news.

News routines can be observed in the editorial conference, in which news and feature staff members meet to decide what will be on the front page and how the stories will be displayed (Clayman & Reisner, 1998). The managing editor is often the chair, with other attendees coming from section editors, graphics, and image makers. Available stories are summarized, compared, and decisions are made: Is a story in or out? On page 1 or elsewhere? Does it have good images or just text?, and so on. Clayman and Reisner note that sociologists' and journalists' analyses of the news process differ greatly. Journalists, they say, either espouse a simple news-as-mirror-of-reality position or a more sophisticated view that journalists, who use professional rules to select and shape news items, are protected from external pressures and work to achieve objectivity. "Sociologists, in contrast, have demonstrated that journalists work within a complex institutional and cultural environment that leaves its imprint on the daily news. Decisions are not made by autonomous journalists, but are rather the product of the framework of social relationships at the newspaper" (Clayman & Reisner, 1998, pp. 196–7).

Defensive Routines

Although news values help gatekeepers select content attractive to the audience, other more defensive routines prevent journalists from offending the audience and their sources.

Fact Checking

Checking that news content is factual has been a long tradition aimed at protecting news media against publishing mistakes, which are a danger to journalists and their organizations. According to Stephen Cooper (2006, p. 21), they make it their duty to check facts in traditional news stories, but he suggests that bloggers may not hold the same professional and ethical norms as journalists, including those journalists who blog:

> In effect, they bring a "fresh set of eyes" to news copy, and thus may point out errors which professional journalists might overlook out of a mild case of groupthink . . . [T]he majority of factual errors in news coverage occur as a result of the shared viewpoints among news professionals, a conformity which may even verge on orthodoxy in some newsrooms. When purported facts are consistent with a shared interpretation of an event, situation, or issue, those purported facts may get far less scrutiny than they should; put another way, their consistency with elite opinion may cause factual errors to be considered presumptively accurate statements.
>
> (Cooper, 2006, pp. 21–2)

He continues to say that this does not imply that bloggers have "purer motives" or are more skilled at checking facts.

The fact checking reform movement has brought new life to the issue of objectivity in the last decade by evaluating claims against evidence. Groups such as PolitiFact and FactCheck.org seek to settle controversies with their own reporting, but as Graves (2012) finds in his ethnographic study of these groups and their "annotative journalism," they remain uncomfortable taking sides and decline to criticize the media themselves. In a polarized world of the networked journalism ecosystem, the fact-checkers seek a continuing role for professional judgment in establishing a legitimate center within the binary logic of the two-party US political system.

Objectivity

As Michael Schudson (2011) notes, the concept of objectivity developed over the late 19th and early 20th centuries. When the American Society of Newspaper Editors formed in 1922–3, the editors adopted "the 'Canons of Journalism,' a code of ethics that included a principle of 'Sincerity, Truthfulness, [and] Accuracy' and another of 'Impartiality,' which included the declaration 'News reports should be free from opinion or bias of any kind'" (Schudson, 2011, p. 75).

In an earlier work, Schudson (1978) notes that competition among newspapers at the turn of the century may have led them to conform to their publics' standards of truth, decency, and good taste.

Objectivity can be viewed as serving a defensive function. Editors and reporters became preoccupied with facts to avoid public criticism and embarrassment for the newspaper. Although a cornerstone of journalistic ideology, it is rooted in practical organizational requirements, making objectivity less a core belief of journalists and more a set of procedures to which they conform in order to protect themselves from attack. Fact checking was once a requirement in news production, but with many people losing their news jobs, fact checking is either laid on the reporter or eliminated. Many bloggers see their roles as checking facts in the offline media.

Gans (1979) suggested that the objective routine, by keeping personal values out, allowed reporters autonomy in choosing the news; otherwise every story would be subject to attack. Similarly, Hallin (1989, p. 67) argued that objectivity helped legitimate the news media. Because they are large, privately owned, and heavily concentrated, with a great deal of power, the media ensure public support through objectivity by claiming that their power has been put in a "blind trust." The Associated Press (AP) is also credited with a strong role at the turn of the century in strengthening the objectivity norm. A uniform style helped it sell its product to a diverse set of client newspapers, which in turn needed to reach a mass but also diverse audience for their mass advertising. Thus the objectivity routine helps organizations in a number of ways to maximize their audience appeal.

Audience Appeal and Narrative Structure

Not only do gatekeepers select information for its newsworthiness and audience appeal, but they also present it in ways designed to meet audience needs. In a newspaper the stories must be readable, the photos arranged properly on the pages, the headlines composed to direct reader attention. Television messages must be visually appealing and hold audience attention. These presentation techniques and formats become important routines of media work.

One of the most enduring routines is the *narrative* story structure. The story must have an inherent appeal, considering the prominence in culture of myths, parables, legends, and oral histories. Perhaps because it is closer to the oral tradition, television news has embraced the narrative story form most easily, with news producers regularly exhorting reporters to tell stories, not write reports. Early on, Epstein (1974) observed the importance in broad stories of having an element of drama, with a narrative structure that captures the audience's attention and holds it.

The story structure represents a routine way of processing what happened, and it guides the reporter in deciding which facts to include. The event must be transformed into a news commodity. Ronald Jacobs (1996, p. 373) suggests that creation of "narrativity" is one of the most important routines in news work.

Framing

Closely related to narrativity is the application of frames in a news story. *Framing* adds contextual information to a factual account: Frames put "isolated factual data into some sort of pattern we understand and find meaningful . . . Journalists weave their factual description of events into a coherent storyline, however nuanced or complex, in order to produce a competent news product" (Cooper, 2006, p. 105). Framing also helps the audience understand the importance and be able to understand the application of the facts to other events. Dietram Scheufele (1999) says that framing colors the content around the facts. As a routine, however, framing is more interesting as a dependent variable; why do journalists use specific frames? The research on media framing has become a vast area within communication research (e.g., Reese, 2007) and beyond the scope of this discussion, but here we regard framing as a routine, to the extent that symbol-handlers do it ritualistically, in a predictably structured way (routinely), and that it adds meaning to a seemingly disconnected list of facts. As journalists write news stories, they can consciously or unconsciously add one frame or another, because that's what they have been trained to do and because frames help the facts make sense.

Although this sounds sensible, there is no widely accepted definition of frame and no cohesive theoretical structure from which to synthesize studies (Scheufele, 1999, p. 103). Is frame merely a synonym for topic? Is frame a cognition such as schema or script?

> No evidence has yet been systematically collected about how various factors impact the structural qualities of news in terms of framing . . . At least five factors may potentially influence how journalists frame a given issue: social norms and values, organizational pressures and constraints, pressures of interest groups, journalistic routines, and ideological or political orientations of journalists.
>
> (Scheufele, 1999, p. 109)

Most significantly, scholars have not agreed on a set of frames that journalists commonly use. Some scholars have suggested that general, "generic" frames include conflict, human interest, consequence (Price, Tewksbury, & Powers, 1995, p. 5); diagnosis, prognosis, and motivation (Gerhards & Rucht, 1992, p. 582); and episodic or thematic (Iyengar, 1991).

Proximity and Scope

Closely related to framing is the scope of a news story. Whereas *proximity* is simply the closeness of the media organization to an event, *scope* is the contextual spin that journalists put on an event. Scope cues readers as to the relevance of an event to them. Cohen, Adoni, and Bantz (1990) suggest that readers' individual perceptions of reality organize news events by "zones of relevance, which differ on the basis of their proximity from the here and now of the individual's immediate environment" (p. 36). Close zones (narrow scope) relate to direct contact, whereas remote zones (broad scope) are abstract and only indirectly known. The congruence of scope and proximity (high if both local, for example, and low if they differ) may influence whether the event is framed as socially significant or deviant (Shoemaker, Lee, Han, & Cohen, 2007, p. 234). Journalists may assume that congruent events are newsworthy, because they require less cognitive effort. When considering an incongruent event, more thinking is necessary.

For example, the journalist finds out that the local mayor died due to breast cancer (local proximity) but that the family asks for donations to go to breast cancer research and the eulogy is about her death as only one example of a nation-wide health problem (national scope). The reporter has a decision to make: Should the story merely cover the mayor's accomplishments and life (narrow scope)? Or should the story emphasize her disease as part of a larger health danger (broad scope)? Because the event is a city official's death, it can be covered with either local or national scope. The readers' understanding of the event differs based on the scope that the journalist applies to the story.

Hun Shik Kim (2002) found that US television journalists use scope as a routine for deciding how to write articles about television shows that reflect their audience's demands. In this study, there was a strong difference in the stories transmitted by local stations and national networks. "Network journalists manifest a global view, selecting international news with diverse themes, while local television journalists adopt a more pragmatic stance due to business pressures and audience demands, choosing international news with a local angle" (Kim, 2002, p. 431).

The local stations, being less proximate to the international event, only covered the event if it could have local scope. The national networks evaluated the event as having global scope, leading them to cover diverse events.

The Audience as Sender and Receiver

The audience is the ultimate consumer of the media product—the end of the news process. However, since news migrated to the Internet, the audience has figured more prominently in the many routines of the news media. Apparently the audience was not receiving what it wanted, because newspaper circulations fell precipitously throughout the last half of the 20th century and only a small percentage of the public kept up with the news in any serious way. A closer examination of 20th century news values reveals that audience appeal was not an important determinant of content. Because news values have been studied by analyzing published news content, they represent only post-hoc explanations, not hypothesis tests.

One way to test the influence of routine news values is to question whether other stories satisfied these criteria, yet did not receive coverage. A more recent approach is to compare news values used by journalists with the news values used by their readers when they select articles to email. Obviously more research on audience news values is needed, especially about the news values of social media users. Although some are targeted at private groups (families, friends) much of the information available on Facebook and Twitter can be used by anyone. The phenomenon of user-generated video going viral is a reflection of the content's deviance, including embarrassing sex videos, babies being mishandled by their parents, or especially cute puppies and kittens. The viral metaphor implies that a disease is spreading quickly. Whoever produced the video shows it to someone else, thereby giving up control over its subsequent distribution. Once on the Internet, it is available to anyone and can diffuse exponentially.

In the early 21st century, we understand that the media are in the midst of change, much of which involves the Internet. Although we cannot predict the architecture of the coming world media system by mid century, we already know that rise of social media has created a sender–receiver–sender model, circular rather than linear. In fact, the linear models of the 20th century (Westley & MacLean, 1957; Lewin, 1943) are largely inadequate to explain the relationship between social and mass media. Information diffuses in patterns that are much more complicated than were the linear communication models of the past.

Organizations as Information Processors

What routines most help media organizations process information that comes to them from suppliers? The media organization must find ways of effectively gathering and evaluating this raw material before sending it to production. Most organizational routines have become part of the news business, giving workers clearly defined and specialized roles and expectations. As with the audience-oriented routines, we assume that organizational routines have developed to meet the needs of the system and that they have become standardized, institutionalized, and understood by those who use them.

Gatekeeping Theory

Following World War II a social psychologist created a theory that has since generated many media sociology studies. Gatekeeping theory includes a model that Kurt Lewin (1943) originally used to study how postwar food choices could be changed: Through what process does food get from its source to the family table, and who is most responsible for making decisions? He called his model "a theory of channels and gate keepers" and suggested that the theory could be used to study the selection and movement of several social artifacts, including news items. The news routine of gatekeeping evolved from this idea. Artwick (2004) provides a useful example:

> A reporter seeking information could run into a roadblock if police or a private individual won't release it. In this case, the authority closes the gate. But a reporter can just as easily stop the information flow when she abandons a story idea to develop another. And a producer can shut a gate when he drops a story from his newscast because he's running out of air time.
>
> (Artwick, 2004, p. 16)

Levin's model is now used to study the news production process—how information about an event is sent from person to person and how each decides whether it might be newsworthy, and all of this can happen before the information is sent to a journalist. The gatekeeping process describes what happens to the information after the event occurs (also see Shoemaker, 1991; Shoemaker & Vos, 2009). Reese and Ballinger (2001) argue that gatekeeping theory was limited by the prevailing notion in the 1950s that the media have only limited effects on the audience (Lazarsfeld et al., 1948).

Every news decision is shaped either by routine practices or by personal opinions, a balance that depends on the type of news. Shahira Fahmy (2005) says that there are few professional rules to guide photojournalists' and photo editors' selection of graphic (violent) images. It is not surprising, therefore, that Kimberly Bissell's research has found (2000, p. 91) that personal opinions often impact image choices more than photographic routines. In the newspaper she studied, primarily local photographs were published, including the stereotypical image of a cute child. Hard news photos were few. Sonenshine (1997) raised concern about the multitude of still and visual images that news media gratefully receive from freelancers and audience members.

> Publishing material shot by freelancers or ordinary folk who happen upon news is not, by itself, a bad thing—as long as there are competent newspeople making informed decisions about when to cover events and how. But news editors' power has waned as more and more information pours in to more and more places. Lost in all the information traffic are the "information cops," who used to be called "gatekeepers." These editors, news directors and publishers would ask the tough questions: where did this material come from? Was it properly obtained? Do we have more than one source on that story? Is it a story?
>
> (Sonenshine, 1997, pp. 11–12)

An alternative channel for information about events is the blogosphere, which supplements information from mainstream news media (Cooper, 2006):

> Just as the mainstream press sets an agenda of topics for the public to consider so does the blogosphere . . . [B]loggers decide which topics to comment on (gatekeeping) and how much to say about them (agenda-setting). When the blogosphere substantially differs from the mainstream media, we can consider this as constituting an alternative agenda. It is apparent that the agenda constructed in the blogosphere is not necessarily congruent with that constructed by the mainstream news media; a good number of posts argue, in essence, that either the mainstream media have erred in their judgment of the relative importance of current events or are willfully ignoring events of consequence.
>
> (Cooper, 2006, p. 129)

Events and issues come to the attention of bloggers, and they pass through gates and channels, eventually to choose events to write about and how to write it up (such as tone, quantity, prominence). Once published to the blogosphere, followers can read and comment. Because many of the followers are bloggers or journalists, there is an overlapping relationship between the content produced by the two—either uncomfortably close or representing the free flow of information, depending on one's point of view.

Gatekeeping can also apply to social media such as Twitter or Facebook (Shoemaker, Cohen, Seo, & Johnson, 2012). These give anyone (who has internet access and abilities) the opportunity to select events for comment and to let both bloggers and journalists know what their readers are thinking. Some have described this complicated situation as the *fragmentation* of the audience: Anyone can be a sender or receiver of information. Consequently, the gatekeeping model has been modified by Shoemaker and Vos (2009) to show that the channels through which information flows (such as traditional journalism, blogging, and the social media) have many opportunities to interact, one of which is to circulate information from channel to channel. Lewin's channels (1943) had high walls, with no movement of information between them. In the revised model, however, the channels have no walls; they are permeable, recognizing the continuous comment and flow of information between them. Although some say the gatekeeping is dead, or at least seriously wounded, Lewin's logic remains a useful structure within which to study the processing of news: information passes through channels and their several stages (sections, in the model). It is selected or rejected, run whole or edited down, written using different styles and tones, and ultimately published in one form or another.

Jane Singer's analysis of online media coverage of the 2000 and 2004 US presidential elections confirmed that newspaper editors used far more of the interactive aspects of the Internet that had developed between the two elections.

> Although they [editors] still see their role as revolving around the delivery of credible information, that information is less likely to be static and more likely to be open to further shaping by individual users . . . These findings suggest that newspaper editors may be reconceptualizing their gatekeeping role as they become more experienced in creating content for the internet, a medium whose open nature obliterated the traditional notion of the professional journalist deciding what information people can and cannot see.
>
> (Singer, 2006, p. 275)

A world in which "everybody" observes everybody else—a fiction, since many people consume little or no news—is not a chaotic world, nor anarchic. Journalistic work could not be accomplished if this were true. Instead, the world of traditional media (both on- and offline), the blogosphere, and the social media looks more like a complex system, so future studies may increasingly gather and analyze data using *system theory* and possibly multi-level modeling.

Decisions

The news service menu may limit the choices made by an editor, but that structuring is precisely what a media organization finds desirable. By subscribing to the AP, Reuters, or other news services, an organization can ensure a steady, predictable stream of a quality product and can reduce the amount of information for which it is responsible. This routine is one of the many that help media organizations operate smoothly. For example, the more constraints a reporter operates under, such as deadlines and geographic location, the narrower is the range of sources relied on for stories (Fico, 1984). Even though constraints affect content, routines help explain how that content is shaped in response to those limits.

Organizations must routinize work in order to control it. As rational, complex entities with regular deadlines, the news media cannot cope with the unpredictable and infinite number of events in the everyday world. Events must be recognized as newsworthy, sorted, categorized, and classified (such as hard or soft news). An organizing routine is especially important for news organizations, which must, in the seemingly contradictory phrase used by Tuchman (1973, p. 111), report "unexpected events on a routine basis."

Many routines are designed to help the organization cope with physical constraints; only a small part of the world can be dealt with. The very term *gatekeeper* suggests adapting to the physical limits of channels, sections within channels, and gates. Given the number of stories and the limited space, decisions must be made to funnel many news events down to a few. Media space is limited for some news organizations and virtually unlimited for others. A printed newspaper can be more flexible in the number of pages it produces, and so the news hole changes in relation to the amount of advertising from one day to the next. Online media organizations are limited only by their bandwidth, allowing them to include longer stories or a larger number of them. Some offline organizations, such as radio networks, extend their reach by creating online self-representations through various websites. This extends service to their audience; in addition to audio, they can now include still and video images and text.

Jane Singer's study (2001) of metropolitan newspapers, online and off, showed that the online versions showed a heavy preference for local news, leaving national and international news for the paper version (p. 78). She suggests that gatekeeping is failing when only such dichotomous decisions are made. She also questions whether the Internet and social media have killed Mr. Gates, but she does note that gatekeeping may be evolving within the social media, as a process to explain content production. Bloggers, for example, rarely make up an event that no one else has seen; instead they play off of traditional news media content. Hence the traditional media can operate as gatekeepers for bloggers.

In all media, the gatekeepers must choose from among many messages. Because of this steady appetite for information, bureaucratic routines help ensure a steady supply. For example, lacking the ability to be everywhere at once, large news organizations establish bureaus at locations most likely to generate newsworthy events. Reporting beats are traditionally at institutions where reliable news can be gathered (police, fire, courts, and so on). In other media, reporters are grouped as teams to make it easier for the organization to cover all aspects of an event.

Time may also be considered a physical constraint, depending on the news organization's deadline schedule. The development of a 24-hour news cycle by organizations such as CNN has created a need for more news content. All-day news scheduling makes timeliness somewhat less important, especially for in-depth reporting. There is, however, still a tendency for satellite television networks to schedule programs that are considered more important than 24-hour headlines, making these scheduled programs still subject to time-bound routines.

Organizations Define News

Although media routines help guide the flow of information into manageable physical limits, they impose their own special logic on the product that results. News organizations are not just passive recipients of a continuous stream of events lapping at the gates. News routines provide a perspective that often explains what is defined as newsworthy in the first place. Before it even gets to the first gate, news workers see some things as news and not others. Through their routines, they actively construct reality.

News is therefore what an organization's routines lead it to define as news. Tuchman (1973), for example, finds that news workers *typify* unexpected events based on how the organization must deal with them. Thus, the hard news/soft news distinction is less a function of the nature of the content than how the event is scheduled. Hard news can be based on either prescheduled events (trials, meetings, and so on) or unscheduled events (fires, earthquakes). In either case, the news of the event must get out quickly. Soft news, also called the feature story, is nonscheduled: that is, the news organization can determine when to carry it, such as on a slower news day. Nonscheduled stories can help fill in those holes where prescheduled stories are slack.

Tuchman (1973) uses the term *news net* to refer to a system of reporters deployed to institutions and locations that are expected to generate news events. Once deployed, this net tends to reinforce and certify the newsworthiness of those happenings that fall within it. Reporters covering these beats promote their stories to their organizations, which uses them if for no other reason than because it has an economic investment in them—the reporter's salary has already been paid. In his observations of a local newspaper, Fishman (1980) found that even when a reporter and editor agreed that nothing was happening on a beat, the reporter was still obliged to write something.

Routines yield acceptable news stories by directing news workers to take facts and events out of one context and reconstitute them into the appropriate format. But in doing so, this process inevitably distorts the original event. A predefined story angle, for example, provides reporters a theme around which to build a story. Reporters work most efficiently when they know what their interview sources will say. This sounds counterintuitive, but it helps explain why reporters reply on familiar sources: They can predict in advance who will give them the information needed to flesh out their angle.

Events Organize News

News is commonly thought to revolve around *events*. An event routine is helpful for the organization because, compared to more abstract processes, events are more easily and less ambiguously defined as news. Events are more defensible as news. Public life consists of an infinite number of occurrences, some of which are promoted into full-blown news events by sources or journalists. News organizations find these events useful as points of reference in the temporal world, to "break up, demarcate, and fashion lifetime, history, and a future" (Molotch & Lester, 1974, pp. 101–2).

Television and videos in particular need events to give the camera something to record. The visual nature of the media demands that something happens at the event. Even issue stories center around a concrete news event peg. Events are useful to news media in providing both a focus for their attention and a schedule of meetings, elections, and other events around which to plan and allocate resources. The organization can schedule coverage, because when and where the event will take place is known in advance. Events are so seductive that the news media will often cover them, even if news values would predict otherwise. Such stories may not be proximate or important, but they appeal to news producers by fitting an unambiguous news event model.

Media Groupthink

Journalists rely heavily on each other for ideas, and this reliance constitutes an important organizational routine, because it provides a reference point with which reporters can compare their own ideas (McCluskey, 2008). When carried to the extreme, however, relying on other journalists may homogenize a story and prevent coverage of other important events. *Groupthink*, or the pack mentality of journalists, may be responsible. Groupthink is "a mode of thinking that people engage in when they are deeply involved in a cohesive ingroup . . . Groupthink refers to a deterioration of mental efficiency, reality testing, and moral judgment that results from ingroup pressures" (Janis, 1983, p. 9). It can occur within a media organization or across journalists who cover one topic—a presidential election, for example. When covering an ambiguous social world, news workers seek certainty in consensus by consulting each other. The groupthink phenomenon makes journalists "insular and self-reinforcing . . . It provides them with a modicum of certitude that enables them to act in an otherwise uncertain environment" (Sigal, 1973, pp. 180–1).

Lacking any firm external benchmarks against which to measure the product, journalists take consistency as their guide: consistency with other news organizations and even with themselves. Subscription news retrieval systems, such as Lexis-Nexis, make it easier for reporters to rely on their own past work for guidance, and the Internet makes it easy to check any newspaper's coverage of an event. This inbred media reliance contributes to the closed system of much reporting. Yet it also provides an essential function, reducing the risk for the organization by ensuring that its product is the correct product.

Twenty-first century journalists have the entirety of the Internet to search. In response to a simple or more complex keyword search, Google and other search engines produce a list of hits, in order of relevance, which is calculated by a proprietary algorithm. Many of these do not provide the wanted information, but journalists scan hits to give themselves access not only to their own organization's work but also to information from around the world. Although the Internet provides a larger and more diverse pool of information, because its relevance and accuracy is in question, journalists still need to compare their work with that of others.

The Pack Versus the Exclusive

The organization must balance the benefits derived from the *pack* routine with the benefits of the exclusive. To understand why a news organization would rather run with the pack than scoop the competition, we have to understand the functions these routines serve. Exclusives do little to enhance the audience appeal of an organization. Newspapers, for competitive reasons, develop exclusive stories or high-profile multipart series designed to attract the attention of Pulitzer Prize judges, plus state and local contests. The very fact that these are exceptional and noteworthy, however, shows them to be the exception to the more common pack coverage.

If the mainstream media all go after the same stories, how is one organization permitted to lay claim to special excellence? Getting first what everyone else wants is the standard in the highly ambiguous process of deciding what is news. Network journalists covering political conventions pride themselves on getting information even a few seconds before the competition. Exclusives also provide a standard of performance by which organizations can evaluate their employees. Schudson notes: "The race for news—a race whose winner can easily be determined by a clock—affords a cheap, convenient, democratic measure of journalistic 'quality'" (1986, p. 3). Yet the reporter does not want to get too far in front of the pack. In coverage of presidential campaigns, for example, national attention is directed at the same candidates and events, causing reporters to be in their greatest synchronization. The desire to be unique is far outweighed by the risk of being different and perhaps wrong in full view of the nation.

In her coverage of the 2000 and 2004 campaigns, Elizabeth Skewes (2007) recalls this anecdote from 2000:

> USA Today's Martin Kasindof . . . was taking down a few quotes from Cheney's speech at a rally at Loras College in Dubuque, Iowa. And, from his perch on the press stand, he was sizing up the crowd. As soon as Cheney finished speaking, Kasindorf and several other reporters in the traveling press corps huddled to negotiate a crowd estimate. Kasindorf put the crowd at 400, someone else said it looked like 600, and the press corps split the difference between the two and settled on 500. Then they talked about the crowd reaction. One reporter asked, "How many would you say were clapping?" "Maybe half," another said.
>
> (p. 108)

Political campaign journalists do compete with one another for different facts or approaches to the election, but the "bubble" they live in—going from hotel to bus or plane and back again together over long hours—necessitates that competition occurs within a framework of shared experiences and norms (Skewes, 2007, p. 109).

Medium-Based Routines

Clearly, different types of media must vary structures in order to carry out their functions. The print and broadcast media, for example, differ in the technology they use to gather and transmit messages, their economic support, how frequently they publish their product, and their political relationships (for example, with the Federal Communications Commission). One way to identify important differences in organizational routines is to observe how workers differ in their behavior and attitudes, differences that can be traced to the nature of the organization they work for.

Although they have a common profession, reporters differ in the ways they deal with their sources. Because television news stations typically have smaller staffs than newspapers in comparable communities, reporters are subject to more demand for daily stories. If the stations also have an internet site, a Facebook page, or a blog, then their reporters are responsible for feeding all of these with daily content. Because television can use a smaller number of stories, television news content may be more deviant than that of newspaper stories. The smaller television gate requires many tough decisions that concentrate news values, whereas newspapers' larger news holes allow more variation. This difference influences both media's selection of events and how the events are portrayed (Shoemaker & Cohen, 2005).

Other effects on content are more subtle. For example, television news stories have traditionally relied on reporter standups, the on-camera appearance of the journalist designed to guide the viewers' understanding of the news event. In providing this commentary, reporters look for snappy language and often fail to provide the usual attribution for their assertions. Because these standups must often be recorded long before the final story is compiled, last minute changes in reports can leave the reporter's claims with inadequate support (Taylor, 1993).

Broadcast reporters have been less likely to say they have regular beats and more that they have freedom to select the stories they work on (Becker, 1982), and they have reported having more editorial decision-making power than their print counterparts (Ismach & Dennis, 1978). Practically speaking, it is harder to change a reporter's video package than to edit newspaper copy. Once the reporter has filed a story, however, he or she must relinquish control to others. Because of the presentation aspects of television news, considerable effort goes into getting the show out, and the reporter's work becomes one element within the larger population of stories.

Livingstone and Bennett (2003) conducted a study to discover whether new technologies have changed television news: Are spontaneous live events covered more than ones planned by officials and bureaucracies? Are official sources used less than they used to be? When "eyewitness" news was promoted by local television stations in the 1980s, critics worried that traditional news values would be gradually de-emphasized, because the technology used to produce live coverage of spontaneous events cost a lot, putting economic pressure on the station to use it. "Thus, technology became something of a stand-alone story element—a means of dramatizing and stimulating story formats, and delivering the promise of the action news brand" (Livingstone & Bennett, 2003, p. 371).

The routines discussed here serve the convenience and needs of media organizations as they produce their product. Of course, the media do not exert complete control over the raw material that goes into that product. To complete the picture of routines, we consider next those that are a function of the suppliers or sources of the raw material.

External Sources and Suppliers of Content

Finally we turn to our third source of routine practices. In manufacturing symbolic content, the media rely on external suppliers of raw material, whether speeches, interviews, corporate reports, or government hearings. Source routines are an adaptation by media organizations to the constraints imposed by their suppliers of information. In some cases, media and sources have adapted to each other's requirements, making it hard to determine which causes the other. Wilson Lowrey (2006) suggests that some sources work to create and maintain relationships with mainstream reporters, but that this kind of relationship is less likely to develop with bloggers (p. 484). Whether bloggers represent a threat to journalists' relationships with sources is questionable: "News organizations may be more interested in containing and directing the blogging phenomenon than in fostering democratic participation. It is unlikely that the content of organizationally sanctioned blogs will have much bite to them, given resource needs and legal concerns" (Lowrey, 2006, p. 493). Jane Singer (2005) found that when mainstream journalists blog, they tend to use many of the same norms and routines as in their news organization, including nonpartisanship and gatekeeping. These blogs, whose architecture includes two-way communication, tend to include many links to other mainstream media sites. She suggests that journalists are "normalizing" the blog (Singer, 2005, p. 173) through the use of old routines, but that they are also increasing transparency by sourcing information through the use of hyperlinks (Singer, 2005, p. 192).

In some cases, source-oriented routines are hardly visible. For example, even highly enterprising investigative reports such as CBS News *60 Minutes* often rely on lawsuits in progress for stories. Notice the number of potential sources in such stories that cannot or will not comment due to impending litigation. Lawsuit-based issues are convenient for journalists to cover. The legal system has essentially laid the groundwork for the reporter and sets the routines. Willing sources (usually on the plaintiff side) are available and committed to a clear point of view. Articulate lawyers are more willing to advance their client's case.

Public Relations

Other source-based routines are more obvious, but less transparent. Photo opportunities and press conferences show more clearly the routines employed by sources
to get into the news. In recent years the public has become wise to many of these
strategies, as indicated by the entry of terms such as media event, sound bite, and
spin doctor. The rise of public relations has played a major role in routinizing and
making more systematic the link between the press and other institutions. During
the early 20th century, newspapers encouraged public relations efforts by using the
handouts and copies of speeches supplied by press agents, even though scorning
those who provided them (Schudson, 1978). The rise of pseudo-events as a routine
in public relations also created a routine for journalists. The pseudo-event does not
arise naturally in the environment, such as a fire or election; instead someone creates it by organizing an event (bank president explains failure), inciting public reaction (protests or walks/runs to raise money), or planting information (officials give
journalists background information). Journalists are easily manipulated by pseudo-
events, due to their dependence on the news flow of public relations-generated
information. Pseudo-events tend to be more dramatic and vivid, because they were
created to be (Boorstin, 1961).

The term *astroturfing* refers to the practice of providing prewritten opinion
columns, talking points, or speeches to supporters of a group so that the supporters
can diffuse the products to others. "It would appear that astroturfing is a play on the
metaphor grass roots, referring to a spontaneous expression of a sentiment shared
among the populace. When the expression is deliberately stimulated through this
sort of communication strategy, it will often be labeled by critics as astroturf" (Cooper, 2006, p. 187). Perhaps the most important effect is that it distorts people's
perceptions of public opinion.

Is this pre-made content different from what a journalist would produce? Probably in some cases, but studies have shown that journalists and public relations
practitioners share the same news values (for example, Shoemaker & Cohen, 2005;
Sallot, Steinfatt, & Salwen, 1998).

Channels of Information

Theoretically, the news media have countless information resources available to
them, including first-hand observation, libraries, polling, and the Internet. Practically, however, they depend heavily on interviews with people for their information.
Sigal (1973, p. 20) defined routine channels as official proceedings, press releases,
press conferences, and nonspontaneous events. Informal channels included background briefings, leaks, nongovernmental proceedings, and reports from other news
organizations. Enterprise channels consist of interviews conducted at the reporters'
initiative, spontaneous events witnessed at first hand, independent research, and
reporters' own conclusions and analysis. The term channel in this context comes
from gatekeeping theory, with channels (and sections within channels) carrying

information about events and shaping it into news (Shoemaker & Vos, 2009). Sigal (1973) found that more than half of the news came through routine channels.

When news media moved to the Internet, in one form or another, the Internet and its browsers became a routine research channel for finding anything from small details to large treatises and on virtually any topic. Internet-based media organizations make their content available to anyone—although some by subscriptions—and so journalists can routinely check what the competition is doing.

Although the Internet is widely available in the Western world and Australia (between 61 percent and 78 percent of people have internet access), diffusion in Africa, Asia, and South America is lower (13 percent to 39 percent) (Internet World Stats, 2012). On the other hand, more than 1 billion people in China have the Internet, twice the US number. The number of users does not define similarity in available content, however; for example, the Chinese government regularly tries to restrict information from the outside world, such as from major US news media (Kahn, 2002), and the news China makes available to its citizens is routinely censured.

Official Sources

The centralization of government power following World War II enhanced its ability to control information, and with that increased ability came routines for institutionalizing the control. The routines imposed by official sources, especially those in Washington, have drawn the most scholarly attention. Newsmakers in business and the professions also attempt to routinize their relations with the news media. Corporate executives hold news conferences to announce a new product; celebrities release information about their latest film or events in their personal lives.

The news making activity of government has nevertheless been of greatest interest, because official behavior is more open to view and study. Corporate executives are less likely to write memoirs than former politicians. The attempts of business to manipulate information, being more diffuse and secretive, provoke less attention than the more easily located government agencies, with their greater tradition of openness and public accountability. Although all sources are becoming more sophisticated in their media relations, official relations have achieved a normalized and institutionalized state.

News content consists largely of statements from official sources. In practice these events are often well choreographed by the sponsoring official, who can set the rules and exert greater control over the flow of information. Questions can be planted, hostile reporters ignored, friendly ones recognized, difficult questions ignored, or evasive responses given.

Informal background briefings may not come through a routine channel, as Sigal (1973) defines it, but briefings create a regular channel through which officials transmit information. These briefings are common in Washington and are governed by generally accepted conventions, such as "off the record," on "deep background" or "background." Off the record information cannot be used in any form; deep background material can be used but not quoted or attributed to the source in any way. Background-only information may be attributed by using a variety of references other than by name (senior White House officials, Pentagon spokespersons, and so on). The objectivity routine normally dictates that reporters name their sources, but they accept these governmental ground rules when their alternative is to get no information at all. Sources find many advantages to giving out not-for-attribution information; foremost among them is the ability to avoid accountability for their statements.

Some officials may go beyond these briefings and pass information to reporters anonymously, in what are called leaks. Presidents complain regularly about leaks in their administration, because as the flip side of the carefully coordinated planned message of the day, leaks threaten the president's unified control of information. Although information passes through leaks less often, they are more routine than exceptional and serve many valuable functions for government officials. Whereas briefings are done on purpose as a part of the overall official strategy, often at the request of reporters, leaks are generally initiated by officials acting on their own as a tactic in intra-organizational infighting; they can be directed at a single reporter at a time, often on an exclusive basis. Hess (1984, pp. 77–8) lists several functions of leaks: to float a trial balloon, to blow the whistle on waste or dishonesty, to promote or sabotage policy, to curry favor with reporters, to carry out a grudge against bureaucratic rivals, and to enhance the leaker's ego by promoting an insider image.

The government provides a convenient and regular flow of authoritative information, which reporters find efficient compared with more labor-intensive research. Reliance on sources reduces the need for expensive specialists and extensive research. Furthermore, Daniel Hallin (1989) argues that professionalization has strengthened the connection between news media and state. Given an objective and disinterested stance on the part of the journalist, government officials provide authoritative validation of the news product. Paradoxically, Sigal (1973) observed that the competitive requirements of journalism also make them reliant on official sources.

Expert Sources

An increasingly important component of the source routine is the expert, the person relied on by journalists to put events into context and to explain the meaning of news. Because the objectivity routine hinders reporters from overtly expressing their points of view, they must find experts to provide the meaning of news events. The choice of experts has an important influence on how that meaning is shaped.

University experts, argued Steel (1990), are particularly attractive to television news producers, who usually have already decided what they want said before calling these sources to "reinforce their own understanding of a story" and to create "the illusion of objective reporting" (p. 28). Although few of these academics provoke or challenge, seeing them gives the impression that something important has been said. Their comments are presumed to lack bias and to be impartial, which helps producers and reporters round out stories and balance sources.

Presidential Manipulation of Routines

In recent years, sources have become more sophisticated in dealing with the news media and in making routines work in their favor. Many of these routines became visible at the presidential level with the rise of the Reagan-era public relations model of information management, although many other sources in government and elsewhere have adopted similar strategies. These routines involve controlling information for government agencies by regulating and shaping the flow of information. Although they may have originated in earlier administrations, such as Nixon's, they became fully developed under Reagan, hiring public relations experts and using the techniques of mass marketing as part of overall political strategy. Simple distancing of the news media constituted an important new routine technique. This included providing visual opportunities of Reagan leaving for Camp David but using the waiting helicopter to drown out reporters' questions, restricting questions during White House photo opportunities, and drastically reducing the number of press conferences and other unscripted encounters.

If they are unable to dictate the news itself, administration sources try to put the most favorable light on events through follow-up contacts with reporters. It has become customary, for example, for party spokespersons (administration officials, senators, and so on) to make themselves available to reporters during conventions and after presidential debates and other campaign events. By presenting a coordinated response, they aim to frame the event in the most desirable manner. Elsewhere officials may engage in damage control by calling network correspondents at the last minute with the White House's point of view, knowing they will be obliged to at least acknowledge it in their closing standups. "The reporters respond to that," communications director David Gergen said in defense of the practice. "They like it. They need it. And you could get them to change their feed" (Smith, 1988, p. 410).

One of the most skillful crafters of Reagan's media image was Michael Deaver, who developed what he called a visual press release, an event crafted to make a visual message: Reagan visiting a job training center during the 1982–3 recession; Reagan visiting a Fort Worth housing construction site to announce an increase in housing starts. According to Hedrick Smith (1988), "deep down, Deaver's goal was to become the de facto executive producer of the television network news shows by crafting the administration's story for the networks" (p. 416). He strove to reach this goal by providing the network with irresistible events and, in the process, developed a new set of symbolic routines. Administrations have become more sophisticated over the years, with President Obama using social media effectively to reach media contacts and citizens.

Bureaucratic Routines

These are the more visible ways in which sources influence the news product. The news media adopt messages from the entire bureaucratic structure of source institutions. Indeed, news can be considered a product of one bureaucracy gathered from other bureaucracies. Sigal (1973) calls government the "coupling of two information processing machines" (p. 4). Thus, in addition to having their news regulated by sources, journalists have information structured for them by other bureaucracies. Out of direct audience and often newsroom contact, journalists adopt the perspectives of the bureaucracies they cover. This highlights some events while rendering others invisible.

Fishman (1980) concentrated on this bureaucratic organization of news work, observing the way in which reporters made their rounds. By systematically organizing their stops during the day (courts, sheriff, police), reporters avoided wasting time. Fishman's reporters, for example, made most efficient use of their time by checking with the courts after checking with the sheriff and police. The court office would not know in advance when cases would be coming up, but police and sheriff offices could be monitored at any time for recent developments. Indeed, reporters who failed to follow this routine were likely to get in trouble with their superiors. As Fishman observed, "the round has a day-in day-out repetitive character, a stability over time. It consists of a series of locations that the reporter moves through in an orderly, scheduled sequence" (1980, p. 43). Fishman argued that the beat routine is constructed around the structure of bureaucracies and directs reporters to certain features of institutions, those points in the system that yield the most efficient concentrations of information. He identifies two kinds of institutional centers in particular that journalists depend on: the media contact, or the meeting. Reporters value meetings for concentrating lots of information into a short period of time.

INFLUENCES ON CONTENT FROM ROUTINE PRACTICES

That all media have routine practices to accomplish their goals is clear. But now we turn to the question of how these routines can impact the quality and quantity of media coverage.

Mr. Gates

One of the earliest and most frequently cited studies is the gatekeeper study by David Manning White in 1950. Although it focused primarily on individual rather than routinized judgments, it began a long tradition of examining the criteria that media decision makers use to select information. White kept track of the stories selected by the last in a chain of gatekeepers, a newspaper wire editor he called Mr. Gates, and later questioned him about his decisions. White felt that scholars should study the subjective, idiosyncratic reasons that explain why the editor chose one story over another. Mr. Gates's comments about the stories he did not select included "not interesting," "b.s.," and "don't care for suicide stories" (White, 1950, p. 386).

White recognized the importance of constraining routines on Mr. Gates, who said, for example, that he preferred stories that were slanted to conform to his paper's editorial policy (1950, p. 390). In a 1956 study of several such editors at 16 Wisconsin daily newspapers, Walter Gieber (1960) found little difference among the papers in story selection and display, concluding that the task-oriented telegraph editors experienced in common the pressures of the newsroom bureaucratic routines. In 1966, Paul Snider went back to the original Mr. Gates and replicated the 1949 study, finding a big decrease in the number of human interest stories used in 1966, and a big increase in hard news, primarily about international and crime. Snider speculated that this change reflected a difference in the social environment. In 1949 the USA was not at war, but by 1966 the media were getting stories about the Vietnam War (Snider, 1966, pp. 426–7). News gatekeeping can result in a mediated reality governed by journalistic norms.

In more recent studies, scholars emphasize the concentric rings of constraints around Mr. Gates. Gatekeeping theory is supported by the strong similarities in news agendas across media, despite the fact that each organization is staffed with its own "subjective" gatekeepers. In a re-analysis of White's data Hirsch (1977) showed that Mr. Gates selected stories in roughly the same proportions that they were provided by the wire service: The menu of crime, disaster, political, and other stories was duplicated on a smaller scale in the editor's selections. Thus Mr. Gates exercised personal choice but only within the format imposed on him by the wire service routines. Did Mr. Gates and the wire service employees simply hold the same individual values as to the relative importance of the news topic categories, or was the wire menu dictating Gates's agenda?

To find out, Whitney and Becker (1982) experimentally presented one group of editors with a set of stories distributed unevenly across seven topics (labor, national, international news, and so on), while another group received an equal number of stories in each topic. The editors closely followed the proportions contained in their source copy when the proportions varied, but used more subjective judgments when given equal numbers of stories in the categories. When story proportions varied, the news routine had an impact by cluing the editors in making their selections. Now that news services no longer dominate the supply of news, more recent research has shown that, although newspapers chose from the same pool of photos of 9/11 and the Afghan War, their choices were different (Fahmy, 2005).

Scott Althaus' study (2003) of gatekeeping and news sources in the 1990–1 Persian Gulf War shows that official sources had less influence on news coverage than expected, with journalists following the routine practice of locating and publishing oppositional sources:

> This discretion did not tend to produce many bold statements of fundamental criticism . . . , but it would be a mistake to infer from this that strategic criticism was thereby marginalized . . . Oppositional context discourse, often initiated by

journalists rather than merely passed along by them, constitutes an important venue for strategic criticism.

(Althaus, 2003, p. 404)

Althaus concludes that "pushover journalism in the realm of foreign affairs still occurs—witness the tepid debate over American involvement in Afghanistan following the 9/11 terrorist attacks" (2003, p. 404), but that administration control is not total.

William Cassidy's (2006) study of gatekeeping in online and print news revealed that journalists' role conceptions were similar, and routine influences explained more variance in predicting role conceptions than did individual influences. This is consistent with findings from Shoemaker et al.'s (2001) study of news coverage of congressional bills, but conflicting results come from Marie Hardin's (2005) study of gatekeeping of women's sports in the southeastern USA, in that sports section gatekeepers' selection of sports events was explained more by their personal characteristics and beliefs, especially their perceptions of what their audiences want. She says that these perceptions may be driven by a negative hegemonic ideology about women's sports (p. 72).

Chang and Lee's (1992) study of newspaper editors' selection of foreign news revealed two functions of roughly the same importance. The first included individual-level variables such as years the editor has worked, the editor's type of journalism training, and political leanings. The second function was more related to routine characteristics of foreign news: threat to the USA, loss of lives and to property, US trade relations, physical distance from the USA, country's military strength, and the country's level of economic development. The authors concluded that "newspaper editors' perceptions of foreign news factors are determined by individual differences and organizational constraints in the newsroom" (Chang and Lee, 1992, p. 560).

Mr. Gates was a lone gatekeeper—if he decided to open the news gate, the event became news. But Lewin's model predicts that multiple items passing through channels must pass multiple gates. Each gate precedes a section in the channel. For example, the journalist may observe an event and write a story for the editor. The editor decides whether to allow the story to pass the is-this-story-newsworthy gate and continue in the channel through another section, perhaps one in which images are selected to pass through the next gate to production, and so on. As Dan Berkowitz (1990) argues:

The metaphor of opening and closing a gate to allow individual news items through didn't provide a close fit to what was observed in the [television] newsroom. Stories that passed through one gate faced still other gates on their way toward being broadcast. Spot news closed the gate on planned event stories. Resource constraints and logistical problems sometimes closed the gate on spot news.

(p. 66)

Berkowitz describes the forces that Lewin predicts as in front of gates. These can be positive or negative and vary in strength. Forces are rarely studied in gatekeeping, but in reality the forces in front of and behind each gate represent variables, such as resources, audience interest, event characteristics, personal opinions and routine directives, and pressures from sources, among others. In addition, there has been too little research attention to the sections within Lewin's channels, each of which represents a step along the way to production. Although Bass (1969) recognized that gatekeeping should at least be divided into "news gathering and news processing segments" (p. 69), there are of course many more sections in the channels that produce 21st century media.

Shaping the Event

Shoemaker and Cohen (2005) conducted a field experiment to assess the similarity of readers' assessments of local newspaper articles to the prominence of the articles in their newspapers. At the end of each focus group, the moderator asked everyone to rank order the newsworthiness of three days of ten local newspaper stories. The stories were selected from each of three days' editions of the newspaper, from the least to the most prominent, measured several months earlier by weighting its length by the story's position in the newspaper. The study found that assessments of each story's newsworthiness by readers, journalists, and public relations practitioners were only marginally related to how prominently the news stories were presented in the newspapers.

Dan Berkowitz (1993) surveyed workers at 12 television stations about their work roles and socialization into journalism—programmers, business staff, and journalists. The three groups shared the view that news judgment should determine news selection, but they differed in predicting whether news judgment would, in the gatekeeping process, be overturned by other factors, such as programming for audiences and economic considerations. Tuchman (1978) concluded that regular routines of newsgathering were less important when an extraordinarily important event occurred, what she called "what a story." Berkowitz (1992), however, found that television newsrooms were able to work by improvising around existing routines, which served two key purposes for this what-a-story. First, routines served as a guide for organizational behavior: By electing to follow a modified version of an everyday news routine, newsworkers could quickly know the appropriate procedures for creating their news product. Second, these routines guided the evaluation of journalistic performance (Berkowitz, 1992, p. 92).

Objectivity has traditionally been a journalistic goal, such that there are separate channels in the media organization for news and for the financial side. Today, however, that separation is either removed, with marketing staff participating in editorial meetings, or the wall between the channels is thin. Most journalists strive to keep their reporting truthful and fair, but the 21st century media can be much more partisan and occasionally unfair, harkening back to Senator Joe McCarthy's control of the media during his anticommunist campaign. His statements were dutifully carried by the news media, even when journalists knew or suspected that he was lying. When objectivity is defined as strictly reporting what people say, it turns journalists into mere conduits. However, when journalists include context and fact checking of sources' statements in their stories, the sources often accuse the media of not being objective, of being biased.

Shoemaker, Seo, Johnson, and Wang (2008) found that stories about normative deviance (such as crime and political conflict), a traditional standard of the front page, are apparently less important to nytimes.com readers when they select articles to email. Instead they select a combination of odd, personally important, and analytical stories or opinions. Readers' ideas of newsworthiness differ from the crime and other normatively deviant stories that editors have favored.

Writing the Story

News stories are written according to judgments about the nature of the event (Tuchman, 1978). For example, stories designated as hard news and soft news are written differently, with the time pressure of hard news events creating a need to get the most important information in the first part of the story. The inverted pyramid form of writing follows this logic by including information in descending order of importance. Its establishment as a news routine comes from its ability to shorten it by cutting from the end rather than rewriting it. Horst Pöttker (2005) studied the *New York Herald* and the *New York Times* from 1855 to 1920 to discern use of different writing styles and compares the chronological, narrative style to the inverted pyramid. The chronological style generally buries the lead, which often comes at the end. Pöttker offers this example of a story about a Swiss event, from the *New York Herald*, January 17, 1850:

> A strange circumstance has just taken place at Herisau, the capital of Inner Appenzell, in Switzerland . . . A young girl of 19, some months back, assassinated her rival. Her lover was arrested with her, and, as she accused him of the crime, both were put to the torture. The girl yielded to the pain, confessed her crime; the young man held firm in his denial; the former was condemned to death, and on the 7th of this month was decapitated with the sword in the market-place of Herisau. This fact is itself a startling one, but the details are just as strange. For two hours the woman was able to struggle against four individuals charged with [carrying out] the execution. After the first hour, the strength of the woman was still so great that the men were obliged to desist. The authorities were then consulted, but they declared that justice ought to follow its course. The struggle then recommenced, with greater intensity, and despair seemed to have redoubled the woman's force. At the end of another hour, she was at last bound by the hair to a stake, and the sword of the executioner then carried the sentence into effect.

> (Pöttker, 2005, p. 53)

If this were written in the inverted style, what would be the lead? Certainly it is not the fact that a crime was committed and justice was carried out. Instead, it is the remarkable struggle of the woman and that her beheading could not occur until she was subdued by tying her hair to a stake. The chronological writing style better fit the soft news story, in which timeliness is less critical.

Some stories are made part of a larger continuing drama. Nimmo and Combs (1983) observed that the Iranian hostage crisis story was treated like a melodrama by the American television networks and suggested that, by increasing the sense of drama in covering a continuing event, reporters are distracted from providing more complete coverage of the conflict. The social media can also increase the dramatics associated with reporting news. When the Egyptian government shut off the Internet during the 2011–12 revolution as a way to slow the flow of information in and out of the country, people used their cell phones to send information via Twitter. The *New York Times* online ran a Twitter-based column that was continuously updated by reporters' short messages. The presentation of real-time and (largely) unfiltered information made the event's coverage much more dramatic and interesting than if routine news stories had continued.

When covering events, reporters often have an anticipated script as to how the story will unfold. The power of this script can be seen in an incident one evening in 1983. A man called a television news operation and said that he was going to set himself on fire, trying to ensure television coverage. A television crew was sent, anticipating a routine story in which the police would arrive in time to subdue the man and take him to jail. The police were delayed, but so strong was their anticipated script that the camera crew began filming anyway, capturing images of the man setting himself on fire and running off in a ball of flame. Critics argued that the crew should have tried to prevent the man from hurting himself, but the powerful routine script overrode individual judgment (Bennett, Gressett, & Haltom, 1985). Of course, trying to fit news stories into familiar forms may blind reporters to other features of the story. Issues don't always lend themselves to the event model, although they are often framed within events. A president's visit to a national park, for example, may obscure the fact that no substantial action has been taken to protect the environment.

Negotiating the News Net

Deadlines force journalists to stop seeking information and file a story, adjusting their work schedules accordingly. Tuchman (1977a) noted that this causes temporal gaps in the news net (in addition to geographic and institutional gaps): Events falling outside normal business hours, for example, have less chance of being covered. As Michael Schudson (1986) observes, the news organization "lives by the clock. Events, if they are to be reported, must mesh with its temporal spokes and cogs . . . News must happen at specified times in the journalists' 'newsday'" (p. 2). With the advent of the 24-hour news day, timeliness is somewhat less important, but still some television news programs, for example, are programmed to show at specific times. Politicians are particularly mindful of this and schedule their own media events early enough in the day to get on the evening newscasts, or on late Friday if they want to minimize coverage, a routine that has evolved with the 24-hour news stream. This focus on timely stories often doesn't encourage journalists to adequately cover slowly developing stories and discourages advocacy journalism: Reporters can address a problem but cannot dwell on it. They must move on to more timely issues.

When in the field, the groupthink routine manifests itself as groups of journalists covering news in packs. Television and print reporters are often seen crowding around newsmakers with outstretched microphones and recording equipment. Not only do reporters tend to cover the same people and stories, but they rely on each other for ideas and confirmation of their respective news judgments. In his oft-cited study, Timothy Crouse (1972) observed how reporters who covered the 1972 presidential campaign relied heavily on each other, particularly on the AP reporter, for help in constructing story leads. The "Boys on the Bus" knew that their editors would question their stories if they deviated too far from the wire service version of an event. Following a primary debate between Hubert Humphrey and George Mc-Govern, newsroom reporters immediately checked with AP reporter Walter Mears, who said he was leading with the candidates' statement that neither would accept George Wallace as a running mate, and most of the reporters followed his example.

Martindale (1984) compared newspaper news stories of campaign events but found that they were not as similar as Crouse's observations might have suggested. Yet the tendency of reporters to follow each other, although strong, is most likely when the stories are based on regular beats and highly predictable events or during crisis coverage when reliable information is scarce (Nimmo & Combs, 1983). Media analyst David Shaw (1989) has reported that the tendency of the pack to follow the common wisdom is even stronger since the publication of Crouse's book, due in part to technology that provides instant access to other reporters' work (such as CNN and computer data services).

Elizabeth Skewes (2007) replicated Crouse's study by following the 2000 and 2004 US presidential elections: "In part, the newsworthiness of the campaign is established by the very presence of reporters from the wire services, the major television networks, and the top newspapers in the nation, who frequently set the agenda for each other, other media organizations, and the public" (p. 3). In her book *Message Control*, she describes a Kerry–Bush debate in St. Louis, where the 500 attending journalists and technicians were not allowed personally to see the debate. Instead they were crammed into the basement of a television studio and watched everything on a bank of televisions. They could have stayed at home and got a better view from their own television. So why were they there? The answer, according to Skewes, lies in the usual news values, especially prominence: One of these men will become president, and thus anything they do is by definition newsworthy.

In her early work on newsworthiness, Shoemaker (1982) asked news and political editors from the 100 largest US newspapers to rate the deviance of 11 political groups, and then she analyzed how politically legitimate the groups were portrayed in the *New York Times*.[2] There was a strong linear relationship between deviance and legitimacy, with the League of Women Voters being the least deviant and the most legitimate and the Nazi group the most deviant and least legitimate. This study showed that the opinions of a general group of journalists can predict other newspapers' content (Shoemaker, 1982, p. 74), suggesting that journalists do share attitudes about people and groups in the news, possibly as a result of groupthink or the pack routine.

The importance of inter-media influence as a routine is demonstrated by its importance in many different settings. Skewes (2007) quotes Richard Benedetto of *USA Today* as saying that journalists on campaign press planes "don't think in terms of what the public wants to know, how can I help them know. They think of it in terms of . . . what does my colleague want to know? What can I show my colleagues that I know that they don't know? (p. 97). Guy Golan (2006) studied inter-media agenda setting by looking at the *New York Times*'s impact on the international content of subsequent ABC, CBS, and NBC evening news shows, finding "that the international news agenda of television news programs may not result from gatekeeping factors or the news values of an event or nation but rather from an inter-media agenda-setting process" (p. 331). The study showed that the international events covered by the television networks had earlier been covered by the *Times*. From an inter-media standpoint, we should ask whether the *Times* is still at the top of the news gatekeeping chain or to what extent it is influenced by yet other media.

There is still a tendency for journalists and bloggers to rely on each other's past content to find story ideas and to help confirm their own judgments, an institutionalized practice. Warren Breed's (1955) classic study of the newsroom observed that newspapermen avidly read other newspapers. Today, they also watch television news and their favorite internet news feeds, blogs, and the social media. Herbert Gans (1979, p. 91) noted that editors read the *New York Times* and the *Washington Post* before entertaining story ideas. If these respected judges of news values have carried a story, then it has been judged as satisfactory, "eliminating the need for an independent decision by the editor" (Gans, 1979, p. 126). In 1986, for example, the *New York Times* helped legitimize the cocaine issue by giving it prominent coverage early in the year. Other media followed in a feeding frenzy as the networks and newspapers converged on the story throughout the summer and early fall (Reese & Danielian, 1989).

Mediating the Mediators

Public relations companies are also media organizations, whose job is partially to shape—some would say "manipulate"—media content, both what is transmitted and its tone. The news media use this material somewhere between not at all and always. Martin and Singletary (1981) found that newspapers used nearly 20 percent of news releases verbatim. The sophistication of public relations (or media relations) strategies and tactics has steadily improved, with corporate spokespersons acting as official sources for their organizations. Shirley Ramsey (1999, p. 95) found that in news of science and technology, organizational spokespersons were far more likely to be sources than the scientists involved in the research.

A more recent study by Youngmin Yoon (2005) examined journalists' perceptions of the legitimacy and expertise of public relations sources and found that together they explain the sources' success in getting their message in the media:

> News sources perceived by journalists as being more legitimate tend to receive news coverage throughout the year, perhaps because journalists regularly seek information and opinions from those sources and routinely include them in their stories, . . . whereas the coverage of less legitimate sources may be limited to a few months of the year when they are probably involved in newsworthy events. More legitimate sources also enjoyed more positive coverage.
>
> (p. 784)

Reporters can get information the hard way through their own legwork and research, or the easy way through inside tips, interviews, and leaks handed to them by officials. Finding the latter far more efficient, they are forced into a bargain that, in exchange for the occasional competitive bone, requires them to accept the more common news delivered through routine channels (Sigal, 1973, p. 53). Other professional perks perpetuate this dependence. Political candidates, for example, use the journalistic reward system as leverage to get what they want in the news media. In the 1988 presidential campaign, Joan Didion (1988, p. 21) observed how political journalists reported clearly "set up" campaign events as though they were not manipulated. Because reporters like covering campaigns—it leads to prestige and advancement and gets them out on the road—they "are willing, in exchange for 'access,' to transmit the images their sources wish transmitted. They are willing, in exchange for certain colorful details around which a 'reconstruction' can be built . . . to present these images not as a story the campaign wants told but as fact."

Controlling and Cajoling

Soley (1992) analyzed the experts featured on network newscasts and concluded that they constituted a narrow, homogeneous, and elite group. Although they are often presented as objective and nonpartisan, these news shapers were largely conservative, associated with Washington-based think tanks, ex-presidents, and prestigious East Coast universities. "It is impossible to avoid hearing or reading their comments that shape the news" (Soley, 1992, p. 6).

Coverage of the 1991 Persian Gulf War showed a similar reliance on a narrow range of experts to help explain the conflict. They came primarily from New York and Washington, especially from think tanks and from a group of retired military officials, many of them with political biases (Steele, 1992). Writing about the later Iraqi war, Althaus (2003) says that although the military wanted journalists to go to officials for information, journalists were quick to take advantage to seek back-ground information from others. Journalists looked for dissenting information to help construct their usual "both sides" narrative (Althaus, 2003, p. 405).

One of the most radical restrictions in news media access came during the 1983 invasion of Grenada. The US administration, breaking a long tradition of military–press cooperation, barred all reporters during the early days of the opera-tion (Smith, 1988, p. 435). Restricted access just increases the media's appetite for other messages, especially from the White House. Hedrick Smith noted that the notion of "scripted spontaneity" originated with Nixon. David Gergen, Communi-cation Director for both Nixon and Reagan, said that when the president spoke, his office wrote the headline and the lead paragraph of the expected prototypical news story, such that his office could get the news coverage they wanted (Smith, 1988, pp. 405–6). In one effort to minimize news editing, the Reagan administration in 1983 began letting news organizations tap into a White House computer for elec-tronic press releases compiled by the communication office. A similar strategy in-volved beaming unedited presidential appearances to local television stations via satellite, thus bypassing the network filter. These strategies have been honed and strengthened to exploit the newer digital technologies.

Although control of media content by the White House is highly visible, other aspects of government at all levels operate in more indirect ways, sometimes ren-dering newsworthy events into nonevents. Fishman (1980, pp. 78–80) observed a meeting of a county board of supervisors arguing about the following year's sheriff's department budget, when a woman stepped up and reported that two deputies had stopped her on the street as she sold ware from a pushcart, handcuffed her, pulled her into their car, verbally abused her, and left her at the sheriff's station for several hours bound hand and foot, before eventually releasing her with no explanation. This startling accusation was deemed inappropriate because it was out of context and irrelevant to a budget meeting. Instead of interviewing the woman, reporters waited for the meeting to resume. They had defined her accusation as a nonevent and it was not reported in the local newspaper, because it did not fit the officials' and reporters' bureaucratic perspective.

Covering the Persian Gulf

The first Persian Gulf War provides a striking case study of how news routines help structure reporting on international conflict in the modern era of information man-agement routines. On the most direct level, the US government imposed severe restrictions on journalists, limiting where they could go and what they could write, building on the rules began in the 1983 US invasion of Grenada. A pool system had been established in 1984 so that representatives from the major news organizations could accompany the military and then were expected to share stories with media not in the pool. Thus, when Saddam Hussein invaded Kuwait in 1990, journal-ists were conditioned to expect, and largely accept, the most restrictive wartime press control of modern times. Reporters were denied access to anything that was not controlled by military handlers, and military public information specialists reviewed all stories. Critics charged that these routines were imposed not solely for reasons of national security, but also to present the military in the best possible light (see Kellner, 1992). These military-imposed restrictions constituted a powerful kind of source-oriented routine, and journalists were obliged to adapt themselves accordingly. Public information officers warned that reporters who asked hard questions could be seen as "anti-military" and that requests for interviews with senior commanders and visits to the field would be in jeopardy (LeMoyne, 1991).

Such restrictive routines emerged largely due to the prevailing suspicious and antagonistic views within the military toward the media, which were widely blamed by military leaders for losing the war in Vietnam. When Vietnam-era officers went on to become senior-level leaders, they brought their views about the media with them. But the news media have their perspective too. The routines approach predicts that the media enter into arrangements that provide the most acceptable content, even if it means conforming to heavy-handed military information control.

Indeed, some (mostly alternative) news organizations tried to contest the Pentagon's restrictions in the Persian Gulf in court, but none of the major news organizations joined the lawsuit filed by the Center for Constitutional Rights on behalf of the publications. In explaining their inaction, Sydney Schanberg argued that the media were scared of criticism by the White House and had been tamed (1991, pp. 373–4).

The routines involved in the media–military relationship have their own logic that shapes news content beyond the simple suppression or censorship of news. They impose an interpretive framework that works against alternative perspectives. As with other media–source relationships, the strong dependence of journalists on the military for information can produce co-optation, leading to uncritical acceptance of military frames of reference. This is often signified in news discourse by using the pronoun *we* and similar terms, which identify reporters with governmental and military interests: we invaded, our troops, our country (see Lee & Solomon, 1991).

Former military leaders and "experts," hired by the television networks to provide context for the Gulf conflict, regularly identified themselves with the Gulf policy—but so did journalists such as Barbara Walters, Tom Brokaw, and Dan Rather. As Kellner argues, using *we* and *our* rhetorically binds the anchors to the military and nation, as it binds the audience to the troops in a sense of shared national purpose (Kellner, 1992). As Ottosen (1993) found, this co-optation can be seen in the military commanders' treatment of pool journalists as "their" journalists, "an integrated part of their own forces" (p. 140).

Media dependence on the military means that the government's definition of success is absorbed uncritically by journalists. Thus, the military is allowed to claim achievements using terms of its own making, crowding out other potential criteria for evaluating the government's policy in diplomatic, economic, environmental, moral, and other areas. By examining the Persian Gulf War we can see how routines developed that served mutual interests, creating a symbiotic relationship between media and military. These interlocking routines help explain the popularity of the high-tech pictures seen at that time on television, made from the "smart bombs" themselves, as they destroyed Iraqi military targets. The military benefited from showing how successfully their weapons had performed. The media benefited by obtaining dramatic footage to grab audience attention. And of course, the defense manufacturers benefited enormously by reaping priceless advertising for their products. In the conflicts to follow in Iraq and Afghanistan, the media–military relationship grew even more routinized, particularly with the embedding of journalists with troops. Putting the faces of top Al Qaeda leaders on a deck of playing cards proved irresistible for the journalists seeking from the military public affairs office a simple and visual way to describe the conflict.

Even in the larger framing of the conflicts the ability of the Bush Administration's ability to effectively promote its view of the policy had serious consequences. The press internalized the Global War on Terror frame promoted by the president, using it as an unproblematic descriptor of a host of related policies. Rather than distancing themselves from the term by calling it the "so-called," or even "US-led" War on Terror, US media embraced the frame label. Interviews with journalists showed that if they did otherwise they would risk seeming argumentative and, worse, not "objective" (Lewis & Reese, 2009; Reese & Lewis, 2009) We examine these issues elsewhere for their institutional and ideological implications. The routines level of analysis draws our attention to how such structured arrangements of information supplying and gathering are highly practical for military and media interests and for their mutual benefit. Identifying these routines gives a clearer picture of the structure underlying news of modern warfare.

SUMMARY

In her book *When News Was New*, Terhi Rantanen (2009) writes about news as a primitive construct:

> News is so widely recognized as news that it is not easy to understand its wider significance. We may look at what is inside news but what we see is what we have been taught to recognize. We may think news is just news, an ephemeral piece that informs about the world. What we may not realize is that, *by following the agreed conventions that makes it recognizable as news*, it sets up a framework within which its predefined elements are related to each other.
>
> (p. xi, emphasis ours)

Routines have an important impact on the production of symbolic content. They form the immediate environment within which individual media workers carry out their jobs. If these highly interconnected routines constrain the individual, they are themselves functions of constraints. The event focus of news, for example, is helpful to the organization in scheduling news but also helps the audience in providing a concrete focus for the message. Many of the same bureaucratic routines that are functional for the media organization are also used and exploited by external sources for their own advantage. Routines of news work provide levers that power centers on the outside can grasp to influence content, and indeed some metaphors describe the press as straitjacketed or handcuffed by its own routines. The more powerful sources can lead members of the media to adapt to their own bureaucratic structure and rhythms. Less advantaged sources must conform to the media routines if they are to have a chance of getting into the news.

Today's entertainment and social media emphasize deviance through their tendency to include violence, as well as interpersonal conflict, celebrity gossip, and oddity. In the social media, people are more likely to communicate the worrisome or unusual parts of their day rather than what was boring and dull. For both news media and social media organizations, surveillance of the environment for deviance is an important routine activity, but not the only force that determines whether an event becomes news. Williams and Delli Carpini (2000) question whether, in the case of extremely deviant events, mainstream news media can maintain their role as gatekeepers of political news. Their study of the affair between President Bill Clinton and a White House intern shows that, in a news environment saturated with information from all possible sources, the traditional media could not control the national political agenda (Williams & Delli Carpini, 2000, p. 79). This has implications for 21st-century media in that the Internet and the social media provide far more information to news consumers than was available from the traditional media alone.

NOTES

1   The popular notion is that they are. The public knows the personal side of gatekeepers best. Journalists are often romanticized as crusading editors or as fearless investigative reporters. For example, in the 1970s the *Washington Post*'s reporters Bob Woodward and Carl Bernstein conducted an investigative study that ended with President Richard Nixon's resignation. They were subsequently given a lot of individual attention by the media (see also Chapter 8).
2   The groups included the League of Women Voters, Sierra Club, Common Cause, the NAACP (National Association for the Advancement of Colored People), the National Organization for Women, the National Rifle Association, Moral Majority, the Jewish Defense League, the Communist Party, the Ku Klux Klan, and the Nazis.

Individuals

At the individual level we ask who are the creators of media content and how do their characteristics affect that creation? We review research at this level, particularly as individual traits may become relevant to their larger professional roles. We consider the issues raised by this level when the individual comes into contact with larger structures. This dialectic interplay between the individual and social structure is an enduring theme in the social sciences, but one with special relevance in the Hierarchy of Influences as we seek to understand the symbolic mediated environment. How can we think about the relative free will, or *agency*, of the individual media workers, even as they operate within larger constraints that also help determine their actions? The very question of constraints may seem out of place in the world of media, which is based so strongly in the public imagination on the creative work and professional decision-making of individuals. And indeed we must fully understand these media people with respect to their individuality and creativity, but must do so within their larger institutional context. Indeed the power of the individual in media settings, although encompassing a wide range of personal traits and idiosyncrasies, expresses itself mainly through professional and occupational channels. Thus, we give these settings particular attention.

INDIVIDUALS AS LEVEL OF ANALYSIS

In the network society era, the connection between individuals and their larger context has changed the way that people relate to their institutional roles. We need to be sensitive to how individuality takes on new significance in this respect, particularly as we try to isolate the factors at work at this level. This shift corresponds to larger global trends rooted in digital communication, which allows intensified connectivity and radical restructuring of social relationships outside of traditional roles and communities, destabilizing old hierarchies (including our own levels of analysis). Individualism plays out in emerging issues of "identity," giving it a new kind of importance and meaning within the Hierarchy of Influences. If before it was possible to identify a media communicator, located within a specific occupation and organization, that task has grown more difficult with developments in media technology and concurrent societal shifts. Social categories and institutional membership—whether based on class, church, family, nation, or career—once were the traditional sources of meaning and identification that helped determine and predict individual attitudes and behavior. And social science relied on those concepts as major analytical tools. As Castells (1996) has theorized, however, the decline in institutions and the rise of networked relationships means that the primary distinction now is between Self and Net.

> Identity is becoming the main, and sometimes, the only, source of meaning in a historical period characterized by widespread destructuring of organizations, delegitimization of institutions, fading away of major social movements, and ephemeral cultural expressions. People increasingly organize their meaning not around what they do, but on the basis of what they are, or believe they are.
>
> (Castells, 1996, p. 3)

Thus, people in advanced societies now construct their identities in ways much less clearly determined by their jobs, which they move in and out of as opportunities arise, feeling correspondingly less loyalty to and reliance on their employers for a personal sense of self. Deuze (2007) sees a rise in "individualization" within these shifts, coupled with a more general fluidity among life, work, and media:

> In the constant remix of times spent on work, life and play in and through media the differences between these spheres of activity get lost. Through the redistribution of risk away from the state or employer to each and every worker, people as individuals become solely responsible and uniquely accountable for running their own lives. The individual, not the firm, has become the organization.
>
> (Deuze, 2007, p. 8)

Although in this chapter we consider how individual factors affect content, these factors are not categorical, fixed, or determinative as they once were. Factors such as social class are still influential, but now they must be understood as operating differently, through networked combinations of interests and affiliations particular to each person and context (something communication research has only begun to address). Although more fluid than ever, personal identity still influences media content, and we identify those individual level influences that have most concerned researchers and present a model for theory building.

Characteristics of Individuals

The questions at this level of analysis could be asked about creative actors in general, including those in the entertainment industry (with some of the earliest work by Cantor, 1971). In the creative process yielding mainstream news, movies, and electronic games, Deuze (2007) extends his analysis of *media work* to encompass four key professions: (1) advertising, (2) journalism, (3) film and television production, and (4) computer and video game development. Historically, however, much previous research has been devoted to describing members of the profession of journalism. And much of this research has been based on surveys, tracking the state of the profession and its trends, as well as more personal issues about its members. The largely descriptive approach characterizing this research provides no single argument or overarching theoretical context to help organize this body of findings—other than, of course, the basic presumption that the characteristics of the profession matter in shaping content. (Indeed, research in this area may be regarded as less explicitly theoretical than the other levels.) Although relatively few in number compared to other professions, journalists have been the subjects of much scrutiny. As professional status grew, and the societal importance of their work received greater recognition, journalists have attracted greater attention from researchers around the world. The growing partisan press and politicization of journalism, particularly in the USA, has also attracted attention to journalists and greater concern over whether their characteristics tend to bias them for or against certain ideas and groups. Thus, much of the research on these questions has flowed from private organizations and been shaped by their particular political and social agendas. As we will see, a closer look at the individual level provides helpful insights in sorting the contrasting claims such scrutiny has yielded.

Meanwhile, the erosion of boundaries between citizens and traditional media workers has made it more difficult to clearly define the professional groups we wish to examine. This could be said for creative media work in general, where with digital media technology easily accessible and mastered, users can easily become media producers: "prosumers." New York University journalism professor and *Pressthink* blogger Jay Rosen has referred to them as "the people formerly known as the audience"[1] But within the journalism profession the issue of definition is particularly problematic. Indeed, now the starting point is the most basic question: Who is a journalist? Studies of journalists pre-dating the technological changes of the early 21st century were able to more clearly define their samples, but more recent research now finds the very subject of their investigation rendered problematic.

We begin with those earlier studies, which generally assume that journalists are people employed by organizations that produce news content. This research provides a valuable foundation for understanding individual level analysis. David Weaver and his colleagues, mounting one of the most prominent research programs in this area, have fixed the definition of journalists as "those who have editorial responsibility for the preparation or transmission of news stories or other information, including full-time reporters, writers, correspondents, columnists, news people, and editors" (Weaver, Beam, Brownlee, Voakes, & Wilhoit, 2007), yielding in the USA a population of about 120,000 members. The third book in their series includes data from a national survey conducted by a larger Indiana University team, an effort that follows others in 1982–3 and 1992 led by David Weaver and G. Cleveland Wilhoit (1991, 1996). Their descriptive and survey-based approach, centered on the construct of *professional role*, has been widely adopted, leading us to use it as a model for this prominent style of research at the individual level. This approach takes seriously the performance of news organizations from the perspective of those who work in them. The makeup of the people populating this profession matters more than others, assume the authors, given how it potentially shapes their perspective on the world.

The work of Weaver and colleagues has documented journalists' characteristics in their longitudinal program of studies, building on the earlier national survey work by sociologists Johnstone, Slawski, and Bowman (1972). Prior to that accounts, where available, were largely anecdotal and historical, with journalists often encouraging a certain mythic image of themselves as rugged individualists, an image continuing to the present and contributing to the anecdotal style of insights. Edward R. Murrow, the patron saint of American broadcast journalism at CBS News, was credited with bringing down communist-hunter Senator Joseph McCarthy during the 1950s, although Murrow was relatively late to the story. Bob Woodward and Carl Bernstein covered the Watergate scandal for the *Washington Post* and are in the public mind the legendary investigators who drove President Richard Nixon from office, even though congressional committee staff carried out most of the impeachment's investigative work. The rise of high profile opinion journalists, such as Bill O'Reilly, Glenn Beck, and Sean Hannity on the Fox News network, brings even more focus on the journalist as personality. When notable media figures reach celebrity status, they capitalize on their exposure to write books about their lives and views of the world. Unlike the more European tradition of journalists as literary figures, this larger-than-life celebrity and personality focus seems counter to the American objectivity principle, which works to render the personal life of the journalist irrelevant to the work itself. In any case, the erosion of that principle has been accompanied by a rise in individual level research attention to these professionals.

Outside of the academy, conservative interest groups have contributed the most research, including numerous surveys, into the character and actions of individual media workers. Many of these reports have accused journalists of revealing their prejudicial personal opinions based on anecdotal exposés. Think tanks such as the Media Research Center or Accuracy in Media present a critique of the culture industry in general, whether the Hollywood film and television industry or the "mainstream" or "elite" journalistic establishment, as being out of touch with the societal values. From a theoretical perspective, media criticism from the right attributes significant importance to individual media workers and the extent to which their personal bias shapes a distorted message (a presumption shared with the Johnstone tradition, although with different conclusions). The irony is that journalists have been willing participants in this critique, defending their work with claims of objectivity, yet still giving a forum, and thus respectability, to their attackers. Why would journalists tacitly endorse their critics? Because the conservative critique suggests that journalists have special professional latitude in deciding the news product (albeit with corresponding blame). This granting of individual responsibility has proved more appealing to journalists than the contrasting liberal critique, based on claims of owner control and corporate domination, which leaves less room for personal agency. Thus, the choice of individual level of explanation has ideological, professional, and theoretical undercurrents.

The Issue of Self-Selection

The basic premise that one's background shapes subjective judgment seems non-controversial. Of course, we all bring to our decisions the totality of life experiences, but to what extent do professional responsibilities and values take precedence? As regards journalists, the question is whether and to what extent personal and professional characteristics influence the content produced. And if they do, is that influence functional or dysfunctional for the journalistic enterprise? Within the Hierarchy of Influences Model, the most important concern is whether such influences are most important relative to other factors. Professional writing and creative story-telling skills appropriately affect media quality, while certain prejudices and ethical failures are regarded as intruding where not wanted. Innumerable studies, inspired by these premises, have documented the ways in which journalists differ from other groups.

By favoring the individual level of explanation, the conservative cultural critique provides a good illustration of the issues at hand. The same issues arise in criticisms leveled at higher education, and, given our positions as academics we are particularly sensitive to such arguments. As with media professionals, negative attention to university faculty has grown over the years, with studies consistently showing that professors differ from other groups. Law school professors, for example, are more likely to vote Democratic than Republican. Campuses and disciplines vary, of course, with humanities and social science faculty more liberal than their counterparts in business, engineering, military science, and agriculture (Cardiff & Klein, 2005). Nevertheless, there is a strong empirical case for both the academic and journalistic professions tilting toward the liberal side of the spectrum—but for what reason, with what result, and with what implied remedy? Benchmarking against the general population may tell us something about a profession's tendencies. Although a uniformity of belief signals a potential problem in any group, making this kind of comparison normatively assumes that the standard of a healthy academic discipline or effective media profession is based on the distribution of member characteristics on a certain (particularly political) variable, which makes little sense in many cases. Certain occupations no doubt attract different-minded people, making the concept of professional roles and personal qualities blend into larger occupational formations. These questions are worth considering further, so that the analytical strategies at this level—particularly regarding professional issues—are clearly understood.

The Ideological Litmus Test

One implication of the conservative critique is that cultural institutions should cultivate greater "intellectual" diversity, a call that invokes liberals' own affinity for affirmative action language, but uses it against them. Professionals (including defenders of higher education) argue, however, that imposing an ideological litmus test for recruiting and admission is to surrender control to outside political interests and that a strong professional autonomy serves as a buffer against those interests, when they seek undue interference in advancing their own interests. Thus, at the individual level, it is important to consider how the profession upholds certain norms and disciplinary procedures, and whether these in turn have the effect of attracting certain types of people. Are media liberal because they contain a significant number of liberal members or does media work have certain features and occupational culture that tend to attract certain people, who happen to be liberal. Our point here is that, at this level of analysis, individuals both shape and are shaped by their larger institutional settings. From a normative perspective, we ultimately must ask whether a profession's attraction of a group profile differing from the general public damages the profession's ethical and disciplinary functioning. We pose these questions to show that, although research at this level is descriptive and, in many cases, often atheoretical, it has a strong underlying normative context.

INDIVIDUALS AS CONCEPTUAL MODEL

To more clearly lay out these theoretical issues, we consider how factors at the individual level can best be understood and examined. We can draw a conceptual distinction between four factors, stable and more or less fixed: personal demographic characteristics, backgrounds and experiences of the communicator (e.g., gender, ethnicity, education, sexual orientation); current attitudes, values, and beliefs of the communicator; background factors, roles, and experiences associated with the professional context of the communicator; and the relative power of the communicator within the organization. We propose a model that outlines these factors, and Figure 8.1 shows their interrelationships. The communicators' personal background and experience are logically prior to their specific attitudes, values, and beliefs, and they also precede specific professional roles and ethical norms. Thus, personal background works through two paths: professional and personal. In one path these factors affect specifically professional background and experiences (e.g., whether to attend journalism school), and in turn professional roles and the ethical norms that guide those roles. In the other path, personal background shapes personal attitudes, values and beliefs, which can directly affect media content. We take up each of these issues now in turn.

Personal and Professional

Personal attitudes, values, and beliefs are considered conceptually distinct here from professional roles, although both affect and mutually reinforce each other, as signified by the link between them. The media professions attract individuals with certain personal views—who find it compatible with their views and work styles—and these views in turn reinforce professional norms, roles, and ethical choices and

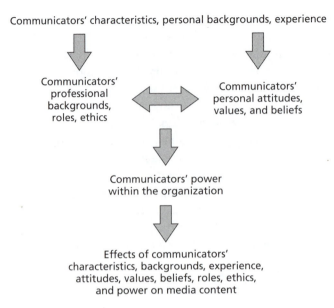

Communicators' characteristics, personal backgrounds, experience

Communicators' professional backgrounds, roles, ethics

Communicators' personal attitudes, values, and beliefs

Communicators' power within the organization

Effects of communicators' characteristics, backgrounds, experience, attitudes, values, beliefs, roles, ethics, and power on media content

FIGURE 8.1 *How factors intrinsic to the communicator may influence content*

outlooks that influence one's work. Thus, the professional affects the personal and vice versa. In previous work, many have depicted the norms of professionalism as more influential than personal idiosyncrasies, calling as it does, at least in its *objectivity* form, for detachment and the suppression of individual prejudices. But the personal and professional are clearly inter-dependent. Thus, in this respect personal attitudes should not necessarily be thought to intrude on the professionalism of the work, but rather more benignly to be a correlate of professional values. There are many places in the world and many media firms where the profession is weak and roles are underdeveloped or can be overridden by other concerns—including the influences at the higher levels we have also described. Both of these groups of individual level variables affect media content to the extent that the individual has power within the organization. That is, these characteristics obviously matter more for some than others, depending on whether they are allowed some range of individual expression or must conform to larger routines and policy. A high-powered media personality may be seen as "overriding" what the professional role would otherwise call for (e.g., an influential media owner like Rupert Murdoch of News Corporation). So, communicators' power is always a factor in whether they are able to shape content along the lines of their professional or personal edicts. Prominent *New York Times* columnist Thomas Friedman and investigative journalist Seymour Hersch were able to advance "counter-frames" against the Bush administration after 9/11, when others in the US media did not or could not (Entman, 2003). The relative influence of these two sets of factors varies with the national and organizational culture, which works to grant or limit communicative power.

Background and Characteristics

The most basic and visible background profile of a profession is demographic. Few occupations have been as concerned as journalism over how representative it is of the public. The American Society of Newspaper Editors (ASNE) in 1986 declared as a goal for each newsroom to mirror its community in minority staffing by 2000 (Haws, 1991), a goal it never reached. There are a number of reports along these lines of demographic profiles of journalists, with the underlying implied appropriateness of comparing the profession with the larger society it serves.

Ethnicity

Revising its diversity goal in 1999, ASNE advocated that the percentage of minorities in daily newsrooms be on parity with those in the general population by 2025 or earlier. Daily newspapers now compare the racial diversity of their news staffs and community on their websites. As of 2004 the Gannett Company (publisher of *USA Today*) was reputed to be doing better than most, according to a Newsroom Diversity Index—computed based on the proportion of journalists of color in the newsroom compared to the non-white share of the population in the newspaper's circulation area. Perhaps most revealing, however, are the several all-white newspapers serving significant non-white communities, such as *The Independent*, in Gallup, New Mexico, which has a 93 percent non-white population (Dedman & Doig, 2004). Knight reports that the first decade of the 21st century saw net increases in Asian, Latino, and Native American journalists, but a decline among African Americans, with an overall minority employment of 13.4 percent (ASNE, 2009). The 2002 Weaver group survey found that 9.5 percent of journalists (not just newspapers) were minorities, compared to the 30.9 percent in the 2000 US census (Weaver et al., 2007). (The 2010 census showed an increase to 33.8 percent as other than "white"[2].) They found some success in recruiting journalists with Jewish and Hispanic backgrounds, but Hispanics and African Americans were still underrepresented. Television had the best minority representation and weekly newspapers the worst. With the US news industry and its hiring in retrenchment, these improvements in newsroom diversity may be difficult to sustain.

Gender

According to the 2002 Weaver survey, 33 percent of all journalists are women, including 54 percent of those hired since 1998. Still, the percentage of women working in journalism has remained constant since 1980, in part because women are more apt than men to leave journalism after a few years, perhaps because they were more likely to weigh work and family demands. Nevertheless, the representation of women in combined managerial and professional occupations was 46.5 percent in 2000 with significant increases in other professions compared to journalism (Weaver et al., 2007). The proportion of women to men has varied by type of medium, with news magazines having the highest proportion of women (43.5 percent) and the news services and radio the lowest (20.3 and 21.9 percent, respectively). The 2008 survey of journalism and mass communication undergraduate programs showed that 63.8 percent were female and 30.6 percent were members of racial and ethnic minorities, the highest percentage yet in these surveys (Becker, Vlad, & Olin, 2009). This gender skew seems to be a worldwide pattern.

Sexual Orientation

The inclusion of sexual orientation as a diversity goal has a relatively recent history. Merle Miller is thought to be the first gay journalist to reveal his homosexuality in print (in a 1971 *New York Times Magazine* article). In the early 1990s "coming out of the closet" was still a calculated risk, with Deb Price, the Washington news editor for the *Detroit News*, becoming the first syndicated columnist to deal exclusively with gay and lesbian issues (Case, 1992a). Now the National Lesbian and Gay Journalists Association has some 1,200 members, and a 2000 survey reported that 90 percent of gay and lesbians are "out" within their newsrooms (Aarons & Murphy, 2000).

Class and Elite Status

Social class is a particularly thorny issue, describing as it does an individual background factor that locates the individual and the profession associated with it in a larger social structure. Beyond simple measures of socioeconomic status, interest in the social class status of journalists has grown over the years. We earlier discussed the extent that journalists participate in an interlocking class structure with other elites. Whether journalists bring a certain class background and outlook to their work, however, easily fits within a discussion of individual factors.

Class: The Myth vs. Reality

Journalists have preferred to project a respectable class image in their own mythology, as courageous reporters and editors sticking up for the rights of the disenfranchised. Streitmatter (1997) encourages this image in his popular textbook *Mightier than the Sword*, which includes early journalists from Thomas Paine and Samuel Adams to the abolitionists and suffragettes, and then to the Progressive Era's muckrakers, who fought Tammany Hall corruption. The Watergate scandal arguably brought journalism to its highest level of public repute, and the heroes of the story, Carl Bernstein and Bob Woodward of the *Washington Post*, are portrayed positively in this and other texts. Yet other scholars have not always had such a positive view. Sociologist Max Weber considered journalists to be a "pariah caste" (Hess, 1981), and Harvard president Charles William Eliot described them as "drunkards, deadbeats, and bummers" (cited in Weaver & Wilhoit, 1996, p. 6).

In his review of journalism in popular culture, Ehrlich (2006) claims that movies have told "romantic, entertaining tales of journalists who uphold their idealized roles as public servants" and provided "models for real-life journalistic conduct, with the film *All the President's Men* a prime example" (p. 502). Beyond this film saga of "Woodstein," he argues that even movies about "bad" journalists, who carry out unprofessional or criminal behavior, "have helped shore up the press's preferred self-image, either by seeing through lies and pretense to the truth or by paying the price of not telling the truth" (Ehrlich, 2006, p. 502).

Certainly journalists in the first half of the 20th century were closer to the working class than they are today, although by the 1930s 80 percent of journalists had at least some college education (Hess, 1981). The image of the hard-drinking, cigarette-smoking social misfit, press pass stuck in the hat brim, and on the margins of polite society journalist is a standard stereotype in films of the 1930s onward, as exemplified in the *Front Page* and other black-and-white classic films (Gersh, 1991). From the disreputable image of early colonial printers and frontier editors to the working class image of reporters during the mid 20th century, journalism has grown to more corporate and professionalized status. The rising importance and status of this professional group can be marked by the first systematic survey of Washington journalists by Leo Rosten in 1937. His sociological portrait showed a press corps more likely to vote for Roosevelt than the general public, a stance at odds with their publishers, from whom they felt pressure to conform (Rosten, 1937). This heavy handed control from their news organizations lessened considerably since then with the rising education and general affluence of the group (in an update by Rivers, 1965). By the 1970s, a third of Washington reporters were graduates of highly selective universities (Hess, 1981).

Average or Elite?

The socioeconomic status of journalists has risen over the last half century, but whether this is a positive development—leading to greater status and professional quality for journalism or an unhealthy arrogance and institutional detachment from ordinary citizens—is a matter of opinion. Concerns over a media "elite" class status are based on normative expectations for journalism: Is journalism a class unto itself and therefore out of touch with the public or, in the more progressive critique, has this media elite grown indistinguishable from other societal elites and therefore incapable of reporting on them with an independent outlook? The eagerness of Washington reporters to don evening wear and hobnob with government officials and celebrities at the annual White House Correspondents' Dinner has been a particularly visible manifestation of the co-optation view, a spectacle that would seem to dispel journalism's adversarial image. When comedian Stephen Colbert spoke at this 2005 event, he lampooned the President and this cozy relationship with journalists: "The President makes decisions. He's the decider. The press secretary announces those decisions, and you people of the press type those decisions down. Make, announce, type."[3] His comments proved to be much funnier with the public than with the audience at hand—reinforcing the disconnect between Washington insiders and the country at large.

Beginning with a widely cited 1986 book, *The Media Elite* (Lichter, Rothman, & Lichter, 1986), the out of touch (liberal outlook), elite view of journalists began to take hold, particularly among conservative media critics. These scholars studied journalists at what they termed the "elite" media: the *New York Times*, the *Washington Post*, the *Wall Street Journal*, *Time*, *Newsweek*, *US News and World Report*, as well as CBS, NBC, ABC, and PBS. They concluded that the "typical leading journalist is the very model of the modern eastern urbanite" (Lichter et al., 1986, p. 20). Since that time, media criticism has often included surveys of journalists, particularly regarding their partisan affiliations (making them correspondingly more sensitive to the issue and resistant to interviews). There is much internal variability within the profession, however, with journalists overall in the nation looking much more like the average American than those working at the elite media in large urban power centers (Weaver et al., 2007). Looking more broadly at the profession as a whole has been typical of academic researchers, and therefore class has been less likely to raise concerns.

Education of Communicators

Closely related to class is education, as a marker of status but also of an intellectual and professional outlook. Education is an important individual level predictor, both as a general background factor but also as signifying a larger issue over how communicators should best be prepared for their careers. Education matters, of course, in shaping the profession and the values practitioners carry with them into their jobs. The issues in US journalism education have direct relevance internationally, where the model—of media skills coupled with some combination of law, history, and social science—has been widely adopted by schools, often staffed by graduates from American universities. The journalism major—and communication more generally—has become a globally popular pursuit for students, notwithstanding the lower employment rates of the early 21st century in the traditional media companies. Annual surveys of US enrollments in university journalism and mass communication programs show that only recently have enrollments begun to slow, with little talk of cutting programs (Becker et al., 2009). As an earlier survey of students showed, the similarity of educational programs contributes to a corresponding sense of unified global professionalism, especially regarding the value of independence and professional autonomy (e.g., Splichal & Sparks, 1994).

Communication programs with a more professional emphasis, as opposed to conceptual (for example, media studies), have grown in number and importance in the training of students, with the employment and hiring links steadily strengthening between the media industries and universities. These schools have brought together various combinations of journalism, public relations, advertising, radio, film and television, the historically separate field of communication studies (once labeled speech communication), and even library and information science, to form academic programs. Often these combined programs represent one of the largest majors on their campuses. These trends have brought visibility and campus resources to journalism-communication programs, making it easier to partner with media industries and raise funds, while bringing new pressures to satisfy those professional communities. Whether highlighted or blended in such programs, the strongest thread in this professional training has been the evolution of teaching journalism at the undergraduate and graduate levels. As the earliest of the communication professions on campus, journalism can perhaps be said to carry the strongest sense of professional ethos—with the longest standing links to the larger profession itself.

Journalism Education

Journalism education has been largely an undergraduate-based program emphasizing entry-level skills, unlike other professions like medicine, law, and theology, organized around and requiring established graduate degrees. Providing the required degree credentials in these areas gives the academy a more meaningful role in controlling the defining ethos in their respective areas. In the 1990s, with strong foundation support generated from the newspaper industry, Reese (1999) argued that the profession was trying to recoup institutional prestige lost during the steady post-Watergate decline in its credibility, exerting sway in the academy to focus education on training, shaping curricula, hiring practices, and programs to be more attuned to industry needs. An over-professionalized approach also has its critics (who decry a "trade-school" mentality), arguing that an overly narrow training may not be in the long-term best interests of young people who will ultimately pursue many careers. In any case, the collapse of the newspaper industry from 2000 onward and the uncertain impact of digital and online technologies has made it more difficult for a chastened profession to dictate terms of education in the academy, yielding a more collaborative spirit, with more engagement and partnership than conflict. The Knight Foundation has recently argued for a "teaching hospital" model for journalism (at schools like Arizona State's Cronkite program), and several schools now are doing much more original and published reporting in partnership with news organizations (Downie, 2012). Journalism education now is likely to have a more equal footing in its partnership with the profession, as both try to discern the future and prepare students bound for media organizations as well as those seeking more citizen-based media literacy skills.

From its beginning the proper education for journalism has been debated hotly both on and off campus: How should it be organized, what are its proper disciplinary allies, what is the proper relationship between the academic field and the professional community, and how should journalists best be prepared? (Reese, 1999; Reese & Cohen, 2000). As a result of its academic evolution, journalism is a hybrid, an interdisciplinary mix of the humanities and social sciences. Even though regarded as a professional program it has a foot in both the liberal arts and professional camps. (Accredited programs require the majority of courses to be taken outside the major.) The debates over the proper direction of journalism education center around key questions: What does it mean to be a professional journalist? How can research be conducted that serves the profession and the society?

The formal origins of journalism education were in 1869 at a short-lived program at the now-called Washington and Lee University, and around the turn of the century several land grant universities established journalism programs (Dennis, 1988). The University of Missouri is given credit for being the first academically separate journalism school, begun in 1908, followed shortly by programs in Illinois and Pennsylvania (Gaunt, 1992). The first two journalism courses at the Ohio State University were taught in 1893, and journalism became a separate academic unit there in 1914, the same year that the University of Texas began its program. These programs evolved from an early focus on basic skills to include more conceptual study in ethics, law, and theory. Today some 480 universities grant bachelor's degrees in journalism and mass communication, a number that has continued to grow over the years (Weaver et al., 2007). The accrediting body for journalism currently has approved 113 programs, with a few outside the USA also seeking the credential (including from China). Defining which programs are considered "journalism and mass communication" is difficult considering the many academic combinations and labels. In their annual survey Becker and colleagues used as a list all programs organized under those labels (in the Association for Education in Journalism and Mass Communication directory), as well as programs which have at least ten courses in "news-editorial journalism" (in the Dow-Jones *Journalist's Road to Success: A Career Guide*), reporting that more than 55,000 degrees were received in the 2007–8 academic year (Becker et al., 2009).

Competing Models

These early tensions between the skills and broader conceptual training perspectives defined the two competing models for journalism education: One advanced by Willard Bleyer at the University of Wisconsin, who wanted journalism to be firmly integrated with the liberal arts, and the other advocated by Walter Williams at the University of Missouri, who wanted practical hands-on training in a real world environment. Wisconsin emphasized research more than Missouri, but Bleyer did not make a strong distinction between theory and professional practice (a distinction that still drives current debates). Bleyer argued that:

> No other profession has a more vital relation to the welfare of society or to the success of democratic government than has journalism. The most essential training which the university can give to a student's thinking of journalism is to equip him broadly with the knowledge of the ages and give him such intellectual power that he will be continually fertile in applying that knowledge to present conditions.
>
> (quoted in Bronstein & Vaughn, 1998, pp. 16–17)

The way journalism, or other communication areas for that matter, is organized on campus makes a difference in how it relates to the professional community. The more integrated programs are within the larger university, and within their relevant scholarly disciplines, the less strongly and exclusively they relate to their professional community. This tug is also seen in law schools, which are often held up as the model of a useful professional training, fully at the service of the legal community and sharing equivalent values and priorities. Even there, tensions have increased as law schools have recruited more faculty holding the Ph.D. and have become more interdisciplinary in their relations with the larger campus, leading to the charges that they have abandoned the practical side of legal education (Reese, 1999).

Wilbur Schramm is regarded as the driving force for establishing communication as an organized institutional presence in the academy. In organizing his programs at the University of Illinois and elsewhere, journalism left its early ties with English and the humanities to join more intellectually with the social sciences. His view of journalism was high-minded:

> I should like to see the kind of School of Journalism that would be not as weak as itself, but as strong as the university . . . a School that would be in the very heart of the university, which would begin with the assumption that the students it wants to produce will be the students in the whole university best equipped to understand and talk about the world.
>
> (Quoted in Medsger, 1996, p. 56)

Schramm's view of journalism's suitable disciplinary allies was persuasive, emphasizing scrutiny *of* journalism, but not without resistance from those advocating keeping the focus on cultural expression *through* journalism.

The Anti-Reflective Profession

To the list of features characterizing a profession, Pelikan (1992) adds a tradition of critical philosophical reflection. This has been a hallmark of academe but has not always characterized journalism. Even critics from within the profession have called it far too self-congratulatory (although these attitudes have no doubt been tempered by the financial and technological crises within the profession). This *anti-reflective* view helps explain the resistance to theory and press criticism within journalism education. Former *New York Times* editor Max Frankel has said, "There (are) too . . . many media critics in business these days. It's ridiculous. If all those people, including me, would go back to work, we'd have a very good press. But instead all we're doing is studying the press" (quoted in Reese, 1999, p. 84). Many industry-originated research initiatives have taken the perspective that more public awareness of journalism's constitutional freedoms and job constraints would make people yield more appreciation of journalists' work—a view exemplified by the Newseum, a museum dedicated to the news business and profession in Washington, DC, and built by the Freedom Forum, a foundation outgrowth of the Gannett newspaper chain, one of the nation's largest and publisher of *USA Today*. The Newseum's goal may be important, but it hasn't stemmed the decline in public trust for media.

The *Winds of Change* report on journalism education (Medsger, 1996), sponsored by the same Freedom Forum, took a strong polemical tone, advocating bringing more news professionals into teaching without so much concern for their academic credentials to help reverse the conversion of journalism into a "generic communications degree." The oversimplified academic-versus-professional dichotomy within the report assumed that the primary source for leadership in this part of the academy lies within the journalism profession itself.

Columbia University has been influential in the communication field, shaped by the sociology of Paul Lazarsfeld, but more recently it has reformed its iconic professional master's program in journalism, which was historically a skills-based, one-year degree. Although not without resistance from professional quarters, the school's offerings have been expanded to offer an additional master's option with more substantive background knowledge for aspiring journalists, more case-study-based teaching, and a Ph.D. program within the school, more oriented toward historical, cultural, sociological, and interdisciplinary work. Journalism educator and dean at the University of Illinois, James Carey, who helped establish the program, long had argued that this was a more logical research focus for journalism than the communication science orientation of Schramm (Carey, 2000).

INFLUENCES ON CONTENT FROM INDIVIDUALS

As we said earlier, it's hard to argue against the proposition that a communicator's background makes a difference in the content produced. Professional values should lead to reporting of higher quality. And yet within the Hierarchy of Influences Model, individual level influences may matter less than one might think. Weaver and Wilhoit (1991) argue that the effect of journalists' demographics on news values and content is probably minor, given the importance of organization routines and constraints, and studies generally show weak relationships between personal factors and news coverage. We might better ask, from among all individual level influences, which are most influential? Are such influences on media outcomes positive or negative? Are there more significant generalizations we can make about individual influences across broader patterns of content?

The increase in women and minorities in the newsroom raises new questions about such influences. At one time, for example, editors questioned whether women should be allowed to cover abortion issues, suggesting they would be naturally biased. Yet similar questions were not asked of men (Mills, 1993). Journalism has often had a conflicted outlook on diversity in the newsroom, seeking inclusion as a matter of justice and implicit purpose of making the product better, but minority professionals often have been restricted from exercising judgments based on their life experience, precisely where it could be most beneficial to a more complete understanding. In other instances, minority journalists experience professional conflict when they confront the issue of whether they should be advocates for their community. This was particularly true early in their period of newsroom inclusion.

For example, at a 1992 meeting of the Asian American Journalists Association, Lincoln Millstein, an editor at the *Boston Globe*, said he was "mildly troubled" by the feeling of "ethnic loyalty versus the pursuit of truth at the gathering. We as a group need to be careful and not go over the edge as an advocacy group, and not become too emotional about what's going on" (Case, 1992b, p. 15). Other news professionals saw a more beneficial effect of some demographic backgrounds, particularly the inclusion of Hispanic journalists, who were regarded as important bi-lingual and bi-cultural bridges to the growing Latino communities. African American journalists have faced similar tension. The New Orleans *Times-Picayune*, for example, launched an extensive series on race in the community, stipulating a policy that each story should be seen by an African American editor, who was to check for unwitting bias by the writer. Of course, that didn't always sit well with the white journalists, who regarded themselves as professionals, capable of writing objectively and fairly regardless of the subject matter (Rosenstiel & Mitchell, 2003).

Pritchard and Stonbely (2007) found that African American reporters at a metropolitan newspaper were subject to "racial profiling" in being assigned primarily to minority issues, while white reporters covered government and business stories. Journalists in that community agreed that the minority experience helped improve the coverage of related issues, but the issue of diversity was confined to "minority" topics and reporters, not as an issue of "whiteness" as it relates to the largely white arena of power. Concerning the influence of gender on reporting, Mills (1997) suggested that women lacked the "critical mass" to alter news definitions and agendas, something that may change when greater diversity is achieved. At least with regard to issues covered, a comparison of news websites carried out by Craft and Wanta (2004) found that female editors' judgments were similar to those made by male editors. In other studies, women editors were less likely to make gender distinctions among reporters in story assignments, and news organizations with predominantly male editors were more likely to cover news with a negative focus. Thus, gender appears to work at a deeper level than just basic issues. All things being equal, newspaper articles written by women are more likely to showcase women within the stories (Armstrong, 2004). Further content analysis by Rodgers and Thorson (2003) has found that reporters' gender does affect their work: Women include more diverse sources, are more positive, and are less likely to employ stereotypes. Their findings led the authors to conclude that:

> Female reporters not only differ in terms of sourcing and reporting styles, but also provide alternative viewpoints that may be critical to diversifying news definitions, as commissioned by the ASNE. We do not mean to imply that the inclusion of women journalists can provide less traditional perspectives that result in a wider variety of sources and viewpoints that may not otherwise be available to news consumers.

> (Rodgers & Thorson, 2003, p. 673)

Personal Values and Belief

Beyond background factors and demographic categories lays the psychological makeup of communicators, their values and more specific, partisan attitudes. Both entertainment and news professionals have been vulnerable to criticism that their values are somehow out of touch with American society, which they are presumed to reflect. Because they are regarded as culture producers and culture regulators, a discussion of values is central to their role in shaping the media products coming out of Los Angeles and New York. In these cases, the values embedded in media products are regarded as directly connected to values embraced by the community of individuals who created those media. Media workers are distributed throughout these culture industries and are not always easy to identify and examine, while journalists are more visible and—given their more explicit democratic role—more easily held to account.

Despite critics who depict them as out of touch with the cultural mainstream, American journalists' larger beliefs and values are carriers of core national and cultural values. In the often-referenced field study of national elite-level news organizations, Gans found that journalists held "motherhood" values of family, love, friendship, and economic prosperity; they opposed hate, prejudice, and war (Gans, 1979). For Paletz and Entman (1981) these values included individualism, free enterprise, competitiveness, and materialism. These may seem like oversimplified generalities, but they emphasize the journalist's role as steward of the status quo.

Although the work of Gans was conducted some time ago, we may take it as a basis for tracing the current status of these strains of belief. If journalists' values take on a political cast, he argues that they line up most closely with those of the early 20th century American Progressive movement. Gans identifies them as ethnocentrism, altruistic democracy, responsible capitalism, small-town pastoralism, individualism, moderatism, social order, and national leadership.

- *Ethnocentrism* refers to the journalists' tendency to value US practices above all others.

- *Altruistic democracy* indicates that most journalists believe that the news should "follow a course based on public interest and public service" (Gans, 1979, p. 43).

- *Responsible capitalism* is what most journalists expect business people to practice—fair competition without unreasonably high profits or the exploitation of workers, and respect for small and family-owned businesses.

- *Small-town pastoralism* is a journalistic ideal representing rural areas and small towns as centers of virtue, craftsmanship, and cohesive social relationship.

- *Individualism* is prized by journalists, who fill feature stories with "rugged individualists"—people who work for the good of society, but in their own way. The individual is the hero who wins despite overpowering odds.

- *Moderatism* acts as a check on excessive individualism—the hero must not break the law or existing norms.

- *Social order* is valued highly by journalists, leading them to include many stories on unrest and threats to the establishment. By pointing out instances in which people disrupt the social order or act contrary to established social values, journalists help define what is acceptable and unacceptable behavior—the normal.

- *Leadership* is also prized by journalists, because leadership is required to deal with social order.

In upholding these values, Ettema (1988, p. 3) has argued that investigative journalism is a conduit through which journalists express "righteous indignation not merely at the individual tragedy (being investigated) but also at the moral disorder and social breakdown which the tragedy represents." The journalist's outrage is often aimed at the "incompetence, indifference, or illegal behavior of public officials and agencies" and frequently results in demands for social reform. These investigative journalists claim not to make moral judgments, but the narrative form is inherently judgmental while ironically juxtaposed with claims of objectivity, of letting the audience decide from the facts. Interviews with these professionals led Ettema and Glasser (1998) to argue that the nature of this form has been: "to affirm traditional conventional interpretations of right and wrong . . . [I]ts essential moral vision is a culturally *conservative* vision in the most fundamental sense of the term—that is to say, committed to the conservation of such values as fair play, common decency, and individual liberty" (p. 114).

The values of journalism are not easy to capture using a one-dimensional ideological scale. As Gans noted, their values reflected both deeply conservative and liberal outlooks. Defense of responsible capitalism could be described as right-leaning liberalism, whereas journalists' respect for tradition, nostalgia for pastoralism and rugged individualism, defense of the social order, and faith in leadership may be regarded as conservative, status quo values (Gans, 1979, p. 68). Journalists obviously vary in the extent to which they adhere to these values, but Gans argued that the values manifest themselves in the news. These values no doubt attracted those to the profession who found them appealing, especially social reform and "do-gooding," which continue to appeal to new generations of students attracted to journalism and media careers. At the same time that they pursue their reformist impulse, journalists serve as custodians of the national order. Even during the Watergate scandal, many journalists engaged in reporting that was damaging to an American president but were still happy to reaffirm the belief that "the system worked" (Schudson, 1993).

Religious Orientations

As more attention has been focused on the culture of the "mainstream media" and whether it is detached from, supportive of, or even antagonistic toward the host culture of the larger society, the role of religion has become a question of greater interest. Historically, many journalistic advocates were motivated by their religious faith, such as during the Abolitionist movement of the 1800s. There were explicitly religious newspapers in the mid 1800s, such as the New York *Christian Advocate* and the *Boston Recorder* with large circulations, and another 100 American cities had explicitly Christian newspapers (Olasky, 1988). By the 20th century, however, the image of journalism turned secular with the rise of the ideology and style of objectivity.

Of the elite journalists surveyed by Lichter et al. (1986), 20 percent were Protestant, 13 percent Catholic, and 14 percent Jewish. Half had no religious affiliation, and 86 percent said they "seldom or never attend religious services" (Lichter et al., 1986, p. 22). A sample of national journalists at about the same period, however, reports them closely resembling the public at large. Weaver and Wilhoit (1991) found that during the 1982–3 survey period 60 percent of journalists were saying they were Protestant, 27 percent Catholic, and 6 percent Jewish. Only 7 percent reported either another or no religious affiliation. Their replication of the study in 1992 showed similar patterns, suggesting that at that time journalists closely matched the public when it came to religion (Weaver & Wilhoit, 1996). That has changed somewhat in more recent years. The percentage of Protestants among journalists declined relative to the American public (46.2 vs. 53 percent, respectively), while Catholics became better represented (32.7 vs. 25 percent). The most recent Weaver survey showed journalists differing significantly from the public in the importance of religion, with 36 percent calling it very important, compared to 61 percent of the public (2007).

Nevertheless, religion is a subject that has not been well covered in US newspapers, although the subject is of great interest to the public. Syndicated columnist David Broder was moved to say that "religion has been the biggest blind spot in newsrooms that I'm familiar with" (Triplett, 1993, p. 36). Coverage of religion is better than it used to be, according to the Religion Newswriters Association, leading executive director Debra Mason to argue that inadequate coverage is not due to an anti-religious bias among journalists, but because religion is a complex issue with too little time to explore it. Now with cuts at most newspapers, the formal religion beat has suffered, although not we suppose because journalists themselves are opposed to it. Religion is complex *and* controversial, making it a daunting media topic. Journalists have been accused of failing to understand important religious stories, such as the rise of the evangelical right, and there is some basis for that— particularly for elite journalists, who are typically based on the east and west coasts. The concentration of evangelicals in southern states creates a cultural division rather than an anti-religious media bias per se. Meanwhile, as with many specialized subjects other platforms have emerged. Religion is increasingly dealt with in online venues, such as the general interest religion online portal site Belief.net or the American Public Media radio program On Being (formerly Speaking of Faith), where presumably journalists speak with more of a "voice."

Political Attitudes

Of all the individual level characteristics, political attitudes of journalists have attracted the most scrutiny. In large part, this has been due to the work of media critics. In the USA this sort of media criticism has become particularly salient given the political polarization of government. Well-funded advocacy groups pursue claims of press bias, which they are convinced runs against their own views, and identifying the political leanings of journalists is crucial to the critique and work of many partisan media watchdog groups (mentioned earlier). While professionals dispute the extent to which their personal views intrude on the end product, an examination of their attitudes does help shed light on the shape and political cast of the individuals behind the news.

In many countries the naturally partisan nature of the press makes bias a non-issue. The US media have caught up in this respect, developing a host of new, more explicitly partisan news outlets, such as on cable television with Fox News, MSNBC, and online with blog sites such as the Huffington Post and BigGovernment (Stroud, 2011). The bias of the journalists and pundits driving these media defines their focus, which is packaged accordingly. Individual level attitudes take on a different meaning in this larger media context. The political stance of those featured in these more opinionated media—and those more freelance figures like cartoonists, comedians, and authors—is more directly synchronized with the ideas they express, yet even in this area one could argue that they are primarily creating a market niche product for consumption, positioning it politically for a desired demographic. In that case the actual political views of the communicator are still relatively inconsequential; they need not believe what they produce, although they may grow to do so. Journalism for many (if not the rank and file) has become a lucrative occupation, on cable news, syndicated columns, and the speaking circuit. Opinion journalists' views are delivered front and center—the analysis for researchers in this case would center not only on describing what is said but also on the validity of their claims or on how their access and views gain favor. The traditional mainstream news media, however, continue to present themselves as objective news brokers (still a strategic niche, as in the case of CNN), attracting continuing attention to the more indirect effects of communicator attitudes, as a more subtle form of influence.

Politically Driven Personal Attitudes

We will take the bias issue up elsewhere, but briefly the left and right critiques of media differ on levels of analysis: The left views bias as rooted in ownership and corporate interests of media while the right seeks it among the individual level attitudes of the media class. Because this latter, politics of journalists view has attracted so much interest and is arguably the most prominent and successful discourse, we first consider how the critique of the "liberal journalist" figures into this discussion. Conservative leaders have adopted the "liberal media" argument as a rhetorical strategy, a strategy that operates above, and in spite of, any supporting evidence (Watts, Domke, Shah, & Fan, 1999). Whatever the general complaints about the media held by the public, many of these are on target: Communicators can be out of touch, culturally and otherwise with their communities, and they are mostly market-driven, leading to the exclusion of important issues. Attaching the word *liberal* to these complaints, however, applies a particular diagnosis, one that summarizes a partisan response to a larger institutional problem.

As we observed earlier, a similar discourse is common among critics of higher education; defining the problem with universities as political "tilt" of the faculty introduces the concept of "balance," suggesting that ideas within the academic disciplines can be placed on the same political spectrum in place within the political arena. Do ideas result from the personnel at work on them, or are they a function of the disciplinary framework through which they are processed—and which attract to them certain kinds of people? This is a key dynamic at the individual level of analysis, and the answer to these questions matters greatly in guiding the policy response.

Whether in media or higher education, the argument of underrepresentation and a call for greater balance from those outside the institution is ultimately an effort to control and naturally runs contrary to the traditional ideas of professional independence, or in the case of the academic world, the autonomy of the scholarly disciplines. Conservatives' interest in the political affiliation of journalists suggests that content product can be regulated by controlling the characteristics of its producers. Several years ago, one of the original conservative media watchdog groups, Accuracy in Media, led a campaign to fire the anchor of the *CBS Evening News*, Dan Rather. This kind of high profile targeting is uncommon today, given the fragmentation of the media landscape and loss of stature of the traditional older networks, but the logic behind the individual focus remains the same. Elsewhere in this book we consider the institutional role of the media in relation to other centers of power in the society, but at the individual level we note that claims about the politics of journalists often say as much about the politics of the critics as they do about any empirical evidence. Beyond offering a diagnosis, such efforts are an attempt to control a profession that doesn't always offer agreeable content. The institutionalized common ground has eroded as the capacity of the profession to provide trustworthy content has been brought into question by its own shortcoming and by the media watchdog culture. Academic research is helpful in providing a more "balanced" empirical view of the state of these professionals.

Media Elites

The book that arguably launched the modern research-based "liberal journalist" critique, *The Media Elite*, was based largely on a survey of journalists at elite media, such as the *New York Times*, and used to paint a negative portrait:

> Today's leading journalists are politically liberal and alienated from traditional norms and institutions. Most place themselves to the left of center and regularly

vote the Democratic ticket. Yet theirs is not the New Deal liberalism of the underprivileged, but the contemporary social liberalism of the urban sophisticate. They favor a strong welfare state within a capitalist framework. They differ most from the general public, however, on the divisive social issues that have emerged since the 1960s—abortion, gay rights, affirmative action, et cetera. Many are alienated from the "system" and quite critical of America's world role. They would like to strip traditional powerbrokers of their influence and empower black leaders, consumer groups, intellectuals, and . . . the media.

(Lichter et al., 1986, p. 294; ellipsis in original)

The arguments about media liberalism centered not around the average journalist, however, but rather around what the authors described in their title as media "elites"—those journalists who work for the most prestigious and influential US media. They found between 1979 and 1980 that 54 percent of elite journalists were politically liberal and 17 percent were conservative. Of those elite journalists who voted in presidential elections between 1964 and 1976, more than 80 percent voted for the Democratic candidate in each year (Lichter et al., 1986, p. 30). This compares with Weaver and Wilhoit's data gathered from a probability sample of US journalists (not just from elites), which shows that in 1982–3, 45 percent of journalists were Democrats, 25 percent were Republicans, and 30 percent were Independents (1991, p. 29).

Although the politics of journalists is a particular obsession of US watchdog and academic analyses, the findings of a left-leaning profession do appear to be consistent around the world. Among Dutch reporters, a majority rate themselves as leaning "a little to the left" (47 percent) or "pretty far to the left" (31 percent) (Deuze, 2002). Australian journalists show a similar "liberal-progressive" skew compared to the public—especially on social issues (e.g., sexual freedom) (Henningham, 1998). Deuze (2002) concludes that this international congruence "suggests that having a 'left' (or perhaps progressive, social-democratic) self-perception is something which can be expected of the 'ideology' related to being a news media professional in a Western democracy" (p. 138). Another survey in five countries showed that journalists in the USA, Britain, Germany, Sweden, and Italy were left of center in their political beliefs, although not extreme, leading Patterson to support Gans' description of journalists as mainstream "progressives" (Patterson, 1998). According to the Weaver group's 2002 survey, journalists were more likely to consider themselves left of center compared to the general public (40 percent vs. 17 percent, respectively), and less likely to describe themselves as right of center (25 percent and 41 percent, respectively). Between the 1982 and 1992 surveys, journalists' political views moved to the left, with middle-of-the-road responses dropping from 57.5 percent to 30 percent. But since 1992, the distribution of political views has been relatively stable, except for a substantial right-leaning shift among executives. On the other hand, in 2002, Weaver and colleagues compared the general public's party identification with journalists, finding that journalists were 4 percent more likely than the public to be Democrats and 13 percent less likely to be Republicans. As in previous studies, journalists were more likely to be Democrats or independent but were closer in 2002 than ever before to the public's distribution; since 1992 journalists have been less likely to self-identify as Democrat (falling from 44.1 to 35.9 percent) and slightly more as Republican (rising from 16.4 to 18 percent) (Weaver et al., 2007).

ANALYZING THE EFFECTS OF INDIVIDUALS

In spite of the many studies of individual attitudes, the influences they have on content have been much less clear. Attitudes don't translate directly into behavior, a rebuttal made many times in defense of the profession in the face of these consistent survey findings, including Gans, in his rejoinder to the Lichter study. In response to this criticism, Robert Lichter wrote,

> We are certainly not saying that attitudes are everything, nor that journalists are ideologues. We're simply saying that news judgment is subjective and decisions about sources, news pegs, and . . . language will partly reflect the way a journalist perceives and understands the social world.
>
> (Face-off, 1987, p. 31)

Such reasoning is intuitively appealing, but the subtleties are lost when it enters the political arena. One could even make the case that some journalists have bent over backwards in the conservative direction of their news content to avoid liberal bias charges, charges which have increased significantly over the years to constitute 95 percent of media bias charges, according to analyses of the 1988, 1992, and 1996 election years (Domke, Watts, Shah, & Fan, 1999). Even a rhetorical charge of left bias can become a self-fulfilling prophesy when it leads to self-policing, and self coverage of the liberal bias rhetoric has a significant impact on public perceptions—an effect documented in analysis of presidential campaigns (Watts et al., 1999). We are led to question whether the influence of personal attitudes on media content may be offset by factors at higher levels of analysis.

In *Deciding What's News*, Gans acknowledged that reality judgments are closely tied to values, which are "rarely explicit and must be found between the lines—in what actors and activities are reported or ignored, and in how they are described" (1979, pp. 39–40). Some years later, however, there was a stronger position in distancing attitudes (perhaps in contrast to deeply rooted values) from judgment:

> Of course, there are some individuals whose attitudes do matter. Henry Luce had some influence on what Time said while he was the editor-in-chief and the owner. William Buckley, another fairly highly opinionated editor, has a great deal of influence, I'm sure, on what the *National Review* puts out. But for rank and file journalists, whether they are reporters or writers or even news

executives, personal attitudes do not affect their work except in unusual circumstances. Moreover, they try to be objective and leave their values at home.

(Face-off, 1987, p. 31)

Although a distinction is made here between the views of elite and more nationally
representative journalists, we may also ask: Do elite journalists have a substantial
impact on media content that is different from the impact of other journalists?
Weaver and Wilhoit say that "it is questionable how much influence [the elite jour-
nalists] exert over the hundreds of smaller news organizations throughout the country. Certainly with regard to local and regional news, the influence of these media
'elites' is likely to be minimal or nonexistent" (1991, p. 25). But, as Reese and Danielian (1989) have shown, there may be substantial media *convergence* on issues of
national concern. In their study of how five newspapers, three television networks,
and two newsmagazines covered cocaine during 1985 and 1986, Reese and Danielian showed that when one elite medium picked up a particular story, other media
were quick to follow. In the same mid 1980s study, they found that the *New York
Times* set the news agenda for the television networks. Now stories can emerge on
the Internet and go viral without the leadership of the prestige press, but in a diverse
media mix we assume there's still a role for elite gatekeepers. Although the influence
of organizations like the *Times* may have been diluted in the more extensive media
landscape, elite journalists' opinions may still have a wide influence—in spite of,
and perhaps because of, the fragmentation of the media outlets.

Perhaps values play a particularly strong role when journalists respond as both
professionals *and* as members of a particular local community. In her analysis titled
Making Local News, Kaniss (1991) pointed out that in news coverage of civic development, journalists' personal values can:

contribute to their willingness to believe the promises made by officials and to
ignore questions of the relocation of existing residents and businesses or considerations of alternative uses of public funds for other neighborhoods outside
of downtown or in the suburbs. As middle-class professionals who often live as
well as work in the heart of city downtowns, reporters are often eager to see the
city made more glamorous and cosmopolitan . . . . Therefore, the personal and
professional bias in favor of downtown development projects, when combined
with the newspaper's need for effective regional symbols, leads to a tendency
for initial coverage of new downtown projects to be positive.

(p. 80)

This kind of influence depends in part on the political culture. In their international
comparative study that presented journalists with different scenarios, Patterson and
Donsbach (1996) concluded that partisan beliefs affected news decisions. Predictably, this influence was strongest in those countries with a tradition of partisan
advocacy—Germany, Italy, and Britain—but they suggest the effect is to shade the
news rather than color it deeply. So, the question is not *whether* attitudes and values
influence the news, but *how* and under *what* conditions?

Journalism as Profession

Finally, we turn to those factors related to professional roles and ethical frameworks (although related in significant ways). We distinguish these factors from more personal features not directly tied to the occupational setting (Figure 8.1). As distinguished from other more general communication occupations, journalism has developed a stronger professional identity. Members are taught these roles in a process described by an early media sociologist, Warren Breed, as socialization. The new journalist "discovers and internalizes the rights and obligations of his status and its norms and values" (Breed, 1960, p. 182). Of course, professional norms and skills are taught more explicitly through formal education, but a strong learn-by-doing "osmosis" mentality has run through the journalism business. Although the balance between them varies, communication professions are reproduced over time by a combination of formal training and on-the-job learning.

This communication of norms within the organization is an enduring concern and important process discussed in Chapter 6 but here it reminds us that professional roles are not intrinsic to the individual but must be learned. The rewards for quickly learning and following policy come from co-workers and employers within the media organization—not from the audience. Socialization has been an ongoing concern in media sociology, providing what Sigal (1973, p. 3) called "a context of shared values" with co-workers. These values, as we discussed earlier, shape the context in which events are viewed and the selection of the aspects of each event that will become the news.

To the extent that we consider these roles important, we must begin with considering the extent to which journalism constitutes a profession. In many respects journalism looks like a profession, which Lambeth (1986, p. 82) defines as having the following characteristics:

- It is a full-time occupation.

- Its practitioners are deeply committed to the goals of the profession.

- Entrance to and continuance in the profession are governed by a formal organization that has established standards.

- Its practitioners are admitted to the profession following prescribed formal schooling and the acquisition of a specialized body of knowledge.

- It must serve society.

- Its members must have a high degree of autonomy.

Similarly, Beam (1990) described professions as organized around a systematic body of knowledge or technique, featuring broad occupational autonomy and authority, emphasizing public service over economic gain, socializing members to a common culture, and producing unstandardized occupational products. Membership in professions is also typically lifelong. To the extent that it lays claim to a high-minded societal role, a set of learned ethical principles, and a strong tradition of independence, journalism conducts itself like a profession—if not quite like the traditional professions of law and medicine, where bodies of knowledge are systematically accumulated in academic settings and then put to use in the field.

Journalism has no credentialing requirements in most countries or other similar barriers to entry. As a First Amendment issue, American journalism has traditionally shunned anything that resembled pre-requisites of an official license to practice, such as that required in many jobs. Many countries have required this journalistic licensing, such as Brazil, although it has recently dropped that requirement in spite of opposition from the universities who contributed to that credentialing. The effect of licensing there had been to mark journalists with a professional allegiance, which they carried with them throughout their life regardless of later career changes. In the USA at least there is no official body that might see to the policing of professional violations. The few attempts at news councils—community organizations that review and judge the merits of press performance, depending on voluntary compliance by professionals—that could provide that function have not been successful. Although independent-spirited, the autonomy of journalists—as a professional prerequisite—is also questionable; journalists don't usually work for themselves (although increasingly they may), and corporate pressures often intrude on individual autonomy.

A profession by formal definition involves a tradition of critical philosophical reflection (Pelikan, 1992), but journalism's strong "learning by doing" streak in its extreme form borders on the anti-intellectual. We could certainly argue that journalism has become more critically reflective and valuing of analysis conducted within its associated academic programs. Often, however, what traditional professions take as deep, critical reflection to determine how practices are working is converted in journalistic learning to the acquisition of "nuts and bolts" knowledge, and the uncritical emulation of former professionals. What should be professional in the reflective sense, often becomes closer to vocational when it becomes unreflective and imitative. Thus, as Weaver and Wilhoit have suggested, journalists are "*of* a profession but not *in* one" (1991, p. 45).

Professional Indices

A number of researchers have developed measures of professionalism in journalism, and considered the extent to which journalists adhere to them. Pioneering work by McLeod and Hawley (1964), for example, measured whether "professional attitudes" were more pronounced than "nonprofessional attitudes," with the assumption that the former should lead to better journalism. The concept of *professionalism* in this context describes how fully a member has internalized the values of the profession, compared to "professionalization"—the process of an occupation undergoing change. Those scoring as more professional on the scholars' index were more likely, for example, to desire the newspaper to be unbiased and responsible, to have greater job satisfaction, and to show better job performance (Becker, 2005). This "trait" approach stemmed from the sociology of the professions, a functional view of how well journalism adhered to its normative criteria. This approach continues to have international appeal, with a recent study, for example, considering how closely Chinese journalists reflected elements of the medical profession in coverage of an earthquake disaster (Lee & So, 2010). This approach, however, largely has given way to a more active, Weberian view of the "professional project," in which social actors convert resources (control over information, access to political elites) into rewards and struggle with other groups for "jurisdiction."

More recently, of course, we must account for journalism's need as a profession to control its boundaries, with the desire to open up the process to a more participatory role for citizens. Professions are based on control over membership and the prerogative to make creative decisions, but new media bring opportunities for anyone to participate in the creation of media messages, so in what sense does the profession continue to exercise control? With professional boundaries breaking down between traditional and citizen journalists, the question now is what shape will a more hybridized professional logic take. In his study of journalism innovation, Lewis (2012) examines this professional-participatory tension, and how a new professional ethic must embrace the involvement of the audience in order to regain its trust. He concluded that the profession must inevitably cede the possibility of control, but that doesn't mean a professional ethic will not remain. We can expect it to be reconstituted around norms of information ethics and transparency and that this is entered into willingly by participants, not enforced by institutional controls. This is more of an organizational and institutional aspect of "professionalization" to be explored elsewhere in this volume.

Professional Roles

Journalists have perceived themselves as being part of a profession and have ideas about what constitutes professional work. To that extent, there are meaningful roles that we seek to describe and explain, with a long tradition of related research. The language surrounding these roles varies, including *belief systems, professional values, ideology,* and *professional identities.* The work of Zelizer (1997) takes a more humanistic approach to these questions, preferring the concept of *interpretive communities* and their shared interpretations and practices. In any case, at the individual level, we are interested in how these views are internalized, and serve as a guide to action. Thus, at this level media sociology most closely resembles the functionalism and methodological individualism that characterized the larger communication field for so long.

A profession does not produce only one kind of role. At its most basic, Bernard Cohen (1963) distinguished between "neutral" and "participant," roles that reflect how the journalist relates to information. In a pioneering representative national survey of American journalists, Johnstone et al. (1972) examined a sample of 1,313 "editorial personnel in daily and weekly newspapers, newsmagazines, wire services, and the news departments of radio and television stations and networks" (p. 525). This study—particularly influential in shaping the line of research conducted by Weaver and colleagues cited extensively in this chapter—found that some journalists considered themselves "neutrals," seeing their jobs as mere channels of transmission, while others saw themselves as "participants," believing that journalists need to sift through information in order to find and develop the story. Neutral journalists saw their jobs as getting information to the public quickly, avoiding stories with unverified content, concentrating on the widest audience, and entertaining the audience. Participants emphasized investigating government claims, providing analysis of complex problems, discussing national policy, and developing intellectual/cultural interests; they were younger, better educated, and worked for bigger media organizations in large cities.

From a political perspective, these roles must be understood within the national context, where journalism is positioned relative to other institutions. Patterson and Donsbach (1996) used two dimensions found to be statistically unrelated to produce a comparative framework: a passive-active dimension and neutral-advocacy dimension. The first concerns the political autonomy of the journalist (passive or active), while the second concerns the positioning as a political actor, whether neutrality is replaced with advocacy. They found, for example, that the straightforward approach of British broadcast news most closely resembled the "passive-neutral" position, while German journalists were more likely to be advocates. With a general trend toward a more active role, they suggest journalism will become a more powerful political actor, but that activity without advocacy may lead to greater mistrust of government—a theme Patterson developed previously in his classic volume *Out of Order* (1993). Another form of this activity without advocacy may be seen in Hallin's view of the "independent insider" role, which he claimed characterized the "high modernism" of US journalism—modeled by the national security beat reporter. This role has now fallen into disrepute following the collapse of political consensus and, more recently, the failure of reporters to be more critical of foreign policy following 9/11. Although not partisan in the traditional sense, Hallin's insider sought access and was granted it in exchange for not being overly critical (Hallin, 1992). The result was to restrict this role to the interpretation of tactical and technical explanation, a tendency that does not meaningfully enlarge the public sphere.

Weaver and colleagues refined these concepts of professional attitudes, extending the dual Johnstone categories of *neutral* and *participant*, to include *disseminator*, *adversarial*, *interpretive*, and later, with a nod to the public journalism movement, *populist mobilizer*. Each role encompassed related expressions of support for various journalistic functions (Weaver et al., 2007).

- The *disseminator* function: getting information to the public quickly, avoiding unverified facts, reaching the widest possible audience, and providing entertainment and relaxation. This function has declined in importance, but the majority still sees as "extremely important" the first two elements, based on quick and factual information. Journalists supporting this role are more ethically cautious, frowning on such practices as hidden microphones, and more likely to have been journalism majors in college.

- The *interpretive* function: investigating official claims, analyzing complex problems, and discussing national and international policies. This remains the dominant professional role of modern US journalists, perhaps rooted in the continuing need for someone to help citizens deal with the information explosion. The strongest support from journalists is most recently for "investigating government claims," with 71 percent saying it's extremely important. Those embracing this role tended to be well educated, liberal, and at larger news organizations.

- The *adversary* function—serving as an adversary of officials or of business—is a relatively minor role. As of 2002, fewer embraced this role, with 20 percent of US journalists strongly endorsing being an adversary of officials and 18 percent being an adversary of business. In their profile, journalists supporting this role were similar to the interpreters but more likely to work for print media.

- The *populist mobilizer* function—let people express their views, develop cultural interests, motivate people to get involved, point to possible solutions, and set the political agenda—is related to the public or civic journalism movement, which encouraged journalists to take a more active role in guiding the conversation with the public. Although clustered together, support for these items varies greatly, from 39 percent endorsing letting people express their views to only 3 percent supporting the setting of the agenda (even if that is what they implicitly do). Mobilizers tend to be liberal, working for print media, and experience a high degree of freedom in their work.

The Online Culture and Journalistic Roles

The newest wrinkle in the Weaver surveys is the online journalist, who is at the vanguard in salary and likelihood of having some graduate education. The online culture seems to have affected the profession by being less likely to "avoid unverifiable facts," more likely to justify any questionable reporting practice, and less caring about reaching the widest possible audience. Compared to their offline counterparts, they were more likely to favor the interpretive function and less apt to see themselves as a populist mobilizer, suggesting the erosion of explicit organizational responsibility for the community. The authors found it surprising that, given the interactive capability of new media, online journalists were less likely to emphasize in survey responses the importance of motivating people to get involved or letting people express themselves. Of course, whether the online world itself *permits* something in its technological capabilities and whether the professionals involved *feel* it's their role to encourage it are two different things.

Many of the trends in the Weaver group surveys have not shown a single direction over time, making it difficult to build to a single overall conclusion. Just when it would be tempting to conclude journalists are becoming more liberal, for example, they take a conservative turn (especially among executives). Just when they seem to more closely mirror the American public on religious views, journalists take a more secular turn. Taken together, the authors find more stability than change, reason for both concern and optimism, and more differences than similarities across organizations and jobs. Thus, these data provide important insights but also raise questions about how we can explain the direction of the profession itself. By providing comparable surveys of the same population over time the Weaver group provides a consistent grid of measures, but the underlying professional object is not static: it is shifting over time and transforming. Since the earliest surveys, much has changed in the professional world. A different kind of person has doubtless become attracted to journalism and others been run off. Journalists are embedded in a variety of new contexts, with many jobs now becoming more editorial, curatorial, and news organizations more algorithmic in their news selection, such as Google News and Yahoo.com, but of course it is still important to have reporters on the ground gathering information. A number of nonprofit sector news projects have taken off in recent years to help supply this need, including the *Texas Tribune* and *Propublica*, with others like the Center for Public Integrity more focused on web-based investigative journalism, and Spot.us an example of an open-source project based on "community powered reporting." Howard Kurtz of the *Washington Post* continued a trend of high profile journalists leveraging their talents across organizations, migrating in 2010 to *The Daily Beast*, an online news-site then in its infancy. This led *New York Times* media columnist David Carr to conclude that "more and more, media outlets are becoming a federation of individual brands like Mr. Kurtz. Journalism is starting to look like sports, where a cast of role players serves as a platform and context for highly paid, high-impact players" (Carr, 2010). In the midst of these changes, the question is what kind of professional ethic will continue to bind them together across these diverse occupational settings.

Perspectives on Professional Roles

The roles perspective brings a normative view of the profession that can seem schizophrenic, implying that journalists should be well educated and competent but not too out of touch with the society overall. Befitting their affiliations with journalism education, the Weaver group implicitly want more status for the profession: Respondents felt better about the work of independent companies and those organizations that valued journalism over profits, they felt better about their jobs with more autonomy, and they still valued substance in their best work and aspirations. Still, it seems these journalists can't win. Increasing education levels and job conditions equate with being more professional, but these could distance journalists from the majority of the population without such advanced learning.

That notion recalls Sen. Roman Hruska's famous anti-intellectual claim: "There are a lot of mediocre judges and people and lawyers," said the Nebraska Republican. "They are entitled to a little representation, aren't they?" Whatever the descriptive profile of media workers, the results must be understood in appropriate theoretical and normative context.

Ethical Issues

Ethics, although rooted in philosophical perspectives, is relevant to the social scientific explanation of how it guides professional actions, directing service to humanity rather than to seek the journalist's own ends (Altschull, 1984). Although journalism as a whole lacks an enforceable code of ethics, this is not for lack of possibilities. In 1992, more than 42 percent of newspapers and 31 percent of television news operations had published standards governing how their staffs should operate (Black, 1992). For example, the *Milwaukee Journal* published its Rules and Guidelines in 1978 to explain that its news-editorial employees are to avoid participating in community activities that could create a conflict of interest "or give the impression of one" (Rules and Guidelines, 1978). Employees also are forbidden to work in public relations and/or for a political candidate. The current statement of the official code of the major professional body puts it this way in its preamble:

> Members of the Society of Professional Journalists believe that public enlightenment is the forerunner of justice and the foundation of democracy. The duty of the journalist is to further those ends by seeking truth and providing a fair and comprehensive account of events and issues. Conscientious journalists from all media and specialties strive to serve the public with thoroughness and honesty. Professional integrity is the cornerstone of a journalist's credibility.

As the key ethical mandates, the code urges journalists to "seek truth and report it," "minimize harm," "act independently," and to "be accountable."[4] Along these same lines, Kovach and Rosenstiel (2001) have taken a somewhat different and broader approach, in a lengthy investigation intended to identify and reclaim the essence of the profession, and recover journalism from the larger world of communication. This work, summarized in *The Elements of Journalism*, has become a widely recognized restatement of the core of the profession, principles journalists subscribe to and citizens expect. These elements include the following:

- obligation to the truth
- loyalty to citizens
- discipline of verification
- independence from those being covered
- independent monitor of power

- public forum

- making significant interesting and relevant

- keeping news comprehensive and proportional

- exercise of personal conscience

A more recent formulation proposed by the Washington News Council, an ombudsman-like group, condenses the fundamental professional responsibility to the acronym TAO: Transparent, Accountable, Open. In advocating this new professional ethic, the group does not promise to follow any particular code, but in its statement of principles declares that when it does it will say so, trusting that enforcement will be carried out by citizens on the Internet.[5]

The most egregious violations of these principles occur when journalists actually fabricate information and deceive readers. Stephen Glass, writer at the *New Republic*, was found to have made up many of his stories in the late 1990s and became the subject of a dramatized version in the feature film *Shattered Glass*. The frequency of these scandals is such that the Freedom Forum keeps an updated, alphabetized list on its website.[6] More subtle violations are becoming more frequent as journalists navigate the new partisan media landscape where issues of truth are more secondary to opinionated commentary. When the National Public Radio (NPR) ousted news analyst Juan Williams for stating on a Fox News program that seeing Muslims on a plane made him nervous, public radio's critics complained that his firing was as an example of "political correctness." Fox supported him and renewed his contract. In justifying its decision, NPR argued that Williams had violated the organization's code of impartiality (a version of American journalism's objectivity); Fox gave this less weight than its preference for point of view commentary. Clearly, the principles of journalism today are not ascribed uniformly across the range of journalistic activity, with the partisan/mainstream division showing particular strain.

For partisan advocates, technology makes it easier than ever to participate in the media conversation. Andrew Breitbart, for example, began a politically conservative group of websites, including BigGovernment.com, dedicated to supporting and distributing information that advances a point of view. He made big news when he provided a platform in 2009 to guerrilla filmmaker James O'Keefe, who purported to find wrongdoing within the community-organizing group ACORN (Association of Community Organizations for Reform Now) when he posed as a pimp with one of his prostitutes seeking business advice. In 2010, Breitbart made news again when posting a video of an official in the Department of Agriculture, Shirley Sherrod, speaking at a civil rights organization event. The two and a half minute video suggested that Sherrod, an African American, had discriminated against a white farmer, leading to her being fired in the ensuing uproar. Later, it emerged that the video had been taken out of context, missing the larger story of racial reconciliation between her and the farmer, but too late for Ms. Sherrod—and even too late for the more objective media that relayed and amplified the initial story. Although there are ethical themes cutting across national professional spheres, the online media world makes it more difficult to have a common conception of journalistic ethics, and the absence of a more unified profession means a lack of enforcement authority even if there was one.

Comparative Global Profession

As journalism has grown more globalized along with other professions, a number of studies have approached these questions from that perspective. Particularly interesting is the question of whether a single global profession is emerging. Most systematic research has been conducted on US journalists, but other surveys have been conducted in other countries as well.

Following in the tradition of his previous surveys, Weaver (1998) has analyzed surveys of more than 20,000 journalists by colleagues in 21 different countries. Although providing valuable insights into specific countries, the nation-by-nation approach does not permit many broader generalizations. The most up-to-date and extensive compilation of such research is contained in his most recent collection, *The Global Journalist in the 21st Century* (Weaver & Willnat, 2012), including surveys from 33 countries but also some attention to emerging cross-national comparative frameworks pointing to the growing popularity of this style of investigation. These conclusions point to as many differences as similarities in the support for professional roles and reporting practices. Considered a different way, in earlier work from the perspective of the new generation of professionals, Splichal and Sparks (1994) found in their survey of 1,800 first-year journalism students in 22 countries that, as they move into their careers, journalists can be expected to become more professional and ethical, better educated, and to value autonomy. One of the most prominent recent comparative projects was launched by Hanitzsch and several international colleagues, mapping "journalism cultures" with interviews of 1,800 journalists in 18 countries (Hanitzsch et al., 2011). And gradually, from these individual and comparative efforts, a picture of journalists around the world has begun to develop. The data provide comparative insights but a mixed picture of the extent to which a globally similar or unified profession has emerged. The Hanitzsch group finds, for example, common support for information reliability and universal ethical principles, but regional differences in support for journalists as agents of social change.

Another way to approach this comparative task is to survey foreign correspondents in the USA for their cross-cultural perspectives. Willnat and Weaver (2003) observe that these journalists from many countries share a similar task, and in general are well educated and experienced, as befits a desirable foreign assignment, but differ in their national professional training. The similarity of their reporting task appears to lead these journalists to agree on the desire for better access to sources, more openness, and high-level briefings from officials—in short, to be allowed to do their job. Reflecting the tension between national and global professional interests, one foreign journalist desired greater trust with sources: " 'I told them many times, I am doing my job, I AM NOT AN ENEMY' " (Willnat & Weaver, 2003, p. 419). Comparing US journalists overall to European and other US-based foreign correspondents shows mixed agreement in support of various professional roles and reporting practices, while comparing European to other foreign journalists based in the USA shows no uniformity in their professional outlooks: "Differing political systems and national cultures still make a difference in which roles journalists consider most important, and in which reporting methods are considered justifiable" (Willnat & Weaver, 2003, p. 419). No matter what increased worldwide professional solidarity may be emerging, as the authors note, is between US journalists on the "inside" and foreign correspondents on the "outside."

In understanding the global journalist, Reese (2001b) notes that a cross-national approach may not adequately capture this emerging phenomenon, given that the stratifications of professional conduct may be more varied within than across countries.

> Elite journalists will likely have more in common with each other, across national boundaries, than with many of their more localized compatriots. More interesting questions may involve considering how this emerging class of "cosmopolite" journalists shares a common standard and understanding of journalism. As transitional commercialism grows, exemplified by firms like McDonald's and Disney, a common monoculture is developing, with media products moving easily across national borders. Global journalism is part of this development, supporting increasingly common understandings of what constitutes the international news agenda.
>
> (p. 178)

As a pervasive and universal aspect of communication, ethics becomes inherently global. Studies of media ethics, particularly of the various professional codes in communication, suggest that there are universal themes that are found throughout the world: "the quest for truth," "desire for responsibility," and "the compulsion for free expression" (Cooper, 1990, p. 3). Of course, how these ethical drives are put into practice varies by international context. Berkowitz et al. (2004) compared American and Israeli journalists on their decisions in various ethical scenarios, that personal and professional factors were less related to ethical decisions than the national context. Although that context appears to continue to be more influential than individual factors, ethical standards can create cultural bridges, leading the authors to suggest that journalists will continue to interact and exchange ideas about "proper" professional behavior.

SUMMARY

We have considered how communicators' characteristics, both personal and professional, influence media content—an individual level approach, which takes it as a given that none of us can escape having our actions affected by our personal subjectivities and life experiences. Many studies connect these traits directly to specific outcomes, but these influences are often implicit in the numerous research efforts that describe media professionals and their characteristics and compare them to the larger society. Thus, we have given special attention to the normative and theoretical issues these studies raise. Describing these communicators and comparing them to the larger society is one thing, but it is another to determine specifically how those individual level factors affect the media message and how they interact. We need to know what relative emphasis to give professional roles compared to personal beliefs and the ways those factors shape each other. As we have shown, demographic factors, such as gender and race, influence content indirectly both through shaping personal attitudes and values and through their links with professional roles and education. Personal and professional factors are closely related, and both help determine content, particularly to the extent that communicators have the power necessary to imprint their own decisions on the product.

NOTES

1 See http://archive.pressthink.org/2006/06/27/ppl_frmr.html. (Accessed April 28, 2013.)
2 See www.usatoday.com/news/census/index?loc=interstitialskip. (Accessed April 28, 2013.)
3 See http://politicalhumor.about.com/od/stephencolbert/a/colbertbush_2.htm. (Accessed April 28, 2013.)
4 See www.spj.org/ethicscode.asp. (Accessed April 28, 2013.)
5 See http://wanewscouncil.org. (Accessed April 28, 2013.)
6 See http://catalog.freedomforum.org/FFLib/JournalistScandals.htm. (Accessed April 28, 2013.)

CHAPTER 9

Studying the Hierarchical Model

Throughout this book we have tried to explain the forces that shape mediated communication of all kinds: social media, mass communication, offline and online, news and entertainment. Admittedly, our emphasis has been more on news than entertainment, but the Hierarchical Model is a rich source of ideas when analyzing any type of mediated content. In addition, we hope that, by seeing the rich and varied sets of ideas and research projects reviewed in this volume, scholars are invigorated to think creatively about their own research programs. We are in a time of great social change with mediated communication at the heart of that change. Change brings opportunities for scholarly and professional careers to be made, and hopefully *Mediating the Message in the 21st Century* feeds those careers by sparking both new ideas and ways to combine old ones.

Now we return to our discussion concerning the theoretical issues raised in plotting out this area of research, particularly in engaging a multi-level approach to media production and control. We offer the Hierarchical Model as a framework through which scholars can discover relationships among old and new studies, because building connections between ideas is one of the first steps in building theory. When these connections are made, the Hierarchical Model becomes a theoretical model, a structure that facilitates the building of many theories by many people. The *Handbook of Journalism Studies* lists the "Hierarchy of Influences" as a "key concept" (Franklin, Richardson, Hamer, Hanna, & Kinsey, 2005), which suggests that there is something about the model that gives it significant value for research, and we assume that this lies in its theoretical utility.

BUILDING THEORY

Perhaps we seem a bit grandiose in talking about building theories, rather than simply doing research, but every theory begins with one idea, and one idea may become one study. As such studies accumulate, scholars think both inductively and deductively to plan and explain the outcomes of their research. The creation of this explanation, however, is not automatic, required, or even likely. There are lines of research in the social sciences that are largely descriptive and amount to an accumulation of data with no explanation for either the commonalities or differences among the projects. As theorists, we find this unsatisfying—a sandwich made of many meats, cheeses, and vegetables but with no bread to hold it together. Crunching numbers can be fun and relatively straightforward, but the more difficult and fulfilling task is being able to explain what the results mean. When quantitative journal articles have discussion (or conclusion or summary) sections that are the shortest part of the publication, it suggests that the authors might not understand how to relate their findings to those of other scholars—or are not interested in doing so. The authors may themselves understand these relationships but cannot communicate them effectively to readers with less expertise, or they may choose not to emphasize their interpretive job. As in other social science disciplines, communication researchers can produce lists of articles that have topics and constructs in common but they do not explain the contribution the studies make to the field.

We believe that scholars, whether they say so or not, want to connect their studies and explain what they contribute—to add them up to a bigger picture and build theory. The Hierarchical Model is intended to help with that, identifying concepts and a common vocabulary for combining and discussing them. By assigning their studies to a level of analysis, scholars then know which studies are directly relevant to theirs and which can be temporarily set aside—until connections within one level are made and explanations for the similarities or differences among studies have begun. Some theories are devoted to one level of analysis, such as the individual (or intra) level for fields like cognitive psychology. Others, in more "variable fields" like communication, can be studied across a range of micro to macro levels; an example of this is gatekeeping theory. Determining an individual study's level of analysis brings clarity, allows better synthesis of results, and therefore turns out to be extremely important in advancing the big picture.

Since the Hierarchical Model was first introduced in *Mediating the Message's* progenitor, Shoemaker's "Building a Theory of News" (1987), and continued in *Mediating the Message's* first (1991) and second (1996) editions, the structure for studying media content on different levels of analysis has helped establish and legitimate an important area of research—and been used by many scholars as a way to tie their individual research projects to a larger intellectual community. Even though based largely on US- and UK-based empirical projects, the theoretical generality and intuitive accessibility of the model seems to travel relatively well, causing it to be cited by a number of international colleagues from a wide range of national settings. Below we analyze how the model has been used in studies of media content and in the building of theory, showing that the model has launched a number of different interpretive strategies.

Many studies have made reference to "Shoemaker and Reese," but these references have been made for different reasons. Since in our work we contribute a combination of synthesis of the research and a proposal for how to better organize it within a hierarchical model, other authors have found different parts of that task useful. Some see the value of having the field mapped out in general, and others use our articulation of particular empirical generalizations, or "findings," from the literature. Sometimes the model itself is used to both locate a study's focus and provide, in more ambitious analyses, a test of factors at various levels in relation to each other.

At the time of our earliest writing, we felt obliged to advocate a focus on media content and control, making a case for research in that area in contrast to the "process and effects" emphasis that had characterized the field. At this basic level, some scholars have simply agreed with us that the area is important without engaging the model as such. Helge (2008), for example, asked how to explain content concerning religion, while Clarke (2005) supported the focus on institutional analysis over content and audience. Now that these questions have been better accepted, the need to justify them has diminished. Now we proceed with more direct tests suggested by the model.

THE MODEL AS FINDING

Given the wide range of literature we reviewed within the hierarchical framework, it's not surprising that it presents a broad citational target for authors seeking an authoritative (we would like to think) basis for their hypotheses. In these cases, the reference to Shoemaker and Reese is often more correctly directed to the underlying research we ourselves covered across a range of levels. Hurley and Tewksbury (2012), for example, in their study of algorithms in news selection, cited us as advocating the importance of the human factor through news gatekeeping. Napoli (1997) has us declaring the importance of ownership interests influencing content in seeking to maximize profit. Outside the media organizational boundary, citations reference the insight that outsiders can exploit media to their advantage—as in Darmon and Fitzpatrick's (2008) study of how corporate interests framed the obesity and health issue. Even more generally, we are found—in a study of Chinese newspapers' coverage of the SARS disease—concluding that the Chinese government controls the media (Zhang & Fleming, 2005) and that geography is important in news coverage (Grimm, 2009). In his analysis of newspaper editorializing in wartime (since World War II), Hallock (2012) cites us as providing evidence of the power of news sources in the manipulation of public opinion, but he also cites us as supporting a power greater than government manipulation—ideology. In helping explain the shape of these editorials, he assigns the government and military promoters to the social institutional level, the newspaper source of the editorials as an organizational influence, and framing as a routines factor, showing how easily adaptable the levels are to even an historically informed project. Such insights have grown over the years to become basic premises for research, and we wouldn't disagree with them. But in these cases we would say that the model provides a helpful taxonomic list to catalog these generalizations.

MODEL AS VALUABLE FRAMEWORK

More specific to the model itself, researchers have found the conceptual framework that the model provides useful, even guiding them to form inductive interpretation of content and other data. They use it as a guide to identifying key concepts, such as the factors that were at work in shaping television coverage of 9/11, including individual level journalistic roles (Reynolds & Barnett, 2003). Kenney (1995) similarly uses the model to suggest inductive explanations for content outcomes, with the race of journalists and their audience helping shape images of Africa in black-oriented and mainstream news magazines. Calling the model of "news determinants" the most useful in the literature, Hackett and Uzelman (2003) suggest hypotheses and locate their summaries of 17 content analyses of media conducted by the media watchdog organization NewsWatch Canada on aspects of media concentration of ownership and corporate power in general. Although criticizing the model as "overly deterministic and under explanatory," Keith, Schwalbe, and Silcock (2010) emphasize the *context* of production in their analysis of images of war across media platforms. Fico and Drager (2001) show how journalists work *in context* and order those influences (with higher levels "constraining" the lower ones). DeVreese, Peter, and Semetko (2001) called the model useful in sorting out different factors in their analysis of television coverage of the launch of the euro currency. In these cases the model has helped impose clarity on otherwise scattered data and insights.

Others use the model more directly to identify and test variables on more than one level. Josephi (1999), for example, looks at the passage of journalism students from school into news organizations, proposing like us to use a "layer model of determinants on media content" (p. 74), collapsing some layers and restricting others—for example, specifying legal and economic determinants (from within the social institutional level). In an analysis of news production in modern Russia, Koltsova (2001) calls our model an important "integrative" effort, combining influences formerly studied separately, and organizes different factors affecting journalism in that country. Koltsova suggests that one must move from the "ideological" level to routines and extramedia factors to understand *how* societal values are structured to serve the power elite. Calling the model a "useful framework" for sorting out context and examining journalism in a global setting, Andresen (2009) examines three levels in an ethnographic study of Kosovo journalists. The individual level includes journalists' memories of war, the routines level captures the idea of inexpensive "protocol new," and the extramedia level was used to refer to the structures of civil society.

Locating Studies

The Hierarchical Model has helped scholars establish a point of reference in locating their focus within the levels of analysis, announcing in effect an analytical strategy. Thus, the hierarchical mapping has facilitated the ordering of studies into generalizations about different categories. Nelson and Signorielli (2007), for example, use our "news content theoretical framework" to underscore the importance of the individual level, in their case journalist characteristics in news decisions, leading them to find gender differences in how women's health issues are covered (women reporters more likely to use a "self-help" frame and use women as news sources). Miller and Ross (2004) cite "Shoemaker & Reese" to anticipate that certain routines privilege certain media frames about Native Americans in the *Boston Globe*, while Keith and Schwalbe (2010) argue based on the model that routines are important in helping explain visual depictions in the US–Iraq war. Shin and Cameron (2003) use the model to locate the level of their study, in the case of the source–reporter relationship, calling it an example of "routines" level research. Similarly, Hollerbach (2009) examines effects *on* advertising to blacks, treating advertising as an extramedia influence and finding that market segmentation hasn't much improved the quality of African American depictions. In examining "influences on media content" in newspaper coverage of a Norwegian church's activities, Angell (2010) examines the individual, extramedia, and ideology levels, while Adam (2007) inductively draws conclusions from a content analysis of EU coverage, finding that differences between French and German media are attributable to nation-state differences—that is, at the societal level of influence.

Interpreting Relative Impact of Constraining Factors

Other authors have used the model as a guide for helping predict the *relative* influence of the various levels. As we discussed previously, we are careful to array the relative influences within the Hierarchical Model to avoid arguing for supremacy of one level over another (and indeed we have proceeded in a different conceptual order this time as we introduced them). Rather, we use more subtle terminology to suggest that one level *constrains* or *conditions* or is *contingent on* the influences at another. Just because one level is *higher* or more *macro* than another doesn't mean that it's more determinative or more important theoretically— although it may be judged to be so empirically in certain circumstances. Of course, simply because of the individualistic focus of much US communication research, incorporating other levels for consideration and placing these individual influences in larger context may have the effect of diluting the theoretical strength of any one of them.

Zeldes and Fico (2005), for example, say in their study of the race and gender of sources and reporters that we suggest occupational socialization has more power than individual factors, and similarly Freedman, Fico, and Durisin (2010) in using the model for "context" interpret it to suggest that influences of journalists themselves are most constrained, yielding to higher-level routine and organizational influences. Likewise, Williams (2002) claims that we give organizational factors more power in explaining bias than personal factors, and Lewis (2008) says that we warn against attributing too much to individual compared to systemic factors. In including economic pressure as an organizational factor, Silcock and Keith (2006, p. 612) use the model to suggest that "organizational constraints such as economics have an even greater influence on media content than media routines." Keith (2011) goes further by critiquing the model for its applicability to the new media era, which lacks the same consistent traditional media routines and features more individual (citizen-based) media production. She suggests that this obviates the influence of the organizational level and takes our hierarchical approach to suggest that some levels—specifically, higher ones—are stronger than others. This leads her to argue that the framework should be thought of as more dynamic when accounting for new media developments.

Another study, conversely, gave us credit for privileging the individual level. Armstrong's (2006) web survey of news producers tested the relative influence of levels by examining reported content produced about women. Individual views were found to be most influential, which was taken as "supporting" a view attributed to us that individual beliefs are core to the concentric rings. Thus, the model has often been interpreted in ways beyond what we necessarily intended.

MODEL AS GUIDE TO INTERPRETATION

The ability to gather data at more than one level within the same research study, as the model suggests is desirable, is relatively difficult. Many studies instead have gathered data at one level (such as with a survey of individual media workers) and interpreted it through the lens of the model. In a study of 11 Dutch correspondents working in Russia, Kester (2010) suggested that the host culture finds its own way of manifesting the influences from these levels on "moments of news selection." The "model was used to formulate sensitizing concepts" for examining in-depth interviews and providing an "organizing principle" for the media content coding. Because journalist surveys have been previously criticized as somewhat atheoretical, placing their responses within the context of the model helps integrate the responses into a larger framework.

Given the importance of public relations in shaping the agenda, Kim and Bae (2006) examine influences based on self-reports from public relations practitioners about what they thought about the relative influence of the various factors in news selections. Fahmy and Johnson (2012), similarly, consider embedded reporters' self-perceptions of influences on Iraq coverage, asking them to assess in a survey various factors, with "professional values and norms perceived to be the top factor" (p. 23). In adapting the model, they suggest that

> The job of the researcher, then, has been to discover under which conditions different levels become more influential and how the different levels interact with each other. But while the theory was developed to try to explain patterns of media coverage, it can be certainly adapted to examine journalists' attitudes.
>
> (Fahmy and Johnson, 2012, p. 25)

The authors state that support for the model is "mixed" when individual level factors were found to be influential. In these cases we can see that studies rely largely on self-perceived relative influences as translated into model terminology.

EVALUATING RELATIVE INFLUENCE OF LEVELS

Given the number of citations to the Hierarchical Model there has not been as much simultaneous testing of the multiple levels as we might expect. Given that the model helps generate hypotheses but makes no explicit theoretical predictions, what does constitute a test? In that sense, there is no conclusive test of the model's "correctness" and no "proving" the hierarchy. Rather, studies examine influences at multiple levels as an empirical question, leaving open the relative superiority of one over the other until subjected to an investigation and empirical test.

Somewhat contrary to the hierarchical top-down interpretation of others, Robertson (2009) takes the model to be a more pluralistic approach to "numerous and contingent" (p. 9) influences, particularly when contrasted with Herman and Chomsky's propaganda model, which he views as a more monolithic approach to predicting elite-serving media content. Comparing five leading UK newspapers in their coverage of autism allows him to pit one influence against another by including both organizational and individual level measures. In one newspaper, lack of strong personal beliefs allowed more standardized patterns, while at another an editor teamed with a "famously contrarian lead writer" (p. 24) to override routines and extramedia factors, findings that were interpreted as supporting our more "pluralistic" approach.

In examining social determinants of media frames in public health poster messages, Beaudoin (2007) empirically tested "multi-level" determinants with country-level indicators across 15 sub-Saharan African countries—including non-media factors such as condom use and HIV rate. In his study of influences on journalists' ethical decision making (rather than influences on content) Voakes (1997) lays out a more direct test, acknowledging that these factors operate simultaneously and that the hierarchy seeks to assign relative value to each (including individual factors and company-level strategies). Multiple regression, with multiple indicators representing different levels of analysis, provides that kind of test of relative strength and shows how one factor may be mediated by another: decision making cannot be understood with reference solely to the individual decision-maker. Indeed, the approach taken by Voakes, testing for the effects of a factor while holding the influence of others constant, is a good analog for multi-level model testing and helps explain some of the appeal of the model to those accustomed to the logic of survey analysis. In multiple regression, each factor or "block" of factors is nested within the hierarchically entered sequence of variables, perhaps starting with the more macro, control factors in accounting for the variance in the outcome measure, or dependent variable. We might want, for example, to know the effects of exposure to political media, while controlling for the effects of education and partisanship.

We wouldn't be saying that partisanship is more important than media, but instead simply wanting to know the effects of one while holding constant the effects of the other.

CONCLUSION

Given the number of studies that have invoked the Hierarchical Model in some way, the above list is certainly not exhaustive. These relatively recent examples are suggestive and illustrate the different approaches scholars have taken. Certainly, it's to be expected that new media developments stimulate additional thinking as to whether such a model is relevant to the current scene, particularly given the blurring of boundaries: professionally, institutionally, and politically. We did not intend to rigidly limit the boundaries of these levels and their interaction or the kinds of phenomena that fit within them. As we have discussed in earlier chapters, many influences are subsumed into each level, each of which is, in effect, underspecified. Thus, scholars need to clearly identify the influences of interest as they elaborate the forces at work within the broad territory mapped out by the model. Earlier, for example, we considered the work of Benson ("Bringing the Media Back In," 2004), who uses Bourdieu's field theory to elaborate the economic and political dimensions within the social institutional, "extramedia" level. With the globalization of the practice of communication research, the adoption of the framework across national boundaries has been intriguing, and it suggests that comparative work across these national contexts may be facilitated. We are pleased that we have been able to advocate for a special emphasis within the communication field on production and control issues in media, and we are even more pleased that the Hierarchical Model we helped to popularize has been a helpful tool in clarifying and provoking theoretical thinking. Clear thinking makes good research, which leads to progress in our understanding. Identifying key concepts, suggesting relationships, and providing a framework to contain empirical generalizations are all important steps in theoretical thinking. Given the rapid change in the media and the global society, capturing the phenomena embodied in the Hierarchy of Influences Model requires that kind of clear thinking and theoretical precision.

REFERENCES

4thestate (2012a). Silenced: Gender gap in the 2012 election coverage. *4th Estate*, April 10. Available online at www.4thestate.net/female-voices-in-media-infographic. (Accessed May 30, 2012.)

—— (2012b). Citizens lack voice among top newspapers. *4th Estate*, May 20. Available online at www.4thestate.net/citizens-lack-voice-among-top-newspapers. (Accessed May 30, 2012.)

—— (2012c). Gender gap among top print journalists. *4th Estate*, May 25. Available online at www.4thEstate.net/gender-gap-among-top-print-journalists. (Accessed May 30, 2012.)

Aarons, L., & Murphy, S. (2000). *Lesbians and gays in the newsroom: 10 years later*. Los Angeles, CA: Annenberg School for Communication, University of Southern California.

Adam, S. (2007). Domestic adaptations of Europe: A comparative study of the debates on EU enlargement and a common constitution in the German and French quality press. *International Journal of Public Opinion Research 19*(4), 409–33.

Aday, S., Livingston, S., & Hebert, M. (2005). Embedding the truth. *The Harvard International Journal of Press/Politics 10*(1), 3–21.

Akhavan-Majid, R. (1991). The press as an elite power group in Japan. *Journalism Quarterly 68*(4), 1006–14.

Akhavan-Majid, R., & Wolf, G. (1991). American mass media and the myth of Libertarianism: Toward an "elite power group" theory. *Critical Studies in Mass Communication 8*(2), 139–51.

Albritton, R.B., & Manheim, J.B. (1983). News of Rhodesia: The impact of a public relations campaign. *Journalism Quarterly 60*(4), 622–8.

Allen, C. (2007). News directors and consultants: RTNDA's endorsement of TV journalism's greatest tool. *Journal of Broadcasting & Electronic Media 51*(3), 424–37.

Althaus, S.L. (2003). When news norms collide, follow the lead: New evidence for press independence. *Political Communication 20*(4), 381–415.

Altheide, D.L. (1976). *Creating reality: How TV news distorts events*. Beverly Hills, CA: Sage.

—— (2003). Notes toward a politics of fear. *Journal of Crime Conflict and the Media 1*(1), 37–54.

Altschull, J.H. (1984). *Agents of power: The role of the news media in human affairs*. New York, NY: Longman.

—— (1995). *Agents of power: The media and public policy*, 2nd edn. New York, NY: Longman.

Amazon Video on Demand (2010). Amazon VOD. *Amazon.com*. Retrieved July 2, 1010 from Amazon.com. www.amazon.com/gp/video/ontv/ontv/ref=atv_getstarted_ontv.

American Society of Newspaper Editors (2009). *US newsroom employment declines*. ASNE, 2009 Census (April 16). Retrieved from http://asne.org/content.asp?pl=121&sl=151&contentid=151. Accessed June 10 2010.

An, S., & Jin, H.S. (2004). Interlocking of newspaper companies with financial institutions and leading advertisers. *Journalism & Mass Communication Quarterly 81*(3), 578–600.

Anderson, C.W. (2010). Journalistic networks and the diffusion of local news: The brief, happy news life of the "Francisville Four." *Political Communication 27*(3), 289–309.

Andresen, K. (2009). Producing "protocol news" in Kosovo's public broadcaster: Journalism in a transitional risk society. *Conflict and Communication Online 8*(2), 1–16.

Andsager, J. (2000). How interest groups attempt to shape public opinion with competing news frames. *Journalism & Mass Communication Quarterly 77*(3), 577–92.

Angell, O. H. (2008). Religion and the media: The cultural role of a church-based welfare agent in a Norwegian local community. *Journal of Contemporary Religion 23*(2), 133–45.

Appadurai, A. (1990). Disjuncture and difference in the global cultural economy. *Public Culture 2*(2), 1–24.

Armstrong, C. L. (2004). The influence of reporter gender on sources selection in newspaper stories. *Journalism & Mass Communication Quarterly 81*(1), 139–54.

—— (2006). Writing about women: An examination of how content for women is determined in newspapers. *Mass Communication & Society 9*(4), 447–60.

Artwick, C. (2004). *Reporting and producing for digital media.* Ames, Iowa: Blackwell.

Artz, L. (2007). The corporate model from national to transnational. In L. Artz & Y. R. Kamalipour (Eds.), *The media globe: Trends in international mass media* (pp. 141–72). Lanham, MD: Rowan & Littlefield.

Associated Press (2010). AP homepage. *Associated Press.* Retrieved June 1, 2010 from www.ap.org/pages/about/faq.html#2.

Atkin, C., Greenberg, B., & McDermott, S. (1983). Television and race role socialization, *Journalism Quarterly 60*(3), 407–14.

Atkin, D. (1992). An analysis of television series with minority-lead characters. *Critical Studies in Mass Communication 9*, 337–49.

Auletta, K. (1991). How General Electric tamed NBC News. *Washington Journalism Review*, November, pp. 36–41.

Austin, D. (1989). Dow Jones & Company, Inc., corporate relations statement, January 6.

Bachrach, P., & Baratz, M. (1962). Two faces of power. *American Political Science Review 56*(4), 947–52.

Bagdikian, B. (1989). The lords of the global village. *Nation*, June 12, 805–20.

—— (2004). *The new media monopoly.* Boston, MA: Beacon Press.

Bai, S. (2010). Constructing racial groups' identities in the diasporic press: Internalization, resonance, transparency, and offset. *Mass Communication & Society 13*(4), 385–411.

Bailey, G., & Lichty, L. (1972). Rough justice on a Saigon street. *Journalism Quarterly 72*(2), 221–38.

Baker, R., & Ball, S. (1969). *Violence and the media.* Washington, DC: US Government Printing Office.

Bantz, C. R., McCorkle, S., & Baade, R. C. (1981). The news factory. In G. C. Wilhoit & H. De Bock (Eds.), *Mass communication review yearbook*, vol. II (pp. 336–90). Beverly Hills, CA: Sage.

Barnett, G. A., Chon, B.-S., & Rosen, D. (2001). The structure of the internet flows in cyberspace. *Networks and Communications Studies 15*(1–2), 61–80.

Barnett, G. A., & Sung, E. (2005). Culture and the structure of the international hyperlink network. *Journal of Computer-Mediated Communication 11*(1), 217–38.

Barstow, D. (2008). Message machine: Behind TV analysts, Pentagon's hidden hand. *New York Times*, April 20.

Baskette, F. K., Sissors, J. Z., & Brooks, B. S. (1982). *The art of editing.* New York, NY: Macmillan.

Bass, A. Z. (1969). Redefining the gatekeeper concept: A UN radio case study. *Journalism Quarterly 46*(1), 59–72.

Beam, R. A. (1990). Journalism professionalism as an organization-level concept. *Journalism Monographs*, 121: 1–43.

—— (2003). Content difference between daily newspapers with strong and weak orientations. *Journalism & Mass Communication Quarterly 80*(2), 368–90.

Beaudoin, C. E. (2007). HIV prevention in sub-Saharan Africa: A multilevel analysis of message frames and their social determinants. *Health Promotion International 22*(3), 198–206.

Becker, L. (1982). Print vs. broadcast: How the medium influences the reporter. In J. Ettema & D. C. Whitney (Eds.), *Individuals in mass media organizations: Creativity and constraint* (pp. 145–61). Beverly Hills, CA: Sage.

—— (2005). Professionalism of newsworkers. In S. Dunwoody, L. Becker, D. McLeod, & G. Kosicki (Eds.), *The evolution of key mass communication concepts* (pp. 79–112). Cresskill, NJ: Hampton Press.

Becker, L., Vlad, T., & Olin, D. (2009). 2008 Enrollment report: Slow rate of growth may signal weakening of demand. *Journalism & Mass Communication Educator 64*(3), 232–57.

Becker, S. (1984). Marxist approaches to media studies: The British experience. *Critical Studies in Mass Communications 1*(1), 66–80.

Bem, S. L. (1974). The measurement of psychological androgyny. *Journal of Consulting and Clinical Psychology 42*(2), 155–62.

Benkler, Y. (n.d.). A free irresponsible press: WikiLeaks and the battle over the soul of the networked fourth estate. *Harvard Civil Rights-Civil Liberties Law Review 46*(2), 311–97.

Bennett, L. (2005). News as reality TV: Election coverage and the democratization of truth. *Critical Studies in Media Communication 22*(2), 171–7.

Bennett, W. L., Gressett, L., & Haltom, W. (1985). Repairing the news. *Journal of Communication 35*(2), 50–68.

Benson, R. (2004). Bringing the sociology of media back in. *Political Communication 21*(3), 275–92.

—— (2006). News media as a "journalistic field": What Bourdieu adds to new institutionalism, and vice versa. *Political Communication 23*(2), 187–202.

—— (2010). What makes for a critical press? A case study of French and US immigration news coverage. *Harvard International Journal of Press/Politics 15*(1), 3–24.

Benson, R., & Neveu, E. (2005). *Bourdieu and the journalistic field*. Cambridge: Polity.

Benson, R., & Powers, M. (2011). Public media around the world: International models for funding and protecting independent journalism. *Special Report from the Free Press*, pp. 1–88.

Berger, B. K. (2001). Private issues and public policy: Locating the corporate agenda in agenda-setting theory. *Journal of Public Relations Research 13*(2), 91–126.

Berkowitz, D. (1990). Refining the gatekeeping metaphor for local television news. *Journal of Broadcasting & Electronic Media 34*(1), 55–68.

—— (1992). Routine newswork and the what-a-story: A case study of organizational adaptation. *Journal of Broadcasting & Electronic Media 36*(1), 45–60.

—— (1993). Work roles and news selection in local TV: Examining the business–journalism dialectic. *Journal of Broadcasting & Electronic Media 37*(1), 67–81.

—— (1997). *Social meanings of news*. Thousand Oaks, CA: Sage.

Berkowitz, D., & Eko, L. (2007). Blasphemy as sacred rite/right: "The Mohammed cartoons affair" and maintenance of journalistic ideology. *Journalism Studies 8*(5), 779–97.

Berkowitz, D., Limor, Y., & Singer, J. (2004). A cross-cultural look at serving the public interest: American and Israeli journalists consider ethical scenarios. *Journalism: Theory, Practice, Criticism 5*(2), 159–81.

Bissell, K. L. (2000). A return to "Mr. Gates": Photography and objectivity. *Newspaper Research Journal 21*(3), 81–94.

Black, J. (1992). Taking the pulse of the nation's news media. *Quill*, November–December, pp. 31, 33.

Bleifuss, J. (1994). Flack attack. *Utne Reader*, January–February, pp. 72–9.

Blumer, H. (1969). *Symbolic interactionism: Perspective and method*. Berkeley, CA: University of California Press.

Blumler, J., & Gurevitch, M. (1995). *The crisis of public communication*. London and New York, NY: Routledge.

Boczkowski, P. J. (2004). The processes of adopting multimedia and interactivity in three online newsrooms. *Journal of Communication 54*(2), 197–213.

—— (2009). Rethinking hard and soft news production: From common ground to divergent paths. *Journal of Communication 59*(1), 98–116.

—— (2010). *News at work: Imitation in an age of information abundance*. Chicago, IL: University of Chicago.

Bohannon, J. (1988). Flashbulb memories for the space shuttle disaster: A tale of two theories. *Cognition 29*(2), 179–96.

Bollinger, L. (2011). Global threat to press freedom. *Foreign Policy*, January 21. Available online at www.foreignpolicy.com/articles/2011/01/21/the_global_threat_to_press_freedom, pp. 1–3. (Accessed July 16, 2011.)

Boorstin, D.J. (1961). *The image: A guide to pseudo-events in America*. New York, NY: Harper.

—— (1971). From news-gathering to news-making: A flood of pseudo-events. In W. Schramm & D.F. Roberts (Eds.), *The process and effects of mass communication* (pp. 116–50). Urbana, IL: University of Illinois.

Boyd-Barrett, O. (1997). Global news wholesalers as agents of globalisation. In A. Sreberny-Mohammadi, D. Winseck, J. McKenna, & O. Boyd-Barret (Eds.), *Media in global context: A reader* (pp. 131–144). London: Arnold.

Boyer, P. J. (1988). *Who killed CBS? The undoing of America's number one news network*. New York, NY: Random House.

Breed, W. (1952). *The newspaperman, news and society*. New York, NY: Arno.

—— (1955). Social control in the newsroom: A functional analysis. *Social Forces 33*(4), 326–35.

—— (1960). Social control in the newsroom: A functional analysis. In W. Schramm (Ed.), *Mass communications* (pp. 178–94). Urbana, IL: University of Illinois Press.

Bronstein, C., & Vaughn, S. (1998). Willard G. Bleyer and the relevance of journalism education. *Journalism and Mass Communication Monographs, 166* (June), 0–36.

Brown, M. (2005). Abandoning the news. In C. Connell (Ed.), *Journalism's crisis of confidence: A challenge for the next generation* (pp. 42–55). New York: Carnegie Corporation.

Brown, R., & Kulik, J. (1977). Flashbulb memories. *Cognition 5*(1), 73–99.

Bulck, H., & Broos, D. (2011). Can a charter of diversity make the difference in ethnic minority reporting? A comparative content and production analysis of two Flemish television newscasts. *Communications: The European Journal of Communication Research 36*(2), 195–216.

Butcher, H. (1981). Images of women in the media. In S. Cohen & J. Young (Eds.), *The manufacture of news: Deviance, social problems and the mass media* (pp. 317–25). Beverly Hills, CA: Sage.

Cantor, M. (1971). *The Hollywood producer: His work and his audience*. New York, NY: Basic Books.

Cantril, H. (1940). *The invasion from Mars: A study in the psychology of panic*. Princeton, NJ: Princeton University.

Cardiff, C., & Klein, D. (2005). Faculty partisan affiliations in all disciplines: A voter-registration study. *Critical Review 17* (3–4), 237–55.

Carey, J. (1996). The Chicago School and mass communication research. In E. Dennis & E. Wartella (Eds.), *American communication research: The remembered history* (pp. 21–38). Mahwah, NJ: Erlbaum.

—— (2000). Some personal notes on US journalism education. *Journalism 1*(1), 12–23.

—— (2002). American journalism on, before, and after September 11. In B. Zelizer & S. Allan (Eds.), *Journalism after September 11* (pp. 71–90). London and New York, NY: Routledge.

Carlson, M. (2007). Blogs and journalistic authority: The role of blogs in US election day 2004 coverage. *Journalism Studies 8*(2), 264–79.

—— (2012). "Where once stood Titans": Second-order paradigm repair and the vanishing US newspaper. *Journalism 13*(3), 267–83.

Carr, D. (2010). A vanishing journalistic divide. *New York Times*, October 10.

Case, T. (1992a). Life from a gay perspective. *Editor and Publisher*, July 11, pp. 13, 33.

—— (1992b). Ethnic loyalty vs. pursuit of truth. *Editor and Publisher*, September 12, pp. 14–15.

Cassidy, W. P. (2006). Gatekeeping similar for online, print journalists. *Newspaper Research Journal 27*(2), 6–23.

Castells, M. (1996). *The rise of the network society*. Oxford: Blackwell.

—— (2007). Communication, power and counter-power in the network society. *International Journal of Communication 1*, 238–66.

—— (2008). The new public sphere: Global civil society, communication networks, and global governance. *Annals of the American Academy of Political and Social Science 616* (March), 78–93.

Caudill, E., & Ashdown, P. (1989). The New England Journal of Medicine as news source. *Journalism Quarterly 66*(2), 458–62.

Chang, T.K. (1989). The impact of presidential statements on press editorials regarding US China policy, 1950–84. *Communication Research 16*(4), 486–509.

Chang, T., Himelboim, I., & Dong, D. (2009). Open global networks, closed international flows: World system and political economy of hyperlinks in cyberspace. *International Communications Gazette 71*(3), 137–59.

Chang, T., & Lee, J. (1992). Factors affecting gatekeepers' selection of foreign news: A national survey of newspaper editors. *Journalism Quarterly 69*(3), 554–61.

Cho, J., Shah, D., McLeod, J.M., McLeod, D., Scholl, R., & Gotlieb, M. (2009). Campaigns, reflection, and deliberation: Advancing an O-S-R-O-R model of communication effects. *Communication Theory 19*(1), 66–88.

Chomsky, N. (1957). *Syntactic structures*. Paris: Mouton.

—— (2003). *Power and terror: Post-9/11 talks and interviews*. New York, NY: Seven Stories Press.

Chuang, A. (2012). Representations of foreign versus (Asian) American identity in a mass-shooting case: Newspaper coverage of the 2009 Binghamton massacre. *Journalism & Mass Communication Quarterly 89*(2), 244–60.

Clarke, S.H. (2005). Created in whose image? Religious characters on network television. *Journal of Media and Religion 4*(3), 137–53.

Clayman, S., & Reisner, A. (1998). Gatekeeping in action: Editorial conferences and assessments of newsworthiness. *American Sociological Review 63*(2), 178–99.

Clinton's the choice (1992). *Editor and Publisher*, October 24, pp. 9–10, 44–5.

Coddington, M. (2012). Defending a paradigm by patrolling a boundary: Two global newspapers' approach to WikiLeaks. *Journalism & Mass Communication Quarterly 89*(3), 377–96.

Cohen, A., Adoni, H., and Bantz, C.R. (1990). *Social conflict and television news*. Newbury Park, CA: Sage.

Cohen, B. (1963). *Press and foreign policy*. Princeton, NJ: Princeton University Press.

Coleman, J.S. (1990). Columbia in the 1950s. In B. Berger (Ed.), *Authors of their own lives: Intellectual autobiographies by twenty American sociologists* (pp. 75–103). Berkeley, CA: University of California Press.

Columbia Journalism Review (1989). Memo, *Columbia Journalism Review 28*(3), 25.

—— (2010). Who owns what? *Columbia Journalism Review*. Available online at www.cjr.org/resources/index.php. (Accessed May 7, 2010.)

Comstock, G., & Rubinstein, E.A. (1971a). *Television and social behavior TV in day-to-day life: Patterns of use*. Washington, DC: US Government Printing Office.

—— (1971b). *Television and social behavior: Television and social learning*. Washington, DC: US Government Printing Office.

—— (1971c). *Television and social behavior: Television and adolescent aggressiveness*. Washington, DC: US Government Printing Office.

Conservatives seeking stock of CBS to alter "liberal bias" (1985). *New York Times*, January 11, p. B4.

Cook, T. (1998). *Governing with the news: The news media as a political institution*. Chicago, IL: University of Chicago Press.

Cooper, S. (2006). *Watching the watchdog: Bloggers as the fifth estate*. Spokane, WA: Marquette Books.

Cooper, T. (1990). Comparative international media ethics. *Journal of Mass Media Ethics 5*(1), 3–14.

Corcoran, F., & Fahy, D. (2009). Exploring the European elite sphere. *Journalism Studies 10*(1), 100–13.

Corry, J. (1986). *TV news and the dominant culture*. Washington, DC: Media Institute.

Cotter, R., de Lint, W., & O'Connor, D. (2008). Ordered images: Cooking reality in Cops. *Journal of Criminal Justice and Popular Culture 15*(3), 277–90.

Craft, S., & Wanta, W. (2004). Women in the newsroom: Influences of female editors and reporters on the news agenda. *Journalism & Mass Communication Quarterly 81*(1), 124–38.

Crane, D. (2002). Culture and globalization theoretical models and emerging trends. In D. Crane, N. Kawashima, & K.I. Kawaski (Eds.), *Global culture: Media, arts, policy, and globalization* (pp. 1–25). London and New York, NY: Routledge.

Crouse, T. (1972). *The boys on the bus: Riding with the campaign press corps*. New York, NY: Random House.

Curran, J. (1990). The new revisionism in mass communication research: A reappraisal. *European Journal of Communication 5*(2/3), 135–64.

Curran, J., Gurevitch, M., & Woollacott, J. (1982). The study of the media: Theoretical approaches. In M. Gurevitch, T. Bennett, J. Curran, & J. Woollacott (Eds.), *Culture, society and the media* (pp. 11–29). London: Methuen.

Curran, J., Iyengar, S., Lund, A., & Salovaara-Moring, I. (2009). Media system, public knowledge and democracy. *European Journal of Communication 24*(5), 5–26.

Czitrom, D. (1982). *Media and the American mind: From Morse to McLuhan*. Chapel Hill, NC: University of North Carolina Press.

Darwin, C. (1936). *The origin of species*. New York, NY: Random House.

Dates, J., & Stroman, C. (2001). Portrayals of families of color on television. In J. Bryant & J.A. Bryant (Eds.), *Television and the American family* (pp. 207–25). Mahwah NJ: Erlbaum.

Davis, A. (2002). *Public relations democracy*. Manchester: Manchester University Press.

—— (2007). *The mediation of power: A critical introduction*. London and New York, NY: Routledge.

De Vreese, C.H., Peter, J., & Semetko, H.A. (2001). Framing politics at the launch of the euro: A cross-national comparative study of frames in the news. *Political Communication 18*(2), 107–22.

Dedman, B., & Doig, S. (2003). Does your newspaper's staff reflect the racial diversity of the community it serves? A John S. and James L. Knight Foundation Report. Presented to the American Society of Newspaper Editors, April 8.

DeFleur, M., & Larsen, O. (1948). *The flow of information*. New York, NY: Harper & Brothers.

Delia, J. (1987). History of communication research. In C. Berger & S. Chaffee (Eds.), *Handbook of communication science* (pp. 20–98). Beverly Hills, CA: Sage.

Dennis, E.E. (1988). Whatever happened to Marse Robert's dream? The dilemma of American journalism education. *Gannett Center Journal 2*, 1–22.

Dennis, E.E., & Ismach, A.H. (1981). *Reporting processes and practices*. Belmont, CA: Wadsworth.

Deuze, M. (2002). National news cultures: A comparison of Dutch, German, British, Australian, and US journalists. *Journalism & Mass Communication Quarterly 79*(1), 134–49.

—— (2007). *Media work*. Malden, MA: Polity.

Didion, J. (1988). Insider baseball. *New York Review of Books*, October 27, pp. 19–31.

Dixon, T.L. (2006). Schemas as average conceptions: Skin tone, television news exposure, and culpability judgments. *Journalism & Mass Communication Quarterly 83*(1), 131–49.

—— (2008). Network news and racial beliefs: Exploring the connection between national television news exposure and stereotypical perceptions of African Americans. *Journal of Communication 58*(2), 321–37.

Dixon, T.L., & Azocar, C.L. (2006). The representation of juvenile offenders by race on Los Angeles area television news. *Howard Journal of Communication 17*(2), 143–61.

Doctor, K. (2008). "Frightsizing" newspapers: What derailed the American newspaper industry? *Global Journalist*, Fall, 26–32.

Domhoff, G. W. (1967). *Who rules America now?* Englewood Cliffs, NJ: Prentice-Hall.

—— (1970). *The higher circles: Governing class in America*. New York, NY: Random House.

—— (1979). *The powers that be: Processes of ruling class domination in America*. Englewood Cliffs, NJ: Prentice-Hall.

Domke, D., Watts, M. D., Shah, D. V., & Fan, D. P. (1999). The politics of conservative elites and the "liberal media" argument. *Journal of Communication 49*(4), 35–58.

Donohew, L. (1967). Newspaper gatekeepers and forces in the news channel. *Public Opinion Quarterly 31*(1), 61–8.

Dorroh, J. (2008). The transformation of NPR. *American Journalism Review*, October/November, pp. 24–31.

Douglas, S. J., & Michaels, M. (2004). *The mommy myth: The idealization of motherhood and how it has undermined women*. New York, NY: Free Press.

Downie, L. (2012). Big journalism on campus. *American Journalism Review 33*(3), 36.

Downing, J. (2007). Terrorism, torture, and television: "*24*" in its context. *Democratic Communiqué 21*(2), 62–82.

Dreier, P. (1982). The position of the press in the US power structure. *Social Problems 29*(3), 298–310.

—— (1983). The position of the press in the US power structure. In E. Wartella, D.C. Whitney, & S. Windahl (Eds.), *Mass Communication Review Yearbook 4*, 439–51.

Dreier, P., & Weinberg, S. (1979). The ties that bind: Interlocking directorates. *Columbia Journalism Review 18*(53), 51–68.

Dumpala, P. (2009). The year the newspaper died. *Business Insider*, July 4. Available online at www.businessinsider.com/the-death-of-the-american-newspaper-2009-7#. (Accessed July 13, 2010.)

Dunaway, J. (2008). Markets, ownership and the quality of campaign news coverage. *The Journal of Politics 70*(4), 1193–202.

Dupagne, M. (1997). A theoretical and methodological critique of the principle of relative constancy. *Communication Theory 7*(1), 53–77.

Editorial (2011, December 23). An all-American misstep. *New York Times*.

Ehrlich, M. (2006). Facts, truth, and bad journalists in the movies. *Journalism: Theory, Practice, Criticism 7*(4), 501–19.

Elasmar, M. G. (2003). An alternative paradigm for conceptualizing and labeling the process of influences of imported television programs. In M. G. Elasmar (Ed.), *The impact of international television: A paradigm shift* (pp. 151–72). Mahwah, NJ: Erlbaum.

Elasmer, M. G., & Bennett, K. (2003). The cultural imperialism paradigm revisited: Origin and evaluation. In M. G. Elasmar (Ed.), *The impact of international television: A paradigm shift* (pp. 1–16). Mahwah, NJ: Erlbaum.

Elbot, E. (1992). The giants in our midst. *Media Ethics Update 4*(2), 5–7.

Entman, R. M. (1985). Newspaper competition and First Amendment ideals: Does monopoly matter? *Journal of Communication 35*(3), 147–65.

—— (1993). Framing: Toward clarification of a fractured paradigm. *Journal of Communication 43*(4), 51–8.

—— (2003). Cascading activation: Contesting the White House's frame after 9/11. *Political Communication 20*(4), 415–32.

—— (2006). Punctuating the homogeneity of institutionalized news: Abusing prisoners at Abu Graib versus killing civilians at Fallujah. *Political Communication 23*(2), 215–24.

Epstein, E. (1974). *News from nowhere*. New York, NY: Vintage Books.

Esser, F. (1999). Tabloidization of news: A comparative analysis of Anglo-American and German press journalism. *European Journal of Communication 14*(3), 291–324.

—— (2008). Dimensions of political news cultures: Sound bite and image bite news in France, Germany, Great Britain, and the United States. *Harvard International Journal of Press/Politics 13*(4), 401–28.

Esser, F., & Pfetsch, B. (Eds.) (2004). *Comparing political communication: Theories, cases, and challenges*. Cambridge: Cambridge University Press.

Ettema, J.S. (1988). *The craft of the investigative journalist*. Evanston, IL: Institute of Modern Communication, Northwestern University.

Ettema, J.S., & Glasser, T. (1998). *Custodians of conscience: Investigative journalism and public virtue*. New York, NY: Columbia University Press.

Exoo, C. (1987). Cultural hegemony in the United States. In C. Exoo (Ed.), *Democracy upside down: Public opinion and cultural hegemony in the United States* (pp. 1–33). New York, NY: Praeger.

Face-off (1987). *Washington Journalism Review*, September.

Fahmy, S. (2005). Photojournalists' and photo editors' attitudes and perceptions: The visual coverage of 9/11 and the Afghan War. *Visual Communication Quarterly 12*(3–4), 146–63.

Fahmy, S., & Al-Emad, M. (2011). Al-Jazeera versus Al-Jazeera: A comparison of the network's English- and Arabic-online coverage of the US/Al Qaeda conflict. *International Communication Gazette 73*(3), 216–32.

Fahmy, S., & Johnson, T.J. (2012). Invasion vs. occupation. *International Communication Gazette 74*(1), 23–42.

Fallows, J. (2011). Learning to love the (shallow, divisive, unreliable) new media. *The Atlantic 307*(3), 34.

Farhi, P. (2007). San Francisco news blues. *American Journalism Review 29*(5), 22–7.

Featherstone, L. (2009). Identity crisis. *Columbia Journalism Review 48*(1), 31–4.

Ferree, M., Gamson, W., Gerhards, J., & Rucht, D. (2002). *Shaping abortion discourse: Democracy and the public sphere in Germany and the United States*. Cambridge: Cambridge University Press.

Fico, F. (1984). A comparison of legislative sources in newspaper and wire service stories. *Newspaper Research Journal 5*(3), 35–43.

Fico, F., & Drager, M. (2001). News stories about conflict generally balanced. *Newspaper Research Journal 22*(1), 2–11.

Fishman, M. (1980). *Manufacturing the news*. Austin, TX: University of Texas Press.

Frankel, M. (2000). The way we live now: The wall vindicated. *New York Times*, January 9.

Franklin, B., Richardson, J.E., Hamer, M., Hanna, M., & Kinsey, M. (2005). *Key concepts in journalism studies*. London: Sage.

Franzwa, H. (1974). Working women in fact and fiction. *Journal of Communication 24*(2), 104–9.

Frazier, J., & Gaziano, C. (1979). Robert E. Park's theory of news, public opinion and social control. *Journalism Monographs 64*, 1–47.

Freedman, E., Fico, F., & Durisin, M. (2010). Gender diversity absent in expert sources for elections. *Newspaper Research Journal 31*(2), 20–33.

Freeman, B. (2006). From no go to no logo: Lesbian lives and rights in Chatelaine. *Canadian Journal of Communication 31*(4), 815–41.

Friedan, B. (1963). *The feminine mystique*. New York, NY: Dell.

Friendly, E. (1967). *Due to circumstances beyond our control*. New York, NY: Random House.

Gade, P.J. (2008). Journalism guardians in a time of great change: Newspaper editors' perceived influence in integrated news organizations. *Journalism & Mass Communication Quarterly 85*(2), 371–92.

Galician, M.L., & Pasternack, S. (1987). Balancing good news and bad news: An ethical obligation? *Journal of Mass Media Ethics 2*(2), 82–92.

Gandy, O. (1982). *Beyond agenda-setting: Information subsidies and public policy*. Norwood, NJ: Ablex.

Gans, H.J. (1979). *Deciding what's news: A study of CBS Evening News, NBC Nightly News, Newsweek and Time*. New York, NY: Vintage.

Gant, C., & Dimmick, J. (2000). African Americans in television news: From description to explanation. *Howard Journal of Communication 11*(3), 189–205.

Garnham, N. (1979). Contribution to a political economy of mass communication. *Media, Culture and Society 1*(2), 123–46.

Gasher, M., & Klein, R. (2008). Mapping the geography of online news. *Canadian Journal of Communication 33*(2). Available online at http://cjc-online.ca/index.php/journal/article/view/1974. (Accessed June 9, 2010.)

Gaunt, P. (1992). *Making the newsmakers: International handbook on journalism training.* Westport, CT: Greenwood Press.

Gerbner, G. (1971). Violence in television drama: Trends and symbolic functions. *Television and social behavior: Media content and control (vol. 1).* Washington, DC: US Government Printing Office.

—— (1972). Violence in television drama: Trends and symbolic functions. In G. A. Comstock & E. Rubinstein (Eds.), *Television and social behavior*, vol. I: *Content and control* (pp. 28–187). Washington, DC: US Government Printing Office.

—— (1988). Reports and papers on mass communication. In *Violence and terror in the mass media.* Paris: UNESCO.

Gerbner, G., Gross, L., Jackson-Beeck, M., Jeffries-Fox, S., & Signorielli, N. (1978). Cultural indicators: Violence profile no. 9. *Journal of Communication 28*(3), 176–207.

Gerhards, J., & Rucht, D. (1992). Mesomobilization: Organizing and framing in two protest campaigns in West Germany. *American Journal of Sociology 98*(3), 555–96.

Gersh, D. (1991). Stereotyping journalists: Whether in the movies from the 1930s or 1980s, newspeople are usually portrayed as rude, divorced, hard-drinking, cigarette-smoking misfits. *Editor and Publisher 124*(40), 18–124.

Giddens, A. (1984). *The constitution of society: Outline of the theory of structuration.* Berkeley, CA: University of California Press.

—— (1997). *The consequences of modernity.* Palo Alto, CA: Stanford University Press.

Gieber, W. (1960). Two communicators of the news: A study of the roles of sources and reporters. *Social Forces 39*(1), 76–83.

Gilens, M. and Hertzman, C. (2000). Corporate ownership and news bias: Newspaper coverage of the 1996 Telecommunications Act. *Journal of Politics 62*(2), 369–86.

Gitlin, T. (1978). Media sociology: The dominant paradigm. In G. Wilhoit & H. De Bock (Eds.), *Mass communication review yearbook*, vol. II (pp. 73–122). Beverly Hills, CA: Sage.

—— (1980). *The whole world is watching: Mass media in the making and unmaking of the new left.* Berkeley, CA: University of California.

—— (1985). *Inside prime time.* New York, NY: Pantheon Books.

GM suspends ads on NBC's news programs (1993). *Columbus Dispatch*, p. 3A.

Golan, G. (2006). Inter-media agenda setting and global news coverage. *Journalism Studies 7*(2), 323–33.

Google (2012). Management team. *Google.com.* Available online at www.google.com/corporate/execs.html. (Accessed July 20, 2012.)

Google Trends (2012). Google Trends homepage. *Google.com.* Available online at www.google.com/trends. (Accessed July 20, 2012.)

Gouldner, A. W. (1976). *The dialectic of ideology and technology: The origins, grammar, and future of ideology.* New York, NY: Seabury.

Grabe, M. E. (1999). A functionalist perspective on television news magazine stories. *Critical Studies in Mass Communication 16*(2), 155–71.

Grabe, M. E., & Kamhawi, R. (2006). Hard wired for negative news? Gender differences in processing broadcast news. *Communication Research 33*(5), 346–69.

Graesser, A. C., Woll, S. B., Kowalski, D. J., & Smith, D. A. (1980). Memory for typical and atypical actions in scripted activities. *Journal of Experimental Psychology: Human Learning and Memory 6*(5), 503–15.

Gramsci, A. (1971). *Selections from the prison notebooks of Antonio Gramsci*, ed. and trans. Q. Hoare & G. Smith. New York, NY: International Publishers.

Greenberg, B. (1980). *Life on television.* Norwood, NJ: Ablex.

Grimm, J. (2009). "Teach the controversy": The relationship between sources and frames in reporting the intelligent design debate. *Science Communication 31*(2), 167–86.

Groeling, T. (2008). Who's the fairest of them all? An empirical test for partisan bias on ABC, CBS, NBC, and Fox News. *Presidential Studies Quarterly 38*(4), 631–57.

Group, G. U. M. (1976). *Bad news*. London: Routledge & Kegan Paul.

Gyatso, T. (2005). *His Holiness the 14th Dalai Lama, essence of the heart sutra*. Somerville, MA: Wisdom Publications.

Habermas, J. (1962). *The structural transformation of the public sphere: An inquiry into a category of bourgeois society*. Cambridge: Polity.

Hackett, R. A. (1984). Decline of a paradigm? Bias and objectivity in news media studies. *Critical Studies in Mass Communication 1*(3), 229–59.

Hackett, R. A., & Uzelman, S. (2003). Tracing corporate influences on press content: A summary of recent NewsWatch Canada research. *Journalism Studies 4*(3), 331–46.

Hafez, K. (2007). *The myth of media globalization*. Malden, MA: Polity.

Hage, J. (1972). *Techniques and problems of theory construction in sociology*. New York, NY: John Wiley & Sons.

Halberstam, D. (1979). *The powers that be*. New York, NY: Alfred A. Knopf.

Hale, F. D. (1988). Editorial diversity and concentration. In R. Picard, J. Winter, M. McCombs, & S. Lacy (Eds.), *Press concentration and monopoly: New perspectives on newspaper ownership and operation* (pp. 161–78). Norwood, NJ: Ablex.

Hall, S. (1982). The rediscovery of "ideology": Return of the repressed in media studies. In M. Gurevitch, T. Bennett, J. Curran, & J. Woollacott (Eds.), *Culture, society and the media* (pp. 56–90). London and New York, NY: Routledge.

—— (1989). Ideology. In E. Barnaouw (Ed.), *International encyclopedia of communication*, vol. II (pp. 307–11). Oxford: Oxford University Press.

—— (Ed.). (1997). *Representations and signifying practice*. London: Sage.

Hallin, D. C. (1986). *The uncensored war: The media and Vietnam*. Oxford: Oxford University Press.

—— (1992). The passing of "high modernism" of American journalism. *Journal of Communication 42*(3), 14–25.

—— (1994). *We keep America on top of the world: Television journalism and the public sphere*. London and New York, NY: Routledge.

Hallin, D. C., & Mancini, P. (2004). *Comparing media systems: Three models of media and politics*. Cambridge: Cambridge University Press.

Hallman, M. (2012). *Traversing philosophical boundaries*, 4th edn. Independence, KY: Wadsworth.

Hallock, S. (2012). *The press march to war: Newspapers set the stage for military intervention in post-World War II America*. New York: Peter Lang.

Hamilton, J. M. (2009). In the foothills of change. *Columbia Journalism Review*, March–April, pp. 51–4.

Hammersley, M. (1989). *The dilemma of qualitative method: Herbert Blumer and the Chicago tradition*. London and New York, NY: Routledge.

Han, K. (1988). *Interlocking directorates of major media corporations: The main determinants*. Austin, TX: University of Texas Press.

Handley, R. (2011). Systematic monitoring as a dissident activist strategy: Palestine media watch and US news media, 2000–2004. *Communication, Culture & Critique 4*(3), 209–28.

Hanitzsch, T. (2007). Deconstructing journalism culture: Towards a universal theory. *Communication Theory 17*(4), 367–85.

Hanitzsch, T., Hanusch, F., Mellado, C., Anikina, M., Berganza, R., Cangoz, I., Coman, M., et al. (2011). Mapping journalism cultures across nations. *Journalism Studies 12*(3), 273–93.

Hannerz, U. (1997). Notes on the global ecumenic. In O. Boyd-Barret, J. McKenna, A. Sreberny-Mohammadi, & D. Winseck (Eds.), *Media in global context: A reader* (pp. 11–18). London: Edward Arnold.

Hardin, M. (2005). Stopped at the gate: Women's sports, "reader interest," and decision making by editors. *Journalism & Mass Communication Quarterly 82*(1), 62–77.

Hart, P. (2009). Fear and favor 2008. *Extra!* April, pp. 10–12.

Hartley, J. (2009). *The uses of digital literacy.* Brisbane: University of Queensland Press.

Hawkins, R. (1997) Prospects for a global communication infrastructure in the 21st century: Institutional restructuring and network development. In O. Boyd-Barret, J. McKenna, A. Sreberny-Mohammadi, & D. Winseck (Eds.), *Media in global context: A reader* (pp. 177–93). London: Edward Arnold.

Haws, D. (1991). Minorities in the newsroom and community: A comparison. *Journalism & Mass Communication Quarterly 68*(4), 764–71.

Healey, T., & Ross, K. (2002). Growing old invisibly: Older viewers talk television. *Media Culture and Society 24*(1), 105–20.

Henningham, J. (1998). Ideological differences between journalists and their public. *Harvard International Journal of Press/Politics 3* (spring), 92–101.

Herman, E., & Chomsky, N. (1988). *Manufacturing consent: The political economy of the mass media.* New York, NY: Pantheon.

Hertog, J., & McLeod, D. (1988). Anarchists wreak havoc in downtown Minneapolis: A case study of media coverage of radical protest. Presented at the 71st annual conference of the Association for Education in Journalism and Mass Communication, Portland, OR.

Herzog, H. (1944). What do we really know about daytime serial listeners? In P. Lazarsfeld & F. Stanton (Eds.), *Radio research.* New York, NY: Duell, Sloan & Pearce.

Hess, S. (1981). *The Washington reporters.* Washington, DC: Brookings Institution.

—— (1984). *The government/press connection: Press officers and their offices.* Washington, DC: Brookings Institution.

Hirsch, P. (1977). Occupational, organizational and institutional models in mass media research: Toward an integrated framework. In P. M. Hirsch, P. V Miller, & F. G. Kline (Eds.), *Strategies for communication research* (pp. 13–40). Beverly Hills, CA: Sage.

Hleft, M., & Barboza, D. (2012). Google shuts China site in dispute over censorship. *New York Times*, March 22, p. A1.

Hollerbach, K. L. (2009). The impact of market segmentation on African American frequency, centrality, and status in television advertising. *Journal of Broadcasting and Electronic Media 53*(4), 599–614.

Hoogvelt, A. (2001). *Globalization and the postcolonial world: The new political economy of development.* Baltimore, MD: Johns Hopkins University Press.

Hovland, C. I., Janis, I., & Kelley, H. (1953). *Communication and persuasion.* New Haven, CT: Yale University Press.

Hovland, C. I., Lumsdaine, A., & Sheffield, F. (1949). *Experiments on mass communication.* Princeton, NJ: Princeton University Press.

Howard, P. N. (2002). Network ethnography and the hypermedia organization: New media, new organizations, new methods. *New Media and Society 4*(4), 550–74.

Høyer, S. (2005). The idea of the book. In S. Høyer & H. Pöttker (Eds.), *Diffusion of the news paradigm, 1850–2000* (pp. 9–16). Gothenburg: Nordicom.

Huckins, K. (1999). Interest-group influence on the media agenda: A case study. *Journalism & Mass Communication Quarterly 76*(1), 76–86.

HuluPlus (2010). What is HuluPlus? *Hulu.* Retrieved July 7, 2010 from www.hulu.com/plus.

Hunt, M. (1961). How does it come to be so? Profile of Robert Merton. *New Yorker*, pp. 39–63.

Hurley, R. J., & Tewksbury, D. (2012). News aggregation and content differences in online cancer news. *Journal of Broadcasting & Electronic Media 56*(1), 132–49.

Internet World Stats (2012). June 2012. *Internet World Stats.* Available online at www.internetworldstats.com. (Accessed June 30, 2012.)

Ismach, A. H., & Dennis, E. E. (1978). A profile of newspaper and television reporters in a metropolitan setting. *Journalism Quarterly 55*(4), 739–898.

Iyengar, S. (1991). *Is anyone responsible? How television frames political issues.* Chicago, IL: University of Chicago Press.

Jackson, J. (1966). A conceptual and measurement model for norms and roles. *Pacific Sociological Review 9*(1), 35–47.

Jacobs, R.N. (1996). Producing the news, producing the crisis: Narrativity, television and news work. *Media, Culture, and Society 18*(3), 373–97.

Jamieson, K.H., & Campbell, K.K. (1983). *The interplay of influence: Mass media and their publics in news, advertising, politics*. Belmont, CA: Wadsworth.

Jamieson, K.H., & Cappella, J. (2008). *Echo chamber: Rush Limbaugh and the conservative media establishment*. Oxford: Oxford University Press.

Janis, I. (1983). *Groupthink*, 2nd edn. Boston, MA: Houghton-Mifflin.

Janus, N. (1984). Advertising and the creation of global markets: The role of the new communication technologies. In V. Mosco & J. Wasko (Eds.), *The critical communications review*, vol. IV (pp. 57–70). Norwood, NJ: Ablex.

Jemison, D.B. (2007). The importance of boundary spanning roles in strategic decision-making. *Journal of Management Studies 21*(2), 131–52.

Johnson, P. (2001). Tim Russert: War changes the rules. *USA Today*, November, p. D.04.

Johnson, R.N. (1996). Bad news revisited: The portrayal of violence, conflict, and suffering on television news. *Peace and Conflict: Journal of Peace Psychology 2*(3), 201–16.

Johnston, V. (1999). *Why we feel: The science of human emotions*. New York, NY: Perseus Books.

Johnstone, J.W.C., Slawski, E.J., & Bowman, W.W. (1972). The professional values of American newsmen. *Public Opinion Quarterly 36*(4), 522–40.

Jönsson, A.M., & Örnebring, H. (2010). User-generated content and the news. *Journalism Practice 5*(2), 127–44.

Jordan, H. (1992). Telling the news in more than black and white. *Extra!* July/August, p. 23.

Josephi, B. (1999). From journalism school to newsroom: What rite of passage? *Asia Pacific Media Educator 1*(7), 74–85.

Juris, J.S. (2005). Social forums and their margins. *Ephemera 5*(2), 253–72.

Kahn, J. (2002). China has world's tightest internet censorship, study finds. *New York Times*, December 4, p. A13.

Kahn, K.F., & Goldenberg, E.N. (1991). Women candidates in the news: An examination of gender differences in the US Senate campaign coverage. *Public Opinion Quarterly 55*(2), 180–99.

Kamhawi, R., & Weaver, D. (2003). Mass communication research trends from 1980 to 1999. *Journalism & Mass Communication Quarterly 80*(1), 7–27.

Kaniss, P. (1991). *Making local news*. Chicago, IL: University of Chicago Press.

Karim, K.H. (2002). Making sense of the "Islamic peril": Journalism as cultural practice. In B. Zelizer & S. Allan (Eds.), *Journalism after September 11* (pp. 131–46). London and New York, NY: Routledge.

Katz, E., & Lazarsfeld, P. (1955). *Personal influence: The part played by people in the flow of mass communication*. Glencoe, IL: Free Press.

Katz, E., Peters, J., Liebes, T., & Orloff, A. (2003). *Canonic texts in media research*. New York, NY: Polity.

Keith, S. (2011). Shifting circles: Reconceptualizing Shoemaker and Reese's theory of a Hierarchy of Influences on media content for a newer media era. *Web Journal of Mass Communication Research 29*, p. 1.

Keith, S., & Schwalbe, C.B. (2010). Women and visual depictions of the US–Iraq War in print and online media. *Visual Communication Quarterly 17*(1), 4–17.

Keith, S., Schwalbe, C.B., & Silcock, B.W. (2010). Comparing war images across media platforms: methodological challenges for content analysis. *Media, War & Conflict 3*(1), 87–98.

Kellner, D. (1992). *The Persian Gulf TV war*. Boulder, CO: Westview.

—— (2004). The media and the crisis of democracy in the age of Bush 2. *Communication and Critical Cultural Studies 1*(1), 29–58.

Kellner, D., & Kim, G. (2010). YouTube, critical pedagogy, and media activism. *Review of Education, Pedagogy, and Cultural Studies 32*(1), 3–36.

Kenney, K.R. (1995). Images of Africa in news magazines: Is there a black perspective? *International Communication Gazette 54*(1), 61–85.

Kessler, L. (1989). Women's magazines' coverage of smoking related health issues. *Journalism Quarterly 66*(2), 316–445.

Kester, B. (2010). The art of balancing foreign correspondence in non-democratic countries: The Russian case. *International Communication Gazette 72*(1), 51–69.

Kim, H.S. (2002). Gatekeeping international news: An attitudinal profile of US television journalists. *Journal of Broadcasting & Electronic Media 46*(3), 431–52.

Kim, Y., & Bae, J. (2006). Korean practitioners and journalists: Relational influences in news selection. *Public Relations Review 32*(3), 241–5.

Kincaid, C. (1988, December 24). The Wall Street Journal's "closet socialist." *Human Events*, pp. 4–6.

Kiousis, S., & Wu, X. (2008). International agenda-building and agenda-setting: Exploring the influence of public relations counsel on US news media and public perceptions of foreign nations. *International Communication Gazette 70*(1), 58–75.

Klapper, J. (1960). *The effects of mass communication*. New York, NY: Free Press.

Klinenberg, E. (2005). Convergence: New production in a digital age. *Annals of the American Political Science Association 59*(7), 48–68.

Koltsova, O. (2001). News production in contemporary Russian practices of power. *European Journal of Communication 16*(3), 315–35.

Konner, J. (2002). Media patriotism provides a shield for Bush. *Long Island Newsday*, January 9, p. A31.

Kovach, B., & Rosenstiel, T. (2001). *The elements of journalism: What newspeople should know and the public should expect*. New York, NY: Three Rivers Press.

Krakauer, S. (2010), ABC News expected to offer "hundreds" of buyouts tomorrow. *Mediaite*. Available online at www.mediaite.com/tv/developing-hundreds-of-buyouts-expected-at-abc-news-tomorrow. (Accessed July 15, 2010.)

Kuhn, T.S. (1962). *The structure of scientific revolutions*. Chicago, IL: University of Chicago Press.

Kumar, D. (2006). Media, war, and propaganda: Strategies of information management during the 2003 Iraq War. *Communication and Critical Cultural Studies 3*(1), 48–69.

La Ferle, C., & Lee, W.N. (2005). Can English language media connect with ethnic audiences: Ethnic minorities' media use and representation perceptions. *Journal of Advertising Research 45*(1), 140–53.

Lambeth, E.B. (1986). *Committed journalism: An ethic for the profession*. Bloomington, IN: Indiana University Press.

Landau, J. (2009). Straightening out (the politics of) same-sex parenting: Representing gay families in US print news stories and photographs. *Critical Studies in Media Communication 26*(1), 80–100.

Lang, A., Dhillon, P., & Dong, Q. (1995) Arousal, emotion, and memory for television messages. *Journal of Broadcasting and Electronic Media 38*, 313–27.

Lang, A., & Friestad, M. (1993). Emotion, hemispheric specialization, and visual and verbal memory for television messages. *Communication Research 20*(5), 647–70.

Lang, K., & Lang, G.E. (1953). The unique perspective of television and its effect: A pilot study. *American Sociological Review 18*(1), 3–12.

—— (2004). Noam Chomsky and the manufacture of consent for American foreign policy. *Political Communication 21*(1), 93–101.

Lasorsa, D., & Dai, J. (2007). When news reporters deceive: The production of stereotypes. *Journalism & Mass Communication Quarterly 84*(2), 281–98.

Lasswell, H.D. (1948). The structure and function of communication in society. In L. Bryson (Ed.), *The communication of ideas* (pp. 243–76). New York, NY: Institute for Religious and Social Studies.

Lawrence, R. (2000). *The politics of force: Media and the construction of police brutality*. Berkeley, CA: University of California.

Lazarsfeld, P., Berelson, B., & Gaudet, H. (1948). *The people's choice*. New York, NY: Columbia University Press.

Lazarsfeld, P., & Merton, R. (1971). Mass communication, popular taste, and organized social action. In W. Schramm & D. Roberts (Eds.), *The process and effects of mass communication* (pp. 554–78). Urbana, IL: University of Illinois Press.

LedeObserver (2009). For big city newspapers, local news sites, symbiosis cuts costs. *Lede Observer*. Retrieved June 13, 2010 from www.ledeobserver.com.

LeDoux, J.E. (1996). *The emotional brain: The mysterious underpinnings of emotional life*. New York, NY: Simon & Schuster.

—— (2000). Emotion circuits in the brain. *Annual Review of Neuroscience 23*(1), 155–84.

Lee, A., & So, C. (2010). Mapping journalistic professionalism in a crisis: The case of Sichuan Earthquake reporting. Paper presented at the International Association for Media Communication Research conference, Braga, Portugal.

Lee, J.H., Han, G., Shoemaker, P.J., & Cohen, A.A. (2005). Here and there around the world: Proximity and scope as news values. Paper presented at the Association for Education in Journalism and Mass Communication Conference, San Antonio, August.

Lee, M.A., & Devitt, T. (1991). Gulf War coverage: Censorship begins at home. *Newspaper Research Journal 12*(1), 14–22.

Lee, M.A., & Solomon, N. (1991). *Unreliable sources*, 2nd edn. New York, NY: Lyle Stuart.

Lee, T.-T., & Hwang, F. (2004). Journalistic ideologies versus corporate interests: How Time and Warner's merger influences Time's content. *Communication Research Reports 21*(2), 188–96.

LeMoyne, J. (1991). Pentagon's strategy for the press: Good news or no news. *New York Times*, February 17.

Lesly, E. (1991). Realtors and builders demand happy news . . . and often get it. *Washington Journalism Review*, November, pp. 20–5.

Levine, J.M., & Murphy, G. (1943). The learning and forgetting of controversial material. *Journal of Abnormal and Social Psychology 38*(4), 507–17.

Lewin, K. (1943). Forces behind food habits and methods of change. *Bulletin of the National Research Council 108*, 35–65.

—— (1947a) Frontiers in group dynamics: I. Concept, method and reality in social science; social equilibria. *Human Relations 1*(1), 5–40.

—— (1947b). Frontiers in group dynamics: II. Channels of group life; social planning and action research. *Human Relations 1*(2), 143–53.

Lewis, N.P. (2008). Plagiarism antecedents and situational influences. *Journalism & Mass Communication Quarterly 85*(2), 353–70.

Lewis, S.C. (2011). Journalism innovation and participation: An analysis of the Knight News Challenge. *International Journal of Communication 5*, 1623–48.

—— (2012). The tension between professional control and open participation. *Information, Communication and Society 15*(6), 836–66.

Lewis, S.C., & Reese, S.D. (2009). What is the war on terror? Framing through the eyes of journalists. *Journalism & Mass Communication Quarterly 86*(1), 85–102.

Lichter, S.R., Rothman, S., & Lichter, L.S. (1986). *The media elite: America's new powerbrokers*. Bethesda, MD: Adler & Adler.

Livingston, S., & Bennett, W. (2003). Gatekeeping, indexing, and live-event news: Is technology altering the construction of news? *Political Communication 20*(4), 363–80.

Lowery, S., & DeFleur, M. (1995). *Milestones in mass communication research*. New York, NY: Longman.

Lowrey, W. (2006). Mapping the journalism–blogging relationship. *Journalism 7*(4), 477–500.

Luhmann, N. (1997). Globalization or world society: How to conceive of modern society. *International Review of Sociology: Revue Internationale de Sociologie 7*(1), 67–79.

Lukes, S. (1974). *Power: A radical view*. London: Macmillan.

Luntz, F. (2000). Public to press: Cool it—America may have a uniquely free press, but a surprising number of Americans don't like the results. *Brill's Content 2* (March), 74–6.

Luther, C. A., & Miller, M. A. (2005). Framing of the 2003 US Iraq War demonstrations: An analysis of news and partisan texts. *Journalism & Mass Communication Quarterly 82*(1), 78–96.

Lynd, R. S. (1939). *Knowledge for what? The place of social science in American culture.* New York, NY: Grove.

MacDougall, A. K. (1988). Boring from within the bourgeois press: Part I. *Monthly Review 40*(7), 13–24.

Mann, L. (1974). Counting the crowd: Effects of editorial policy on estimates. *Journalism Quarterly 51*(2), 251–7, 294.

Marchington, M., & Vincent, S. (2004). Analysing the influence of institutional, organizational and interpersonal forces in shaping inter-organizational relations. *Journal of Management Studies 41*(6), 1029–56.

Martin, C. R. (2008). "Upscale" news audiences and the transformation of labour news. *Journalism Studies 9*(2), 178–94.

Martin, W. P., & Singletary, M. (1981). Newspaper treatment of state government releases. *Journalism Quarterly 58*(2), 93–6.

Martindale, C. (1984). Newspaper and wire-service leads in coverage of the 1980 campaign. *Journalism Quarterly 61*(2), 339–45.

Martins, N., Williams, D., Harrison, K., & Ratan, R. (2009). A content analysis of female body imagery in video games. *Sex Roles 61*(11–12), 824–36.

Marx, K. (1938). *Capital: A critical analysis of capitalist production*, vol. I, trans. S. Moore & E. Aveling, ed. Dona Torr. London: Swan Sonnenschein, Lowrey, & Co.

Marx, K., & Engels, F. (1970). *The German ideology.* London: Lawrence & Wishart.

Massing, M. (2004). Now they tell us. *New York Review of Books*, February 26.

Mastro, D., & Stern, S. (2003). Representations of race in television commercials: A content analysis of prime-time advertising. *Journal of Broadcasting and Electronic Media 47*(4), 638–47.

McAllister, M. P. (2007). Girls with a passion for fashion: The Bratz brand as integrated spectacular consumption. *Journal of Children and Media 1*(3), 244–58.

McChesney, R. W. (1992). Off limits: An inquiry into the lack of debate over the ownership, structure and control of the mass media in US political life. *Communication 13*(1), 1–19.

—— (1993). *Telecommunications, mass media, and democracy: The battle for the control of US broadcasting, 1928–1935.* Oxford: Oxford University Press.

—— (2002). September 11 and the structural limitations of US journalism. In B. Zelizer & S. Allan (Eds.), *Journalism after September 11* (pp. 91–100). London and New York, NY: Routledge.

McChesney, R. W., & Nichols, J. (2010). *The death and life of American journalism: The media revolution that will begin the world again.* Philadelphia, PA: Nation Books.

McCombs, M. E. (1987). Effect of monopoly in Cleveland on diversity of newspaper content. *Journalism Quarterly 64*(4), 740–92.

—— (1988). Test the myths: A statistical review, 1967–86. *Gannett Center Journal 2*(2), 101–8.

McCombs, M. E., & Shaw, D. (1972). The agenda-setting function of mass media. *Public Opinion Quarterly 36*(2), 176–87.

McGarty, T. P. (2004). The impact of broadband options on the disaggregation of the media industry. Draft paper for the Angevin Group, pp. 1–31.

McGovern, A., & Lee, M. (2010). "Cop[ying] it sweet": Police media units and the making of news. *Australian and New Zealand Journal of Criminology 43*(3), 444–64.

McLeod, D., & Hertog, J. (1992). The manufacture of "public opinion" by reporters: Informal cues for public perceptions of protest groups. *Discourse and Society 3*(3), 259–75.

McLeod, J. M., & Hawley, S. E. Jr. (1964). Professionalism among newsmen. *Journalism Quarterly 41*(4), 529–38.

McLuhan, M. (1962). *The Gutenberg Galaxy: The making of typographic man*. Toronto: University of Toronto Press.

McManus, J. (1994). *Market-driven journalism: Let the citizen beware?* Thousand Oaks, CA: Sage.

McQuail, D. (1986). Diversity in political communications: Its sources, forms and future. In P. Golding, G. Murdock, & P. Schlesinger (Eds.), *Communicating politics* (pp. 133–49). Leicester: Leicester City Press.

Mead, G. H. (1934). *Mind, self, and society: From the standpoint of a social behaviorist*. Chicago, IL: University of Chicago Press.

Medsger, B. (1996). *Winds of change: Challenges confronting journalism education*. Arlington, VA: Freedom Forum.

Merton, R. (1949). *Social theory and social structure*. Glencoe, NY: Free Press.

Meyers, O. (2011). Expanding the scope of paradigmatic research in journalism studies: The case of early mainstream Israeli journalism and its discontents. *Journalism 12*(3), 261–78.

Miller, A., & Ross, S. D. (2004). They are not us: Framing of American Indians by the *Boston Globe*. *Howard Journal of Communication 15*(4), 245–59.

Mills, C. W. (1956). *The power elite*. Oxford: Oxford University Press.

—— (1959). *The sociological imagination*. Oxford: Oxford University Press.

—— (1963). Two styles of social science research. In I. Horowitz (Ed.), *Power, politics, people* (pp. 553–67). New York, NY: Ballantine.

Mills, K. (1993). The media and the year of the woman. *Media Studies Journal 7*(1–2), 18–31.

—— (1997). What difference do women journalists make? In P. Norris (Ed.), *Women, media, and politics* (pp. 41–55). Oxford: Oxford University Press.

Molotch, H., & Lester, M. (1974). News as purposive behavior: On the strategic use of routine events, accidents and scandals. *American Sociological Review 39*(1), 101–12.

Mosco, V. (2004). *The digital sublime*. Cambridge, MA: MIT Press.

Mosco, V., & Herman, A. (1981). Radical social theory and the communication revolution. In E. McAnany, J. Schnitman, & N. Janus (Eds.), *Communication and social structure* (pp. 58–84). New York, NY: Praeger.

Mundorf, N., Drew, D., Zillman, D., & Weaver, J. (1990). Effects of disturbing news on recall of subsequently presented news. *Communication Research 17*(5), 601–15.

Murdock, G., & Golding, P. (1977). Capitalism, communication and class relations. In J. Curran, M. Gurevitch, & J. Woollacott (Eds.), *Mass communication and society* (pp. 12–43). Beverly Hills, CA: Sage.

Napoli, P. M. (1997). A principal-agent approach to the study of media organizations: Toward a theory of the media firm. *Political Communication 14*(2), 207–19.

Nelson, D. E., & Signorielli, N. (2007). Reporter sex and newspaper coverage of the adverse health effects of hormone therapy. *Women and Health 45*(1), 1–15.

Nelson, J. (1993). *Volunteer slavery: My authentic negro experience*. Chicago, IL: Noble.

Netflix (2010). Watch movies and TV episodes instantly. *Netflix.com*. Retrieved on July 7, 2010 from www.netflix.com/WiMessage?msg=99.

Newhagen, J., & Reeves, B. (1992). This evening's bad news: Effects of compelling negative television news images on memory. *Journal of Communication 42*(42), 25–41.

Newspaper Death Watch (2010). Homepage. *Newspaper Death Watch*. Available online at www.newspaperdeathwatch.com. (Accessed June 16, 2010.)

Nimmo, D., & Combs, J. E. (1983). *Mediated political realities*. New York, NY: Longman.

Nixon, R., & Jones, R. (1956). The content of non-competitive vs. competitive newspapers. *Journalism Quarterly 33*(3), 299–314.

Nohrstedt, S. A., & Ottosen, R. (2000). Studying the media Gulf War. In S. A. Nohrstedt & R. Ottosen (Eds.), *Journalism and the new world order*, vol. I: *Gulf War, national news discourses and globalization* (pp. 11–34). Gothenburg: Nordicom.

Notice of 1989 Annual Meeting and Proxy Statement (1989). *New York Times Company*.

Olasky, M. (1988). *Prodigal press: The anti-Christian bias of the American news media.* Westchester, IL: Crossway.

Oshima, H. (1967). Growth and unemployment in Singapore. *Malayan Economic Review 12*(2), 32–58.

Ottosen, I. (1993). Truth: The first victim of war. In H. Mowlana, G. Gerbner, & H. Schiller (Eds.), *Triumph of the image: Persian Gulf War in global perspective* (pp. 243–65). Boulder, CO: Westview.

Owens, L. (2008). Network news: The role of race in source selection and story topic. *Howard Journal of Communication 19*(4), 355–70.

Paletz, D., & Entman, R. (1981). *Media, power, politics.* New York, NY: Free Press.

Pan, Z. (2000). Spatial configuration in institutional change: A case of China's journalism reforms. *Journalism 1*(3), 253–81.

Pardee, T. (2012). Is gay too mainstream for its own media? *AdAge*, March 12, pp. 1–3.

Parisi, P. (1992). Critical studies, the liberal arts, and journalism education. *Journalism Educator 46*(4), 4–13.

Park, R. (1999). News as a form of knowledge: A chapter in the sociology of knowledge. In H. Tumber (Ed.), *News: A reader* (pp. 11–15). Oxford: Oxford University Press.

Paterson, C. (1997). Global television news services. In O. Boyd-Barret, J. McKenna, A. Sreberny-Mohammadi, & D. Winseck (Eds.), *Media in global context: A reader* (pp. 145–61). London: Edward Arnold.

—— (2011). *The international television news agencies: The view from London.* New York, NY: Peter Lang.

Paterson, C., & Domingo, D. (2008). *Making online news: The ethnography of new media production.* New York, NY: Peter Lang.

Patterson, T. (1993). *Out of order.* New York, NY: Knopf.

—— (1998). Political roles of the journalist. In D. Graber, D. McQuail, & P. Norris (Eds.), *The politics of news: The news of politics* (pp. 17–32). Washington, DC: CQ Press.

Patterson, T., & Donsbach, W. (1996). News decisions: Journalists as partisan actors. *Political Communication 13*(4), 455–68.

Peer, L., & Ksiazek, T. (2011). YouTube and the challenge to journalism. *Journalism Studies 12*(1), 45–63.

Pelikan, J. (1992). *The idea of the university: A reexamination.* New Haven, CT: Yale University Press.

Pepitone, A. (1976). Toward a normative and comparative biocultural social psychology. *Journal of Social Psychology 34*(4), 641–53.

Perez-Pena, R., & Arango, T. (2009). They pay for cable, music, and extra bags. How about news? *New York Times*, April 8.

Peters, J. (2008). Institutional opportunities for intellectual history in communication studies. In J. Pooley & D. Park (Eds.), *The history of media and communication research* (pp. 143–62). New York, NY: Peter Lang.

Peterson, T. (1981). Mass media and their environments: A journey into the past. In E. Abel (Ed.), *What's news* (pp. 13–32). San Francisco, CA: Institute for the Contemporary Studies.

Pew State of the News Media (2009). Newspapers. *Pew Research Center.* Available online at www.stateofthemedia.org/2009/narrative_newspapers_intro.php?cat=0&media=4. (Accessed June 16, 2010.)

Pfetsch, B. (2004). A theoretical approach to comparative analysis. In F. Esser & B. Pfetsch (Eds.), *Comparing communication: Theories, cases and challenges* (pp. 344–66). Cambridge: Cambridge University Press.

Phillips, G. (2011) Reporting diversity: The representation of ethnic minorities in Australia's television current affairs programs. *Media International Australia 139*, 23–31.

Picard, R., Winter, J., McCombs, M., & Lacy, S. (Eds.) (1988). *Press concentration and monopoly: New perspectives on newspaper ownership and operation.* Norwood, NJ: Ablex.

Pollock, J. C. (2007). *Tilted mirrors.* Cresskill, NJ: Hampton.

Pottker, H. (2005) The news pyramid and its origin from the American journalism in the 19th century. In S. Høyer & H. Pöttker (Eds.), *Diffusion of the news paradigm, 1850–2000* (pp. 51–64). Gothenburg: Nordicom.

Price, V., Tewksbury, D., & Powers, E. (1995). Switching trains of thought: The impact of news frames on readers' cognitive responses. Paper presented at the Annual Conference of the Midwest Association for Public Opinion Research, Chicago, IL, November.

Pritchard, D., & Stonbely, S. (2007). Racial profiling in the newsroom. *Journalism & Mass Communication Quarterly 84*(2), 231–48.

Pritchard, D., Terry, C., & Brewer, P.R. (2008). One owner, one voice? Testing a central premise of newspaper-broadcast cross-ownership policy. *Communication Law and Policy 13*(1), 1–27.

Raley, A.B., & Lucas, J.L. (2006). Stereotype or success? *Journal of Homosexuality 51*(2), 19–38.

Ramsey, S. (1999). A benchmark study of elaboration and sourcing in science stories for eight American newspapers. *Journalism & Mass Communication Quarterly 76*(2), 87–98.

Rantanen, T. (2009). *When news was new.* Malden, MA: Wiley-Blackwell.

Ravi, N. (2005). Looking beyond flawed journalism: How national interests, patriotism, and cultural values shaped the coverage of the Iraq War. *Harvard International Journal of Press/Politics 10*(1), 45–62.

Raymond, J.E. (2003). New objects, not new features, trigger the attentional blink. *Psychological Science 14*(1), 54–9.

Reese, S.D. (1990). The news paradigm and the ideology of objectivity: A socialist at the *Wall Street Journal*. *Critical Studies in Media Communication 7*(4), 390–409.

—— (1991). Setting the media's agenda: A power balance perspective. In J. Anderson (Ed.), *Mass communication review yearbook*, vol. XIV (pp. 309–40). Beverly Hills, CA: Sage.

—— (1999). The progressive potential of journalism education: Recasting the academic versus professional debate. *Harvard International Journal of Press/Politics 4*(4), 70–94.

—— (2001a). Framing public life: A bridging model for media research. In S.D. Reese, O.H.J. Gandy, & A.E. Grant (Eds.), *Framing public life* (pp. 7–31). Mahwah, NJ: Erlbaum.

—— (2001b). Understanding the global journalist: A hierarchy-of-influences approach. *Journalism Studies 2*(2), 173–87.

—— (2004). Militarized journalism: Framing dissent in the Persian Gulf wars. In S. Allan & B. Zelizer (Eds.), *Reporting war: Journalism in wartime* (pp. 247–65). London and New York, NY: Routledge.

—— (2007a). The framing project: A bridging model for media research revisited. *Journal of Communication 57*(1), 148–54.

—— (2007b). Media production and content. In W. Donsbach (Ed.), *Communication* (pp. 2982–94). Malden, MA: International Communication Association.

—— (2009a). Finding frames in a web of culture: The case of the war on terror. In P. D'Angelo & J. Kuypers (Eds.), *Doing news framing analysis* (pp. 17–42). London and New York, NY: Routledge.

—— (2009b). Managing the symbolic arena: The media sociology of Herbert Gans, L. Becker, C. Holtz-Bach, & G. Reust (Eds.), *Wissenschaft mit Wirkung* (pp. 279–94). Wiesbaden: VS Verlag fuer Sozialwissenschaften.

—— (2010). Journalism and globalization. *Sociology Compass 4*(6), 344–53.

Reese, S.D., & Ballinger, J. (2001). The roots of a sociology of news: Remembering Mr. Gates and social control in the newsroom. *Journalism & Mass Communication Quarterly 78*(4), 641–58.

Reese, S.D., & Buckalew, B. (1995). The militarism of local television: The routine framing of the Persian Gulf War. *Critical Studies in Mass Communication 12*(1), 40–59.

Reese, S.D., & Cohen, J. (2000). Educating for journalism: The professionalism of scholarship. *Journalism Studies 1*(2), 213–27.

Reese, S., & Danielian, L. (1989). Intermedia influence and the drug issue: Converging on cocaine. In P.J. Shoemaker (Ed.), *Communication campaigns about drugs: Government, media, and the public* (pp. 29–46). Hillsdale, NJ: Lawrence Erlbaum.

Reese, S., Grant, A., & Danielian, L. (1994). The structure of news sources on television: A network analysis of *CBS News*, *Nightline*, MacNeil/Lehrer, and *This Week with David Brinkley*. *Journal of Communication 44* (2), 84–107.

Reese, S.D., & Lee, J.K. (2012). Understanding the content of news media. In H.A. Semetko & M. Scammell (Eds.), *Handbook of political communication* (pp. 749–67). Beverly Hills, CA: Sage.

Reese, S.D., & Lewis, S.C. (2009). Framing the War on Terror: Internalization of policy by the US press. *Journalism: Theory, Practice, Criticism 10*(6), 777–97.

Reeves, R. (1993). *President Kennedy: Profile of power*. New York, NY: Simon & Schuster.

Reporting, F. & A. (2004). *How public is public radio? A study of NPR's guest list*.

Reuters (2010). Reuters news agency factsheet. *Thomson Reuters*. Retrieved June 1, 2010 from http://thomsonreuters.com/products_services/media/media_products/.

Reynolds, A., & Barnett, B. (2003). This just in . . . How national TV news handled the breaking "live" coverage of September 11. *Journalism & Mass Communication Quarterly 80*(3), 689–703.

Rivers, C. (1993). Bandwagons, women and cultural mythology. *Media Studies Journal 7*(1–2), 1–17.

Rivers, W. (1965). *The opinion makers*. Boston, MA: Beacon Press.

Robertson, J.W. (2009). Informing the public? UK newspaper reporting of autism and Asperger's syndrome. *Journal of Research in Special Educational Needs 9*(1), 12–26.

Robertson, L. (2006). Adding a price tag. *American Journalism Review*, December/January. Available online at www.ajr.org/article.asp?id=4004. (Accessed July 13, 2010.)

Robinson, C., & Powell, L.A. (1996). The postmodern politics of context definition: Competing reality frames in the Hill–Thomas Spectacle. *The Sociological Quarterly 37*(2), 279–305.

Rodgers, S., & Thorson, E. (2003). A socialization perspective on male and female reporting. *Journal of Communication 53*(4), 658–75.

Rogers, E.M. (1986). History of communication science. In E.M. Rogers (Ed.), *Communication technology* (pp. 68–115). New York, NY: Free Press.

Rose, A. (1967). *The power structure*. Oxford: Oxford University Press.

Rosenberg, A. (2012). *Philosophy of social science*. Boulder, CO: Westview Press.

Rosenberg, B., & White, D.M. (1971). *Mass culture revisited*. New York, NY: Van Nostrand-Reinhold.

Rosenstiel, T., & Mitchell, A. (2003). *Thinking clearly: Cases in journalistic decision-making*. New York, NY: Columbia University Press.

Rosten, L. (1937). *The Washington correspondents*. New York, NY: Harcourt Brace.

Rules and Guidelines (1978). *Milwaukee Journal*, p. 3.

Rusher, W. (1988). *The coming battle for the media: Curbing the power of the media elite*. New York, NY: William Morrow.

Ryfe, D.M. (2006). Guest editor's introduction: New institutionalism and the news. *Political communication 23*(2), 135–44.

Sallot, L.M., Steinfatt, T.M., & Salwen, M.B. (1998). Journalists' and public relations practitioners' news values: Perceptions and cross-perceptions. *Journalism & Mass Communication Quarterly 75*(2), 366–77.

Salovaara-Moring, I. (2009). Dead ground: Time-spaces of conflict, news, and cultural understanding. *The Communication Review 12*(4), 349–68.

Sampson, E.E. (1977). Psychology and the American ideal. *Journal of Personality and Social Psychology 35*(11), 767–81.

Schanberg, S. (1991). A muzzle for the press. In M. Sifrey & C. Cerf (Eds.), *The Gulf War reader history, documents, opinions* (pp. 368–75). New York, NY: Times Books/Random House.

Scherbaum, C.A., & Ferreter, J.M. (2008). Estimating statistical power and required sample sizes for organizational research using multilevel modeling. *Organizational Research Methods 12*(2), 347–67.

Scheufele, D. A. (1999). Framing as a theory of media effects. *Journal of Communication 49*(1), 103–22.

Schillinger, E., & Porter, C. (1991). Glasnost and the transformation of Moscow News. *Journal of Communication 41*(2), 125–49.

Schlesinger, P. (1978). *Putting "reality" together: BBC news.* London: Constable.

Schramm, W. (1960). *Mass communications: A book of readings,* 2nd edn. Urbana, IL: University of Illinois Press.

Schramm, W., Lyle, J., & Parker, E. (1961). *Television in the lives of our children.* Palo Alto, CA: Stanford University Press.

Schramm, W., & Roberts, D. (1971). *The process and effects of mass communication.* Urbana, IL: University of Illinois Press.

Schudson, M. (1978). *Discovering the news.* New York, NY: Basic Books.

—— (1986). *What time means in a news story.* New York, NY: Gannett Center for Media Studies.

—— (1993). *Watergate in American memory: How we remember, forget, and reconstruct the past.* New York, NY: Basic Books.

—— (2011). *The sociology of news,* 2nd edn. New York, NY: Norton.

Schwartz, J. (2010). Whose voices are heard? Gender, sexual orientation, and newspaper sources. *Sex Roles 64*(3–4), 265–75.

Scott, B. (2005) A contemporary history of digital journalism. *Television and New Media 6*(1), 89–125.

Scott, D. K., Gobetz, R. H., & Chanslor, M. (2008). Chain versus independent television station ownership: Toward an investment model of commitment to local news quality. *Communications Studies 59*(1), 84–98.

Shaheen, J. (2003). Reel bad Arabs: How Hollywood vilifies a people. *Annals of the American Academy of Political and Social Science 588*(1), 171–93.

Shannon, C., & Weaver, W. (1949). *The mathematical theory of communication.* Urbana, IL: University of Illinois Press.

Shapiro, M. A., & Fox, J. R. (2002). The role of typical and atypical events in story memory. *Human Communication Research 28*(1), 109–35.

Shapiro, M. A., & McDonald, D. G. (1995). I'm not a real doctor, but I play one in virtual reality: Implications of virtual reality for judgments about reality. In F. Biocca & M. R. Levy (Eds.), *Communication in the age of virtual reality* (pp. 323–45). Hillsdale, NJ: Erlbaum.

Shaw, D. (1989). How media gives stories same "spin?" *Los Angeles Times,* August 25.

—— (1999). Crossing the line. *Los Angeles Times,* December 20.

Sheehan, N. (1988). *A bright shining lie: John Paul Vann and America in Vietnam.* New York, NY: Random House.

Sherizen, S. (1978). Social creation of crime news: All the news fitted to print. In C. Winick (Ed.), *Deviance and the mass media* (pp. 203–24). Beverly Hills, CA: Sage.

Shin, J. H., & Cameron, G. T. (2003). The interplay of professional and cultural factors in the online source–reporter relationship. *Journalism Studies 4*(2), 253–72.

Shoemaker, P. J. (1982). The perceived legitimacy of deviant political groups: Two experiments on media effects. *Communication Research 9*(2), 249–86.

—— (1984). Media treatment of deviant political groups. *Journalism Quarterly 61*(1), 66–75, 82.

—— (1991). *Gatekeeping.* Newbury Park, CA: Sage.

—— (1996). Hard-wired for news: Using biological and cultural evolution to explain the news. *Journal of Communication 33*(5), 32–47.

—— (2006). News and newsworthiness: A commentary. *Communications: The European Journal of Communication Research 31*(1), 105–11.

Shoemaker, P. J., & Cohen, A. (2006). *News around the world: Content, practitioners and the public.* London and New York, NY: Routledge.

Shoemaker, P. J., Cohen, A. A., Seo, H., & Johnson, P. (2012). Foreign and international news. In F. Esser & T. Hanitzsch (Eds.), *Handbook of comparative communication research* (pp. 341–52). London and New York, NY: Routledge.

Shoemaker, P.J., Eichholz, M., Kim, E., & Wrigley, B. (2001). Individual and routine forces in gatekeeping. *Journalism & Mass Communication Quarterly 78*(2), 233–46.

Shoemaker, P.J., Hyuk Lee, J., Han, G., & Cohen, A.A. (2007). Proximity and scope as news values. In E. Devereux (Ed.), *Media studies: Key issues and debates* (pp. 231–48). London: Sage.

Shoemaker, P.J., Johnson, P.R., Seo, H., & Wang, X. (2010) Readers as gatekeepers of online news: Brazil, China and the United States. *Brazilian Journalism Research 6*(1), 55–77.

Shoemaker, P.J., Riccio, J., & Johnson, P.R. (2013). Gatekeeping. In P. Moy (Ed.), *Oxford bibliographies in communication*. Oxford: Oxford University Press.

Shoemaker, P.J., Seo, H., Johnson, P., & Wang, X. (2008). Audience gatekeeping: A study of the *New York Times* most-emailed news items. Paper presented at the Conference on Convergence and Society: The Participatory Web (3.0), October, University of South Carolina, Columbia, SC.

Shoemaker, P.J., & Vos, T.P. (2009). *Gatekeeping theory*. London and New York, NY: Routledge.

Shoemaker, P.J., Vos, T., & Reese, S.D. (2009). Journalists as gatekeepers. In K. Wahl-Jorgensen & T. Hanitzsch (Eds.), *Handbook of journalism studies* (pp. 73–87). London and New York, NY: Routledge.

Siebert, F., Peterson, T., & Schramm, W. (1963). *Four theories of the press: The authoritarian, libertarian, social responsibility, and Soviet communist concepts of what the press should be and do*. Champaign, IL: University of Illinois Press.

Sigal, L. (1973). *Reporters and officials*. Lexington, MA: D.C. Heath.

Signorielli, N. (1983). The demography of the television world. In G. Melischek, K. Rosengren, & J. Stappers (Eds.), *Cultural indicators: An international symposium* (pp. 137–57). Vienna: Austrian Academy of Sciences.

—— (Ed.) (1985). *Role portrayal and stereotyping on television: An annotated bibliography of studies relating to women, minorities, aging, sexual behavior, health and handicaps*. Westport, CT: Greenwood.

—— (2004). Aging on television: Messages relating to gender, race, and occupation in prime time. *Journal of Broadcasting and Electronic Media 48*(2), 279–301.

—— (2009). Race and sex in prime time: A look at occupations and occupational prestige. *Mass Communication and Society 12*(3), 332–52.

Silcock, B.W., & Keith, S. (2006). Translating the tower of Babel? *Journalism Studies 7*(4), 610–27.

Simonson, P., & Weimann, G. (2003). Critical research at Columbia: Lazarsfeld's and Merton's "Mass communication, popular taste, and organized social action." In E. Katz, J. Peters, T. Liebes, & A. Orloff (Eds.), *Canonic texts in media research* (pp. 12–38). Cambridge: Polity.

Singel, R. (2009). FYI, Pandora makes your music public. *Wired*. Available online at www.wired.com/business/2010/05/pandora-privacy. (Accessed June 13, 2010.)

Singer, J.B. (2001). The metro wide web: Changes in newspapers' gatekeeping role online. *Journalism & Mass Communication Quarterly 78*(1), 65–80.

—— (2005). The political j-blogger. *Journalism 6*(2), 173–98.

—— (2006). Stepping back from the gate: Online newspaper editors and the co-production of content in campaign 2004. *Journalism & Mass Communication Quarterly 83*(2), 265–80.

Sivek, S. (2004). The framing of Iraq war reporting by embedded and unilateral newspaper journalists. Paper presented at the Association for Education in Journalism and Mass Communication annual conference, Toronto.

Skewes, E. (2007). *Message control: How news is made on the presidential campaign trail*. Lanham, MD: Rowman & Littlefield.

Slaughter, A.-M. (2004). *A new world order*. Princeton, NJ: Princeton University Press.

Sloan, D. (1990). *Makers of the media mind: Journalism educators and their ideas*. Hillsdale, NJ: Erlbaum.

Smith, A. (2008). *An inquiry into the nature and causes of the wealth of nations: A selected edition*. Oxford: Oxford Paperbacks.

Smith, H. (1988). *The power game: How Washington works*. New York, NY: Random House.

Smith, J. (2010). Hurrah for Murdoch: Paid-for news keeps democracy alive. *The Independent on Sunday*, March 28.

Smith, S., Pieper, K., Granados, A., & Choueiti, M. (2010). Assessing gender-related portrayals in top-grossing G-rated films. *Sex Roles 62*(11), 774–86.

Snider, P. B. (1966). Mr. Gates revisited: A 1966 version of the 1949 case study. *Journalism Quarterly 44*(3), 419–27.

Soley, L. (1992). *The news shapers: The sources who explain the news*. New York, NY: Praeger.

Son, J., & McCombs, M. (1993). A look at the constancy principle under changing market conditions. *Journal of Media Economics 6*(3), 23–36.

Sonenshine, T. (1997). Is everyone a journalist? *American Journalism Review 19*(8), 11.

Sparrow, B. H. (1999). *Uncertain guardians: The news media as a political institution*. Baltimore, MD: Johns Hopkins University Press.

—— (2006). A research agenda for an institutional media. *Political communication 23*(2), 145–57.

Speed, L. (2010). Loose cannons: White masculinity and the vulgar teen comedy film. *Journal of Popular Culture 43*(4), 820–41.

Sperry, P. (1995). A changing information market. *Investor's Business Daily*, March 27.

Splichal, S., & Sparks, C. (1994). *Journalists for the 21st century: Tendencies of professionalization among first-year students in 22 countries*. Norwood, NJ: Ablex.

Squires, J. (1993). Plundering the newsroom. *Washington Journalism Review*, December, pp. 18–24.

Standish, K. (1989). Lean times continue; Painless ways to economize. *RTDNA [Radio Television Digital News Association] Communicator*, April, pp. 18–23.

Starkman, D. (2011). Confidence game: The limited vision of the news gurus. *Columbia Journalism Review 50*(4), 121–30.

Steel, E., & Vascellaro, J. E. (2010). Facebook, MySpace confront privacy loophole. *Wall Street Journal*, September 26.

Steele, J. (1990). Sound bite seeks expert. *Washington Journalism Review*, September, pp. 28–29.

—— (1992). TV's talking headaches. *Columbia Journalism Review*, July/August, pp. 49–52.

Stelter, B. (2009). Can CNN, the go-to-site, get you to stay? *New York Times*, January 18.

Stephens, M. (1980). *Broadcast news*. New York, NY: Holt, Rinehart & Winston.

Stepp, C. S. (2007). Transforming the architecture. *American Journalism Review*, October/November, pp. 15–21.

—— (2008). Maybe it's time to panic. *American Journalism Review*, April/May, pp. 22–7.

Stewart, D., Blocker, H. G., & Petrik, J. (2013). *Fundamentals of philosophy*. New York: Pearson.

Stocking, S. H. (1985). Effect of public relations efforts on media visibility of organizations. *Journalism Quarterly 62*(2), 358–66, 450.

Straubhaar, J. (1997). Distinguishing the global, regional and national levels of world television. In A. Sreberny-Mohammadi, D. Winseck, J. McKenna, & O. Boyd-Barrett (Eds.), *Media in global context* (pp. 284–98). London: Edward Arnold.

Streitmatter, R. (1997). *Mightier than the sword*. Boulder, CO: Westview Press.

Stroud, N. (2010). Polarization and partisan selective exposure. *Journal of Communication 60*(3), 556–76.

—— (2011). *Niche news: The politics of news choice*. Oxford: Oxford University Press.

Tankard, J. W. Jr. (1984). *The statistical pioneers*. Cambridge, MA: Schenkman.

Taylor, S. (1993). The standup syndrome. *American Journalism Review*, July/August, pp. 35–8.

Thagard, P. (2005). *Mind: Introduction to cognitive science*, 2nd edn. Cambridge, MA: MIT Press.

Thompson, J. (1990). *Ideology and modern culture: Critical social theory in the era of mass communication*. Palo Alto, CA: Stanford University Press.

Thorson, E., & Friestad, M. (1989). The effects of emotions on episodic memory for TV commercials. In A. Tybout & P. Cafferata (Eds.), *Cognitive and affective responses to advertising* (pp. 305–26). Lexington, MA: Lexington Books.

Thussu, D. K. (2007). *News as entertainment: The rise of global entertainment.* London: Sage.

Tichenor, P. J., Donohue, G. A., Olien, C. N., & Clarke, P. (1980). *Community conflict and the press.* Beverly Hills, CA: Sage.

Tierney, K., Bevc, C., & Kuligowski, E. (2006). Metaphors matter: Disaster myths, media frames, and their consequences in Hurricane Katrina. *Annals of the American Academy of Political and Social Science 604*(1), 57–81.

Triplett, W. (1993). Visitation rites. *American Journalism Review 15*(September), 33–6.

Tuchman, G. (1972). Objectivity as strategic ritual: An examination of newsmen's notions of objectivity. *American Journal of Sociology 77*(4), 660–79.

—— (1973). Making news by doing work: Routinizing the unexpected. *American Journal of Sociology 79*(1), 110–31.

—— (1977). The exception proves the rule: The study of routine news practice. In P. Hirsch, P. Miller, & F. G. Kline (Eds.), *Strategies for communication research* (pp. 43–62). Beverly Hills, CA: Sage.

—— (1978). *Making news.* New York, NY: Free Press.

—— (1981). The symbolic annihilation of women by the mass media. In S. Cohen & J. Young (Eds.), *The manufacture of news: Deviance, social problems and the mass media* (pp. 169–85). Beverly Hills, CA: Sage.

Tunstall, J. (1971). *Journalists at work.* London: Constable.

Turk, J. V. S. (1986). Public relations' influence on the news. *Newspaper Research Journal 7*(4), 15–27.

Turner, F. (2005). Actor-networking the news. *Social Epistemology 19*(4), 321–4.

Turow, J. (1984). *Mass media industries.* New York, NY: Longman.

—— (1997). *Media systems in society,* 2nd edn. Boston, MA: Allyn & Bacon.

Turpenien, M. (2000). Customizing news content for individuals and communities. Unpublished doctoral dissertation. Helsinki University of Technology, Espoo, Finland.

Usher, N., & Lewis, S. (2011). What newsrooms can learn from open-source and maker culture. *Nieman Journalism Lab Blog,* October 7. Available online at www.niemanlab. org/2011/10/what-newsrooms-can-learn-from-open-source-and-maker-culture. (Accessed July 10, 2011.)

Veronis, C. R. (1989). Research moves to center stage. *Presstime,* November 11, pp. 20–6.

Vliegenthart, R., & Walgrave, S. (2008). The contingency of intermedia agenda setting: A longitudinal study in Belgium. *Journalism & Mass Communication Quarterly 85*(4), 860–77.

Voakes, P. S. (1997). Social influences on journalists' decision making in ethical situations. *Journal of Mass Media Ethics 12*(1), 18–35.

Wagner, T. (2008). Reframing ecotage as ecoterrorism: News and the discourse of fear. *Environmental Communication 2*(1), 25–39.

Waisbord, S. (2011). Can NGOs change the news? *International Journal of Communication 5,* 142–65.

Wallerstein, I. (1993). The world-system after the Cold War. *Journal of Peace Research 30*(1), 1–6.

—— (1997). The West and the rest. *International Sociological Association Presidential Newsletter No. 6,* April.

Wartella, E., & Reeves, B. (1985). Historical trends in research on children and the media, 1900–60. *Journal of Communication 35*(2), 118–33.

Watts, M. D., Domke, D., Shah, D. V., & Fan, D. P. (1999). Elite cues and media bias in presidential campaigns: Explaining public perceptions of a liberal press. *Communication Research 26*(2), 144–75.

Weaver, D. H. (1998). *The global journalist: News people around the world.* Creskill, NJ: Hampton.

Weaver, D. H., Beam, R., Brownlee, B., Voakes, P., & Wilhoit, G. C. (2007). *The American journalist in the 21st century: US news people at the dawn of a new millennium.* Mahwah, NJ: Erlbaum.

Weaver, D. H., & Wilhoit, G. C. (1991). *The American journalist: A portrait of US news people and their work.* Bloomington, IN: Indiana University Press.

—— (1996). *The American journalist in the 1990s: US news people at the end of an era*. Mahwah, NJ: Erlbaum.

Weaver, D., & Willnat, L. (2012). *The global journalist in the 21st century*. London and New York, NY: Routledge.

Weiner, D. (2005). *Reality check: What your mind knows, but isn't telling you*. Buffalo, NY: Prometheus Books.

Weiner, N. (1948). *Cybernetics; or control and communication in the animal and the machine*. Cambridge, MA: Technology Press.

Weis, W. L., & Burke, C. (1986). Media content and tobacco advertising: An unhealthy addiction. *Journal of Communication 36*(4), 59–69.

Wertham, F. (1954). *Seduction of the innocent*. New York, NY: Rinehart.

West, K. (2011). Who is making the decisions? A study of television journalists, their bosses, and consultant-based market research. *Journal of Broadcasting and Electronic Media 55*(1), 19–35.

Westin, D. (2010) Text of a memo to all ABC News employees. *Mediaite*. Available online at www.mediaite.com/tv/developing-hundreds-of-buyouts expected-at-abc-news-tomorrow. (Accessed June 12, 2010.)

Westley, B. H., & MacLean, Jr., M. S. (1957). A conceptual model for communication research. *Journalism Quarterly 34*(1), 31–8.

Weston, M. A. (2003). Post 9/11 Arab American coverage avoids stereotypes. *Newspaper Research Journal 24*(1), 92–106.

White, D. M. (1950). The gatekeeper: A case study in the selection of news. *Journalism Quarterly 27*, 383–90.

Whitney, D. C., & Becker, L. B. (1982). "Keeping the gates" for gatekeepers: The effects of wire news. *Journalism Quarterly 59*(1), 60–5.

Whorf, B. (1956). *Language, thought and reality*. Cambridge, MA: MIT Press.

Wicks, R. H. (1995). Remembering the news: Effects of medium and message discrepancy on news recall over time. *Journalism & Mass Communication Quarterly 72*(3), 666–81.

Wilhoit, G. C., & Auh, T. S. (1974). Newspaper endorsement and coverage of public opinion. *Journalism Quarterly 51*(4), 654–8.

Wilke, J. R., Heimprecht, C., & Cohen, A. (2012). The geography of foreign news on television. *International Communication Gazette 74*(4), 301–22.

Williams, B., & Delli Carpini, M. (2000). Unchained reaction: The collapse of media gatekeeping and the Clinton–Lewinsky scandal. *Journalism 1*(1), 61–85.

Williams, D. (2002). Synergy bias: Conglomerates and promotion in the news. *Journal of Broadcasting and Electronic Media 46*(3), 453–72.

Williams, R. (1977). *Marxism and literature*. Oxford: Oxford University Press.

Williams, W. S. (1992). For sale! Real estate advertising and editorial decisions about real estate news. *Newspaper Research Journal 13*(2), 160–8.

Willnat, L., & Weaver, D. H. (2003). Through their eyes: The work of foreign correspondents in the United States. *Journalism: Theory, Practice, Criticism 4*(4), 403–22.

Wilson, C., & Gutierrez, F. (1985). *Minorities and media: Diversity and the end of mass communication*. Beverly Hills, CA: Sage.

Windhauser, J. W., Norton, W., Jr., & Rhodes, S. (1983). Editorial patterns of *Tribune* under three editors. *Journalism Quarterly 60*(3), 524–8.

Winseck, D., & Cuthbert, M. (1997). From communication to democratic norms: Reflections on the normative dimensions of international communication policy. In A. Sreberny-Mohammadi, D. Winseck, J. McKennan, & O. Boyd-Barrett (Eds.), *Media in global context* (pp. 162–76). London: Edward Arnold.

Wirth, M. O., & Wollert, J. A. (1976). Public interest program performances of multimedia owned TV stations. *Journalism Quarterly 53*(2), 223–30.

Wolfsfeld, G. (1984). Collective political action and media strategy. *Journal of Conflict Resolution 28*(3), 368–81.

Wollert, J. A. (1978). Programming evidence relative to the issues of the NCCB decision. *Journalism Quarterly 55*(2), 319–24.

Xu, J. (2012). Trust in Chinese state media: The influence of education, Internet, and government. *Journal of International Communication 19*(1), 69–84.

Yoon, Y. (2005). Legitimacy, public relations, and media access: Proposing and testing a media access model. *Communication Research 32*(6), 726–93.

Zeldes, G. A., & Fico, F. (2005). Race and gender: An analysis of sources and reporters in the networks' coverage of the 2000 presidential campaign. *Mass Communication and Society 8*(4), 373–85.

Zelizer, B. (1997). Has communication explained journalism? In D. Berkowitz (Ed.), *Social meanings of news* (pp. 23–30). Thousand Oaks, CA: Sage.

—— (2011). Journalism in the service of communication. *Journal of Communication 61*(1), 1–21.

Zhang, E., & Fleming, K. (2005). Examination of characteristics of news media under censorship: A content analysis of selected Chinese newspapers' SARS coverage. *Asian Journal of Communication 15*(3), 319–39.

Zhang, J., & Cameron, G. T. (2003). China's agenda building and image polishing in the US: Assessing an international public relations campaign. *Public Relations Review 29*(1), 13–28.

Zhao, Z., & Postiglione, G. (2010). Representations of ethnic minorities in China's university media. *Discourse Studies in the Cultural Politics of Education 31*(3), 319–34.

Zoch, L., & Molleda, J. C. (2006). Building a theoretical model of media relations using framing, information subsidies and agenda building. In C. H. Botan & V. Hazleton (Eds.), *Public relations theory II* (pp. 245–72). Mahwah, NJ: Erlbaum.

ABOUT THE AUTHORS

Pamela J. Shoemaker has been John Ben Snow Professor in the S.I. Newhouse School of Public Communications at Syracuse University, New York, since 1994. Her books include *Gatekeeping Theory* with Tim Vos (2009), *Gatekeeping* (English with Mandarin annotations) with Yonghua Zhang (2007), *News around the World* with Akiba Cohen (2006), *How to Build Social Science Theories* with James Tankard and Dominic Lasorsa (2004), *Mediating the Message: Theories of Influence on Mass Media Content* with Stephen Reese (1991, 1996), *Gatekeeping* (1991), and an edited volume *Communication Campaigns about Drugs* (1989). In addition, Shoemaker and Michael Roloff have edited a top-ranked journal, *Communication Research*, since 1997. She has been invited to speak in Brazil, Canada, China (ten universities), Germany, Israel, Mexico, Peru, Portugal, Russia, South Africa, and the UK and has given conference papers in many others. She is a past president of the Association for Education in Journalism and Mass Communication and formerly a head of its communication theory and methodology division; she also received the Kreighbaum Under-40 Award for teaching, research, and service. She is also a former chair of the mass communication division of the International Communication Association. Prior to joining the Newhouse School, Shoemaker was Director of the School of Journalism at Ohio State University (1991–4) and was on the faculty at the University of Texas at Austin (1982–91). Her Ph.D. in mass communications is from the University of Wisconsin at Madison (1982), with her MS in communication and BS in journalism from Ohio University, Athens (1972).

Stephen D. Reese is Jesse H. Jones Professor and Associate Dean for Academic Affairs in the College of Communication at the University of Texas at Austin, where he has been on the faculty since 1982 and where he was previously Director of the School of Journalism. His research on issue framing, media sociology, political communication, and the globalization of journalism has been published in numerous book chapters and articles, and includes his edited volume, *Framing Public Life: Perspectives on Media and Our Understanding of the Social World* (2001), *Mediating the Message: Theories of Influence on Mass Media Content* with Pam Shoemaker (1991, 1996), and major edited section, "Media Production and Content," in the International Communication Association's *Encyclopedia of Communication* (2008). He has chaired the Political Communication Division of the International Communication Association and two divisions of the Association for Education in Journalism and Mass Communication, and was awarded that organization's Krieghbaum Under-40 award for teaching, research, and service. He has lectured internationally at universities in Brazil, China, Colombia, Finland, Germany, Israel, Mexico, and Spain, and was Kurt Baschwitz Visiting Professor at the University of Amsterdam. He received his Ph.D. from the University of Wisconsin (1982) and his BS in Communication from the University of Tennessee (1976).

INDEX

Note: 'n' after a page number indicates a note; 'f' indicates a figure.